T0398849

The Changing World of a Bombay Muslim Community, 1870–1945

The Changing World of a Bombay Muslim Community, 1870–1945

SALIMA TYABJI

OXFORD
UNIVERSITY PRESS

OXFORD
UNIVERSITY PRESS

Great Clarendon Street, Oxford, OX2 6DP,
United Kingdom

Oxford University Press is a department of the University of Oxford.
It furthers the University's objective of excellence in research, scholarship,
and education by publishing worldwide. Oxford is a registered trade mark of
Oxford University Press in the UK and in certain other countries

First e-book edition published in India in 2013 by Cinnamon Teal Publishing

First Edition published in 2023

Published in the United States of America by Oxford University Press
198 Madison Avenue, New York, NY 10016, United States of America

British Library Cataloguing in Publication Data
Data available

Library of Congress Control Number: 2023930673

ISBN 978-0-19-286974-6

DOI: 10.1093/oso/9780192869746.001.0001

Contents

Characters in Alphabetical Order

Abbas, grandson of Tyabjee Bhoymeeah, through his second son Shumsuddin. Married to Amina, Badruddin's eldest daughter. Judge of the Baroda High Court.

Amina, granddaughter of Bhoymeeah, through his fifth son Badruddin; wife of Abbas Tyabji of Baroda.

Amiruddin, youngest of six sons of Bhoymeeah. Married to Hamida, his elder brother Shumsuddin's widow, and guardian of Shumsuddin's six orphaned grandchildren.

Atiya (Fyzee), great-granddaughter of Bhoymeeah through his eldest son Shujauddin; writer, intellectual, patron of the arts. Married to Samuel Rahamin, celebrated painter.

Badruddin, fifth son of Bhoymeeah, successful lawyer, and one of first Indian judges of the Bombay High Court. Married to Rahat, daughter of Sharaf Ali of Cambay.

Camruddin, third son of Bhoymeeah Tyabjee, first Indian solicitor to practise in Bombay. Played an important part in setting his family's progressive views and way of life.

Faiz, third son of Badruddin, literary tastes, active in keeping Badruddin *akhbar* alive. Judge of the Madras High Court, Bombay High Court. Married to Salima Latif.

Hafiza, one of Badruddin's elder daughters, who died at the age of seventeen.

Halima, daughter of Badruddin, married to A. A. Fyzee, brother of Nazli, Atiya, and Zohra.

Hamid, great-grandson of Bhoymeeah Tyabjee, through his second son, Shumsuddin. Orphaned and grew up in Amiruddin Tyabji's household. ICS. Married Abbas' daughter Sharifa.

Husain, second son of Badruddin, educated at Downing College, Cambridge, practised in the Small Causes Court in Bombay. Married to Mahmuda Futehally, his cousin.

Jabir, great-grandson of Bhoymeeah Tyabjee, through his son, Shumsuddin. Orphaned and grew up in Amiruddin Tyabji's home, like his siblings Hamid, Camrunissa, Salim.

Mohsin, Badruddin's eldest son, first Muslim member of the ICS. Married to Tahira Lukmani of Baroda.

Rahat, wife of Badruddin, mother of Mohsin, Husain, Amina, Sakina, etc.

Safia, Badruddin's youngest surviving daughter. Married to Jabir Ali.

Sakina, second daughter of Badruddin, married to Badruddin Lukmani. Social activist, and leader of the Congress women's group in Bombay.

Surayya, elder daughter of Badruddin, leader of her age group. Married to cousin Aly Najmuddin.

Illustrations

Front cover: From left to right, Safia Jabir Ali, Akhtar Salahuddin Tyabji, and Saada Salman Tyabji, descendents of Tyabjee Bhoymeeah, c.1910.

Foreword

Nasir Tyabji

Despite the impressive body of work on various aspects of the growth of nineteenth and twentieth century Bombay that has appeared during the last 25 years, there has been a noticeable absence of research on the Gujarati-speaking Islamic communities that migrated to the city in the nineteenth century. Published work on Bombay has focussed on the physical aspects of the development of the city, its structures of governance and its cultural and literary life[1]. Tantalisingly close to the subject of this book, but veering off in its own quest, is a recent study of Bombay's role as a centre generating urban reformist Islamic practices, stretching across to East Africa.[2]

A 1974 review of Christine Dobbin's *Urban Leadership in Western India* began by saying that the 'book, in spite of the title, is about the activities in Bombay city of tiny, mainly Gujarati-speaking, minority groups.'[3] Although generally appreciative, the review was infused with an underlying scepticism of the significance of the focus of the book. Did the activities and the aspirations of a tiny group, within a minority at that, really matter? Dobbin's book had followed both Jim Masselos' PhD thesis of 1965, published in 1974 and Anil Seal's study of Indian nationalism.[4] Both these monographs had drawn attention to the growth and political importance of an educated stratum of Muslim and Parsi Gujaratis who entered the public sphere in Bombay, and the fraught relations they had with wealthy merchants, also largely from Gujarat.

Subsequently, academic interest in South Asian Islamic communities seems to have moved towards the much more numerous (and hence the purportedly more significant) communities of Northern and Eastern India.

However, a cursory survey of the more prominent Gujarati-speaking families professing Islam who had settled in Bombay, the Tyabjis, Currimbhoys, Peerbhoys, Fazalbhoys, Rahimtoolahs, and Sayanis indicates that a major field of research in the history of Western India remains to be investigated. To the extent that many members of these families resisted the call for Pakistan, they (also) played a major role in that canonical measure of the significance of Muslims in South Asia, that is, their role in events leading up to partition.[5] Indeed, with the Gandhian phase of the national movement, many women of the Tyabji family were also taking a militant part in the national movement.[6]

The Gujarati Islamic communities were culturally and historically quite distinct to their fellow believers in North and East India, not least in being unhesitant in acknowledging their origins as converts from Hinduism. Indeed, this was to be the basis for an appealing (and logical) argument against the Muslim League's slogan of Hindus and Muslims forming two separate nations.[7] Equally significantly, evolving from the trading communities of the western coast, their rise in both economic and social status (their embourgeoisement) was distinct to the lateral movement of the land-owning communities of North India, which movement was largely based on access to modern education. Such a lateral movement left many residues of an inherent right to a privileged existence and, of course, drew substantial numbers of them towards the Muslim League's separatist ideology.[8]

It is within this largely unexplored field, of the social change accompanying the bourgeois transformation of urban communities professing Islam, that the significance of the personal accounts of both men and women members of the Tyabji family included in this book can be appreciated.[9] The main body of the book, based on the personal memoirs of Safia Jabir Ali, one of Badruddin Tyabji's younger daughters, is revealing in its description of the treacherous route towards modernity.[10] Unlike the situation in Japan, where an indigenous government supported a Japanese path to a bourgeois identity, modernity in behaviour and values in colonial India could only be based on the pre-existing model available, that presented by the British representatives in the upper reaches of the civil service and the judiciary. Thus, being English in deportment and behaviour and allowing women access to a public life became important markers of urban civility.

Particularly important here was the effort to overcome resistance to women appearing in public without the purdah.[11] Here again, the consciousness that flowed from the knowledge of their status as converts allowed for a flexible and common sensical approach to matters of social reform, where they came in conflict with tenets of religious orthodoxy.[12] From the time of his return from England in 1867, Badruddin Tyabji had voiced his opposition to this practice, culminating in an open declaration he made as the President of the Muslim Educational Conference in 1903 that purdah had no religious sanctity. In this campaign, the example of European practices as also those of the Parsis were held as exemplars. In fact, while in the early nineteenth century, Parsis had followed the practice, it had been abandoned in the course of the century.[13]

If there was a desire to emulate British social norms and civility in personal matters there was, of course, the ever-present racial discrimination, which affected all strata of Indians, however wealthy and established they might be.[14] Anger at this visceral display of the logic of colonial rule was underscored by the competition of established expatriate interests in both professional and commercial spheres of activity. There was thus a subjective and an objective basis to the initial wariness towards, and later questioning of, colonialism. Further, at times of political tension, being wealthy and established did not save Muslim families from humiliation. It is surely significant that Tyabjee Bhoymeeah, the figure from whom the Tyabji family emerged, though a person who was granted easy access into the presence of the Governor of Bombay (John Elphinstone), was also shunned by his friend Jamsetjee Jeejeebhoy during the fraught years after the 1857 uprising.[15] It may be noted here that Elphinstone's entry in the Dictionary of National Biography mentions that he '... discovered a more serious conspiracy in Bombay itself, of which he held the threads until the right moment, when he seized upon the ringleaders and prevented the conspiracy from coming to anything.'[16] Tyabjee Bhoymeeah had approached Elphinstone for help in securing the release of a relation arrested in Ahmedabad on suspicion of being 'sympathetic' to the uprising. Although he managed to get a letter of introduction from the Governor by which he eventually secured the release of his relation, the interest and determination he showed would surely not have escaped the Governor. When incorporated into family folklore, such incidents fed the alienation from British rule evident in the mood of some of the personal accounts that form the basis of the book that follows.

Given the social prominence he had attained (and wealth which on his death in 1863 amounted to Rs 5 lakhs) the decision of the Tyabjee

Bhoymeeah family to change their *family* language from Gujarati to Hindustani in 1859 is not immediately comprehensible.[17] Not only was Jamsetjee Jeejeebhoy a personal friend but so was Cowasji Jehangir. There was an extended social group in Bombay across communities where Gujarati was not only the language of communication but also of intellectual and literary expression.[18] While Bombay Hindi was inevitably to become the lingua franca of daily life in the city, there was no substantive reason to change the language of *intra family* communication to Hindustani. In fact, the resistance this change faced, both at the time and even 40 years later, is recorded.[19] Writing in 1865, six years after the family decision, Badruddin Tyabji argued that India needed a national language and, as Hindustani was the most widely spoken, it should become the national language. This was an early recognition of a *national* sentiment.[20] But he also felt that to aspire to leadership of India's Muslims, it was essential to master the idiomatic Urdu spoken in Lucknow.[21] There is here a clear instance of the difficulties in charting a course towards a national urban modernity within a colonial context, while refashioning the individual's location within a community.

The objective of advancing the process of a Hindustani-based identity formation was exemplified by the decision to make Hindustani the medium of instruction at the educational institutions established under the Anjuman-i-Islam.[22] While the initiative was driven by the evidence of the low Muslim representation in government schools and colleges in the 1870s (and thus of opportunities of modern education), 78.5% of Muslims in Bombay city were Konkani or Marathi speakers, while a further 20.7% were Gujarati speakers, amounting to 99.2% in all.[23] It would seem that the appropriate response would have been to provide modern education within separate language sections of the school in the family language of the children, rather than introducing Hindustani as the medium of instruction.[24]

Somewhat at odds with the tendency towards a Hindustani-speaking Islamic identity was the emphasis placed, not only on modifications in behaviour in accordance with the norms of British civilian life in India but also education in English medium schools, not only in Bombay, but also in England. A notable feature here was the equal treatment given to both the girls and boys in terms of educational opportunities and in expectations of engaging in active recreational hobbies. The two appendices in the book also point to the close observation of family lives in both Britain and the European continent by members of the family on their visits to these countries, which must also have helped shape the process of forming of the overall identity which emerged within the Tyabji family in the course of the twentieth century.

The final element that made for this identity was the engagement with the national movement, more direct in some cases but always affecting the attitudes of individuals within the family up to the time of Independence.[25] In sum, three processes were underway in the formation of the worldview, which underscores the accounts in this book: an aspiration to model important features of family life on European models; a tendency to view Hindustani as the marker of an Islamic identity; and the emotional if not active engagement with the national movement. The effects of all three processes are evident on various occasions in the book.

Notes

1. Dossal (1991); Dossal (2010); Gupchup (1993); Patel and Thorner (1995a); Patel and Thorner (1995b); Masselos and Patel (2005); Ramanna (2002); Ramanna (2012); Kidambi (2007).
2. Green (2011).
3. Robb (1974).
4. Seal (1968); Dobbin (1972); Masselos (1974).
5. Apart from active participation in Congress activities, some members of the Tyabji family, with the encouragement of the Congress leader, B.G. Kher, remained in the Muslim League with the intention of influencing its policies, until the Pakistan resolution was passed. See also Tyabji (1946).
6. Pym (1930); Lukmani (2000); Bredi (2003).
7. Tyabji (1946): 14, 16. The economic (and social) context of the rise of the trading communities in Bombay is described in Farooqui (1996).
8. The various competing views on what 'Indian Muslim' identity might mean and the tortured trajectory by which the Islamic communities of North and East India came to terms with nationalism is portrayed in Jalal (2002).
9. The Tyabjis are Suleimani Bohras, a minority community amongst the Bohras. See Lokhandwalla (1955). Recently, there has been detailed analysis of both the personalities and the public and political roles of two women members of the larger Tyabji family, in which the dilemmas of being modern in a colonial context are exemplified. See Lambert-Hurley and Sharma (2010); Lambert-Hurley (2014).

10. Badruddin Tyabji (1844–1906) was a barrister, social reformer, educationist and Judge (and Acting Chief Justice) of the Bombay High Court. He played a major role in the Bombay Presidency Association and was the President of the Indian National Congress at its Madras session in 1887. See Tyabji (1952); Noorani (1969); Shakir (1987).

11. Tyabji (1930).

12. Tyabji (1930).

13. There are accounts of the social life of the Parsis in Mody (1998) and Palsetia (2008).

14. An incident involving Badruddin Tyabji is vividly described in Tyabji (1952): 46–49.

15. Fyzee (1964): 17.

16. Henry Morse Stephens 'Elphinstone, John (1807–1860) (DNB00)'. Accessed 27 September 2015. https://en.wikisource.org/wiki/Elphinstone,_John_%281807-1860%29_%28DNB00%29. There is an unabashedly colonial view of the manifestations of the uprising Bombay in Albuquerque (1986).

17. Tyabji (1952): 14–15; Fyzee (1964): 3; Karlitzky (2002).

18. At least until the late nineteenth century, Bombay was the centre of both reformist social movements and of intellectual activities amongst Gujaratis. See, for example, Mallison (1995); Shukla (1995).

19. Tyabjee Bhoymeeah's wife, Hurmat Wali, refused to speak in Hindustani and insisted in responding in Gujarati (Fyzee 1964: 3); two generations later, in 1900, Salima Tyabji (nee Latif) started a letter to her husband, Faiz Tyabji, son of Badruddin Tyabji, in Gujarati (Karlitzy 2002: 193).

20. Tyabji (1952): 22.

21. Tyabji (1952): 20.

22. The Anjuman-i-Islam was an educational initiative in which Camruddin Tyabji, his brother Badruddin Tyabji, the Konkani merchant, Nakhoda Mohammad Ali Rogay, Munshi Hidayatulla and Munshi Ghulam Mohammed were its founders. A boy's school was established in 1880. A girl's school had to wait until 1939 to be started.

23. Data drawn from Masselos (1971): 46.

24. However, in 1902, 22 years after the establishment of the institution, the Secretary of the Anjuman announced that taking into account the fact that Gujarati was the family language of the trading sections of the community, it had been decided that instruction in arithmetic and geography would be in Gujarati. He prefaced his remark by disclosing the fact that in this, the school was deviating from the Government's standards for the curriculum. This information was provided by Qazi Kabirudin on the occasion of the inauguration of the Makba Gymnasium at the Anjuman by the Governor of Bombay, Henry Northcote. *Times of India*, March 20, 1902, p. 5. I am grateful to Danish Khan for bringing this item of information to my notice.

25. Karlitzy (2004). Despite numerous factual inaccuracies and haphazard referencing, this is, perhaps, the only recent study of this subject.

Bibliography

Albuquerque, Teresa. *Urbs Prima in Indis*. New Delhi: Promilla and Co., 1986.

Bredi, Daniela. 'Continuity and Change in Women's Role in Indo-Muslim Society Seen Through a Few Female Members of the Tyabji Family'. *Annali di Ca'Foscari XLII*, no. 3 (2003): 223–41 reprinted in Beckerlegge, Gwilym. *Colonialism, Modernity and Religious Identities: Religious Reform Movements in South Asia*. New Delhi: Oxford University Press, 2008.

Dobbin, Christine E. *Urban Leadership in Western India: Politics and Communities in Bombay City, 1840–1885*. London: Oxford University Press, 1972.

Dossal, Mariam. *Imperial Designs and Indian Realities: The Planning of Bombay City, 1845–1875*. Mumbai: Oxford University Press, 1991.

Dossal, Mariam. *Theatre of Conflict, City of Hope: Bombay/Mumbai 1660 to Present Times*. Delhi: Oxford University Press, 2010.

Farooqui, Amar. 'Urban Development in a Colonial Situation: Early Nineteenth Century Bombay'. *Economic and Political Weekly* 31 (1996): 2746–59.

Fyzee, Asaf A. A., ed. 'The Autobiography of Tyabjee Bhoymeeah: Merchant Prince of Bombay, 1803–1863'. *Journal of the Asiatic Society of Bombay* (New Series) 36–37, Supplement, (1964).

Green, Nile. *Bombay Islam: The Religious Economy of the Western Indian Ocean, 1840–1915*. Cambridge: Cambridge University Press, 2011.

Gupchup, Vijaya V. *Bombay: Social Change, 1813–1857*. Mumbai: Popular Book Depot, 1993.

Jalal, Ayesha. 'Negotiating Colonial Modernity and Cultural Difference: Indian Muslim Conceptions of Community and Nation, 1878–1914'. In *Modernity and Culture: From the Mediterranean to the Indian Ocean*, edited by Leila Tarazi Fawaz and C. A. Bayly, 230–60. New York: Columbia University Press, 2002.

Karlitzky, Maren. 'The Tyabji Clan—Urdu as a Symbol of Group Identity'. *The Annual of Urdu Studies* 17 (2002). Accessed 16 April 2015. http://www.urdustudies.com/Issue17/index.html.

Karlitzky, Maren. 'Continuity and Change in the Relationship Between Congress and the Muslim Élite: A Case Study of the Tyabji Family'. *Oriente Moderno* 84, 1 (2004): 161–175.

Kidambi, Prashant. *The Making of an Indian Metropolis: Colonial Governance and Public Culture in Bombay, 1890–1920*. Aldershot: Ashgate Publishing, Ltd., 2007.

Lambert Hurley, Siobhan, and Sunil Sharma, eds. *Atiya's Journeys: A Muslim Woman from Colonial Bombay to Edwardian Britain*. Delhi: Oxford University Press, 2010.

Lambert-Hurley, Siobhan. 'The Heart of a Gopi: Raihana Tyabji's Bhakti Devotionalism as Self-Representation'. *Modern Asian Studies* 48, no. 3 (2014): 569–95.

Lokhandwalla, T. 'The Bohras: A Muslim Community of Gujarat'. *Studia Islamica* 3 (1955): 117–35.

Lukmani, Yasmeen. 'The Role Played by the Tyabji Women in the Freedom Movement'. In *Women in India's Freedom Struggle*, edited by Nawaz B. Mody, 219–38. Mumbai: Allied Pub. Ltd, 2000.

Mallison, Francoise. 'Bombay as the Intellectual Capital of the Gujaratis'. In *Bombay: Mosaic of Modern India*, edited by Sujata Patel and Alice Thorner, 76–87. Delhi: Oxford University Press, 1995.

Masselos, Jim. 'Bombay in the 1870s: A Study of Changing Patterns in Urban Politics'. *South Asia: Journal of South Asian Studies*: Series 1, 1 no. 1 (1971): 29–55.

Masselos, Jim. *Towards Nationalism: Group Affiliations and the Politics of Public Associations in Nineteenth Century Western India*. Bombay: Popular Prakashan, 1974.

Masselos, Jim, and Sujata Patel, eds. *Bombay and Mumbai: The City in Transition*. Delhi: Oxford University Press, 2005.

Mody, Nawaz B. *The Parsis in Western India: 1818–1920*. New Delhi: Allied Publishers, 1998.

Noorani, Abdul G. *Badruddin Tyabji*. New Delhi: Publications Division, Ministry of Information and Broadcasting, Government of India, 1969.

Palsetia, Jesse S. *The Parsis of India: Preservation of Identity in Bombay City*. New Delhi: Manohar Publications, 2008.

Patel, Sujata, and Alice Thorner, eds. *Bombay: Mosaic of Modern Culture*. Bombay: Oxford University Press, 1995a.

Patel, Sujata, and Alice Thorner, eds. *Bombay: Metaphor for Modern India*. Bombay: Oxford University Press, 1995b.

Pym, Michael. 'India's Women Who Stand with Mahatma Gandhi'. *The New York Times*, 25 May (1930).

Ramanna, Mridula. *Western Medicine and Public Health in Colonial Bombay, 1845–1895 (New Perspectives in South Asian History)*. Hyderabad: Orient BlackSwan, 2002.

Ramanna, Mridula. *Health Care in Bombay Presidency 1896–1930*. Delhi: Primus Books, 2012.

Robb, Peter. 'Review'. *Bulletin of the School of Oriental and African Studies* 37, no. 1 (1974): 248–49.

Seal, Anil. *The Emergence of Indian Nationalism: Competition and Collaboration in the Later Nineteenth Century*. Cambridge: Cambridge University Press, 1968.

Shakir, Moin. *Muslims and Indian National Congress: Badruddin Tyabji and His Times*. Delhi: Ajanta Publications, 1987.

Shukla, Sonal. 'Gujarati Cultural Revivalism'. In *Bombay: Mosaic of Modern Culture*, edited by Sujata Patel and Alice Thorner, 88–98. Delhi: Oxford University Press, 1995.

Tyabji, Faiz B. 'Social Life in 1804 & 1929 Amongst Muslims in Bombay'. *Journal of the Bombay Branch of the Royal Asiatic Society* 6 (1930): 286–300.

Tyabji, Husain B. *Why Mussalmans Should Oppose Pakistan: Indian Affairs No 3*. Bombay: Padma Publications, 1946.

Tyabji, Husain B. *Badruddin Tyabji—A Biography*. Bombay: Thacker and Co., 1952.

Preface

This study initially arose from my curiosity about how I, brought up as a Muslim, could have the freedom, intellectual and otherwise, that was popularly supposed to be denied to Muslims, women in particular. The freedom was far greater I thought than that enjoyed by many of my non-Muslim friends, and I was certainly not the only beneficiary. Many women of my generation, certainly of my family, brought up in the same traditional way, had the same views on life and values, and the same liberty to act on them.

My curiosity was whetted further by a casual reading of a nineteenth-century family journal, in which there were entries by women who had the same zest for life and intellectual curiosity that I used to think marked my generation. The only difference seemed to be our style of dress.

I am therefore most grateful to Gail Minault and to Ravinder Kumar, then Director of the Teen Murti House archives, who generously encouraged me to pursue this line of enquiry. At that point I'd planned to structure it around the lives of two pairs of sisters, one pair who were intellectuals and social reformers, Nazli and Atiya Fyzee, and the other Gandhian activists and nationalists, Sakina Lukmani and Safia Jabir Ali.

It was my good fortune to learn from Amiruddin Ali, Safia Jabir Ali's son, that his mother had copied out a series of family journals dating from the late nineteenth century to the mid-twentieth, and had also kept a journal of her own, which were given to the Teen Murti House Archives. It is this body of work on which I have focused here, following the leads as they emerged from the material, without any preconceptions in mind. Professor Irfan Habib made me realize the importance of looking at my source material myself, without intermediaries. I have also looked at several other family journals, but found that although they will certainly repay close study, for my purposes these two sources were rewarding enough. I am deeply indebted to Amiruddin Ali for sharing this material with me, and for the time that he has spent in fleshing out this material with his own recollections of the period.

As my views took shape, Aparna Basu provided much time and advice, and V. N. Datta was unstinting in his efforts to help me bring my ideas into coherent form. An early version of Chapter One was read to a meeting of the Forum of Independent Scholars, Delhi, in 2004, and I benefited from the lively discussion that followed. Uma Chakravarty was a constant source of encouragement, and stressed the importance of including passages from the journals, and letting people's voices be heard, for which I'm deeply grateful. Finally, my friend David Baker unleashed his editorial claws on the script and made me pull it into shape. To Aparna and Michael, for their unstinting support and every sort of encouragement, I owe a huge debt. Ram Guha found the time to read the script and made important suggestions which I am most grateful for.

Without Theodore Wright's wonderfully detailed family tree of Bhoymeeah and Fez Hyder's descendants, I would have been completely lost in trying to work out the lines of descent. I'm most grateful to him for giving me a copy of it.

For help with the translations, I am greatly indebted to Amiruddin Ali; to V. N. Datta, and Ausaf Ali, for the Persian and Arabic quotations; Muzaffar Alam worked through a thicket of indecipherable and incomprehensible language, a mixture of Arabic, Gujarati, and Bambai ki Zabaan, to provide a very careful rendition of an 1877 account, for which I am most grateful; Syeda Imam and Monis Kidwai provided similar help for the account of the 1903 Anglo-Mohamedan Conference, and Monis Kidwai I have to thank in addition for drawing my attention to a biography of Shaikh Abdullah from which I obtained fascinating insights into the problems faced by the great educationist. Poonam Datta did me a great service by telling me of Lady Nora Scott's diary, which was invaluable in helping me to structure my own thoughts in the second chapter.

The staff of the Teen Murti Archives were unfailingly helpful and courteous, and I must record my special thanks to N. Balakrishnan and Deepa Bhatnagar for their aid in providing access to the archival material as well as in overcoming hurdles with regard to the photographic archives, from which several of these photographs have been taken. They were originally part of the Faiz B. Tyabji Collection. The remaining pictures are from the collections of Amiruddin Ali, Habib and Sakina Futehally, and Yasmeen Lukmani.

Zishaan Akbar Latif provided the photograph of Tyabjee Bhoymeeah, advised about the illustrations, and designed the cover. My grateful thanks to him.

Introduction

There has been no independent study so far of the 'Bombay Musulmans'—a disparate and unwieldy community in the Bombay of the nineteenth century, as Husain Tyabji has pointed out.[1] The Islam that was professedly held in common by various groups could barely provide a sense of unity or cohesion to people so widely diverse in terms of language, customs, and also of forms and practices of belief. This heterogeneity among the Muslim community was a reflection of the nature of the town: the rapid growth of Bombay—which had emerged in the course of the century as a commercial metropolis and a centre for ship-building, replacing Surat as the most important port on the western coast—attracted traders, shipbuilders, artisans of many kinds from the hinterland, Gujarat, the Konkan, and further south, making it a centre of heterogeneous culture.

By the middle of the nineteenth century, a class of wealthy ship owners, shipbuilders, and merchants, belonging to the varied communities that constituted the city, of which Musulmans formed an important part, had emerged. This class was outward-looking, 'modern,' and generally reformist in outlook: Parsi, Gujarati, or Maharashtrian, its goals of social reform, education, as well as political awareness, were gradually beginning to be perceived as goals held across communities, and increasingly across different regions.

The questions that were being raised in the social turmoil of the period in the Hindu community were over issues of female education, the age of marriage, widow remarriage, female seclusion.[2]

These issues were not foreign to the Muslim community; and the part played by Muslim leaders in Bombay in discussing and negotiating them was not an insignificant one, taking into account the size and relative backwardness of the community.[3]

The documents which form the basis of this study show the beginning of such awareness among elite circles of Muslims. Further evidence of the rise of social consciousness among wealthy Muslims lies in the

The Changing World of a Bombay Muslim Community, 1870–1945. Salima Tyabji, Oxford University Press.
© Nasir Tyabji 2023. DOI: 10.1093/oso/9780192869746.001.0001

establishment of the Anjuman-Islam, a trust founded in 1872 as a means of establishing schooling for Muslim children on the lines already set up by the Parsi, Gujarati, and Maharashtrian communities.

Within this context, I attempt to trace the evolving identity of a Bombay family and its changing social and political views in the late nineteenth and early twentieth centuries, using three main sources: their family journals, an individual memoir/journal, and letters written home from Europe.

The most intriguing and unusual source is that of the family journal, or *akhbar ki kitab*, a tradition which originated in this family in the mid-nineteenth century, and continues to exist till today. *Akhbar ki Kitab* literally means news book, but is better understood as a sort of family journal. The material I have drawn from these journals covers the period 1877 onwards.

The second source, related to the first both in its nature and authorship, is a memoir cum journal, intensely private in its revelations, yet also clearly meant to be read by others, or rather by the family, as were the original family journals. This was written between the years 1920 and 1945, by a member of the family who had earlier, as a six- or seven year old, been an eager contributor to her father's *akhbar* book.

The third type of source that I have drawn on is a series of letters written from Europe, in English, by two outstanding male members of this family, of different generations. The letters are separated by a gap of 60 or so years—1870 and 1929—but they are written by two individuals who had a great influence on others, Amiruddin Tyabji, and his great-nephew Saif. It is significant that they were both more at ease writing and communicating in English than in Urdu. These letters need little introduction or explanation; they stand by themselves.

I hope also to show that while there is no similar record for other families, there are enough indications that the subject family was not unique in its responses to social and economic change—one can infer that there was a fairly wide current of opinion among Muslims of similar views.

The study falls into four parts. In the first, I examine the nature and significance of this *akhbar*, the purpose it served in the life of an urban westernizing family in a period of rapid social and political change. In the second part, I focus on the family's opinions on issues such as marriage customs, purdah, the Urdu language, dress, and other matters as they filter through usually light-hearted entries on family activities. The following chapter contains translations of some important entries, many written by the women in their capacity as guardians of the hearth, of family tradition, as they themselves constantly emphasize. They range from an account of life on a coffee estate in south India in 1877, to the great eclipse of 1898, descriptions of the discussions on purdah at the Anglo-Mahomedan Conference held in 1903, a lively account of travels in Europe in 1893, to a detailed account of the last illness and death of their mother in 1905. The Badruddin Tyabji *akhbar* comes to an end with the report of an excursion to the Jog Falls in Mysore written in 1907. I hope these passages will convey something of the tone, as well as the range of interests that the *akhbar* books cover.

The third part consists of a translation of a journal written between 1926 and 1944, essentially a continuation of the *akhbar* tradition; in many ways it exemplifies what the family culture was all about. I have taken the liberty of deleting the more humdrum details of daily life in Bombay in the early 1940s, but hope some of the liveliness and charm, the intellectual curiosity, and passionate love of country, has been adequately conveyed.

Finally, come letters written from France to his family in Bombay in 1870 by Amiruddin Tyabji, who had been sent to school in England as a young boy, and was then, as a 22 year old, entrusted by his elder brothers with running the family business from its branch in Havre. These letters are full of fun, but intensely serious as well on matters of marriage, religion, responsibility to family. Such views would undoubtedly have shaped the opinions of the large family he brought up; his family *akhbar* provided some of the liveliest accounts of contemporary events; moreover, he figures as a very important figure in the early life of Safia Jabir Ali (whose memoir forms the third chapter), for whom he stood in place of the father she lost at the beginning of her girlhood.

Saif Tyabji, whose letters from Europe written in 1929–30, form an Appendix to this study, also played a powerful and influential role in his family's life, as is evident from Safia Jabir Ali's memoir—most especially in his passionate and determined espousal of education for girls. The letters quoted here fall into a different category from his uncle Amiruddin's: they are an account of a young Muslim Indian's reactions to Europe—it is largely European culture that he is absorbed in experiencing and appraising. What the two writers have in common, as they do with all the earlier contributors, is the knowledge of being firmly rooted in their own culture; and of being at ease in writing and expressing themselves. Perhaps this was due to the discipline imposed by having to write in the *akhbar*.

Such narratives, whether cheerfully spontaneous, or consciously magisterial, provide us with insights into the changing world of India at several levels. The most immediate is the effect on individuals, through them their families, and thereby their communities. Husain Tyabji has pointed out the extraordinary influence Badruddin Tyabji was able to exert on the religious leaders of the Sulaymani community, showing them how change in trivial matters like the use of cutlery, or of tables and chairs, was not to be feared, it was to be welcomed, for these were changes that the Prophet himself, the icon of progress, of common sense, would have approved of.[4]

The occasional references to other leading Muslim progressives in the field of social reform and education for women in Bombay are especially valuable in that they support the presumption that this clan would not have been isolated in calling for change.

Such fundamental changes in the attitude of a family that was among the pioneers in social and educational reform were in fact symptomatic of the changes taking place throughout India. Hence, these narratives have a significance that goes beyond familial, community, or religious boundaries.

Bhoymeeah's descendants were reacting to currents of thought that were part of a sweeping realignment of attitudes among those who were subject to British rule.

1

The Tyabjee Family and Its *Akhbar*

The focus of this study is the very large extended family that was formed largely by the descendants of two brothers, Tyabjee Bhoymeeah (1803–63) and Faiz Hyder (1805–52), Sulaymani Bohoras from Cambay in Gujarat.

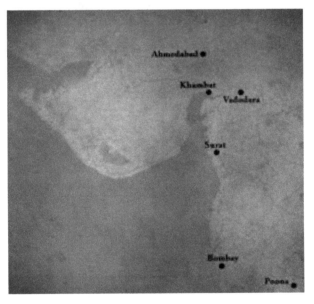

Sketch map of south-west Gujarat, showing the port of Cambay (Khambhat) in relation to major centres of Sulaymani settlements.

Cambay was then an important port for trade with China in cotton, opium, and carnelian. The Sulayman community by the mid-nineteenth century had spread from Cambay to the major mercantile centres of Surat, Bombay, Ahmedabad, and Baroda.

The Changing World of a Bombay Muslim Community, 1870–1945. Salima Tyabji, Oxford University Press.

Tyabjee Bhoymeeah, Liverpool, 1853.

Starting off as a small trader, with his family based in Surat, Tyabjee Bhoymeeah had with outstanding resourcefulness and hard work established himself in Bombay by the mid-nineteenth century as a man of property, and of culture. He was a recognized leader of the Muslim community, as well as a close friend of the Governor of Bombay, and a Justice of the Peace.[1]

While a pillar of the establishment, Tyabjee was also a man of exceptionally open views. He very quickly recognized the importance of contact with Europe, of acquiring European professional skills, as well as social manners. Having himself travelled to Europe and then performed the Haj in 1853, he sent his younger sons to England to acquire the appropriate skills for the new world that was opening before them. Camruddin, his third son, was sent to England in 1852 and returned in 1858 having qualified as a solicitor; Badruddin, his fifth son, in 1867 returned to India as a Bar-at-Law. They were the first Indians to practise law in Bombay,[2] while his youngest son Amiruddin, also educated in England, joined his elder brothers in the family business of S. Tyabjee and Co.

By 1870 two of Tyabjee's grandsons were studying in England; moreover, by then two of his granddaughters[3] were sufficiently at home in

English to be able to correspond in that language. This was in marked contrast to the fear of English education, of the western Christian culture that prevailed in traditional Muslim society in the nineteenth century throughout most of India. By the mid-1870s almost all the children, girls as well as boys, were studying at mission schools, St Xavier's for the boys and the Zenana Mission School at Girgaon and later the Alexandra School for Girls in the Fort area of Bombay; they also received lessons at home in writing and reading Urdu and Persian, and of course the Quran.

Camruddin Tyabjee, c. 1860.
After Husain B. Tyabji.

Camruddin (1836–89), who was the first professional in the western sense, of the family, returned from England having qualified as a solicitor in 1858. According to his brother Najmuddin's account, it was at Camruddin's insistence that the family, at that point consisting of Bhoymeeah's 10 children, began the tradition of writing *akhbar* books. Five volumes covering the period 1860–78, written in English, Bambaiya Urdu, and occasionally Gujarati, were thus produced, the *Akhbar Tyabia*.[4] There was a volume kept in the country home at Chembur, near Bombay, which was also well contributed to because of Camruddin's efforts.

By the mid-1870s, at least four of Tyabjee's six sons had felt the need to began a separate family book of their own: Shujauddin, the eldest (1829–78), a wealthy ship owner and merchant, and head of the family firm S. Tyabjee and Co. by about 1873; Camruddin himself c. 1875 began an *Akhbar Qamariyya*, as did Najmuddin (1842–c. 1902). Badruddin (1844–1906), and Amiruddin (1848–1917), kept a separate book wherever they lived.[5] The granddaughter of Tyabjee's eldest daughter Zainab, who married the Baroda doctor Mohamedi, also kept one, and Nudrat-ul-Nairn, Tyabjee's youngest daughter, started one with her husband, Shaikh Fatehali, in their Kihim house in 1890; while, in Karachi he had begun one by 1877.

By virtue of belonging to the small Sulaymani Bohora community,[6] which, like other Muslim kinship groups in Gujarat and elsewhere, formed a tightly knit group that frowned on intermarriage with other Muslims, a family network evolved that encouraged continuous inter-marriage between first and second cousin. Hence, by the second generation, more than half the marriages were with the sons or daughters of maternal or paternal siblings. An important consideration in arranging these inter-family marriages appears to have been the question of finding suitably 'advanced' or 'modern' mates for the children.[7]

I The Genre of Family House Journals

The special interest of the *akhbar* lies in the fact that this genre of family house journals seems, as far as I am aware, to be unique to the branch of the Sulaymani Bohora trading community hailing from Cambay (Khambhat) in Gujarat. The only comparable material in Urdu is a family magazine, which, started initially by the men of a well-to-do Navayyut family in the early 1900s in Hyderabad, was then restarted by the women in the 1930s, and used as a forum for discussing issues such as female education and professional employment.[8]

From the time of Akbar, there was a well-established tradition at the Mughal court of writing a formal daily *akhbar* and of recording the Emperor's activities; the custom spread to the regional courts, was followed by important nobles and merchants, and continued under the British East India Company into the nineteenth century.[9] Parallel to this formal *akhbar* was the custom initiated by the Mughals, and dating back perhaps to Timur, of writing autobiographies and memoirs that dwelt not merely on the political or military achievements of the ruler; but contained deeply personal and self-critical passages of reflection, and comments on their achievements and failures. Babur's memoirs are part of the tradition that was possibly established by Timur himself,[10] and we know from his daughter Gulbadan's memoirs that the importance of observing and recording, of offering critical accounts of day-to-day events was part of the culture of the Timurid family, not restricted to the male rulers, but that the women, at least of the ruling classes, were as literate and well-informed as the men.

Of a different nature but equally great importance were the *khatas*, account books, kept by merchant families as well as small traders; in Gujarat the peculiar homogenized culture of the merchant traders led to many of these books being written in the Perso-Arabic script, but in the Gujarati language. The value of the written tradition was also evident from the scrupulous care with which *pandas* maintained records of birth and death, as did the administrators of *masjids* and trusts.

It is unlikely that the highly literate and sophisticated family of Tyabjee Bhoymeeah would have been uninfluenced by or unaware of these traditional practices. Allowing for the fact that their *akhbar* was a highly personal one, revolving around family events, one would expect that some reference would be made to, at least, the earlier courtly tradition of *akhbar* writing.[11] Especially since each volume has a formal beginning and dedication—but these tend to state that the purpose of the exercise is to record pleasant and joyful moments in the family for the benefit of posterity! Although the importance of recording events such as births and deaths is also noted. The number of journals kept by various branches of the family indicate how seriously this duty was taken.

One can only speculate as to why Camruddin took the writing of *akhbar* books so seriously. He may have been influenced by the English and European custom of keeping guest books, in which visitors not merely signed but also wrote accounts of their doings during their stay. He would undoubtedly have met people who kept such family books themselves. (There is an important distinction of course between these 'public' family journals, which lay invitingly open to any member of the household, and the custom of keeping a diary, which was essentially or ostensibly of a private nature, at least during the diarist's lifetime.)

Camruddin's great-nephew, A. A. A. Fyzee, an authority on Arab literature and the Quran, dismissed the idea of this being a purely Western custom adopted by the family. Many years later, in 1942, at a family reading of some passages written over 50 years earlier (which had already been 'lost' and found again) he explained that this was in fact an Arab custom which had travelled to the West and returned to us through British channels.[12]

Together with the importance attached to recording events that were significant to them was the corresponding requirement of preserving what was written. This need to preserve and conserve varied according to individual natures and their understanding of the historical process: some were handed over to libraries or collections of archival material; some locked up like monsters in great cupboards, and their existence never divulged; others kept swaddled in cloth, lovingly preserved, although inaccessible to the owners because of the language in which they were written, and yet not parted with—and variations thereof.

II The Language of the Journals

Abbas Tyabji's biographer states that the clan, if not the entire Sulaymani *jamaat*, decided in the mid-nineteenth century to change their mother tongue from Gujarati to Urdu on account of Camruddin Tyabji's influence. Asaf Fyzee has recorded that 'in 1859 it was decided formally at a family gathering that Gujarati was too be abandoned … everyone bowed to this decision and spoke in Hindustani.'[13] Tragically, Camruddin's own *Kitab-i Qamariyya* has disappeared (although Asaf Fyzee was able to consult it in the 1960s). It would undoubtedly have thrown light on the reasons for such a drastic linguistic and cultural change, one which also had political significance. This was a switch that could not be accomplished quickly or ever with complete success—the family's spoken and written language has always differed from the pure elegant Urdu of Delhi and Lucknow. Of all Tyabjee's sons, Badruddin was perhaps the most conscious of the importance of speaking and writing in an educated and cultivated manner; but his own family, as well as his brothers' and sisters' continued to speak a kind of vulgar pidgin Urdu, more accurately described perhaps as 'Bombay language,' which marked them out from their North Indian compatriots. Badruddin and some of his elder daughters were painfully conscious of this deficiency which they were not able to eradicate totally from their spoken language, although they read widely, and were familiar with the work of all the great Urdu and Persian poets. A further impediment was the greater daily practical importance for both men and women of speaking English correctly and well. However, the language of these journals, with its odd awkward syntax, its mixture of sophisticated Persianized Urdu with Gujarati and Marathi words, of idioms translated literally into Urdu from English, has a strange ungainly charm and vivacity, and enhances the general impression of a unique world into which one is entering.

III The Need to Keep Journals

Whatever the original source or inspiration, for some of Tyabjee's descendants the need to keep journals seems to have fulfilled a special need: one reason for the vehemence with which family members or visitors are exhorted to write about their daily activities was perhaps the swift and hotly debated changes then taking place, brought about by anglicization, modernization, social and religious reform. There might thus have been a general sense of immense and profound change, of excitement at the progress in the political and social arena, which would have impinged on all members of the family, young and old, men and women, even if it is not explicitly mentioned. They knew they were in the vanguard of change, and it was perhaps these changes which made the family feel that it was important to draw the defining line between themselves and others, to preserve their family identity by means of what emerges from some of these records to be fairly rigid ideas about what constituted enjoyment, fun, fair play, etc., that is, the norms of familial, and therefore social values.

However, one should not think that it was an effortless commitment on the part of young and old to record their family history. The books are replete with complaints about young people being careless, being sloppy when they actually wrote, of long gaps in the family records, of exasperation and punishments.

IV Varying Approaches of the Writers

The elders' attitudes to the stated purpose of these records varied a good deal: Badruddin remarked rather solemnly on 10 May 1901 in his introductory entry to a new volume, that such a volume would be an important reminder of the *gammath* (fun) that his family had had. Similarly, when Amiruddin, his younger brother, started his own book in 1876 on a coffee plantation in the Nilgiris, he wrote enthusiastically that there were so many wonderful and strange things happening, they had to be recorded, and his certainty that the household would rush to write of their experiences with tigers and snakes.

Rahat Badruddin, c. 1890.

On the other hand, Rahat, Badruddin's wife, rebukes her children for not having taken their duties seriously, leaving important matters like the death of their uncle Camruddin, unrecorded. In September 1889 she wrote: 'I'm extremely upset that for some days now, in fact for quite a long time, no one has written in this book through sheer laziness. It's very necessary that this custom be kept up, in a responsible way, and respecting certain norms. This means that those who choose to write take the trouble to do so correctly, and record in a responsible manner those things that are important for our descendants to know. Now there are many things that have not been recorded, and I think I must write about them [gives account of Camruddin's illness and death].'

Rahat's daughter Hafiza also complained of the struggle it was to keep up the book: 'Goodness me,' she writes, 'look at this—so many people have written. The two worst culprits were really Sakina and Husain[14]—nothing had any effect on them at all, neither threats nor strict instructions that they had to write once a week. And then, on Sunday morning, I made them do *uth-baith* (push-ups), when we were all gathered for breakfast, and this had a most satisfactory result.'

In keeping with this more serious approach, one finds that the women tend to use the journals to reflect on social customs and changes within the family—for instance, Rahat writes about the suitable age for marriage, Surayya, an elder daughter of Badruddin's, on the importance of breaking away from rigid restrictions on marriage within the *jamaat,* Rahat again on the importance of diversity of dress. However, as noted earlier, the very nature of this family record would automatically exclude references to the world outside. For instance, Badruddin was a close friend of the scholar, judge, and social reformer, Ranade, and would have been deeply concerned over contemporary social and political issues; Camruddin played a leading part in the effort to protect a young Maharashtrian girl from the consequences of child marriage. But such issues seldom surface in the family books.

The last half of the nineteenth century saw battles being fought by reformist Hindu groups over issues such as widow remarriage, child marriage, or female education, issues which impinged on the lives of all communities. At the same time, women like the Parsi Cornelia Sorabjee, Vidyagauri Nilkanth of Ahmedabad or Kadambini Ganguly from Calcutta were striding ahead in the field of education and employment; and there were of course vigorous discussions on the role of Muslims in newly politically aware India. These concerns were being raised in public, through letters to the press, tracts, autobiographies, written by women and men in Marathi and Gujarati as well as English, revealing an altogether different kind of life and of struggles for emancipation of a kind that our women seem not to have faced, or not to have been aware of facing.[15] The reason for these lacunae in the *akhbar* may have been that the family women were as aware as the men that this was a family book, the purpose of which was to celebrate and enshrine the family culture; it was not a forum for discussing the fundamental changes or reforms that were taking place outside this space. Hence it would be a mistake to judge, merely on the basis of these writings, this particular genre, that the family as a group was impervious to serious concerns relating to other communities.

However, from time to time, important national events do disrupt the saga of family events: we have a tantalizing glimpse of this when Badruddin's eldest son, Mohsin,[16] made a revealing comment on Badruddin's attitude to the Congress session over which he presided in 1887: 'Father is going to Madras as President of the Congress with much *taqaza,* in fact under compulsion.' However, he continues, 'This is a very wonderful thing, and a great source of pride for all Muslims, and especially for our *qabila* (tribe, family), from amongst all the Hindus.'

Badruddin himself wrote, rather self-consciously: 'I haven't written in this book for a long time, partly because... the children were writing in it [keeping it up] so I didn't think it was necessary for me to do so. But today I think it wouldn't be inappropriate for me to write a brief account of my trip to Madras.' He continues with an account of his activities there which he felt was appropriate for a family journal.

Similarly, this is not a forum for displaying the tensions, the traumas experienced, for instance, by young women married into an uncle's household that turned out to have an alien culture, or accounts by women who felt their own world was becoming increasingly remote and isolated from that of their menfolk, of those who longed for more traditional lifestyles and questioned the need to be modern and successful in a Westernizing world. There were tragic deaths or unhappy marriages, and from the matter-of-fact way in which these events are recounted we can assume that much is being left unsaid.

The need to write about themselves also indicates a certain sophistication in the family's assessment of itself and its social values. Underlying the wish to record for posterity accounts of picnics and games of badminton and croquet, or of family gatherings where plays were performed or of musical evenings, one might sense the feeling of being special. What was this based on?

It was a highly cultivated and progressive group, one that was eager to see what the West had to offer, but very clear-sighted about its deficiencies; a group where both men and women were equally at home climbing trees and in putting up plays, in playing the sitar and the violin, singing *ghazals* or English songs at the piano; declaiming Milton or verses from Saadi or Ghalib; where each new daughter-in-law was introduced to the family culture by being taken out to ride every morning. And where the children regularly participated in the annual sports at the hill station of Matheran.

Most of all, it was a group that believed in the importance of the written word, and this is of special interest in a culture where preservation of material objects has generally been considered to have little value.

2

Currents of Change 1876–1939, as revealed in the *Akhbar*

The Badruddin Tyabji family books, which cover the period 1880–1907, run to over 800 pages of Urdu in foolscap. Each of Badruddin's three homes, in Bombay, and the hill stations of Matheran and Mahabaleshwar, had a separate book allotted to it. The Amiruddin Tyabji books, started in Bombay, Wayanad, Coimbatore, are less impressive in length—although they cover a longer period, 1876–1939—but are equally lively and almost indistinguishable in tone and content. The Fyzee Yali *akhbar* and the Latifa, Fatehali, and Mohamedi volumes show the intermittent vitality of this tradition, but it is the Badruddin and Amiruddin *akhbars*, with their thoughtful and serious comments on contemporary issues, on which I have largely based one portion of my study.

One question that arises when one confronts the enormous amount of material produced by one family about itself is whether the enforced practice of writing, of recording, makes a marked difference to the family's attitude to the written word. Does it lead to unusually great respect for personal records, for keeping diaries, preserving account books and letters? Was there any long-lasting, deeper impact of childhood training in this area? If not in terms of writing, in terms of preserving? Are there large amounts of family records still secreted away?

But of greater interest is the expectation that through these *akhbar* books, one may find answers to questions of a type that it is rarely possible to ask: for instance, what light is thrown on the social relationships between men and women within the family, and to what extent can we presume that these would hold for other communities of the same social standing? How much did friendships made in school, particularly by the girls, contribute to greater contact between the varied communities, which seem to have led somewhat isolated lives, except when there were functions in the homes of

The Changing World of a Bombay Muslim Community, 1870–1945. Salima Tyabji, Oxford University Press.
© Nasir Tyabji 2023. DOI: 10.1093/oso/9780192869746.003.0002

British officials?[1] How did the growing national and social reform move-ments, fostered almost entirely by men, affect the women? To what extent did the women of this family feel it was important to utilize the forums provided by the ladies' clubs in Bombay or the women's magazines pub-lished from Aligarh and Lucknow to give expression to their views on is-sues like the age of marriage, or girls' education or purdah? Did they restrict themselves to questions affecting only the Muslim community, or had the growing sense of political unity also affected their understanding of there being social issues faced in common by Indians of all communities?

What reaction would independent-minded girls have to European notions of purdah society being a deprived one? Where would women of this highly sophisticated culture look to for role models: would the North Indian aristocratic culture be a more seductive one than that of the western woman? Is there any hint of their feeling that purdah did indeed deprive them of important functions, such as the ability to take part in public life? Did they think that as women they could indeed do so? Has the idea of women only being a power behind the scene receded some-what? What was happening in other communities? What views did they have about Urdu? Were they self-confident and at ease with their col-ourful local version of the language? If not, if correct Urdu was important for them, what might the reasons be? Finally, is there any suggestion that the men discussed these issues *within* the family?

Even if the *akhbar* do not provide definite answers to such questions, there may be hints and indications which would flesh out our knowledge of the social realities of the period, during which such enormous social and political changes were taking place. Comments on these issues are of special interest when they emanate from the women, particularly so in the absence of similar material on other Bombay families.

I The Creation of Family Identity and the Need to Record

Although all the elders of the family made intermittent attempts to keep up the custom, for the Badruddin family it was notably Rahat, Badruddin's wife, and her elder daughter Hafiza who showed special concern that the family chronicle should be properly maintained in the early years. Finally, it was a son, Faiz, for whom it became an obsession and to whom we owe the rich material of the 1890s. Faiz, then a young college student, took it on himself to discipline his family including visiting cousins and potential in-laws and force them to write, especially in the Matheran book.[2]

What made him do so? What sort of importance had these books acquired for him? It seems that a very strong sense of family identity, distinct even from that of maternal or paternal relations, was beginning to emerge, and the Badruddin branch of the family was developing its own subculture. For Faiz, it was important to reinforce this by recording all the activities that went into the creation of this culture. His uncle Najmuddin saw in him a successor to Camruddin, the founder of this family tradition. Was Faiz alone in this project? Were there counterparts in other branches of the family? For the Amiruddin Tyabji family, his cousin and contemporary Hamid became a demanding editor: in the Amiri book too, the material from the 1890s is particularly rich.

Faiz became something of a tyrant, but appears nevertheless to have been adored by his younger siblings, however, much of a nuisance the elder ones found his regime. 'Write! Write! That's alone hears about as soon as one arrives!' commented an irritable elder, who had apparently heard tales about the kind of literary frenzy prevailing in this household, and thought it was overdone. There was for instance a bulletin board on which everyone's names figured, giving the day each person was to write in the Book.

But not everyone was able to exercise the same authority, regardless of their age and seniority.[3] What's at stake here was not male against female, elder against younger, but, it appears, beneath the horseplay and *tamasha*, a reassertion of authority of the group 'Leader'. He was the one who decided what the day's activities were to be, what was 'sporting' or not, what was out of sync with the family culture that was being evolved through games, walks, and other entertainments: a status that was unquestioningly given Faiz, and that probably led to his autocratic decisions being accepted with reasonable good will.

Faiz was more than a mere bully as far as forcing people to write went; he was properly an editor, who decided who should write on what topic or event, and in this, he and his sister Surayya, who were perhaps the intellectuals of the family, worked together. For instance, Surayya suggested to her eldest sister, Amina (Mrs Abbas Tyabji), that she write about her encounter with an English woman in the train from Matheran to Bombay;

Faiz decided that his eldest brother Mohsin should write a description of the great eclipse of 1898; Amina was similarly bullied into writing accounts of her travels in Europe for both the Badruddin and the Amiruddin books; it was probably Faiz who decided that Sakina should write the long detailed 'official' account of their mother's sudden illness and death; and finally Faiz who asked another sister, Halima (mother of A. A. A. Fyzee) to write the very fine account of her excursion to the Jog Falls with which the Badruddin books end (see Chapter 3). An appropriate piece to end with, as that account encapsulates much of this family's culture: a sense of adventure, great sensitivity to natural beauty, and physical hardiness.

II Differences in Attitude to the *Akhbar*

It's clear that the *akhbar ki kitab* was regarded by members of both Badruddin's and Amiruddin's families either as a nuisance, a pound of flesh being demanded every week or as a convenient forum for settling scores; for thoughtful comment on social change and reform; or a place to record important events which impinged on the family's life, whether deaths, eclipses, or Congress meetings. While the stated purpose of the books remained to record the fun the family unit had, an astonishing variety of personalities emerge, with varying perspectives and interests.

A Young Girl's Perspective

A counterpart to Editor Sahib for the Badruddin books was his elder sister Surayya, one of the most consistently thoughtful writers on issues of general interest. Born in 1875, she experienced directly the radical changes affecting the practice of purdah, of modern schooling for girls, of reforming the practice of child marriage, that took place in many modernizing families in the last decades of the nineteenth century.

Her contributions to the book start about 1886 when she was 11, and continue till the Badruddin family books end, in 1907, soon after his death. It is fortunate that she, one of the most gifted of his children: artistic, very musical, highly sensitive to natural beauty, an energetic young woman with a great sense of fun, but also someone who engaged seriously with the issues of the time, saw the *akhbar* books as a forum for her views. There are a number of photographs taken of her over a period of 30 years or so, which have a strange effect on the viewer: they bring home very sharply the fact that this modern young woman, with her zest for life and eager responses to fresh experience, lived in a different age, beset with what appear to be crippling conventions, symbolized perhaps in the elaborate, beautiful clothes. But the clothes did not hinder their vigorous activities (see Chapter 3).

Sakina (standing) and her younger
sister Surayya, about 1890.

Our first introduction to Badruddin's family's lifestyle is through Surayya's contributions to the *akhbar* books in the mid-1880s when she and her elder sister Hafiza (1870–87), young girls of 11 and 16, rushed desperately to the *akhbar* book to be the first to record accounts of outings, or other significant events; these were largely of visits to English homes, with wistful comments on the elegance of the ladies' drawing rooms, their furniture, paintings, carpets, etc., from which one may infer that their own home was lacking in what they perceived as style.

She also commented on the fact that their father's large house had a garden which needed a lot done to it; here too the model was the gardens of English officials, with a rose garden, a shrubbery, a gymkhana area, etc., rather than a Mughal Garden (for which in any case the slopes of the Bombay hills would not have been very appropriate).[4] Here the rather disparaging comment made by Nora Scott, the wife of an English judge of the Bombay High Court in 1882, on Badruddin's home, helps us to understand the kind of unease the young girls must have felt about their home. Lady Scott, a sensitive and sympathetic observer of the Indian scene, remarked in her diary that '[The] veranda was furnished with sofas and a gaudy carpet', that the drawing room was furnished in the European style, 'but not prettily' and she found that 'the little girls' dresses were like those of children in a circus in England'.[5]

Halima, fifth daughter of Badruddin Tyabji c.1890.

III Music: Its Place in the Family Circle

Surayya's great passion was music. In keeping with the highly anglicized culture of her immediate family, it was the piano that she learnt to play. She doesn't mention where she had her lessons, whether in an English lady's home or whether she had a teacher coming to the house, but it's clear that her instrument (probably a grand piano) had an important position in the drawing room, called the hall. She would practise with fervour and for many hours, to the irritation of some members of the family who many years later remembered the sound of her piano reverberating through the house.

On the evenings that the entire extended family met at Badruddin's house, music played an important part, and it seems that Surayya, and a cousin, Jafar (brother of Akbar Hydari) played duets on the violin and piano. Perhaps she played the accompaniment, or sang herself, English songs, for singing *ghazals* or playing the *sitar* were not, at that point, acceptable in Badruddin's household. A decade later, by the mid-1890s, it seems that things had changed: his younger daughters and daughter-in-law were learning to play the *sitar*, to sing Urdu *ghazals*, and always performed at family gathering. Badruddin's earlier views were probably influenced by the colonial perception of Indian dance and music that it was performed on by professional singers and performers who were also courtesans. Safia Jabir Ali's memoirs don't contain any comment on this although she writes at some length about her family's taste in music and 'accomplishments' (see Chapter 4). None of the younger girls seem to have had lessons in drawing, painting, or embroidery although these accomplishments had been an important part of their elder sisters' life since the 1880s. This was perhaps because of the increasing demands of a convent school education.

Tahira (*right*), then engaged to Mohsin Tyabji, with Sharifa, daughter of Abbas Tyabji, Baroda, *c.*1895.

Currents of conservative thinking existed within the larger family, noticeably in the family of Badruddin's sister; Sakina, whose husband, Jiwabhai, had such strong views on music, theatre, and certain kinds of entertainment that whenever he was to be a guest, Surayya remarked sorrowfully the piano had to be shrouded. This happened not only at Badruddin's gathering but also at those held by his elder brother, Camruddin. Such views were generally deplored if not derided by other members of Badruddin's larger family, as is evident from a comment made by the young and irreverent youngest brother, Amiruddin, who wrote from Le Havre in 1870 to his family in Bombay how much he was enjoying meeting French ladies and going to dances and the theatre, in spite of the disapproval of certain relations at home, to whom he would never dare to confess all this.[6] The Sulaymani Jamaat had taken a conservative stand on such issues. Badruddin and Camruddin, successful members of the Bar, could afford to ignore their religious leaders' dicta, but not so other members of the community who were in humbler positions, where the community's approval and patronage were of social and financial importance.

IV Modernity: Education, Exercise, and Fun

Education

A basic plank in the nineteenth-century social reformers' programme, which under missionary influence was common all over India, was the need for female education. Hence, Badruddin was at one with contemporaries such as Ranade[7] in believing in the importance of educating the women in his family. Although he had strong support from some wealthy members of the Muslim community in Bombay, the reluctance to educate girls was as pronounced and widespread amongst Muslims as in other communities, and hence it required very strong convictions to act upon. Badruddin's convictions probably arose, as did his elder brother Camruddin's, from his experiences in England, as well as the influence exercised by the Governor's wife, Lady Reay.

His wife Rahat was literate in Gujarati and Urdu; she read the papers in Gujarati, and loved to hear Urdu and Persian poetry. She wrote with great facility in Urdu. There is no record of her attempting to learn English but she was, family anecdotes indicate, a strong-willed lady, who might have felt no need to add to her skills. In 1876 the first girls' school, the Zenana Bible Mission School, was established in Bombay. All three of Badruddin's elder daughters, Sakina, Hafiza, and Surayya, attended the school, the first Muslim girls to do so. Other cousins, Nazli and Atiya Fyzee amongst them, also joined. The school course would have included arithmetic, geography, history, English, and probably some kind of physical exercise. In addition, they had lessons in sketching, portraiture, landscape painting, at the homes of English ladies. One of the skills Sakina acquired was the art of colouring or tinting photographs: a specimen of her work, a portrait of her father, survives in a family collection. Two of Badruddin's younger daughters, growing up in the early years of the twentieth century, were removed from a school because he was appalled at the poor teaching of English.

For Badruddin's daughters, communicating with or entertaining his Western or Parsi friends would not have been difficult, not only because of being at ease speaking English but also for the sense of confidence their mission school education would have given them. Nora Scott has commented on how well Badruddin's elder daughters stood in for their mother as hostess at parties.[8]

Exercise

It was understood that fresh air and exercise were as important for women as learning to read and write. Ramabai Ranade describes Ranade's insistence that she have an airing and a walk every evening, however greatly it offended the women in his conservative family. The emphasis on exercise, on outings, was equally marked at the court of the Begums of Bhopal, where social reforms affecting women went hand-in hand with a conventionally Islamic lifestyle.[9]

Safia, Badruddin's youngest daughter, writing many years later (see Chapter 4), remarked that she thought the main influence on the Tyabji clan in this area was exercised by a cousin, Badruddin Lukmani, who had studied medicine abroad, and come back greatly impressed by the western emphasis on fresh air and exercise for good health, as was Badruddin himself. Whatever the reasons, the entire clan, men and women, girls and boys, took to badminton, croquet, climbing trees, riding, going on long excursions, with great zest. (There were some exceptions who made their distaste for exercise known, but they were outnumbered.) Cricket was not a game played by this innovative family in the nineteenth century; team games were confined to *bhirokho* and *ata-pata* (Chapter 4). Nor do we hear of their swimming, even though they lived near the sea. However, other members of the clan who had bought property by the sea south of Bombay, notably the Fyzee family, went bathing every day (see Atiya Fyzee's entries, Yali *Akhbar*). They probably had a separate set of clothes for this exercise, of which unfortunately we have no record.

The entire clan was keen on physical activity of every kind: Surayya specifically mentioned her uncle Camruddin's encouragement of her riding, so much so that he presented her with a pony. His own daughter was also a fine rider. Certainly Badruddin, by the end of the 1890s, felt that it was important for his daughters-in-law to learn to ride and took each young woman out with him in the mornings for a ride, while the others walked to their picnic spots.

The girl selected as a bride for his eldest son, Mohsin (who had done outstandingly well in the ICS exams in London in 1885), was Rahat's brother's daughter, for Badruddin's wife had strong views about not having her children marrying into *nawabi* families, but wanted people of good solid bourgeois stock (Laeeq Futehally, pers. comm.). Tahira was invited to spend some time with her future family to be indoctrinated appropriately into the family pursuits of riding, walking, and playing croquet. Initially she'd found her new family's daily routine of brisk walks and rounds of badminton exhausting but eventually became a good energetic walker herself, excellent at croquet, and a fine rider.

By the 1880s, Badruddin's practice had made him a very wealthy man. So one may assume that the layout of the extensive gardens of his house on Cumballa Hill was influenced by the new anglicized tastes. The garden included a gymkhana area, where there were tennis courts, and a little later, badminton courts, as well as shrubberies, a rose garden, and little knolls with summer houses (see Chapter 4). The girls preferred badminton to the more strenuous tennis, except for Surayya who continued to play with her brothers and cousins. There was such a passion for badminton that the men apparently played all day, even through hot and sultry afternoons, but the girls preferred the mornings, often before going to school, or the evenings when there was a breeze. Nora Scott gives us a vivid picture of the 'little Oriental damsel' (Nazli Fyzee, aged about 12) playing a vigorous game of badminton in the courtyard of her Bombay home, which was a fairly modest house, near Babulnath. Croquet, a little later, also became a great favourite. There were badminton and croquet grounds in the homes of most family members in Bombay as well as in Matheran and Kihim, the village by the sea where many family members owned homes.

A game of croquet at Dilkusha, Najmuddin Tyabji's house in Kihim, c. 1890.

Apart from walking, riding, playing badminton, Badruddin's own family went on long, strenuous excursions to places like Vihar Lake (now absorbed into Bombay city) that were in those days several hours' journey away, involving travelling by train, bullock cart, and walking, to reach the picnic spot. Rahat, in spite of the frail health caused by constant childbearing and her weight, joined in many of these expeditions and wrote a detailed account of them (see Chapter 3). These expeditions were ones where Badruddin's entire family—his married children and their children—was together for long periods, where the children and adults developed the same tastes and values, and a strong unifying sense of family culture arose, a culture that was both distinctive and binding.

Some years later, describing her younger siblings' behaviour in Matheran, Surayya remarked dryly that with all the climbing about on trees, eating *jamun*, and raucous singing of choruses, they were behaving like their monkey ancestors. But there's a tinge of approval, if not pride, at such simian behaviour. As for more public activities, all the four little girls took part in the sports at Matheran and came home to heap the hall table with their cups and prizes, although for at least a couple of years, there was formidable competition from the Allana[10] family girls, who walked off with a couple of prizes that Badruddin's daughters had tended to think was their family property. There were different sports days for British and Indian children. There's no comment in these books on this segregation—perhaps it was taken for granted as a fact of life.

How common was this new interest in exercise and fresh air? Did it apply fairly generally to all families of the same westernizing social class? A comment of Surayya's on an evening spent with a Parsi friend of hers suggests otherwise. Surayya took her guest for a stroll, perhaps a brisk walk, in the garden and was disconcerted to find that her friend didn't enjoy it at all. They came back early and probably sat and had sherbet and sweets in the veranda. So Tahira Lukmani from Baroda was not an exception at finding walking and riding an unusual pastime.

However, this incident is of particular interest as it's one of the very few involving an 'outsider', in this case, a Parsi, whom Surayya must have made friends with in school. She would have belonged to the same social class, of modernizing professional families, and we would therefore expect that they would have more or less the same ideas about pastimes, exercise and fresh air, derived from their mission schools and English models. If one can generalize on the basis of these two experiences, it's evident that changes that affected the concept of womanhood would take time to be adopted, regardless of the community.

Fun

Fun, amusement, is a concept related to the aristocracy: Mughal princesses and noblemen's wives had fun hunting and riding, shooting deer and tiger, playing chess, listening to music, and smoking the *huqqa*. It was not an idea that fitted into middle-class Indian society, where women's sole function appeared to have been to bear children and please the household gods, or *mullas*. Camruddin, the first member of the clan to be educated abroad, played a very important part in introducing the idea of fun, of independence, to the women of the household. Camruddin seemed to have taken a special interest in encouraging his young nieces to enjoy themselves outside the house—a revolutionary concept for those times. Surayya relates joyfully that her uncle presented her with a pony of her own, having discovered when she visited him in Mahabaleshwar, the fashionable hill station for Bombay officials, how much she enjoyed riding. (His own daughter, Dilshad Begum, was also a fine rider.)

More, he encouraged Surayya and her two closest friends within the family, Nazli and Atiya Fyzee, to found a club, the sole purpose of which was going for outings and enjoying themselves. It was both a joke and a matter of envy to their brothers and sisters or female cousins who were excluded from the club, that the three of them should set off in the evenings, go for a drive and gorge themselves on *ganna* (sugarcane). This was a far cry from the general belief that the role of women was to become efficient managers of their families' welfare and essentially to remain inconspicuous spouses or mothers within the family context.

But Camruddin or perhaps Badruddin himself also instructed the three founder-members on how a club functioned: the members therefore formulated a proper constitution, setting out the aims of the club, its rules, fees, etc., and the importance of keeping proper accounts. By the 1890s, membership had been expanded to include four more young women of the clan, and the club was named the Akhde Surayya (the Pleiades); by the 1910s, they had a printed rule book. 'Having fun' was taken for granted, they now stated the specific ways in which this fun was to be obtained: by organizing badminton tournaments, picnics, and excursions. Male cousins were allowed to participate in these activities. From comments made by other members of the family it appeared that Surayya was not only the founder and main spirit behind the club but also an extremely determined if not autocratic secretary, not inclined to give way to suggestions from others, or even admit her elder sisters to the club in the early years.[11]

V Social Reform

Age of Marriage

To what extent were Badruddin and other members of the clan directly affected by the social reformist movements regarding child marriage and widow remarriage? There is no direct evidence regarding this in the *akhbar*, but probably the reason not one of his daughters, apart from the eldest, Amina, was married till she was 18 was because Badruddin was greatly influenced by the reformist opposition to child marriage.[12]

Sakina, later to become a prominent social worker and Congress activist, was over 20, and Surayya at least 18 before their marriages took place. And although Mohsin, Badruddin's eldest son, was engaged to a girl who was about 14 they did not marry till she reached the age of 17 or 18. When, in 1894, two of her nieces got married when they were only 14, Rahat expressed her views very strongly in the *akhbar*: she wrote with feeling about the hardships faced by girls being married against their will, thrown into strange homes when they were so young, and, in the case of marriages with 'outsiders', to a man who would be a total stranger. In both instances her apprehensions were borne out.[13]

Both Nazli Fyzee and her elder sister Zahra were divorced (Zahra from the son of a first cousin, Camruddin Tyabji). So was Camruddin's sister, Kulsum bi. In later generations the practice became even more common. Does this reflect something of Arab social customs, where divorce, from the earliest times (cf. Sukayna, Hazrat Husain's daughter) to the present day is common and carries no social stigma? As against North India, where rather than divorce and remarry, it was more common to take a second wife? Is that what Badruddin and Rahat wanted to protect their daughters from?

Regardless of how gravely Rahat viewed the marriage of her two young nieces at such a young age, and despite the fact that both ended badly, there is no doubt that one at least enjoyed herself thoroughly at her wedding. Here is an account, given by a disapproving older cousin, Badruddin's daughter Hafiza, probably aged 17 or thereabouts, of her cousin Nazli's wedding in December 1886.

'We tried to go early to Begum Sahiba's splendid and *nawiz* wedding. Nazli wasn't yet ready—but that didn't matter. But something else happened that was so strange that we couldn't quite take it in, or believe that it was really happening. And this was that Nazli just didn't behave at all decorously and *sharmao* as she should have done. It wouldn't have mattered too much if she'd at least just sat quietly—but no, there she was, laughing and chattering away! We felt it was just so very odd and improper—quite terrible. And then, even when she was dressed up and looked a proper *dulhan,* she carried on in the same way! She just wouldn't sit still, or stop talking. We kept on gesturing to her to behave properly, and eventually, Bibi Amirunissa and Zahra [her mother and elder sister] had to speak to her quite sharply. But it didn't have any effect on her. I didn't say anything to her because there were a lot of English and Parsi ladies there, but she didn't behave any more decorously then either. Eventually I just couldn't contain myself, and ticked her off, and her reply was "Oh heavens, what can I do? I don't feel *sharmilee.* So tell me what to do." Oh we just didn't feel that it was a wedding at all.'

What Hafiza doesn't comment on, but her sister Surayya and cousin Camrunissa in the Amiruddin *akhbar* did, was that this was the first marriage of a girl outside the *jamaat,* and strongly disapproved of by the Hazrat, the religious head of the community, who refused to per- form the *nikah*; and that not only members of the community, but close relations such as Camruddin himself, stayed away. Camruddin's family was in Matheran, a hill station within easy reach of Bombay, but made no effort to be present—only Badruddin's and Amiruddin's families at- tended the wedding, although there were a number of English and Parsi guests (no Hindus are mentioned). Surayya, who was very attached to both Nazli and Atiya, doesn't discuss the issue at length, but the other cousin, Camrunissa, writes with great approval of this radical change in marriage customs, hopes that there will be more such marriages, and that people will gradually change their narrow-minded attitudes. The disapproval of the marriage, even though it was such a grand one, was probably based on the fact that the Nawabs of Janjira were Sunnis. It seems that Amiruddin Tyabji was responsible for arranging it—the Nawab was one of his cronies, who had originally wanted to marry one of Badruddin's daughters, had Badruddin's wife Rahat countenanced the idea.

Individuals and Social Reform

Although the social reform movements in India regarding women's rights were generally initiated and led by men, there were in each community remarkable women who were in the forefront of these struggles. In the Muslim community in Bombay, the Fyzee women played an outstanding part in the early twentieth century in the area of female education, the practice of *purdah*, the importance of exercise and so on.

Nazli Fyzee, when Begum of Janjira, made a name for herself by establishing schools for girls, encouraging women to be active and take part in sports, and herself indulging in the family pursuits of riding, walking, shooting (her cousin Salman describes her shooting a buck when he was on a visit to Janjira). Her husband encouraged, or at least did not prevent her from travelling to Aligarh, Lucknow, Bhopal, and other places to meet others keen on social reform within the Muslim community; she wrote extensively on the need for female education, contributed generously to Maulana Shibli's Nadwa in Lucknow, and had the Maulana coming to stay at Janjira.[14] She also travelled widely in Europe with her husband, visited Istanbul, was given the order of the Nishan-e-Shafqat by the Sultan. She was able in every way to make use of the freedom and opportunities she had had in her parental home to even greater profit in her new station.

Her divorce, which took place about 1914, is also of interest because of the light it throws on the Fyzee sisters' commitment to social reform. It appears (Suhaila Habib, oral communication) that although the Nawab was devoted to his wife, the necessity for an heir forced him to marry again. Nazli Begum was told that her status as the elder Begum would remain untouched. However she was unwilling to make this compromise. Her younger sister, Atiya, who with Nazli herself had campaigned, spoken, and written about the restoration of Quranic rights to women, which included the restriction of polygamy to extreme cases, persuaded her older sister not to concede this right to her husband. Nazli Begum then asked for a divorce and obtained a generous settlement from her husband. Her life as an intellectual, patron of the arts, and social reformer does not seem to have been affected by the change in her status; she continued to travel widely, in Europe, the US, and Japan with her sister, and was in touch with the leading French intellectuals of the day.

VI European Stimulus to Social Reform

The concept of public service, of charitable work unrelated to caste or community, was a novel one for Indian society in the nineteenth century.

Women of the middle classes would normally distribute alms on auspicious occasions, food and clothing at Id or Diwali. The wealthy would endow masjids, build gardens, rest houses for pilgrims, but to take up charitable work outside the home, work that would benefit women of all communities was a revolutionary idea, and an area where European influence, both missionary and from leading members of the government, played a very fruitful role.

Rahat describes parties given by Lady Northcote, wife of the Governor, to which she would have taken her young English-speaking daughters and mentions that apart from such parties, the ladies of different communities met at English ladies' homes to have discussions on social issues, and also, for instance, to raise funds for the Victoria Memorial.

In August 1890, when she was 19, Sakina wrote of a Committee of Women, set up so that purdah Muslim women could take part in social reform activities. They met at the home of Lady Thomas Thomason. Rahat and Mariam Khatoon (Mrs Najmuddin) were members. They intended to visit girls' schools and collect money for deserving students. This indicates that interest in and support for reform was no longer restricted to their own communities. The girls' schools referred to might have been mission schools, although that seems unlikely; were they perhaps informal classes, such as the ones set up by Ramabai Ranade at the Sewa Sadan in 1890. In this way, an understanding of the restrictions of being in purdah began to emerge.

In Sakina's words: 'The European Ladies have started a new interest for us; for years, the Indian National Congress had been having meetings which only the gentlemen ran; we haven't been able to attend because of purdah. And now we want to take part too—this of course applies only to Muslim women—the others have been active for years. Now they have set up a separate committee only for women and we have taken up certain tasks, which we can handle. One of them is to go to girls' schools and give them whatever aid we can. A number of family women are on this committee; and we had a meeting at Lady Thomas Thomason—which Mother and Chachani Saheba Maryam (Mrs Najmuddin Tyabji) also attended. We all contributed Rs 10 a year, and this money will either go towards prizes in a girls' school, or to fund a poor bright girl.'

The Sewa Sadan provided another forum where women of all communities could meet and work together. (This was an institution that the

Tyabji family was closely associated with till the 1970s.) A similar initiative with a different purpose was the Club founded by the Maharani of Baroda for women. The concept here was that women should get out of their homes, and amuse themselves, and also in the process meet women of other communities and backgrounds. Amina wrote of the beautiful Hindu Ladies and their daughters who had responded to the Maharani's efforts, but that sadly, there were no Muslim women apart from herself and one other lady. The sense she conveyed was of Muslim women being cocooned from outside influences. Such were the first slight but significant steps towards developing a sense of social cohesiveness, that was later to provide the foundation, especially amongst the women, of a sense of national consciousness.

VII Changing Views on Purdah

Was there any change in the understanding and practice of purdah that paralleled the other significant changes in social consciousness? With all the vigorous activity mentioned above and the free mingling of cousins at games and family entertainments, it is something of a surprise to find that the girls were in fact in purdah. It seems that girls over 13 did not appear before strange men in public: Nora Scott described how although, 'as a great concession' her husband, whom Badruddin greatly respected, was allowed to be present, 'but when Mr Peterson looked in for a minute of his way to a dinner party, to see his children performing, Mr B. did not approve'. She had noted in May 1884 that she had been called on by some 'purdah' ladies. 'The husband of one of them, Mr. Ameeroodeen Tyabjee, came with them, and he was very pleasant, friendly and merry, evidently pleased to come and bring his women kind.' Asked if either of the ladies had been to England, 'No,' he replied, 'we wish they would, but they will not come out of purdah, and I think the last few years it is worse than ever—our ladies keep so close'.

Since the girls led such full and active lives within their own family, and took part in school activities—for instance, at a school exhibition held in December 1887, Sakina, in purdah, by which we assume that there were no men in the audience, read the Prologue, sang, and played the piano—it's difficult to tell whether they felt the restrictions of being in purdah.

In fact, some years later, in January 1891, Surayya wrote in her spirited way that at *zenana* parties the first and biggest question from the 'Angrez' women tended to be, 'But how can you get on without men? What is there in life without them???' But, she continues, 'they forget our club motto— that the world is for women too, and that we can perhaps manage without them! We're not their ragged little tails [*dumchiyan*]! Ha!' The 'club' was probably the Society started by the American, Dr Ryder, with the motto: 'Tell the men the world was made for women also.' Sakina commented: 'not only is it true that women can do everything just as well as men, if not better, but unlikely that men can compete with women.' Her namesake, Sukayna, the Prophet's great-granddaughter, would certainly have agreed. She can be held up as the model of the liberated Muslim woman—she debated in mosques against the Umayyad usurpers of the imamate, changed husbands, and in her marriage contracts had it written that her husband would not have the right to polygamy. Further, she stipulated that she would not obey her husband against her will.[15]

The first negative reference to purdah is made rather wistfully by Badruddin's fourth daughter, Jamila (Surayya's partner in a badminton match) about 1898. She describes the events at the annual Matheran Sports, and says she's not able to take part in the riding event for which one of her brothers had entered, or even watch it properly, since she had to sit in the purdah enclosure, which would of course have been at some distance from the grounds, and also curtained off by chiks (apart from the Badruddin family, there were also some girls from a Khoja family, probably the Allanas). We see here a delicate balancing of the feeling that while all was very well with their world, there were also new vistas of activity opening up which were still closed to them.

However, by the turn of the nineteenth century, there was a marked change in attitude, and the practice of purdah became a topic of heated controversy. Badruddin himself took the lead at the Anglo-Mohamedan Educational Conference held in December 1903, when he denounced the practice of purdah in India as being far removed from the Quran's injunctions. In a controversial speech, one which was a landmark for the emancipation of Muslim women in India, he 'attributed the backwardness of the Musulmans largely to the religious and literary prejudices and the absence of female education.' He strongly urged that the education of Muslim girls should be taken in hand. Musulmans had lagged behind because of the restrictions of purdah which had been extended far beyond the demands of the Shariat. 'There are', he said, 'no doubt plenty of passages in the Koran and in the traditions of the prophet which lay down the highest principles of morality and modesty, which inculcate modesty and decorum, which prohibit the ostentatious display of beauty and ornaments, which upbraid impropriety of conduct, but I have not been able to discover anything in the Koran which either directs or even sanctions the system of purdah in all its strictness as it obtains among us to the present day.'[16]

In a notable instance of the women of the family utilizing the *akhbar* to record their views on public events, we have two entries in the Badruddin Akhbar (see Chapter 3) which relate graphically the intense agitation caused by calls for the need to establish girls' schools and the doing away of purdah. We also have an account by Surayya describing with great feeling the fetters which they had begun to feel bound them, and which they realized were not imposed by their religion, but rather by social convention. Technically they were already out of purdah, in that they travelled freely in Europe without burqas.

In 1893 Amina, Badruddin's eldest daughter, whose husband Abbas, judge at the High Court of Baroda, and later Chief Justice, was a close friend and confidant of the Gaekwar of Baroda, was invited to accompany the Maharani on her first trip to Europe. Since the Maharani had lived in close seclusion and was unfamiliar with European customs, it was felt that Amina, with her knowledge of English and familiarity with European ways, would be a helpful aide and companion on the journey. They were evidently good friends and in a relationship of trust which paralleled the relationship between their husbands.

Amina's first cousin, Zubeida, whose husband, again a first cousin, was an engineer, travelled in Europe and England, went to plays, met Queen Victoria, went to fancy dress parties, and to the theatre. They must both have revelled in the freedom. Back at home, they had to observe purdah, but the *akhbar* books don't indicate that they were restive about this; perhaps because, apart from the Parsi community, most other women of equivalent status would have practised some form of seclusion.[17]

VIII Relations with the British

Relations with British officials were inevitably complicated by conflicting impulses within the family: on the one hand there was a strongly independent streak within the clan; moreover, they were Muslims, and hence viewed with suspicion at a time of great political upheaval; on the other there was evident admiration for British values, the sense of fair play, the openness of British society, and so on.

This ambivalence is captured in an account given by Abbas Tyabji's biographer of a boyhood experience of his in the home of his grandfather, Tyabjee Bhoymeeah. An Englishman had apparently intruded into Bhoymeeah's compound one day, and shouted at his servants. Abbas, then about 8 or so, ran to tell his grandfather about it. Bhoymeeah did not appear to react, but, as Abbas recalled it, a few days later, when the Englishman walked in again, apparently to complain about a leaking water tap, and used very abusive language, Bhoymeeah's servants caught hold of him and gave him a thrashing. The Englishman didn't cry out—instead he calmly counted out each stroke one, two, three. Abbas, watching open-mouthed with his young cousins, was not particularly struck by this stoic behaviour—they stood there, mimicking him. Eventually the Englishman, who Bhoymeeah ordered should be taken to the police chowky, managed to twist out of the servants' grasp and escaped, never to reappear.

This incident occurred perhaps in the early 1860s, soon after the 1857 Rising, at a time when the fearsome reprisals against those suspected of supporting the rebels would have been fresh in everyone's memory.[18] To have taken such action against the *sahiblog* required great self-confidence; but, as Asaf Fyzee's translation of Bhoymeeah's memoir makes clear, Bhoymeeah was a man for whom authority, unless rightly exercised, had little value.[19] This incident, and the fashion in which Abbas recounted it many years later to his biographer, played a very important part in moulding Bhoymeeah's family's attitude to the British. Abbas Tyabji's biographer specifically comments on the fact that was never any fear thenceforth of the *gora* in this family.[20]

It's a striking feature of many of the incidents recounted in these books, by both men and women, that there seems to have been no instinctive awe of the red-faced roaring Angrez, but a remarkable sense of dignity and self-confidence in several kinds of encounters. One of the earliest of these is an experience that Badruddin's eldest daughter Amina had in a railway carriage when travelling back to Bombay by train from Matheran. Hasan, her younger brother and escort, put her into a first class ladies' carriage, which was occupied by an English couple. The gentleman had to move out, which he did with bad grace. At every station, to Amina's amusement, the man would come up to ask solicitously how his wife was faring, and she would recount to him how tiresome it was for her to have to get ice, etc. for herself, and probably also complained about the insufferable behaviour of these Indians, daring to address English people so. This performance was repeated all the way to Bombay and only at the very end did Amina address the lady in English, and convey that she'd understood every word, causing consternation. A similar incident involved Husain, Badruddin's second son, who had newly returned from England after having eaten his dinners at the Bar: He was infuriated at being pushed out of the way by a European at the station in Bombay when he was trying to buy a ticket for Matheran. Both these events were felt to be important enough for the 'editor sahib' to request a detailed account of them. Yet again, in the Bombay Branch of the Royal Asiatic Society Library, a young cousin, Aly Najmuddin, later married to Surayya, was elbowed out of the way by an Englishman. Aly was enraged enough to take the man to court, but lost his case on a matter of procedure.

The variety of situations is interesting: a lady in purdah, and two young men in public places. There would have been few Indian members of the Asiatic Society at that date, and it was probably unusual also for a well-off Indian to be standing in a queue buying a ticket for himself. (But this latter incident took place soon after Husain's return to India after seven years abroad; he was sufficiently influenced by the western lifestyle not only to wish to buy his ticket himself, but also to organize long hikes in Matheran with his cousins, when they carried their own food and water with them, instead of feasting in a *nawabi* way on food brought to them by servants.)

However, the clan's relations with the British were not always antagonistic: Badruddin's extended family was on very cordial relations with many English people, and it is striking that at Nazli Fyzee's wedding, which many members of her own family and the entire Sulaymani community refused to attend as it was with a non-Sulaymani, many of the guests were English or Parsi ladies. One of Badruddin's wife's closest friends was her doctor, Mrs Phipson, who had delivered many of her eighteen children. She was a guest of Badruddin's family in Matheran, spending four days there in 1895.

Apart from this, contact with British officials as well as missionaries, American or British, widened the clan's understanding of the world outside the charmed circle. There were of course purdah parties of which this is a representative account: ' "The wife of the barrister and member of council, Mr Budroodeen Tyabji, is rather a stout cheery-looking person, and seemed very ready to talk and be pleasant, although all our remarks to each other had to be interpreted. She brought three daughters with her, one a girl of thirteen," "just beginning purdah," as her uncle explained to us. She wore the sari or long scarf which goes over the head and can at any moment be drawn over the face ... The little girls' dresses were very much like those of children in a circus in England ... she could speak some English, and so could the other girls. They go to a mission school and the mother said they were very happy there. The ladies all took something, but Mrs Badroodeen did not seem to know what to do with her dessert knife and fork—she held them both in one hand.'[21]

How much the ladies, Indian or English, enjoyed such formal encounters, one can only imagine, but the little girls must have had fun, and enjoyed these experiences of strange food and drink and lifestyles. (There's seldom any reference to food in these books, but one may assume that at home, amongst themselves, Badruddin's family did not use cutlery and had meals cooked in the traditional Cambay style.)

The Working Committee, Women's Section, for the Bombay Exhibition, 1899. Women from leading families in Bombay: Sakina Lukmani, seated left, Rahat Tyabji, fourth from left, Wazirunissa Latif, standing middle. The communities, Parsi, Gujarati, Bohra, Maharashtrian, are distinguished by their dress.

Lady Scott continues: 'One lady [Kumraniessa], husband's name Azra Achmet (Mirza Ahmed) spoke English; they had "a merry little chat together". At another party given by her (in January 1885) 'the first arrival was a carriage with two draped figures within, who looked young, bundled up as they were.... They threw off their cloaks, and two girls, of about ten or twelve appeared-daughters of the barrister and member of Council, the Honourable Budrudeen Tyabji. These girls speak English, so there was no difficulty in entertaining them.... Mrs Ameeroodeen Tyebjee and her two nieces came' and Lady Scott 'had a long talk with Mrs Ameeroodeen, taking her round the drawing room and showing her the pictures.'[22]

There is no hint in any of these family documents of other visits between the women of such professional, modern families, no suggestion of an acquaintance with them; and where indeed could such encounters between Indian women take place? One possibility is at the purdah parties held by English officials' wives; the other is the kind of society founded by Dr Ryder that has been referred to earlier. Here, the chances of women talking to each other with some ease was greater than at an official formal party.

The evidence from the *akhbar* suggests that social contact amongst women was restricted to interaction with English and Parsi ladies. There are numerous references to calls paid on or by them. They have discussions, probably in a mixture of Hindustani, Gujarati and English, with emancipated Parsi ladies such Lady Petit, Khurshidbai (Surayya's close friend from school), and Lady Readymoney, who had come to visit Rahat in Matheran, and consult her about preparations for the Prince and Princess of Wales' visit to India.

One suggestion was that a sketch book showing the clothes worn by different communities could be presented. Rahat comments in the *akhbar* that if women come out of purdah, that would affect their style of dressing, and what a shame if everyone started dressing uniformly! She felt strongly about the importance of diversity, and regretted uniformity so much that she wrote to the *Tehzeeb e-Niswan* about this as Surayya tells us in the Matheran akhbar book. Rahat herself was described as being 'Largely instrumental in bringing together women of the numerous Indian communities of Bombay, Hindus, Parsis, Khojas, Memons, Kokins [Konknis?], Dawoodis, Sulaimanis, Moghals and Arabs'; she was also very active in giving zenana parties.

What language would they have spoken in? By the 1880s, most Parsi girls would have been to English medium schools, and a few Bohra and Khoja families' daughters too, so one may assume that the younger children would have communicated with each other in English. What about their mothers? Rahat certainly could not speak English, and must have relied heavily on her daughters to translate and interpret for her. Amina came especially from Baroda to Bombay in April 1899 to act as her mother's hostess at a party held for Lady Sandhurst, the Governor's wife. Similarly, she accompanied her mother to pay calls on, and also receive visits from Lady Jenkins, the Chief Justice's wife, Mrs Pherozeshah Mehta, Mrs Crowe, and the wives of other leading officials in Matheran. Lack of a common language would have been a severe handicap in inter-community intercourse, and perhaps what happened at many gatherings was that the Marathi, Gujarati, and English-speaking circles were cut off from each other, an isolation that the men would not have suffered from.

One of the few references to friendships with Parsi girls is made by Jamila in 1905, when she asked a friend called Ferozbai Pestonjee to stay with her at Somerset House and help her nurse her two young sisters through an illness while the rest of the family was in Matheran. In his efforts to become part of the social group created in British official circles, Badruddin would have found his wife's lack of English and unfamiliarity with Western customs, such as handling a knife and fork, and possibly even a plate (though he had magnificent monogrammed dinner sets of his own—were these only used at mixed parties that his wife would not have attended?), a liability?

IX The Urdu of Bombay

What about their Urdu? Why should the family, or the entire Sulaymani Jamaat, as it now seems, have switched from their native Gujarati to Urdu in the mid-nineteenth century? Was it a question of status, of feeling that speaking Urdu was an indicator of social superiority? Was it because of directions from their Dai in Yemen, with a theological objective? Or was it because the feeling of being part of a pan-Indian community was fostered by speaking Urdu, the language of the cultivated aristocratic Northern

Indian Muslim? While Gujarati was only spoken by the low-class trading (convert) communities? According to both Abbas Tyabji's biographer, Hadi Dehlavi, and Najmuddin Tyabji, it was Camruddin, on his return from England, who suggested and implemented this major change. The Sulaymani archives in Bombay might yield interesting insights into this decision.

How successfully was this switch made? Husain Tyabji has given an amusing account of how, in London in the 1870s, Badruddin approached a gentleman known for his scholarship, and knowledge of Arabic and Persian (Amir Ali) and asked for lessons in Persian. Was quite taken aback to be told by the gentleman that he should first learn Urdu. But I know how to speak Urdu, he protested. No, no, said the other, what you speak is Gujarati not Urdu. Learn Urdu first!

Throughout the *akhbar* books, we see traces of Badruddin's consciousness of his family's faulty speech, and of the efforts he made to get them to drop Gujarati and Marathi words and phrases, going to the extent of fining those who used them; nobly paying up himself when his youngest daughter caught him out, in a moment of great exasperation in a game of whist.

Surayya described at some length her father's attempts to improve his family's vulgar pidgin Urdu: adults gathered regularly to read and listen to Urdu and Persian, which improved their spoken language, so that, as she says they would no longer have to sit shamefaced and tongue-tied in the presence of cultured ladies from the North. As for the younger children, their regular lessons in writing and reading with Ustad Amir Ali, who even accompanied them on their holidays to Matheran, gave them a great advantage over their elder brothers and sisters. Certainly, the language used by Badruddin's younger children in their *akhbar* entries was purer and more correct than their elders', which appears to have embarrassed them by its ungainly mixture of Urdu, Marathi, and Gujarati idioms, turns of phrase, and vocabulary.

The version of the Badruddin *akhbar* copied out by Safia Jabir Ali contains explanatory notes on some of the language used by her elder sisters. On the other hand, Badruddin's family prided itself on writing in Urdu and were scornful about other cousins being more at home in English and using English for their *akhbar* entries. This seems to have applied to Camruddin's children, Mirza Aqa in particular.

As for the other language of Bombay, Marathi, it seems that the Fyzee sisters were the only ones to take it seriously enough to take lessons in speaking and writing it. (Perhaps this was because of the Janjira connexion.) The Nawab of Janjira's family ladies, who were 'Hinduized' enough to wear saris as Hafiza, one of Badruddin's older daughters, remarked rather scornfully, might well have spoken Marathi or some kind of Hindustani rather the Urdu of aristocratic Muslim families.

X Family Values

One of the aspects of family life that emerges very clearly from the books is the ritualistic, almost ceremonious sense of fair play: punishment for wrong-doing was meted out regardless of age or status. One future brother-in-law writes of the punishment given Mrs Lukmani [Sakina] for daring to issue a note threatening that if the *Akhbar ki Kitaab* wasn't written in by the evening, the wrong-doer would be *tinpooted* (some sort of forfeit). A meeting was called and the 'leader' (who was actually the culprit), spoke eloquently and at length on the crime. The punishment was for Sakina to tear up the paper at Echo Point, and throw it into the valley, which she reluctantly did; the pieces were then gathered up, put into a match-box, set on fire, and thrown down. 'This impressive sight was witnessed by our army in deep silence, and Mrs Lukmani shed bitter tears.'

On another occasion, a special court was constituted to try Mr Justice Badruddin for the crime of losing his temper when playing whist. His wife was the judge, his brother Amiruddin the plaintiff, and the jury consisted of his daughters, who found him guilty and condemned him to taking the whole lot out for a treat in Bombay. Similar instances of such 'family courts' recur in many of the *akhbar* books kept by the expanding family, which, by the 1930s, consisted of branches of the Tyabji, Latif, Fyzee, Ali, Futehally, and Mohammadi families.

Another striking feature of the clan culture is that even into adulthood, because of the constant interaction with a large number of male relations, the girls would have developed a feeling of equality, of a new kind of self-worth. Participation in the same amusements as the male members of the family would have led to relationships of a different kind from those where adolescent girls were curtained off and restricted only to suitably refined, untaxing pursuits, such as reading poetry, sketching or doing embroidery, if they weren't making *puris* and sweets in the kitchen (like their Hindu counterparts).[23]

The boisterous nature of this equality can be gauged from an account, written about 1885, of a game of badminton played between Badruddin's younger son, Hasan (later renamed Faiz) and his two elder sisters, Surayya and Jamila, all aged between 15 and 18. The two girls played against him, the forfeit being that whoever lost would have their nose rubbed in the dust. The girls won. A week or so later, the match was repeated, the girls lost, and there was no question of their being let off their share of the punishment, or Faiz being gentle with his sisters.

XI Political Views

Such a family's political views would be of interest. These family papers don't contain any lengthy comments on issues of concern to the outside world, although this doesn't mean the men were not involved: Amiruddin Tyabji, representing the family firm of Tyabji and Co. in Le Havre in 1870, for instance, had commented impatiently in one of his letters written from Le Havre, that his brothers in Bombay never wrote to him about the pressing concerns of the day, which at that point would have been the Turkish question (see Chapter 3). We also have two significant remarks on this, from Shujauddin, Badruddin's eldest brother, and Fatehali, his younger brother-in-law, who commented on the anti-British feeling being built up by Britain's stand on this issue. They are brief, but particularly striking in a family journal where outside concerns received little mention.

Amiruddin himself developed very strong views on the Franco-Prussian war which broke out when he was in Havre. He wrote to his family during that period that he admired the Germans greatly, found little to admire in the French, and wasn't surprised at the French collapse. Although his elder brothers regarded him as a frivolous, irresponsible ladies' man, traces of a deeply serious responsible person appear even in his early letters home (see Chapter 5). It's not surprising that although he was a keen sportsman and companion of rajas and nawabs (in 1902 he was a guest of the Raja of Kasimbazar at the Coronation Durbar in Delhi) he also played an important part in the Bombay Municipal Council, an early attempt at introducing self-government at the local level in India. In his *akhbar*, Amiruddin gives an account of the petition presented by the Musulmans to the Queen, which contained sentiments of loyal support to the Sovereign, whom the Musulman community considered their legitimate sovereign.

One of the few political statements contained in the Badruddin and Amiruddin *akhbars* is actually one by Badruddin himself, describing his visit to Madras in 1887 as President of the Indian National Congress, suitably tailored for a family book. His eldest son, Mohsin, by then a District Judge, commented: 'Father is going to Madras as President of the Congress with much *taqaza*, in fact under compulsion. This is a very wonderful thing, and a great source of pride for all Muslims, and especially for our *qabila*, from amongst all the Hindus.' Badruddin's account went:

'I haven't written in this book for a long time, partly because of the trouble with my eyes, so that the doctors had forbidden me to read or write, and also because the children were writing in it [keeping it up] so I didn't think it was necessary for me. But today I think it wouldn't be inappropriate for me to write a brief account of my trip to Madras'

'I left for Madras on the 22nd December, having been chosen President of the Indian National Congress, and reached Madras on the 24th morning. I had never been to Madras before, and was keen to see it, and as if to fulfil this wish, the annual session of the Congress being held there, and my being chosen to preside over it, gave me an excellent reason to go'

'The arrangements there were excellent, and I was honoured and feted in every possible way. Two or three Congress representatives met me a few stations before the train reached Madras, and at Madras itself, I got a wonderful reception from a large crowd of Hindus, Muslims and English people, all gathered to welcome me'

'At first, I thought I'd stay with Mr Norton, Bar-at-Law, but after two days I moved to the Carter[?] Hotel, because it was rather far away [from the Congress meetings]'

'The Congress sessions started on 25 December, and ended on 30 December. All the sessions went, on the whole, well and smoothly; it was an extraordinarily brilliant gathering, in which over 700 delegates of every community and district of India took part. Practically everyone who had made a name for himself in public service was there. Although at first the Madras Muslims, like the Calcutta ones, were wary of the Congress, after discussions with them they were all convinced [of the importance of joining Congress], and indeed most enthusiastic.

'There were fine speeches made at these sessions, all of which have appeared in the papers. I was very troubled and anxious when I left Bombay for this session, not knowing how I'd be able to handle such an important and tricky business, but thank God, so far as I can tell, no-one has as yet found fault with my handling of affairs'

'There were any number of parties, too, given by Norton, Subrahmanya, Mudaliyar, etc., and we enjoyed them very much. And, especially important, there was a long discussion with the Governor, Lord Connemara, about government's policies in general, and particularly about Muslim welfare. The governor held a garden party for all the delegates, and was most charming and gracious to everyone'

'The Muslims too did us proud, and honoured us with magnificent parties (amongst others, Mir Ghulamuddin Khan Bahadur), who belongs to Tipu Sultan and the Karnataka family. There were so many parties in our honour, that the last two days, I think I had to go to ten every day'

'Apart from all this, I also went to several *madrassas*, and one in particular, the[?], held a function for me, and I addressed a few words of advice to them on the aims of the Muslims, and presented them with Rs 100'

'So, I came back happy and satisfied beyond my wildest expectations, my only regret being that I couldn't spend a couple more days there, and see the town properly, or to attend the Governor's party, or to get to the Deccan, despite being so close to it. To my delight, my great friend Banerjea was also there—what a nice man he is—if only more Bengalis were like him!'

Badruddin was ill at ease on the national political platform, and the following year, despite repeated and intense efforts to persuade him to preside over the fourth session of the Congress, he declined to do so. There were many conflicting claims on his time. In addition, the Anjuman-i-Islam, of which he was then President, was reluctant to accept his political leadership in the face of the challenges presented by the extremely influential North Indian Muslim political leader, Sir Syed Ahmed Khan. Sir Syed urged the need to preserve a separate Muslim identity, both culturally and politically, and feared a political alliance with the Hindus.[24]

Although he had no further link with the Congress, and devoted himself to his large practice as far as his failing sight would permit, he did in 1903 play a leading part in the Anglo-Mahomedan Educational Conference as has been noticed earlier, where he spoke very forcefully about the correct understanding of purdah, and about women's education, urging that the Prophet's message be correctly understood, and in any case letting his own family out of purdah the very next day, as Surayya states in the *akhbar*.

After his wife's unexpected death in June 1905, followed by that of his daughter Jamila, Badruddin's health deteriorated sharply. He was advised to travel to Europe, accompanied by one of his sons where he met his two younger daughters, both at school. He died of a sudden heart attack in London, just as he was about to be appointed Chief Justice of the Bombay High Court. And that more or less brought to an end the Badruddin *akhbar*, the chief source of my study, although there were entries made in it as late as 1907 (see Chapter 3).

Amiruddin Tyabji survived his brother; and his family *akhbar* continued intermittently till 1939. While there are lively discussions and spats between the writers, as in the Badruddin *akhbar*, there are also long gaps, and of course a smaller number of contributors, which make it a less useful source of material than the Badruddin books. The last entry was made by Amiruddin's niece Farhat, in 1939. It ends with an account of the condolence meeting held for Hasham Yar Khan, the eldest of Amiruddin's adopted family, who had become a leading lawyer in Hyderabad and was granted this title by the Nizam.

3

Passages from the *Akhbar*

Translated from the Urdu

This chapter contains passages from the Amiruddin and Badruddin books which convey an idea of the life led by this family, the good spirits, the sense of family togetherness, and their energetic pastimes. They are not entirely representative of the entries since many of those are hastily scribbled and of no special interest. I have also not included the numerous entries on plays, or musical evenings, as none seemed to be of special merit although these entertainments played an important part in their time at Matheran and Mahabaleshwar, and also in Bombay.

Below are three entries on the Turkish crisis of 1876–77 in the *Akhbar-e-Amiri*; the opening entry in the Wynad Akhbar made by Amiruddin Tyabji (1877); an account of family picnics given by Rahat Tyabji (1891); Amina Tyabji's descriptions of her travels in Europe in 1893–94; Mohsin Tyabji's account of the solar eclipse in 1898; three passages about the fierce discussions on purdah at the Anglo-Mahomedan Educational Conference of 1903; Sakina Lukmani's detailed account of her mother's last illness and death; and the last important piece in the Badruddin books, Halima Fyzee's description of a visit to the Jog Falls in 1907.

I have included the final brief entry by Halima as it gives an idea of the family continuing to hold a place in Bombay society even after Badruddin's death.

I have also included Safia Jabir Ali's own comments made many years later as they provide a poignant comment on the lasting value of these books, and also provide a bridge to her own memoir which follows in Chapter 4.

The Changing World of a Bombay Muslim Community, 1870–1945. Salima Tyabji, Oxford University Press.
© Nasir Tyabji 2023. DOI: 10.1093/oso/9780192869746.003.0003

I 1877 The Turkish Crisis

The following entries by Shujauddin Tyabji, Sheikh Fatehali, and Qamrunissa, their niece, are unusual in that they focus on a political issue—rare for a family journal largely devoted to domestic interests. The strong identification with the caliphate that was felt by some sections of Muslims in India may not have been shared by other members of this family: the bitterness and anger expressed by all three writers here form a sharp contrast to the bland entries on illnesses, deaths, and social functions that they're sandwiched in between, as well as the family tone of Badruddin's account of the 1887 Congress session. They also indicate a powerful Muslim identity. Both men had close connections with Turkey; Fatehali had lived in Istanbul for several years from the 1870s. Shujauddin's son-in-law Hassan Ali spent many years there, and had a Turkish wife.

It is also of interest that the third emotional entry is by a young woman with evidently a sharp awareness of concerns beyond those of the immediate family circle. The strong criticism of Britain's stand is preceded by an entry describing the visit of several people, including Camruddin, Badruddin, and Abbas, to Delhi for the 1877 Durbar. These were evidently the loyalists. Shujauddin and Fatehali seldom write in Badruddin's *akhbar*.

The British claimed to have fought the Crimean war against Russia to preserve the Ottoman Empire. The Turks therefore thought of them as their allies against the depredations of Russia, and the neutrality of the major powers of Europe. However, reports reaching Britain of the excesses committed by Turkish irregular troops against Bulgarian Christians in the course of 1876 aroused very strong protests in England, which initially were summarily dismissed by Disraeli. Gladstone's passionate indictment of Turkish rule in a pamphlet titled *Bulgarian Horrors and the Question of the East* created such a furore that Lord Salisbury, a member of the Cabinet, wrote to Disraeli that concessions would have to be made. Disraeli refused to consider any drastic measures, and the Balkan crisis soon appeared to be 'a duel between Britain, as defender of the status quo', and Russia, 'the self-appointed champion of Balkan liberation'.

Intense diplomatic activity took place all through 1876, culminating in a Russian ultimatum to Turkey in October of that year. This resulted in an armistice; an international conference was held in Constantinople in December 1876 and January 1877, attended by European powers. The Europeans presented terms which were the 'irreducible minimum' acceptable to them—the partitioning of Bulgaria, independence for Bosnia-Herzegovina, and other major losses for Turkey.

The Turks rejected the proposals outright, taking a very strong stand because of the wave of public opinion in their favour, in Constantinople as well as London and St Petersburg. It is this stand that Qamrunissa applauds. However, war broke out again between Russia and Turkey later in the year.

6 January 1877

By the grace of God, all the courage and manliness we'd expected from Turkey have turned out to be appropriate, [but] it was all really a matter of chance that such an event should take place at all [in the existing circumstances].

Russia is trying to drive Turkey out of Europe, and all the other states are supporting Russia in this, and the representatives of these great and independent countries are gathered together in Constantinople for consultations about this at this moment. What they have decided unanimously on Saturday, and have presented to Turkey is something that, if Turkey accepts it, will mean that its independence and greatness will totally disappear. The British, who have otherwise been allies of Turkey, have now also become turncoats, and together with the other states have warned Turkey, saying 'Either you agree to this, or we will cut off our support to you.'

We were all very anxious that Turkey would not be able to carry on a war against all these states, and would cave in, but against all expectations we heard yesterday by telegraph that Turkey has refused to accept these humiliating terms desired by the Christian states, and this has been resolved upon. This means that war is imminent. Let us hope that Lord Beaconsfield doesn't go back on the spirited assurances he gave in the Guildhall, that Britain would not renege on the commitments of the 1856 Treaty of Paris, and that it would not allow the greatness and independent status of Turkey to be in any way damaged. But it seems that Britain has forgotten all these promises and joined Russia. Turkey will not behave this way. It will stick by what it has said, and if it is indeed driven out of

Europe, it won't happen without a hard fight. It won't act in a contempt-ible and cowardly manner.

May it end according to god's will. Shujauddin
Note: copied 21 April 1958 Safia

7 January 1877

The way the poor Turks have been treated by the British, more than the Turks, it's the British who will suffer from this disgraceful deceitful letting down. We all knew that this lot was intent on their own gain, but what they have done to the Turks now is the height of double-dealing and trickery. A lot of people say, Oh poor things! What can the leaders do now, they have to be guided by popular feeling [in Britain]. My view is that if that is indeed the case the whole lot of ministers should have resigned, and when the new lot came to power they could have reconsidered openly the earlier decision made by the Prime Minister, and that would at least have covered over some of the treachery of this decision.

Fatehali

20 January 1877

Oh wonderful, wonderful brave Muslims! Your courage and determination are quite incredible. May god preserve it long, and may it bring you victory! The last telegram from Europe aroused in us an extraordinary hope and enthusiasm. May god preserve this Usmania Empire in its full glory and power, and the flag of Islam be kept flying high! And the infidels be prop-erly punished for their treachery and selfishness. Amen Qamrunissa

II 1877 Amiruddin Tyabji's Opening Entry in His Wynad Book

This *akhbar* was started at a coffee estate in Coimbatore, near Wynad, where Amiruddin had been sent on family business, probably by his elder brother Shujauddin, to explore the possibilities of establishing links with coffee growers. The entry is as usual full of hope that people will respond to the wonderful opportunities to write, which is as usual disappointed. Amiruddin's ebullient style is in interesting contrast to his brother Badruddin's manner. Amiruddin Tyabji himself played an active part both in the Anjuman-i-Islam Educational Trust and in Municipal committee affairs some years later. Alas there is no reference to these activities in his *akhbar*. However, Amiruddin makes it a point to mention his household staff by name, whether in *akhbar* entries, or captions in photographs.

The Wynad *Kitab* begins:

1 September 1877—[Safia's hand]

In the name of God. What a wonderful thing, I'm surrounded by family wherever I look. The hall [drawing room] and Pathree? [veranda?] are teeming with people, enough to put the fear of god into our enemies. I'm going to ask each of them to sign below—it'll be a useful record. And I'm sure that the *akhbar* book will be full of lots of entries, and that each of them will do their utmost to keep it up. And write every day about the interesting things that have happened. And I'm especially sure that our young ladies will work hard at their pieces, and do their best not to let the book down. Amen Amiruddin.

Signatures: (1) Najmuddin Tyab Ali (2) Maryam, daughter of Al Haj Mohammad (3) Nuzratul Naeem, daughter of Tyab Ali (4) Amiruddin (5) Muizuddin (6) Safia, daughter of Najmuddin (7) Zubeida bibi, daughter of Futehally (8) Fatima Khatoon Najmuddin (9) Ali Najmuddin (10) Saada, daughter of Najmuddin And the servants brought from Bombay: Mama Hafeeza, Mama Halima, Mama Kariman Najoo, Cook, Ghulam Husain Sipahi [Indecipherable date]

I was so pleased by the thought that people would write such lovely long accounts in this book, but it's already evening, and no one's yet written. Oh well, I'd better write the second piece too, and I'm really surprised that there are such exciting things to report here, and all the time, but no one seems to want to write about them!

The day before yesterday, that is on Thursday, at about ten in the morning, when Bhai Najmuddin and Muiz were with their Malayalam teacher; and I was busy with Nuzrat, Safia, Zubeida and Aly, teaching them arithmetic, we heard a terrific commotion outside, with people shouting and cries of 'Oh she's been bitten by a snake, she's been bitten by a snake!'

I was of course horrified when I heard this, and I leapt up from my seat, and took my loaded rifle with me, and oh dear reader, do please remember that we're living in a place where we always need a loaded gun, and I saw that all the *mamas* [women servants] were wailing away, and saying, 'Oh Bibi [Maryam] has been bitten by a snake!' Now, sirs, please remember that we are living on a coffee estate, on top of a hill, in Coimbatore. When I asked where Bibi was they said, 'Oh, she fell down!' or 'We don't know what happened!' So then Bhai Najm and Muiz, and the children, Bahen Nuzrat and I, and then the *sipahi* Ghulam Husain and Najoo, we all rushed down. A little later we saw Najoo and the *sipahi* coming up with Bhabi Maryam. And Bhabi was weeping away. You cannot imagine our state.

Anyway, when we had all calmed down, and Bhabi Saheba had recovered somewhat, we learnt that what had happened was this: Bhabi Saheba had wanted to have a chicken killed and then found that all the chickens had gone down to the bottom of the hill. So then our brave Arab sister-in-law decided that she would call the chickens back up, and she set forth on her own, went down the hill, along some path where the grass was waist-high, where there was a monster [lit., dragon, possibly a python] which thought that Bhabi Saheba would be a good morsel, and so it came out and caught her by the leg, but she raised such a din that he let go of her; and then pursued her all the way up! So there were the two of them racing each other: At which point Najoo and the *sipahi* arrived, so it went off. I went in search of it with my gun, but he had disappeared. I would certainly have sent him to hell if he'd appeared. Really what a ghastly thing this was. Thank goodness that Bhabi Maryam escaped being harmed by that accursed villain. I cannot begin to describe what an effect this horrifying event had on all of us.

May God preserve us all from such dangers and keep us in sound health, and shower a few lakhs of rupees on us so that we can, thanking him for his goodness, go back safely to Bombay Amiruddin

III 1891 Rahat Badruddin Tyabji's Account of Family Picnics

Rahat's family chose to entertain itself energetically over the Christmas and New Year holidays. Vihar and Bhandup (now suburbs of Bombay, with Colaba and Worli parts of Bombay proper) were evidently in the late nineteenth century places for excursions and outings. In the 1890s there must have been large tracts of open land around the Malabar Hill/ Cumballa Hill bungalows. Badruddin is referred to as 'Sahib', a practice that is still common among Muslim families.

This is a matter of fact account but it contains fascinating information. On account of Christmas, Sahib got a few days' holiday, in fact a week. We had a lot of fun then. On Thursday we went to Warli, to Mangaldas' bungalow, which he'd allowed us to use. We'd gone there very early in the morning, at five. We'd tried to get some *neera* [fresh unfermented toddy], but there wasn't any, however we had a good breakfast otherwise, and then set off to explore the seashore and the surrounding jungle, which was beautifully peaceful, and we had a lovely time. Our party consisted of: Bhai Amiruddin, Bhabi Hamida, Zeenuth and her children, Bhabi Begumsaheba [Camruddin's wife], Khanum Koochik, Agha Koochik, Mirza Jan, Hyder Mian, and Muizuddin. And of course the whole lot of us, apart from Husain who's gone to Kihim for a few days with Bahen Nuzrat [Badruddin's youngest sister]. Anyway, we spent the whole day there, and walked about, and ate a lot of *targolas,* and then after dinner, we got back home at about 9 in the evening. It was a lovely day altogether, full of fun and merriment.

Then on Friday we went to Colaba, and as that was also some distance away, we set off at two in the afternoon, and got to Colaba at three or half-past. We found a pleasant terrace (agassi) where we had our tea, and then we walked about and enjoyed the sea breezes, and got home after dark having enjoyed the moonlight there. The Band Stand was on the way and that day the band was playing, so we stopped there for a while and listened to the music. That day our party consisted of very few people— there was only Bhai Amiruddin, and Hamid and Hashoo [Hashim]. But from here there were Jamila, Halima, and Salman, and they all enjoyed themselves very much. Saeeda and her *mama* Ayesha were also with us, and she found a whole lot of *jhame* (a kind of pumice) to scrub her feet with. And had a great time.

On Saturday morning we went to the Victoria Gardens. Things are greatly improved there, and the animals are also far better looked after which we were very pleased about. We had a pleasant time there, and got back home at about ten. They've decided to have an entrance fee for these gardens, which is one anna per person.

Party at Chembur. On Sunday we had a good time at Chembur [now a built-up suburb but practically a hill station in those days], where a whole lot of people had gathered. A number of them had decided to spend three days there, and Bahen Sahiba Zainab [Badruddin's eldest sister] was there with her whole family. So was Bhai Sahib Najmuddin, and some people were there all three days and others just for two. The arrangement was that everyone should pay for their food while they were there. We'd thought of going there on Sunday and celebrating Hasan's [Faiz's] birthday there, and making everyone our guest. He was pleased and so were we.

We spent Monday peacefully at home, and on Tuesday early in the morning, at a quarter to five, we set off for Byculla station to catch the 5.30 train to Bhandup, which we reached at about 6.30. From there we had to go by bullock cart to Vihar lake, and we'd sent two men ahead of us the day before to arrange for this so we could get there without any delay while it was still cool. But it wasn't easy to arrange for these carts as the village was some distance away, and the villagers were busy trans-porting *chuna* (lime plaster) in their carts and there just weren't any free for us. We got three with great difficulty, and even these weren't enough. We needed one for the baggage, and the other two were so small that you could barely fit three people into one of them, while there were nine of us who needed them. We'd sensibly not brought any of the smaller chil-dren along because we'd known there might be problems on the way, and we'd also kept our party pretty small—just as well as otherwise it would have been really difficult. It was dark and walking wasn't pleasant and there was also the question of catching the train back. Terrible if we'd missed it. This was why we'd thought it a good idea to have transport. So people took it in turns to sit in the carts, and a number of them walked all the way—Badruddin Sahib walked all the way in the morning and sat for a short while on the way back, and so did Bhai Najmuddin and Bhai Amiruddin. The carts were so very small that there was no question of everyone getting into them. Well anyway, we started from Bhandup at 7 and got to Vihar at 10. The lake and the countryside around was cer-tainly very beautiful, but because by that time it had got rather hot and we were tired, we had a bit of a rest. We'd had breakfast on the way, in a pretty spot. After lunch we had a siesta, and then we set out on the lake in a boat and saw a good bit of the surroundings, and then at five we set out on the return journey, some walking, some in the carts. I couldn't join the walkers, but everyone else took it in turns to walk and then ride. We had dinner … Our first-class compartment wasn't large enough to seat all nine of us, so we had two separate compartments, and it didn't occur to anyone that it would be better to be all together as we had to have dinner. Now Bhabi Maryam, Bhai Amiruddin and Sakina, and the others were in the other compartment, and we wanted them to come into my compartment. The train was so slow that it stopped at every station, but for such a short time that it was very difficult to get off it and then get back into one's compartment. Now hardly had those people settled comfortably in their carriage that they started hearing calls, 'Come on, come on, get into our compartment and quick!' And they couldn't make out what had happened. Anyway after several attempts we managed to get them to move and we all had a good meal and got home safely. It had taken us three hours to get from Bhandup to Vihar by bullock cart, and two on the way back. Altogether we had a lot of fun, and we missed those who hadn't been able to join us. Rahat

IV 1894 Amina Tyabji's Account of Her Travels in Europe

Amina, Badruddin's eldest daughter, accompanied her husband, Abbas Tyabji, then a judge at the High Court of Baroda, to Europe in 1893. Abbas was a close friend and ally of the Gaekwar, Sayaji Rao, under whom Baroda had become a model for other princely states as well as British provinces. When the Gaekwar decide to travel with his wife to Europe, Abbas Tyabji was asked to accompany him with Amina, so as to help the Maharani to adjust to European customs, and also assist with the language, perhaps. For both women it would have been their first visit out of the country, but it seems that Amina's knowledge of English, and of Western ways of behaviour and etiquette was greater, probably because of the opportunities she had had in her father's home in Bombay to meet and entertain English people.

The party left for Europe in 1893, travelled together in France and Italy, and Amina and her husband then continued to London, where they met Badruddin and Husain, who was then at Cambridge. They went to the theatre, visited friends in the country, and went about in hansom cabs.

Nowhere in Amina's account is there a hint of the fact that she was among the first Muslim women to be travelling out of purdah. The very first Indian Muslim woman happened to be her first cousin, Zubeida, who'd been invited to tea at Buckingham Palace, and then won the first prize at a fancy-dress ball.

In neither of these cases is there any indication that the women were reluctant to come out of purdah, that they'd been dragooned into it. On the contrary, when Zubeida was invited by the Queen to call on her, jubilant telegrams were flying about in Bombay announcing the event.

Amina had to write in both the Badruddin and Amiruddin *akhbars* on account of the fierce editorial rivalry between them. I have included both.

Zubeida Ali Akbar, London, 1893.

Hasan [Faiz] has been after me for days to write a nice long account in the *akhbar* book but unfortunately I've just been too lazy to do so, and am quite ashamed of it. But because I'm leaving for Baroda this evening, I've taken up a pen, overcome my laziness, and decided to organize my thoughts ... Heaven help me. I hope I produce something that will satisfy my brother Hasan.

I have first to thank almighty God that together with all the other blessings I have been showered with, I should also have had this great good fortune, which makes one's heart swell with happiness and pride, and raises one's spirit to the heavens. Actually, it is a great cause of pride for all Indians that Father [Badruddin] has been chosen from among all the other barristers to this great office and dignity of being a Judge. And of course for us children it is an especial cause for gratitude to God. May he continue to protect and guard us, and fulfil all our dear Mother's deepest desires and wishes. Amen.

For your goodness towards me I am most deeply thankful.
How can I possibly offer adequate thanks for your goodness towards
    me, O God [Persian quotation]

Thank goodness that Father is quite well again—the trip to Europe has made such a difference to his health generally, and his eyes. I was so very lucky as to have a whole month and a half with Father in London, doing all sorts of lovely, interesting, amusing things, having fun! Dear Husain also joined us for two weeks. And oh, how much we saw and did, what fun we had together! We'd spend the whole day looking at the sights in London, the buildings, the theatres and shows, and also go to parties. In fact, we did so many things those last two months that it's difficult for me to conceive of it now. We'd spent the previous six months on the Continent with the Maharaja [Gaekwar of Baroda] and Rani Saheba, and had done a lot then too, but it was nothing compared to this! I'm really amazed that I had so much energy—France, Italy, Switzerland—in all those places we saw all sorts of wonderful things, natural and man-made, and it would be a huge task to give even a short description of it all. And today I don't have the time, or otherwise I would have tried to give some fragmentary account of it all. Just thinking about it overwhelms me. What incredible, over-whelming scenes we saw in Switzerland, in Italy what historical sites, so fascinating, and so saddening too; very especially, Mount Vesuvius, and St Peter's Cathedral, and its breathtaking views still swim before my eyes. In lovely, delicate, bride-like Paris, we would spend half the night looking at the shop windows, so beautifully dressed with wonderful things, and then we would watch absolutely mesmerized, people drinking coffee in the cafes, in their *faqirah* (elegant) clothes—in Nice too we had a great time—we were there with Maharaj in the full season—and that was where we met our dear Mrs Morris, whom we got to know so well, and became so attached to that I'd call her Nani (grandmother), as she asked me to, and she herself would treat me so lovingly, just as if I were her child—what a dear sweet lady—we all adored her. And I can't write to her, or read her letters without getting quite overcome! There were many other loving and affectionate people whom we got to know very well, and it would be so wonderful to be able to meet them again. But I must stop for now.

Amina in the Akhbar I Amiri

Mr Hamid (Hamid Khan) has brought along this *akhbar* [to Badruddin's house] and is forcing me to write in it! I was very pleased to see it, and would love to look at all the amusing and interesting pieces in it, but there's no time for that, so I'll just write a few sentences, and keep that for another time. Everyone is very keen that I should write about the delightful and very interesting time we had on our trip to Europe.

We set off with the Gaekwar and Maharani Saheba last year (1893), on 16 December, on this journey. We spent six months travelling in Italy, France, Switzerland. After that we went off to England, while Maharaj and Rani Saheba and their party stayed on in France.

In London, we found Father; and Husain, who was at Cambridge, joined us for a fortnight. So the four of us had an absolutely wonderful time together. We met a lot of good friends [of Father's] whose kindness to us cannot be described, and we went to all kinds of places, plays, shows. We also went to the country, and stayed with very hospitable people. So we were feted and welcomed greatly, and then we left Husain and Father and England, and set off on the way back home.

Bhai Ali Akbar and Zubeida were also in London, but as Zubeida wasn't keeping very well, we weren't able to go about together as we'd have liked to, and in fact we hardly saw them.

From London we went to Paris, and the six days we had there to go to the museums and other beautiful sights and places were scarcely enough. What an exquisitely beautiful place it is! London and Paris are two such great famous cities, but what a difference between them! When we first got to London, those dark smoking chimneys and foul air was so alarming. But when we once became familiar with it, and began enjoying ourselves, we really began to love it. It's a place where everyone is so busy—everyone is rushing about all day. The London police is really most impressive. The way we'd run across the streets, dodging between vehicles, even thinking about it really gives me a heart attack now. How Husain would drag me along, avoiding horses' mouths and carriage wheels—oh god!

As for Paris—as soon as we arrived, we were overcome by its beauty and elegance. What can one possibly say about it—it's truly a fairy land. From Paris we went to Rome and saw all the historic buildings there—I was quite overcome by St Peters Cathedral. When we came out, I wanted to sit down and weep with emotion! What an effect it had on me! From there we went to Naples, and did something very wonderful there—we climbed up Mt Vesuvius at 11 in the evening, and saw the most extraordinary natural fireworks. From there we went to Brindisi and took the steamer on 1 August, and after a comfortable voyage we came back to our loved Hindustan on 20 August. And I can't possibly describe what it was like to meet our dear people again. It was a miracle to be with such happiness. I spent a month in Bombay and then went to Baroda, returning to welcome Father back on 26 October. By god's grace he's come back looking very fit and well. I plan to return to Baroda in a couple of days.

Amina 19 November 1894

Amina seated right, Zubeida beside her, Amina's husband Abbas behind, standing, with Badruddin, Ali Akbar (Fyzee), and Husain. London, 1894.

V 1898 Mohsin, Commanded to Write the 'Official Account' of the Eclipse by Younger Brother Editor Faiz

The Eclipse
In margin: Date Sunday 23 January

I'm ashamed to see that I haven't yet written even once in this book—though for those who have to read my writing, it's probably a blessing. I've been in Sind for seven years, in fact longer than that, and have now just been posted to Thane, and since that's only an hour away by steam train, let's hope I'll be here for a while.

Yesterday, a party consisting of parents, Sakina, Halloo, Hasan, Mohammad Akbar Hydari, Bahen Amina and I went to Jewar to see the eclipse of the sun, a natural wonder, and something which wouldn't occur again for 200 years, and so we thought something worth making an effort to see from a place where we'd get a good sight of it. And I think that all of us, including the servants, would agree that all the trouble and expense and effort of going there was well worthwhile. The railway authorities had laid on three special trains last Friday night for those who wanted to go and see the eclipse from Jewar. We took the 10 p.m. train from here and reached Jewar at 11 [the next day]. About 500 people had gathered there to see this unique sight. The Governors of Bombay and Madras and one other governor had also come. So we weren't wrong in deciding to come: [Persian quotation]:

When grief surrounds one,
One forgets one's own grief

That is, we were all in the same boat.

The eclipse started at about five minutes past twelve at Jewar. It reached its height at 1.13, if I'm not wrong, and at about 2.35 or 2.40 it ended. We saw that lots of people were using pieces of glass that had been blackened to look through. Mohammad Akbar got us this kind of darkened glass, which was very useful, as without it it would have been dangerous to look directly. Even when the moon had covered the sun, even then the sun's size and light wasn't diminished. We were standing about idly when

Father called out to us that the eclipse had started, and we saw that the sun was indeed partially covered by the moon, on the right, and it looked as if a slice had been cut out of it on that side.

Gradually, very gradually, the visible part of the sun shrank, till it looked like the new moon, but it looked red. As the moon covered the sun, the night and the heat lessened, and everything, the sky, the earth, the trees, people, all looked different. Instead of the clear bright sun's heat, we had the pale chilly light of the moon. And apart from all this, there was a strange effect on people, which it's difficult to describe, but was quite clearly marked then—a kind of sadness or desolation. Everything looked for a brief moment altogether different—it was the way it is when the sun sets—and the light was like that of the full moon.

The sky was grey, the moon was grey, and when it finally covered the sun fully, the moon itself had turned quite black, and one felt one needed only to stretch out one's hand to touch it. And it seemed to be quite solid *(sakht)*. When the moon was quite black, it had a white circle around it, and from the circle issued arrow-like rays, and there were red spots on this white circle. When the moon had completely covered the sun, its shape began to change again, until it had completely recovered its former shape. It's a great shame that when the moon had completely covered the sun, we didn't think of using the binoculars. We men saw the sight through the telescope, and I hope someone else, for instance Hasan, will describe what we saw. This account has already become so long that I don't think I should make it any longer. There are lots of others who will be able to correct my mistakes, and add all those things that I've forgotten to mention.

[A diagram of this follows].

Now I'll tell about the problems I'd mentioned in the beginning— they were that the picnic baskets we'd brought along with us full of good things kept on occupying our attention, and the efforts we made to deal with them are evident from the condition they're in.

Mohsin Badruddin Tyabji

VI 1904 Purdah

There are two *akhbar* entries on the discussions on purdah at the Mahomedan Conference of December 1903, a brief one by Rahat, a longer one by Sakina. There is also an impassioned detailed account by Surayya that formed part of her diary which contains references to the non-Muslim participants in the Conference. They appear to have been written spontaneously—'Editor sahib' is not referred to. This was a crucial issue for which the women desperately needed a forum to express their views.

February [1904]

Rahat wrote:
'*Muslim Conference*'
We had just recovered from the wedding [Faiz to Salima Latif] when we took part in a large and very important conference, attended by many leading scholars. We were very keen to attend such a meeting, and what a wonderful occasion it was. We were able to listen to distinguished *maulvis* express their views about education and upbringing, and we greatly enjoyed the opportunity. Almost all the family women attended regularly, and the Khoja ladies from the Allana family also came here. Mrs Nasrullah and ... Ali's wife and mother-in-law also came. What a wonderful woman she is. She is very progressive, speaks well, and is nice-looking too. But she lives in Hyderabad, and in such strict purdah, it's very difficult for her, and she hopes ardently.... People are now making full use of Badr Bagh [Sulaymani community masjid and meeting-place]; there was a wedding held there recently. That's enough from me; I hope someone else will write more.
Rahat
Sakina Lukmani wrote:
As dear Mother has written, truly what a wonderful occasion. This Mohammedan Educational Conference was held in Bombay this time. It seems that the Aligarh lot had been wanting to hold such a session in Bombay for a long time, and for dear Father to preside over it. But both because of his poor health, and the difference in views, it had not been possible till now. What a good thing that it's finally taken place, and that we were able to take part in it.
  From ... till ... there were meetings every day. These would usually start at 11 every morning, with a break for *namaz* at 2 p.m., resuming

at three and then going on till 6. It was a pretty heavy schedule, and for those unfortunates who had to be there all day, it must have been quite exhausting. It was such a great shame that Father was so unwell the very day that the Conference was to start—he had a high temperature, and was aching all over, but he forced himself to attend. He'd lost his voice, and was also very weak, so he wasn't able himself to make the speech he'd prepared, but he had to ask Bhai Abbas to read it for him. How very fortunate that he should have written out his speech for the occasion, on account of journalists' requests, much against his own practice. What a problem it would have been otherwise, at the last minute. This speech is going to be pasted in here. [Not done]. So I'm not going to say any more about it. Bhai Abbas read it very well; it was the first time that he's spoken in public, at such a large gathering; and we must congratulate him on this effort.

Some other young people from the family also made suggestions or resolutions, so we had a chance to hear them speak; Bhai Husain also spoke well.

The biggest controversy was over purdah, and to what extent the Shariat requires it, and what the Quran says about it. Father said that the Quran did not justify such strict purdah—in fact he read out seven *ayats,* in which it is clearly stated that women should cover their bodies decently, leaving their hands and faces free; and that nothing of their appearance or clothes should be visible to strangers; and so on. In fact, he challenged the *maulvis* to come up with proof from the Quran justifying the severe purdah which is now customary in India. Everyone was quiet save for the hot-headed young man (whose name I don't know), who said there were definitely verses justifying such purdah in the Quran, and he wrote them down for Bawajan [Father]. And it turned out that they were the very same ones that Father had read out! Anyway, there was a terrific debate over this question—and a lot of Muslims got very agitated over it all. Some even said that by opposing purdah, they had lost all their respect for Father! Now, how can it be that they could possibly continue to follow and respect a man whom they had admired so much, whose steps they wished to follow in every way—well how could they possibly continue to admire him? Religion on one side and Badruddin Tyabji on the other! Anyway, they all got very worked up, and several wrote exceedingly silly things about it all in their papers. So this terrific controversy went on for a few days.

It was also considered extremely improper for women to attend the Conference—and several articles were written about it all.

And in the *Tehzeeb-i-Niswan*, the number one paper, which is published from Lahore by Mrs Mumtaz Ali, well in that too there was a lady who expressed great dismay and shame that women from Bombay should be so lacking in virtue as to do such things out of purdah! And embarrass her so greatly!

We were very amused by all this, and we're looking forward to the day coming soon when everyone will express surprise, and say 'But what was there wrong in doing this?' and the women—oh, I meant ladies, of dear Hindustan, will share in this astonishment.

We heard Maulana Nazeer Ali Ahmed lecture, and Hali and Shibli's speeches with great interest. We admire their writings, and it was wonderful to hear them in person. And in fact, all sorts of people, who would never otherwise come to Bombay, were present at the Conference, and it was a great chance for us. We are just sorry we couldn't see more of them. And in fact Maulana Hali actually went off to Baroda for a few days, where Bhai Abbas showed him the Muslim Girls' School, which he was very impressed by, and said he wanted to do something on the same lines.

A lady called Chand Bibi had sent a paper, which was read out by Miss Kabrajee. In this, she largely pointed out the problems created by purdah, and advised on the importance of educating girls. Miss Susie Sorabjee also spoke very well on the same lines. Oh our poor Lahore and Aligarh *walis* were lectured like anything on loosening purdah! Let's hope it has some effect.

Sakina

Surayya Tyabji's account of the Anglo-Mohammedan Educational Conference, 1903
This is not part of the *akhbar*, but is preserved in the Akhde Surayya records

Bismillah ur Rehman ur Rahim
Today the Mohammedan Anglo-Oriental Educational Conference came to an end, with the last session starting at 2.30 p.m. It had begun on 27 December 1903, and the esteemed President was our dear father.

They'd made arrangements for women in purdah to attend—they'd put up *chiks* in front of a very narrow alley running along the Anjuman hostel.

There was a fine arrangement for the men, with a pavilion that was beautifully decorated. But the arrangements for us were in such a narrow and confined space, that for five days we had to stand on chairs all day to hear and see what was happening—there were two or three women standing on each chair, that was the only way we could accommodate everyone, and give them a chance to see and hear.

We were in a bad way, legs and backs aching like anything, it was only our interest and passionate involvement that kept us going through all those five days. Anyway, to cut a long story short, all the women took a keen interest in the Conference, and they'd be there every day from 11 onwards. Apart from us, there was the wife of Qasim Ali Allana, Sakina Bai, and Dost Mohammad Allana's two daughters; Mumtaz Begum, who used to be called Rabia before her marriage, and who is Nakhuda Rogay's daughter—and some other Khoja ladies—Haji Mohammad Ismail's family, and Mirza Mahdi's family, Kazi Kabiruddin's, Haji Mirza Abdulhusain's daughter, and his daughter-in-law—they would all come, as did Adam Alki's wife and mother; a couple of times.[1] [M. I. Dalvi for this information.]

The Conference was certainly extremely successful, and some fine resolutions were passed. For instance, there was one by [Khwaja] Ghulam us-Saqalain, father of Ghulam us-Sayyadain, who I believe is Hali's grandson, who put forward a resolution with great feeling and sincerity and conviction, very well articulated, that whatever destructive customs might have crept into us Muslims—for instance, the useless expenses at times of weddings or mourning, well beyond one's means, that everyone attending the Conference should be required not to spend any money this way, and more than that, should stop others from doing so, and also urge them to use this money for children's education. Of course, everyone was very taken with this idea, and it was proposed and passed with great enthusiasm. Then one Sikander Abadi proposed, and this was seconded by Bhai Mohammad Akbar, that each person would be give fifteen minutes to make his point. Now Ghulam Mustaqlain [sic] had exceeded his time, and although lots of indications were made to him that he should stop, he just kept on and on. The bell didn't work either; he just kept on talking. At last Father was forced to get up and go to him and say 'Enough', and made him sit down. He was so deeply offended by this and in fact so outraged, that he took off his hat and flung it down, quite beside himself with rage. Bhai Mohammad Akbar, who was a great friend of his, did everything in his power to calm him down, and Faiz [Badruddin] and some other friends tried too, but it was no use. They told him he'd get more time to speak, but he really was so upset he just wouldn't listen till Father sent for him and said, 'Now you can speak', and he was satisfied. In short, it was *bar i gamath*—a lot of fun. It seems that he has worked very hard and in a very committed fashion, on such matters. And that was another important resolution that was passed. Someone called Ba Aqsa proposed that girls' schools should be established with Hindustani, with strict enforcement of customs, modelled on the kindergarten system, where religious instruction would also be given. Now, one may start schools, and make all kinds of excellent arrangements for everything, but the biggest hurdle is that these shouldn't be just for show, so that we can say, 'Oh, look at our schools, we have them too.' But the point is, who is to get the girls to go, that's where the real problem lies, to persuade the parents and those others who are in charge, to actually send the girls to school.

I hope that all these wonderful ideas find fruition, and that Islam takes some steps forward, and those committed to this idea are able to persuade those Muslims who claim loudly to be Muslims simply by reciting the Qalma and that's all, Oh God, show them what Islam truly means, and what the Prophet's message truly is, what its aim is, certainly not that one can enter Paradise by simply intoning 'La illaha illalah . . .' and, oh God, when one sees the wretched condition of Muslims all around, and the awful beliefs and customs they have taken to, how can they ever be taken to the right path, and what lies ahead of them, just to think of it all fills one's heart with the utmost depression and grief. One begs God to protect this people, out of his mercy and compassion and kindness. Amen.

Father had said in his speech that was read out on the first day of the Conference that the biggest hurdle towards girls' education was purdah. I won't say any more about this as I'm going to stick into this book all the speeches and resolutions that were made at the Conference. But we heard that there was an uproar over what he'd said, and that all the *maulvis* and *qazis* were up till 1 or 2 in the morning, screaming and shouting and saying, 'Yes, Badruddin Sahib was also opposed to purdah and said it should be dropped, and last year at the Conference the Aga Khan had said the same thing—what does this Conference mean that purdah has to stop—We shall walk out of it.' And other silly and destructive things. These reports reached Father; and a lot of people came to see him and said, 'I've got to do something to calm them down, they just won't listen to whatever we say to them.' So the next day Father had to write and explain that whatever he'd said were his personal views [on purdah], and that there was no question of imposing them on anyone, or forcing people to agree with his views, but that he did want to counsel that the kind of purdah being practised then, which meant that women couldn't leave their homes, or have any fresh air or exercise, that none of this was based on the Quran or the Shariat, it was merely a custom which had to be dropped. Everyone had a right to do what they wanted with their wives or daughters. All this was written in Urdu. The first day's speech was in English, which Bhai Abbas had read out, as Father was very unwell that day, and it wasn't certain that he'd even be able to go to the Conference. He had a very bad cold and a temperature. Thank goodness he was able to attend the session. The combination of Faiz's wedding and the preparation for the Conference was very mentally taxing and exhausting for him.

Bawajan [Father] read the six *ayats* from the Quran relating to purdah, and then threw the question open for discussion, so that whoever could find a seventh *ayat* or *hukm* should present them to the audience. A chap called Riazuddin B.A., got up and claimed he could. He was asked to write them down, and when he did, Father said, 'But they're the same' [as the ones already read out]! But he was such a madman that it wasn't surprising that he kept on bursting out with objections. It was a great problem making him sit down. This chap was terribly insulting, and talked very arrogantly to a very respectable gentleman who was speaking—he said to him 'Why are you speaking in English? Don't you know that most of the people here don't understand English?' He yelled this out and was very rude—and on that occasion too Father had to speak sharply to him and tell him to sit down. If he had to say anything, he should speak in a fitting and respectful manner: And this reprimand must have angered him.

[Father emphasized]: 'Now the *ayats* in the Quran regarding purdah are only these, and they are commandments: 'Messenger; tell the Musulmans to keep their eyes lowered and to be modest in their behaviour; and dress. That is virtuous behaviour; and God knows all that they do. They shouldn't reveal their charms to the world.' 'Tell Muslim women also to lower their eyes, and not display their physical charms, except when it is fitting. They should closely cover their breasts with a *dupatta*. Apart from husband, father; father-in-law, son, husband's son, brothers, brothers' and sisters' sons, acquaintances, slave girls, servitors, eunuchs, or children, with everyone else they should not expose their physical beauty, and when they walk they should do so quietly, and not let the sound of their ornaments draw attention to them even when they are indoors.' 'Oh Muslims, follow these commandments in the presence of God, and you will earn His blessings ... Oh Messenger! Tell your wives, your daughters, and the women of the Musulmans that they should veil themselves with their *chadars,* so that it will indicate that they are Muslims [women of standing] and they will not be molested. God is infinitely merciful.'

[Father continued]

'Now please pay attention to these *ayats*. In the first it is simply stated that women should not expose their bodily charms, and that they should cover themselves with a chadar in such a way that the shape of the bosom is not evident. Those parts of the body that can be exposed according to the law, are the mouth and hands; nothing else is to be visible. *Only in front of the Qazi is* it *permitted to speak.*

'According to tradition, all the women in former times would come out of their houses, they would travel. Till the end, the Messenger of God would go on journeys with his wives accompanying him. In India, the way purdah is practised, the women penned up within the four walls of the house, like some strange animal, and the *tamasha* there is when they travel by train, on the platform, none of these things have been taught by Islam. Now, in Arabia, Egypt, Syria, all of the Islamic world, women ride out on horseback, they cover their faces, and then this *burqa,* whether a good thing or bad, is not compulsory for them, nor did it start at the time of the Prophet. The way that four walls [four schools of law] have been built around the Kaaba [in the same way], the custom of wearing a *burqa* arose later. There is no Islamic compulsion. So in fact there is no commandment in the Quran to hide one's face—although of course in the *sura ahzab* it is commanded. This shows that just as in Delhi and Lucknow, merchants' wives go on foot, in groups to the river, the bazaar, or to places of worship, with the *ghunghat* [veil covering the face], in the same way the Quran says that Muslim women should go about veiled, not display their physical beauty, and should cover themselves modestly.

'Even if we accept that this is the correct meaning, the way we practise it in India is not according to the Shariat.'

[Then the following spoke and expressed these views]:

1. Maulvi Nazeer Ahmed Dehlavi: 'Women should cover themselves with their *chadars.*'
2. Maulvi Shah Waliullah: 'Women should draw a veil over their faces.'
3. Maulvi Rafiuddin: 'Draw your larger *chadar* close over yourselves.' and
4. Shah Abdul Qadar: 'Cover the lower half with a *chadar.*' (Draw your larger *chadar* close over yourselves).

Maulvi Nazeer Ahmed has stated plainly what Maulvi Abdul Qadar has hinted at. But in Maulvi Rafiuddin's translation there is no hint that the face should be veiled. The purpose of this *sura* being revealed is, that when the women of Medina went out, people would stare at them and make fun of them. For people would notice women of gentle birth, and if there was nothing to distinguish them from slave/servant girls, then there would inevitably be problems arising from the confusion. So it was declared that when ladies went out, they should cover themselves with a *cloak/chadar,* as had earlier been the custom among the Arabs, then there would be no possibility of being mistaken for a slave and annoyed or molested.

At that time there was no question of veiling themselves, one doesn't know from where it arose. If in Arabia Muslim women had been veiling their faces, there'd have been no question of their being teased.

In any case, Muslim women have as much right to move about freely as European women, the only difference being that the Europeans leave their heads and necks uncovered, and do not have a veil/scarf over their bosoms. That is contrary to the Shariat; if they were to do so, then their clothes and behaviour would be according to Muslim observances. Some Hindus claim that the custom of purdah came to India with Islam, but this is totally incorrect. From Arabia to Kabul, nowhere do we see the severity of the purdah that exists here among the Hindus and the Muslim gentry. From this it is clear that the custom of purdah as we know it now was already established in India, that the Muslims adopted it, and then increased it so greatly that it exceeded whatever the Hindus practice was. And so on. So we need no further proof that our views on purdah are in consonance with those of God and his beloved Prophet ... [some repetition]

We will of course follow the teachings of the beloved Prophet. Never has there been any change which hasn't been greeted with anger, abuse, threats, and murder. As if in the Prophet's days there was any less vituperation and insult! And for the same reason, that he wanted to show men the true way, to save them from going astray. In my view, it's nothing new, the kind of disgusting vilification that this family has been subjected to. Something good will come of it all, inshallah! We believe that God is with us, and we rely on his aid and protection. The kind of immoral rubbish that's being written in the papers, the filthiest of filthy comments-don't deserve a glance.

Maulana Hali, Maulana Nazeer Ahmed, Maulana Shibli, and Maulana Phulwari had come especially for this Conference, and there were lots of delegates from all over India. So the gathering was a very impressive one. When will there ever again be such an opportunity to hear scholars gathered together from the entire country, discussing each other's points of view? We were really very lucky. What wonderful *vaz* and speeches we heard, all of which will be reported in detail in the official report.

Maulana Hali read out a portion from the *Musaddus i Hali*, mourning the fall of Muslims from their former glory, and urged people to awake from their sloth and look around them and see what progress has been made, while they slumbered unaware. And so on. He spoke so very beautifully on this topic. He gives the impression of being a very gentle, very quiet person, dressed very simply; he was wearing a gown, and had a grey shawl thrown over his shoulders, and a black cap.

Nazeer Ahmed's style is very amusing. He read out from a book, interspersing the reading with jokes and anecdotes, and he had the audience in fits of laughter. Then there was a riddle, which he directed especially at Bawajan, saying, 'You are great at making difficult judgements in court, now let's see what you can make of this knotty problem!'

[Riddle in verse relating to spelling of word '*char*', followed by explanation]

He explained it to us with great gusto, and we all laughed heartily, and had fun at Father's expense too. They say that Nazeer Ahmed is a great mimic, and he can imitate ladies' talk so well that no-one can tell whether it's a woman talking or not. He was wearing a *saya* made of a shawl, and an *angarkha* resembling ours, and he had a red Turki hat [fez]. He has an uncanny resemblance to Chacha Sahib Najmuddin, and when he tells his jokes the resemblance is particularly striking. Hazrat Zia Ali Saheb [head of the Sulaymani Jamaat] also frequently attended the conference, and in fact it was he who had invited Nazeer Ahmed to come from Delhi.

Maulana Shibli also made an impressive speech, although I did not fully understand his argument. He seemed to be saying that religion cannot flourish/be established without wealth, or political power, and gave many examples of this, and he also said that no other religion could compare with the great kings and nobles that Islam was able to win over. This seems to be rather strange—and we were on the whole rather disappointed with his speech.

Maulana Phulwari Sahib once recited a *vaz,* starting at nine in the evening and going on till well past midnight. That was a terrific day for us, starting out for the Conference at ten in the morning, and getting back after midnight. Haji Mohammad Ismail pressed us to stay for dinner, and some of us did stay on, while most of the others went home. What a wonderful experience it was, listening to the *vaz,* something that will *never* leave our minds and hearts. It is impossible to convey the way he recited from the Quran, the sweetness, and the power of it. One wanted him never to stop. We were completely transported by it. It was such a great shame that so many of the women had left, and lost the chance of hearing something quite extraordinary.

He also spoke a bit about purdah, and how in the Prophet's time, women would go to tend wounded soldiers in the field, and others needing succour, and bring them water. Unfortunately, no one got up to ask how this was compatible with purdah. He was of course in favour of purdah, but his examples countered his argument! At the end, he read out some *duas* for about five to ten minutes, his hands outstretched, in the most extraordinarily moving way, so that even as I write this there are tears in my eyes as I recall the experience, the way in which he called out to God fifteen or twenty times, in the most heartfelt way, for all of humanity.

There were two Muslim women who had taken the opportunity of sending their views on purdah to be read out at the Conference. One was a lady called Chand Bibi, wife of Mir Sultan Mohiuddin, who is Deputy Collector in Madras, and the other was Mrs Nasiruddin from Hyderabad. Unfortunately Chand Bibi's paper was in English, goodness knows why, her

English was very poor, not even correct, and what she had to say wasn't that great either, basically an appeal for funds. She has herself contributed Rs 50 towards the fund, and the idea is to have a *meta*, or some kind of bazaar held every year in the grounds where the Conference was being held, where handicrafts would be sold, and the money raised go to charity. It's a good idea, but let's see how successfully it's implemented. Quite a lot of money was raised for the fund that day. An old *faqir* from Delhi donated a rupee towards it, which was auctioned for Rs 300 to Haji Mohammad Ismail!

Then there was a speech in Urdu written by Mrs Nasiruddin, which was really a very fine one. In it she made a heartfelt appeal to the Muslim community to tell her why, when Muslim women were intensely eager, even in purdah, to attend this Conference, why should they not be given permission to do so? What sin had we committed? When you consider that when performing the Haj men and women travel together in a ship, nor is purdah practised during Haj. When we are all taking part in such a learned Conference, and all sorts of learned and edifying discussions are taking place, why can we not attend if we observe purdah?

We used to observe all the proceedings from the purdah enclosure, but what tremendous efforts went into arranging for it. What hurdles were put in our way. And for those of us who were there, the insults, satirical and obscene comments that were made were quite unutterably shocking. Allama Mehndi Ali himself and his brother did not allow their wives to attend, and Mohtarma Fakhrul Haji Begum and others used to attend surreptitiously. These are all truly terrible practices—the true meaning of purdah has disappeared altogether; but people are ready to come to shed blood and worse over this.

This Mrs Nasiruddin seems to be a very liberal progressive lady, and a cultivated and cultured one. There were a number of family people who spoke on various issues, such as Chacha Sahib Amiruddin [Tyabji], Bhai Ali Akbar [Akbar Hydari], Husain, Faiz, Hashim Muizuddin, Shammoo bhai [Shumsuddin Tyabji], Abbas Tyabji. Bhai M. Akbar had passed a resolution at the beginning to place the proceedings on a sound foundation, and he spoke about the need and the usefulness of such a conference. He spoke very well. Chacha Sahib Amiruddin spoke briefly, and then Hashim Mian [Muizuddin] really made a very good speech, in Urdu, about girls' education. There was one resolution that was passed with great enthusiasm, which was for a special university for Muslims, where there is already a college, and there was wild enthusiasm for this idea. Just to set up such a university would require a crore of rupees, and then what about the need for professors, and staff?

Bhai M. Akbar was going to speak against this, but fortunately he didn't eventually. He would just have been shouted down, and no good would have come of it. These people say that Muslims are so different from Hindus anyway, so then where is the sense in setting up a separate university for them and increasing the differences? And secondly wouldn't it be better to have more colleges and schools to start with, which barely exist now? Rather than an ambitious project for a big university? But the Aligarh people were so dead keen on the idea, and there was such enthusiasm for it, that no one could possibly oppose it.

Miss Sorabjee, who had come especially from Poona to take part in this Conference, made a very impassioned speech, speaking very forcefully about the need for girls' education. We heard that many Muslims found it very insulting, but really with what conviction she speaks, and what a powerful voice she has! She is one of three Parsi sisters who have converted to Christianity, and each is more capable than the other. They have spent their lives campaigning for girls' education. One of them has qualified as a barrister; and she had wanted very much to practise here in the High Court. But thank goodness that this wasn't possible! Because surely the world will come to an end when we reach the stage when women can argue in court, and become judges!

There was a gentleman by the name of Ba Akaza, who made a very eloquent speech. What a gift these people have, their words pour out of them as effortlessly and clearly as a stream of water!

Other people who had come especially for the Conference were Miss Ghoshal from Calcutta, and Amena Begum from Rajkot. Amena's husband is Mr Ghulam Muhammad Munshi. Amena Begum is the sister-in-law of my friend, Tyaba Begum, the daughter of Syed Husain Bilgrami. They were staying with Amena [Hydari] and Bhai M Akbar in Mazagon, while poor Mr Munshi is in a hotel. Miss Ghoshal belongs to the famous Brahmo Samaj Ghoshal family, and is a quite wonderful person. She is working tirelessly for girls' education, and she writes a lot too. Now there is a new activity—they have opened in Calcutta a large shop which sells only swadeshi articles. She also sings marvellously well, Urdu, Farsi, and Hindi songs, which I have set to an accompaniment in the Western fashion, and they are really wonderful and novel. That quality which you normally find in our singing, the low pitch and monotony, has been improved upon, and it is more lively. The British also enjoy this singing. She has such a wonderful voice that one could listen to her for hours on end and not tire.

She is certainly implacably opposed to the British. She says that the British behave so rudely with Indians, that there is no bearing it, and all the Hindus have become very anti-British. There is absolutely no agreement between them. Let alone agreement, it's come to blows—what a pity!

VII 1905 The Death of Rahat Badruddin Tyabji

There is no better way of conveying what happened to this cheerful, triumphant, active family in the course of 1905–1906 than by quoting the last few pages of the Badruddin Somerset *akhbar*, the Bombay *akhbar*, in Safia's version.

The description of Rahat Tyabji's last illness and death is by Sakina, who had stayed on in Bombay while the rest of the family went to Matheran.

1905, March

Mother isn't too well. That lump is causing her a lot of discomfort. Dr Dimock, who came yesterday to see her, has said that an operation can't be avoided, and perhaps this will be in three or four months' time. Mother and Father are now planning to go to Belgaum, and from there to Matheran, and on their return, *inshallah*, the operation will take place. Pray God it will be successful.

Sakina

Safia: Copied out about the tenth of October 1958

1905, April

Father, Mother, and [blank] have left for Matheran today. Dearest Mother plans to spend a long time there. Because on the 15th of May Nasima and Rafia will leave for England with Bhai Camruddin [Latif] and Bahen Vazirunissa [future parents-in-law], and Mother will definitely come to Bombay to see them off.

Sakina

[In margin, Safia] April 1905

What an awful, extraordinary thing. We've just had the news that Bhai Camruddin has the plague. They're staying at the moment at Badr Bagh [the Sulaymani *jamaat* community centre], as they've let out their house and furniture in preparation for their stay in England. Poor Vazir Bahen was having such an awful time getting ready for this trip, and now she had this ordeal to face.

May God in his mercy help them, back to health and prosperity.

Sakina

[In margin, Safia] May 1905

Thank God that Bhai Camruddin has made such good progress that the Doctor has advised him to have a change, and since Bahen Vazir had expressed a desire to come here for a few days, they may perhaps arrive tomorrow. They'll leave for England on the 15th of May.

Mother won't come to Bombay as it'll be terribly hot, and as she's not been well, they're afraid that it might affect her badly. How terrible it must have been for her to have to say goodbye to dearest Nassoo and Raffoo two or three days before they actually leave. May God return us these dear children quickly and happily and safely.

Sakina

[In margin, Safia] 15 May 1905

Today dear Nasima and Rafia left for England. May God make their trip a successful one, and they return with all kinds of knowledge and loads of culture. Dear Father went with them to Bombay on the 12th, and he'll perhaps be back tomorrow. Together with Bhai Camruddin and Bahen Vazir, there are Sarhan, Tehmina, Nasima, Rafia; they boarded the ship today.

Sakina.

[In margin, Safia] 22 May 1905 corresponding to AH???

Safia: *God give me the strength to copy this.*

I see that no one has touched this akhbar book for ages. And how could anyone possibly have the heart or strength to write about such a terrible, heart-wrenching event. But it has to be done. Poor poor Somerset has been orphaned, left desolate, hopeless. Oh god, why did dearest Mother all of a sudden go away from us? Here we were rejoicing that the operation was successful, and that we'd be able to see her in a couple of days, happy, not in pain, and then we suddenly get the news that there's no hope, come and see her for the last time!

Oh God, only you can know what it did to poor Father, and all of us unfortunates, and why that dear spirit was taken away from us. We would have done everything possible to prevent it—but who can fight the will of God? However desperately we fight, however much we resist, in the end we have to give up and accept it.

On April [blank] the whole family, that is dear Father, Mother, and almost all the children except for Nasima, Hanifa, Rafia, Safia, and Hatim and me went to Matheran, and darling Mother had promised me that she'd be back on the 10th of May to see off Nassoo and Raffoo, and also to keep an eye on me and Afzal who was on the way! We fully expected her to come as she'd said she would. But then she was so unwell and it was so terribly hot here, that we eventually wrote and told her not to strain herself, and dear Father thought so too, so we managed to persuade her not to come. So she had to say goodbye to dear Nassoo and Raffoo, who'd gone to Matheran for a fortnight, in Matheran, and I heard that she was terribly upset by this. But she kept up a brave front, and kept on saying that I'm not in the least upset that they're going, just so as not to spoil their excitement and happiness. But the grief of it left her quite weak, and it appears that the tumour which she had suffered from for a good five years, suddenly got enlarged as a result of this parting. One evening after dinner they were playing whist, and she was watching with great interest as she always did, when all of a sudden she had this terrible pain and almost fainted with it. Father; Bhai Ali Asghar [Fyzee], Bhai Mirza Aqa *[bin Camruddin Tyabjee]* and Husain were there, and they carried her with great difficulty to her room.

And the pain was so terrible, she was unconscious [Safia explains this]. The whole night was an agonizing one, but the next day she was a bit better till in the evening the pain started again, and it just would not die down. They'd sent for a doctor from the hospital there, and also sent a telegram to Dr Lukmani in Bombay to come. He brought with him a very experienced doctor, Dr Nariman, as a consultant. But nothing helped. Then, very anxiously, arrangements were made to bring her to Bombay. I forgot to mention that the day the pain started, Father had written straight away to 'him' [her husband, Dr Badruddin Lukmani] saying that the operation was now urgently needed. [Dr Lukmani] then went and met Dr Dimock, and it was decided that he and Dr Quicke would perform the operation as soon as it was possible. [Dr Lukmani] went to Matheran on Sunday, and on Monday dear Mother was brought down to Bombay by Father. That morning the medicine finally had some effect on her, and she was feeling slightly better so that the journey wasn't too much of a strain for her. She even enjoyed the trip in the *palki*, and said to us when she got to Bombay that after so many days of being cooped up, she found the fresh air, the trees, and the greenery all around her immeasurably refreshing. She thoroughly enjoyed the views as they descended the ghat, and the train journey was also a comfortable one. She was delighted to see Nurse De Joss on the platform at Bori Bunder [Victoria Terminus], and of course it was a great relief for Father, to have her taking charge of dear Mother. Well anyway … They got home, but that cursed pain had only let up for a short time, and it started again. And my god, what a night we had. May God grant that no one should ever live through such an experience.

The next day, Dr Dimock and Quicke came, and decided to operate the very next day, at eight in the morning. That very day Bhai Abbas arrived from Baroda—it was so wonderful to have him here. Anyway. We were of course all on tenterhooks, but the amazing thing was to see how dear Mother took it all. She was so calm, so cheerful, so resolute in the face of this awful thing that lay ahead of her. She was keenly involved in every little detail of the preparations that were being made—and she wanted to be consulted about them, and she wasn't in the least nervous or anxious. The doctors wanted to use Father's room for the operation—they needed a lot of light. So the whole room was washed out and scrubbed, the furniture removed, till it sparkled like a mirror. This was necessary for an operation of this kind.

The next day, Tuesday 6th June, preparations started from early morning. Cart loads of stuff began arriving. And at eight o'clock we all went to dear Mother to see her before she was taken to the operating room. We were all in a terrible state, but she was just so amazing—she wasn't in the least little bit anxious or nervous. Rather, there was a kind of relief and happiness that at last this awful pain was going to be got rid of. She got up on her own and went and sat in the chair in which she was then carried to Father's room. And this was the last time we saw our dear Mother conscious. And oh god, oh god, those hours that passed while the operation was going on—how did we survive them! But when we heard that the operation was safely over, and that it had gone much better than expected, that the tumour was not malignant as had been feared—oh the rejoicing and happiness then—not at Id or any wedding can there be a tenth of the joy we felt then. But we were not allowed to see her for three days—but what did it matter, we were happy enough, we'd be seeing dear Mother in three days, without any pain. The afternoon passed peacefully (this was 6 June), but then in the evening she began to feel uncomfortable again, her legs were hurting and she suffered from thirst and dehydration. And then, before dawn, her legs and feet began to lose their warmth. By the morning, there was no pulse left in one hand. Dr Dimock came at about [blank], and he and Dr Badruddin did whatever was possible to bring life and warmth back into her. But it was all in vain. Her heart could not stand the strain of all that she had endured, and became weaker and weaker. When we first heard of this frightful condition, we begged to be allowed to meet her just once. But the doctors felt that she might not be able to withstand the strain of meeting her loved ones, and that she might collapse as a result. They were not willing to take any risks while there was the slightest possibility of her recovering her strength. But after hours of struggling, they realized that the matter was now in God's hands, and that he was calling her to him. Then Dr Dimock came down, and sent Father and all of us up to her; when we went we saw no sign of life in her eyes … so then what was there left?

May God grant her the finest place in Heaven, and our dear Father the patience to endure. Amen. Sakina

Safia: Note The idyllic life we'd had as children began to change from now. I was twelve years old then, and although 53 years have passed since then, more than dear Mother's death, what has left an indelible impression on me is memories of the happiness of learning that the operation was successful, people's radiant faces, especially dear Father's, and then the fearful news that followed. To see Mother drawing her last breaths, Hattoo bhai fainting, and to face the sorrow that we had not

imagined could exist, to live life without our Mother! Oh heavens, God
is our only help.

Amina 19 November 1894

Rahat Badruddin, 1899.

VIII 1907 A Visit to the Jog Falls

October 1958 Hijri Year

Safia: After dear Mother's death no one could even think of touching
the akhbar book, and then Halima bahen wrote an account of a trip
she'd made. A very full and good account

I'm writing this at the request of dear Hussoo bhai [Faiz]. We've just returned from seeing the most marvellous Falls, that is the Geersuppa Falls.
It happened in this way:

Since last year, Bhai Akbar [Ali Akbar Fyzee], Ali Beg [Asghar Ali
Fyzee, Halima's husband] and various other gentlemen had been talking
about it. I'd gone to Belgaum in August with dear Father, and Bahen

Surayya, and Hanifa. Father could only stay for twelve days, he had to go back then, but Bahen Zubeida urged Hannoo and me to stay. Hannoo left after a few days, but I spent a whole two months in Belgaum. I felt much better in that lovely place with the good air. That was when Bhai Akbar and Bahen Zubeida urged me to join the Geersuppa excursion. At that point I didn't think much of it, but when I got back to Bombay, in the middle of the October heat, people said to me that I shouldn't give up such a wonderful opportunity. I'd heard so much about it that I was keen to go myself, and decided to join the [expedition]. Our party was to have been much larger initially—Mr Panse, Mr Madgaokar, and Bhai Mohsin were all keen to go. Bhai Mohsin then had to drop out because Bhabi Tahera was very unwell. As for the other two what happened was that we had initially planned to go by steamer to Karwar, but because of the stormy weather we had to change our plans and travel by train. We went first to Belgaum by train, where we'd initially hoped that Bhai Akbar and Bahen Zubeida would join us straightaway and come on to Goa with us. We had no idea of what had been happening while we were travelling! Bhai Akbar and Bahen Zubeida who came to meet us at the station told us that they had been bombarded with telegrams telling them that it was very very stormy, there were high winds, and that the Goa steamer had been cancelled!

We had to get down at Belgaum, and spend the day there, and we set off the next day for Goa. We spent three days there—the first day, we arrived quite late, at about 10 o'clock. The following day was spent in sight seeing in Goa and Panjim. It's a very interesting place. And in Old Goa we saw a wonderful temple, called the San Francisco, in which the saint or *pir* himself lies buried. There is some wonderful ornamentation in gold, which looks very beautiful on blue and silver columns. And there are other things worth seeing too.

The day after we returned from Goa, we set off for Geersuppa. At one point, there were so many problems that we didn't know whether we would get there at all. One problem was that it turned out that after reaching Shimoga on the Mysore Road, we would have to travel 60 miles or so by cart, *tanga* or *jhutka*. We didn't think that Bahen Zubeida would be able to handle travelling in these contraptions, and also we didn't know quite what they were. And then one day a gentleman who'd come to dinner said, 'But why don't you take a rickshaw along?' We all thought this was a great idea, and we took a rickshaw along with us. We were also grateful to this gentleman for his idea, because Bahen Zubeida would never have been able to handle travelling in those carts. We started off on Wednesday 26 October, by the 9.30 Mail.

We were: (1) Bhai Akbar; (2) Bahen Zubeida; (3) Major Bholanath; (4) Mrs Bholanath; (5 and 6) her two sons; (7 and 8) the two of us. We travelled in a second-class compartment, and saw all kinds of wonderful and new places (mulk), and we had such excellent company! It was great fun. We reached Barnir station that night at 11 p.m., where we had to change trains, and catch the train to Shimoga which was waiting there. We went to sleep comfortably in it, and the train started at five the next morning. We'd had a good rest all night, and got over our tiredness, and we rested comfortably in the Shimoga train till we reached Shimoga at 8 in the morning, and then went by cart to the rest house, which was nice and comfortable, and with a lovely location. We had lunch there, and at 4.30 in the afternoon we got into carts, four of them, and set off. Two carts held our luggage, and in one Mrs Bholanath and her sons travelled, in the other, there was Bhai Akbar Ali, Beg and myself. Major Bholanath was on his bike, and Bahen Zubeida in her rickshaw!

From here, there was a good road, and five rest houses on the way. The first was Kumsia, about 15 miles distance; the second at Anandpur, also at 15 miles distance; the third was Sagar, another 15 miles; the fourth at Telgappa, 9 1/2 miles away, and the fifth the one at Jog Falls, also 9 1/2 miles away. In all, we had to cover a distance of 64 miles in these carts. Major Bholanath on his bicycle was a great comfort, he'd cycle up and down, keeping an eye on everyone!

One major problem for us was that no one there could understand what we were saying. And we'd do our best to convey our meaning gesturing away, but that still didn't work! We spent the first night at the Kamsi rest house, lunched there, and then left after lunch for the next stage. There was an excellent road all the way from Shimoga, there were large beautiful trees, and so on, but oh, the road from Kamsi onwards—we were in ecstasies, enraptured. For about five or six miles we went through a huge bamboo jungle, and it is quite impossible to convey the beauty of their shapes, the denseness, the different forms, and then, the majesty of that jungle in the evening light—it is truly a wonderful sight. How I missed dear Father and all the others. The forests were so dense that one couldn't see anything inside at all—who knows what sorts of animals lurk inside them! At first we used to be rather nervous at travelling through this kind of dense jungle in the evening, but then we got used to it.

At the Anandpur rest house we met a padre sahib, a nice simple good man, but we had a bit of a problem about accommodation. There were only two rooms in the rest house, and he had one! But we made good use of the dining room and the veranda instead. There were lots of mosquitoes here, in fact we could hardly sleep all night. In the morning, Bhai Akbar and Ali Beg went for a shoot, while the women spread out a *shatranji* (durree) under a shady tree, working and chatting away.

We set out again in the afternoon from here, having had lunch at the rest house, and got to Telgappa. Oh, I forgot to mention that Sagar is quite a big town, and we got all kinds of provisions there. We'd set off from here at about 9.30 or so, and got to Telgappa in the most marvellous light. This rest house is situated on a high hill, looking down on a lake which is full of water lilies, and it has a lovely view. And as we reached it that first evening, we saw the new moon shining through the huge trees. We had travelled through such thick forests, and at one point, where there was a bit of a clearing, we saw the moon again, and it was so beautiful, we will never forget it. What sights we saw, the forests, the trees, the hills, the *maidans* and fields, what an absolutely fantastic trip that was. We didn't stay long at that place, but set off immediately after lunch. Once again, for a couple of miles, we passed through incredibly beautiful scenery, it was out of the question for anyone to stay sitting in the cart, so I got out and walked a long way. It was great that the road was in such good condition. Bhai Akbar was also very sad that he hadn't thought of bringing along his bicycle. Oh how wonderful it must have been to cycle along that way!

At sunset we reached the river Sharavathi, where there was a large barge [tarapa] on which we climbed with our carts and bullocks, and were ferried over to the other side, and then continued on our way, till we reached the borders of Mysore State. There were then again tremendous forests of great majesty and might -it arouses such awe and fear in one. Any moment an animal might have sprung out at us. And the thing was that ours was the only cart on the road—all the others were well ahead of or behind us. And we could hear the sound of water from here, and kept on wondering when shall we see it!

After crossing the river, we had to go on another two miles, and then we reached the bungalow. It was a splendid and very comfortable place, belonging to Mysore State. Each such rest house had two bedrooms, a dining room and veranda. From here we had a good view of the Falls. As we reached, what did we see but Bhai Akbar and Bahen Zubeida stretched out on chairs in the veranda and doing the Goba puja! We got out and did the same thing, and in fact that evening we had to be content with sitting and watching the scene from there. We were quite tired too. We went straight off to bed after dinner. Oh, I made a mistake—there were four rooms in this guest house, each with its attached bathroom, and the rooms were nice and spacious. Two are perhaps rather smaller.

The next day we started looking at the Falls in every kind of light, from early morning, before dawn, all day. Quite close by, there was a little point from where we could watch, called Lady Curzon's Seat, from where we had a good view of the Falls. These Falls are right on the borders of Mysore State, and the rest house faces them. There is Dame Blanche or White Lady, who very delicately pours down—it really looks as if there were lengths of chiffon floating down. Quite close by, there are two Rocket Falls, looking just like *phooljharries*, or strings of pearls. One really can't begin to describe the sight. At a little distance there is the Roarer, an amazing, stormy flow, which hardly flows but seems more to beat against the rocks, and halfway down it meets and joins the Raja. All the noise and turbulence comes from it, because there is a lot of water flowing through a narrow channel, and then when the channel widens out a bit (*khulasi*), it seems to burst out with its fury, while Raja flows calmly along with such dignity and majesty, carrying along thousands of pearls! And to see all these falls together! It is truly worth making this effort to see them.

The very first day, when we were at lunch, Ali Beg read out an account from a book according to which in the middle of the afternoon, a rainbow appeared over them. This spectacular sight was not to be missed. So he wanted to go straightaway to see this. And then he called out to all of us to come. A lot of people were quite annoyed, they thought is this a thing to do, to pull us away from our meal, we can finish our meal and then go to have a good look at what there is. But Bahen Zubeida and I couldn't resist it—we ran out. And truly, what a sight it was—I just have to describe it!!! The water was sparkling in the sun, and the sun's rays light it up in such a way that each drop looked like a pearl. Oh, it was marvellous, marvellous.

I must also mention that in the morning, that is before the sun rises, the Falls don't look so wonderful, because they're shrouded in a kind of mist, and the water flows so fast that it becomes a kind of foam. This is especially so with Raja, who has a lot of such habits. But right in the middle of the afternoon, between noon and about four p.m. he can be seen quite clearly! We were so thrilled by the sight that we decided, as soon as lunch was over, we should go down and look at the Falls. There's a path here which leads right down to the Falls, and we'd actually planned to go there this morning, but the caretaker there warned us that it would be quite wet and slippery in the morning, and advised us to go later in the day. None of the others were willing to go down in the heat of the afternoon, but the two of us, that is Ali Beg and I, decided to go. We took along a bottle of soda and some biscuits! Although it was only 12.30 then, the path was so well shaded with those magnificent trees, that we didn't feel the heat at all. And it was so beautiful. The path had been cut through thick jungle. From time to time, wherever the trees thinned out, we'd have glimpses of the Falls. There was also a Point from where one had a fine view. We got right down to the Falls and sat on a nice shaded rock.

The path was okay for a short while, but for most of it one had to walk over very large rocks which was not however difficult. One had to be careful how one placed one's feet. At first we'd thought that Bahen Zubeida could be carried down on a chair, but it would be quite impossible to carry a chair down, there's no foothold at all. And oh heavens, when we finally got down, what a sight greeted us! We could hardly breathe. All around us, and so near, were the Falls, and then when we went further down and looked in front there were these huge mountains, surrounding us on all sides, so that one felt quite giddy. I sat absolutely still, unable to say a word. So overpowering was the whole scene, and so shaken and full of gratitude were we that we sat dumbly, in absolute thankfulness. The unique thing about Raja is that it falls 930 feet straight down into a gorge, and in one second, 1200 tons of water flow down.

We spent the whole day looking at the Falls; the men went down still lower till they got right down to the bed of the ravine. We took off our shoes and socks too, and were ready to join them where they stood, but the men were quite clear that we shouldn't come down, as it was so very slippery. Major Bholanath slipped once, and hurt his leg quite badly. If it hadn't been for Major Bholanath I would certainly have gone, but I didn't have the courage to defy him. When the men came back they were quite dazzled, in transports (*wajd*) over it all. The water fell directly on to them, and they said that what you saw from there was quite incomparable to anything we had seen from here! However we were quite contented. The men were absolutely drenched with the water.

We left quickly so that we should get back up before sundown, and had quite a taxing climb back up. It reminded me of Ram Bagh, in Matheran! Half way up we had a rest, and had some tea, and recovered a bit. There's one thing I haven't mentioned at all—I'd forgotten about the rainbow! When we'd first climbed down, this was lying as if it were at our feet, at the bottom of the Falls. And then it slowly rose, so that by the evening, at sunset, it was on Raja, and then it went straight up, and then it vanished. And when it disappeared, we were left with the strangest sense of loss: as if it had carried away not only the spirit of the Falls, but of all of us as well! Oh, the way the water sparkled in the sun!

I so wish that everyone who reads this *akhbar* can go and see it for themselves. These Falls are also called the Jog Falls from a village that is quite close by. How wonderfully green those hills are—and sometimes the spray from the Falls would drench us as if it were rain, and indeed it was difficult to believe it wasn't raining.

The next day we set off at 7 in the morning after a cup of tea to go to the 'Angrezi Bungla' and see the Falls from there. A few people walked, and the others went by cart. It was wonderful to be able to walk, and to look at each tree, each leaf, and the flowers properly. After a couple of miles, we crossed the river again, and after that I got into the cart, as we were getting late. The path was so good and so shady that there was no question of getting tired, nor was it hot. It wasn't cold either; except of course for the early mornings and in the evenings when it would get a little chilly. Yes, I forgot to mention that after we'd crossed the river; and since we were well ahead of the others, we climbed on to a large black stone in the middle of the river, which from a distance you would mistake for a tree. We sat absolutely still on the rock, and looked at the water, and we began to feel that we were at one with the water, and flowing away with it. This river is really very very beautiful; the thick forests surrounding it on all sides give it both qualities.

We had breakfast at the Bungla, and then taking someone from the rest house with us, we went to see the waterfalls. One can't see all the falls from this spot—only Lady and Rocket. One has to go down to be able to see them all from different angles. We first had a wonderful view of Lady; and in fact, from this spot we had a completely different view of all the Falls. We also got a fine view of Rocket, and as for Roarer, of which we'd seen only half earlier, we now had a full view of it from this spot, and of the terrific force with which its waters descend.

Finally, we went to see Raja. Oh heavens, what a magnificent sight that is! How can I possibly begin to describe it! We went quite close to where the water was flowing, and beside it there were huge bald stones, on which we stretched ourselves out, while someone held us firmly by the feet, as it seems people can get dizzy looking down. It was impossible to tear oneself away from the sight. The sight of those pearls flowing down constantly, and what volumes of water! They say 1200 tons in one second! It is quite marvellous. And then, the water isn't of one colour, the colour keeps on changing, cream, to green, to dark green. We were there in the middle of the afternoon, with the sun beating down on our heads, and in the sun the water shone. A strange thing was that just below where the water flowed, a large piece of rock had broken off, and there's just about room for a man to stand on it under the rushing water. You can see right into the heart of Raja. Zubeida Bahen wasn't feeling too well that day, so we'd thought we wouldn't bring her down to see all this. But after this sight, we felt she just must come, so Bhai Akbar went up to fetch her.

At this point, we found another strange and wonderful rock: Ali Beg and I had thought that while we were waiting for Bhai Akbar and Bahen Zubeida to join us, we'd look for a nice shady tree to protect us from the sun, and this is how we found the rock. There was a little cave inside it, and when we went in and sat down, there was such a delicious cool breeze flowing about us, it was difficult to believe that outside the noon-day sun was beating down! Then we eagerly called out to everyone to join us there, and we had our picnic there. I'd written earlier that we had breakfast at the bungalow, but I was wrong—we'd brought a picnic with us which we had in the cave. You can imagine how large the cave was, that we should all of us have fitted in so comfortably.

Bahen Zubeida also loved the place, and a lot of people wanted to stay there and have their afternoon nap! Then we had a last look at Raja, and were transported once again with rapture! Then we made our way back to the bungalow, and since it was very very hot, we had a bit of a rest there, but then we thought longingly of our Mysore bungalow, and decided to set off immediately in spite of the heat.

The following day we left this wonderful place with a heavy heart, on our way to Shimoga. On the way back we travelled fast, we did nineteen miles the first day, thirty the next, and in this fashion we reached Shimoga very quickly. We spent one day in Belgaum, and then on Monday the three of us, that is Bahen Zubeida, Ali Beg, and I left by the 5 o'clock Mail for Bombay and reached the next day. We found everyone well—dear Father had just returned the day before from Mahabaleshwar, and I went and met him that very day. It's very upsetting that although Father has just come back from Mahabaleshwar, his eyes are bothering him a lot, and he can barely see to read. May God protect dear Father and make his eyes strong and fit again.

Halima (aged 24)

IX The Final Entries in the Badruddin *Akhbar*

Amina in the Badruddin *Akhbar*

On 9 November, the Prince and Princess [of Wales] came to Bombay. We saw it all very comfortably from the Taj Mahal Hotel. The next day, the tenth, there was a reception for them at Government House. The Princess was extremely gracious. Yesterday there was a reception given for her by the Indian ladies, which went off very well.

I won't say any more, as I'm sure someone will write a full account of it all.

25 November 1905

Today dear Father left for Europe with Husain by steamer. They will go straight to London to consult an eminent eye doctor, and then perhaps travel on the Continent. He will be away for a whole year. May God bring him back quickly, so we can soon be sitting listening for the sound of his approaching carriage wheels. And may his presence bring life and joy back to Somerset.

Sakina

Safia: I finished copying this out on Sunday, 12 October 1958, at 4.30 in the afternoon. I thank God I was able to complete the task. Hijri year....

12 October 1958

Safia writes as she completes her work:

Our hopes were not fulfilled, and God did not grant us our prayers. We had not overcome the sadness of our mother's death, when we lost him too, in London on 19 August 1906; it left us all helpless and desolate. It took us many years to recover from the shock of this loss. And although we did get over it, it took strength to enter into our new lives with confidence, and to stop being overcome by memories of the past; to live in fact in the present, and *rejoice* in it. And to be content. But God is indeed great—for after all the losses and grief, I can say that I am indeed happy, I am indeed content, and full of thankfulness! Alhumdolillah. Safia

4

A Modern Woman: The Journal of Safia Jabir Ali, 1926–45

Translated from the Urdu

Introduction

Safia was Badruddin Tyabji's youngest daughter; and an avid reader and writer in the family *akhbar* by the time she was eight. So her journal could be viewed as the result of the literary tastes instilled in her from her childhood, when reading and writing was a normal and pleasant part of the daily routine.

There was a long gap between 1926 when this memoir was begun, and 1942 when she resumed writing. The circumstances in which she lived during that period, hardly referred to in the latter half, barely a backward glance thrown at that time, must nevertheless have played a part in shaping her views.

This was the period during which Safia's husband, Jabir, a close cousin and ardent Gandhian, began to take an active part in the Non-Cooperation Movement, was jailed, and then devoted many years of his life to public work. She showed great determination and self-confidence in running their farm, looking after the household, and caring for their son Amiruddin while her husband was in jail. This gap in her memoir has been bridged here by her son Amiruddin, a contribution that is in keeping with the joint nature of the earlier *akhbar* books.

Safia's *akhbar* starts off as another 'set-piece'—a joyous celebration of the happiness of youth, of achievement, of adventure, and of toughness—another important characteristic of this family. As time passed, for the writer it became important to remember the past, to record memories, both for herself, perhaps to reinforce her sense of herself, and also, as she states, for her son to read and cherish.

The Changing World of a Bombay Muslim Community, 1870–1945. Salima Tyabji, Oxford University Press.
© Nasir Tyabji 2023. DOI: 10.1093/oso/9780192869746.003.0004

The poignant memories of her idyllic childhood, of the adored father, give way to her statements about her no less idolized husband. The account of their early courtship, playful, intimate, astonishingly candid, the ecstasy of union, is extraordinary in its charming openness, in its desire to share the rapture of love with her child. This develops into a celebration of conjugality, equally unusual in our society.

Was she influenced somewhat by European writing, at a time when the romantic, individual element within a marriage had begun to find acceptance as nuclear, urban family units began to emerge in India? Or was it a question of her reaffirming her belief that her life had been one of great happiness, in spite of evident physical and emotional stress? Of equal interest is her frank acceptance of youthful sexuality, however low-key her statements.

Although she wrote fairly diligently over a period of two years or so, and managed to persuade both her son Amir, and her adopted son, Ustad Sahib Samad, to write, it's really astonishing that her husband, a man of stature in the nationalist movement, as well as within the family, contributes not a word. It is her view of the world, and her view of her husband, that create this *akhbar*. It's also a very spontaneous record of her feelings and views—we learn with each new entry what it was that preoccupied her at that moment—leaping from accounts of her childhood in her parents' home in the 1890s, to her life in Tavoy in 1917, to descriptions of the humdrum details of cooks and *dhobis* and the price of food (which she was well aware of the importance of recording), to accounts of cultural events, *mushairas*, etc., that she attended or books that she was reading.

Safia was, like most women of those times, a female living through her men, in many ways impotent except within the house, or within well-defined parameters, such as certain forms of political protest. It's also of interest that in spite of her intellectual vigour and independence of mind, she did not take up issues of social or political reform as did her cousins Atiya and Nazli, or her elder sister Sakina, whom one might describe as activists. Life beyond the home meant for her 'her country'. Clearly, her early childhood and whatever political views she'd absorbed in her parents' household played an important part in shaping her sense of identity as an 'Indian'; it was equally clearly the views of the adored husband that reinforced and sharpened them. As it happened Badruddin, her father, retired early from the national political stage—but that had little to do with his deep commitment to the idea of his community being part of the nation.

This is what his daughter's memoir makes very clear.

In the name of the Merciful and Beneficent
Chembur
Tamheed

I

Begun on 22 February 1926

For some days now, Jabir and I have been talking about how we must start keeping some sort of diary. We've spent such delightful, such happy and good times in this enchanting place that we feel we must write it all down, every single thing, so that in later years we should have this detailed account to refresh our memories of these wonderful times.

I must admit that we're both surprised that, the world being the dreadful place it is, it should then turn out to be so wonderful!—that, after all our tribulations and sorrows, we should now have our heart's desire. Jabir has always been very interested in agriculture and horticulture and took his degree in agriculture [Cambridge, c. 1909]. But then, after having tried for many months to get the right kind of job, after such a degree, had eventually to turn to business. In this he was helped by Salah Mian [Abbas S. Tyabji's elder son] to set up a business in Burma.

When Jabir returned from Rangoon, not only without a penny, but worse, in debt, we had a very anxious time deciding whether he should start a new hardware (ironmongery) business, or whether to take up a job. In any case, we needed somewhere to stay—and our relations were very good to us over that. We could have stayed with them for as long as we liked, but, for one thing, we didn't want to be a burden, and for another, one's own home is something quite different. It's all very well when one's on holiday and wanting to enjoy oneself, but for everyday living there's nothing like having one's own home.

Safia before her marriage, aged 16. Bombay, 1909.

Jabir had great difficulty in getting a job, so he started his own business but had enormous problems because of not having any capital; we were both reluctant to borrow from anyone, especially as we were already burdened with debts. At that point, Jabir had an idea—one that had actually occurred to us earlier, but we'd never seriously considered it before—there'd been no occasion to. And this was to go and live in Deonar [part of present-day Chembur], on the family property there, and farm it, while carrying on with whatever other business Jabir had in Bombay.

The more we thought about it, the more attractive the whole thing became. Jabir had always been keen on farming, and I loved the idea of having a garden, a home of my own, of living in the country amidst wide open spaces, greenery, and cool breezes, where one could be what one wished, and do what one wished, away from the hustle and pressures of the city. There were problems, of course. Not a soul in the family agreed with us that one could live in Chembur all the year round, and everyone, of course with our interests at heart, tried to dissuade us from what they saw as being incredibly foolish and stubborn behaviour. The house was completely dilapidated, the land an overgrown jungle, the place completely isolated, the nearest station a couple of miles away—and of course there was no question of our being able to afford a car or even a carriage. In the rains, we'd be even more isolated, because the roads would be deep in mire, and we wouldn't even be able to walk—and that is certainly true! Also, there was a lot of malaria and fevers of all kinds, especially when the rice is ripening, and, as for the mosquitoes, you couldn't even sit except under a mosquito net! There were any number of poisonous snakes and scorpions and as if that wasn't enough, there was always the danger of marauding Pathans. The house was so leaky that if it rained there'd be real ponds inside.[1] White ants were such a nuisance that even if you swept the house twice a day you couldn't get rid of them, and they'd eat up everything.

We were told of all kinds of problems, but none of this had any effect on Jabir, who brushed it all aside, and was determined to go ahead with his scheme. At first, I vacillated. I was attracted by the idea, but then people's warnings and advice would make me change my mind—but Jabir's unwavering commitment to the idea affected me eventually, and also, I didn't have the fears many people have of feeling cut off and of being on my own a great deal, though I was a bit unnerved at the thought of the rainy season, and how we'd handle that. We also had to get the family's permission to live here, and build a house, and have the options of buying the land off them. They all agreed to this happily, and one or two of them even gave Jabir their portions.

Jabir had been in Bombay since 25 December [1924], and two months had passed in all this uncertainty, which we'd passed with Badr Bhai [Lukmani] in great comfort. It was on 25 March 1925 that we went to Chembur to clean the house up. Jabir had been there earlier on his own several times. There was so much rubbish in the old house that just thinking of it now makes my heart sink, but at that time we were so enthusiastic, we thought nothing of it. We were young and fit, by god's grace, and nothing deterred us. We'd each take up a *jharoo* and sweep away. The tenant would occasionally help us, but it was mostly us who did the work. The roof and every corner was full of rubbish and muck—cobwebs, ants, lizards, mice, squirrels—every kind of noisome, horrible creature had contributed its bit and I really can't begin to describe the condition of the house. It took us days and days to get the house into a condition that we could think of moving into. The furniture was also in the same state, and needed a lot of repairing before it could be used. But it was awfully useful: wooden beds, chairs, some tables, mattresses, bathroom fittings, vases, brass trays, garden tools, and also some tableware, but nothing for the kitchen. In fact, there wasn't a kitchen, and the first thing we did was make a little room and put in a *chulha*. At first we had a cook called Abdul Qadar, who used to work for Hasan Mian [Ali] and Camoo [Jabir and Salim Ali's elder sister], and now is with Adnan [Futehally]. He was an excellent cook, and would make the simplest things quite delicious, and was a quiet unassuming sort of person. He was also very good at coping with the fact that there was no kitchen and no stove—he'd go off into the jungle and cut firewood, and cook on a stove made of a few bricks.

After the place had been thoroughly cleaned up, we moved in. At first we made do with the absolute minimum, and then slowly brought in more stuff, including what we'd brought back from Rangoon—beds, my dressing table, almirahs for clothes, silverware, book cases, a safe, and other odds and ends, which we'd stored in Bombay, and which fitted quite well into this little house. Camoo had gone to Japan and we'd bought her cane-bottomed furniture off her then. All our brassware had been locked up for ages, and had gone quite black. It took a long time to get it to sparkle again, and when it did, we were so pleased! Initially, when we had no other servant, Bibi [elder sister Sakina Lukmani] had loaned us her Mohammad for some days, then, in the first week of April we got a servant called Abdul Ghani, who's still with us, and very responsible and willing. May god's grace be on him, and may he stay that way.

From the very beginning, we loved the place. The more problems we had, the more enthusiastically we tackled them. The house itself had been cleaned up, but there was a real jungle surrounding it, and all over the land. We started clearing it, and making huge bonfires every day after sunset, and sitting down, tired out, looking at what we'd achieved during the day and feeling happy. No one who's not done it themselves can quite realize what hard work it is to clean out undergrowth, and how long it takes. The two of us would be at it for two or three hours at a time. Sometimes we took on hired labour, but it still took us months to get the basic clearing done. And now, as I write this, although there've been great changes, there's still a lot to be done. All four sides around the house have been cleared, and since this bit's swept out every day, it looks fairly neat, but everywhere else it's still terribly overgrown. In the monsoon, a patch that's just been cleared will, in a couple of days, be so full of jungle again that it's difficult to believe that it had all been cleared at all, with all that effort. Then there was the business of opening up our baggage, all packed in large wooden crates. For some time the house was just full of it all, and though it was exciting opening them, and finding our things again, there was also a lot of heart burning, because so many things had got damaged on the way, either by damp or sea water seeping into them, and books and pictures had either been eaten up by white ants or mice or cockroaches, but that anything remained at all was a godsend, nothing short of a miracle. And when you have your loved possessions all around you, it's like having old friends back, and a source of joy, and our house became even more our home.

As I've said earlier, we had a tiny income within which we had to manage. We didn't of course have to pay any rent, which was a great saving, and though we ate very simply, there was always more than enough, but our lives were so active and energetic and in this wonderful place we were always hungry, and needed lots of food. We had two servants: a cook, whom we paid 25 rupees a month, and a 'boy' for 18 rupees. In addition, we had to allow for transport to Bombay, for repairs to the house, etc., so we made a budget and managed to stick to it, thank goodness. I'm leaving a blank page for monthly accounts [left blank]. Our greatest anxiety was about how to manage during the monsoon. It wasn't just a case of repairing a leaky roof—the whole house was one [bloody] veranda! The rain beat in from all four sides—what could we do about that? Then there was the worry about fevers, snakes, scorpions, mosquitoes—and we just had to find a solution to all this. We had the roof repaired but not very well, and that was a real problem all that season, but we hung canvas along the verandas and that really worked very well. We were able to sleep in the verandas, as usual, but my goodness, the storms and buffeting winds! We didn't suffer from fevers, but the poor servants had a bad time, though we did what we could to help them with medicines. Everyone around and in Bombay was complaining about it too, so we weren't the only sufferers. Mosquitoes were a real nuisance. At night, mosquito nets kept us safe, but during the day it was only by burning great piles of *katal* that we could keep them at bay. This is a wonderful thing that was a real boon. We also burned neem leaves and rubbed all kinds of oils all over us, but nothing was as effective as *katal*. We killed lots of scorpions and snakes too, and the servants were bitten too, but only when the roof was being repaired, and years later, when we had the roof redone, and the tiles turned over, we found lots of scorpions nestling inside. We had this done in October, after the rains, and I hope that next year we'll be more comfortable and the roof won't leak. We tackled the other essential repairs slowly, month by month. The floor was completely broken, and we had to dig it up, and about half the flooring was re-laid. The crumbling walls were broken down, replastered, and repaired. The bathrooms were [totally dilapidated]—we had them floored and white-washed, which made a great difference. Also, the rooms were very dark and airless, so we broke open the walls at the top, and instead of having *roshandans,* we had expanded metal fittings installed, which made a great difference. The doors and windows we painted and varnished ourselves, and all these little changes and improvements to the house quite trans-formed it.

I'm writing all this after a long break. It's now over a year since we moved in, and we've lived through another monsoon. The front veranda which is our living and dining room (and sometimes our bedroom too), now has cane furniture, a *takht,* Jabir's writing table at one end, mine at the other, three bookshelves, three or four small tables with small orna-mental objects on them, generally brass; all these things suggest that we're happy living here. We've started a small garden in front, too. There aren't many flowers at the moment but we have some roses, and bamboo, and several kinds of creepers. We've made a road to the front for cars and car-riages, which we'll make into an avenue with flowering trees, and we've planted gulmohur, rain trees, and *amaltas (cassia fistula).* To the west we've planted lichee, pineapple, and banana, and to the south there are fields with papaya. One field has been planted with rice. One plot has been cleared near the well, where we shall have an orchard of oranges, sweet lime (mosambi) and papaya. Last year we'd planted some veget-ables, but they didn't do too well because there wasn't anyone to tend them. This year we've decided to concentrate on the fruit trees alone. It's such an effort to keep the jungle at bay—we labour all year long to keep the land free of weeds, and then, some showers of rain, and overnight, it's all overgrown again. We were terribly disappointed by the mangoes this year—we got only one mango, an alphonso—from all those trees. We set a great price on that mango! Azeem [Husain Tyabji] had just come from Adnoor, badly mauled by a tiger; he had very courageously saved

Shammoo bhai's life and his own. He is now in hospital, and we gave it to him. He said it was very delicious!

What ingratitude from the mango trees, tho', after all the trouble we'd taken over them; we'd given them manure, kept them free of weeds and creepers, and grass. Perhaps next year we'll have better luck. Here, there were two or three chicku trees, and a couple of lime trees, from before, which had been totally neglected. Jabir has attended to them very diligently, and we hope that they'll give us plenty of fruit soon. We've had to cut down about forty trees so far, of which there were four or five very close to the house, mangoes, all of which but one were alphonsoes. It was sad to have to cut them, but it's made a great difference to the house, and the front portion of the garden looks much pleasanter. There was a huge wild mango tree, which it was a real labour to cut down—heaven knows how many days it eventually took. The branches spread right over the house, and the roots must have spread very far. We now have a badminton court there, and a few cannas and lilies *(gul-e shabboo)*. How I long to have some proper flowers! But there are some bushes of jasmine (mogra).

20 July 1926 One of the first things we did when we settled here was work out ways of levelling the ground. High ground was dug up and low-lying stretches filled in. There were rice fields already, and the *bunds* surrounding them were used to fill them up. This went on for several months, with two or three men employed solely on this work. The smaller mounds Jabir attacked himself, or got one of the domestic servants to do. And I'd help too. It'd be difficult to explain where all this filling in has been done without a large-scale plan, so I'm leaving space on the next page for such a plan. [Blank page] In front, where there was a rice-field, we've now planted roses—25 Lamarque, 25 [another variety of rambler], and 25 Marshal Neill. There's a large *garh* (drain) all round the compound, so that water doesn't collect. To the west, there's a boundary of barbed wire, which we'll slowly extend all round, and we've just had the hedge of euphorbia (mingot) mended. We've kept a few chickens as well, not more than twenty-five or so. We've hatched a number of chicks, but the first time we tried we had a horrid experience, as the eggs were all eaten up by some animal, but we were successful later on, and got quite large chickens. We have one excellent kind called Minorca—black and very large, and it lays very large eggs too, which we hatched, and got seven or eight chicks from them, which hawks and other predators killed. But

there are still three left, which are doing very well. Last year we got [blank] eggs, on some of which we set the hens and ate the rest. We don't have a proper hen-house yet, and the hens wander all over the place, and peck at the flowers; we're hoping to have a proper fenced-off area for them soon, though heaven knows when that'll be. We've started work on one bit, but then other more urgent jobs took precedence.

On the east, right in front of the house, there's a little portion we've made into a flower garden; on one side, there are roses, which bloom quite beautifully, and gladden one's heart; and on one side, in the middle, there's a kind of cave of bamboo, on which we have *chameli* (a variety of jasmine) and other creepers. We'd planted some last winter, and another couple now. As soon as it rained, they did very well, especially the convolvulus; we're hoping to put in other pretty ones soon. There are flower beds all around, where we'll have seasonal plants, but also flowering trees, small ones, like the lagerstroemia. We managed to put down a few annuals this last year, and they made such a difference to the place. We've now planted balsam, asters, sunflowers, and marigold by seed.

On the western side of this patch, where we have the roses, we plan to have other flowers too, and make a garden of it. We already have a row of cannas, which run parallel to the house, and will have another row of roses on this side, and in between at the moment we have balsam, and as a background, we'll have a raintree on one side, an *amaltas* on the other; and, in between, a [blank]; the raintree has just been planted, about a couple of weeks ago, and is doing very well. We have great plans for the garden, and so enjoy ourselves planning it all. I do hope it all happens, and the garden's soon bursting with fruit and flowers. Amen. As for the mangoes, apart from keeping the trees clear of weeds and grass, they've been given fertilizer, basic slag and ammonium sulphate. Let's see what sort of effect it has.

II

There is now a considerable gap in Safia's account. To cover the years that passed before she returned to her book, her son Amiruddin Ali writes:

It is unfortunate that the period 1928–1942 is left blank in these diaries. It was a very important period in the lives of Safia and Jabir Ali. This was the time when Jabir plunged fully into the national struggle. Also at this time Amir was born, and the next five years must have been a very busy time for Safia. She had to look after her young son, and also was in charge of the farm. Between 1929 and 1935 Jabir spent nearly four and a half years in gaol, in three instalments. Fortunately there were loyal servants in the house, and for farm work. This was a great help. It was also fortunate that Safia's elder sister Sakina Lukmani had come to live in Chembur in 1928. Her husband, Dr Lukmani, a medical practitioner, had purchased a big house with about three acres of land, about two miles from Safia and Jabir's farm. Here he and his family lived till 1973. Sakina Lukmani, nearly 25 years older than Safia, had been a second mother to her after her real mother died in 1905.

Safia had a horse carriage in which she drove to her sister's house at least four times a week after the day's work at the farm was over. Dr Badruddin was a lover of Urdu and Persian poetry. He often recited the ghazals of Ghalib and Zauq, or lines from Hafiz and Sadi. Safia also loved Urdu poetry and listening to Bhai Badar, as she called him, gave her great pleasure. By 1930, Dr Lukmani was already over 60 years old, and did not practise very vigorously as a doctor. He therefore spent many hours every day with his books of poetry and literature.... Sometimes she would go by her carriage to Andheri to her sister Hanifa, who also lived in a house with a big garden. Nearby was the house of her elder brother Husain... while her brother Faiz and his wife Salima were more like friends. There and in her elder sister Halima's household were nephews and nieces with whom she had an excellent relationship. They were often asked to go to Deonar Farm in groups of two or three. Here they would climb trees, go wandering in the fields and meadows, climb the hills behind the farm, and help to make the house cheerful, even when Jabir was in gaol.

On some evenings Safia would walk alone across the fields to the hills about a mile away. This is a small range of hills which has played an important part in the life of the family. The biggest hill rises to 1000 feet above sea level, and was covered with dense vegetation in the past. Safia would climb one of the lower hills from where she watched the sun going down on the Western horizon, then walk back home as it was getting dark. The great ornithologist Salim Ali and his best disciple Humayun Ali spent many days in these forests, recording the bird life of the area. Salim, Jabir's youngest brother, was a very frequent visitor. He and his wife Tehmina lived in a cottage in Kihim near the town of Alibag, but they often came and stayed at Deonar at Chabootra (name given to their house by Jabir and Safia). Safia was very fond of both these people, and was very happy when they came to stay. She also went and spent many days with them in Kihim with her son Amir.

When Jabir was out of gaol, there were many activities connected with the national movement. He used to spin regularly and both of them went around selling khadi cloth. Bahen Sakina along with Safia and several nieces joined in the salt satyagraha. They also took part in picketing liquor shops. Jabir and Safia attended two open sessions of the Congress—Karachi 1930 and Ahmedabad in 1931—where they were able to renew friendships with some national leaders, and also made some new friends. After 1935 Jabir was not arrested though he continued as an active member of the Congress Party, and was President of the Taluka Committee for many years.

The interesting event during the gaol years was a week's stay in Matheran in 1932–33. Jabir was released from gaol on the express condition that he would not go out of the Bombay suburban district, except to Bombay city. Matheran was part of Kolaba district, and therefore out of bounds. At that time Jabir's elder brother Hamid, who was Collector of Kolaba district (he was in the Indian Civil Service) sent a message to a cousin in Bombay to say 'For God's sake ask Jabir to keep away from me because if I see him I will have to arrest him.' For Safia the visit to Matheran was like getting back to Paradise—the long walks through the thick woods when she often heard the *shama* singing, renewing her contacts with places she had known so well in her childhood, picnics by the lake.

Around this time a badminton court was prepared on the western side of the house. Jabir was a champion player. He won the All England Handicap Doubles in 1909 with his cousin A. H. Fyzee as partner, and the Triple Crown at the Bandra Gymkhana Championships in 1926, '27 and '28, nearly twenty years later. Many cousins, nephews, and nieces came to stay at Chabootra and play badminton. Badminton was played early in the morning, just after sunrise when there is no breeze, and after an hour of vigorous games everyone went in for a good breakfast of eggs, *chapattis,* and porridge made from *bajra* or wheat. Safia was a very keen player but not a champion. In later years, especially after 1940, several young people from the growing suburb of Chembur would drop in to play badminton. Safia continued playing up to 1950 or 1952 when she was 58 years of age.

The years 1935–37 brought many changes in the lives of Safia and Jabir. In 1935 Amir was admitted to a small school in Chembur. This school was run by the Catholic Society of Chembur, which was a new development. Housing plots had been given on lease to a cooperative society of Roman Catholics about the year 1927 or 1928. By 1934 they had started a school where a devoted young lady taught about a dozen children. School admission for Amir brought his parents into contact with the Roman Catholic community. In political matters there were wide differences between Jabir and Safia and the Catholics, but at the social level it was much easier to interact with them. One or two of their leaders were quite sympathetic to the national movement. The most active of the leaders was Professor A. A. Soares, who later took an important part in the Goa freedom movement. He had a very high reputation among educationists. Safia became a regular visitor to many homes in the Catholic colony especially at festivals. Both of them were often invited to weddings.

In 1935, a Jewish family, the Reubens, came to settle in Chembur. The senior Mr Reuben had retired as a judge from a state in Kathiawar (now Saurashtra). His eldest son, David Reuben, was in the ICS and known to several members of the Tyabji clan. The three daughters of the elder Reuben became good friends of Safia, but it was Rebecca Reuben, the eldest, who became one of her closest friends. She was a great educationist, and a highly educated, scholarly person. For twenty years or more Safia spent two or three evening a week with Rebecca.[2] In fact she spent as much time with her as with her beloved sister Sakina.

When Rebecca died in 1957, Safia wrote to her sisters, 'Dear Rebecca has always been a true friend to me in every sense of the word. I have gone to her with the joys and sorrows and troubles that life brings to all of us. She always shared these with me, sympathised and understood, gave me her sisterly affection, allowed me the privilege of looking into her noble soul.'

In 1936 another important friendship bloomed which had a life-long effect on Jabir and Safia. Jabir's old Cambridge friend, Jal Naoroji, grandson of the great Dadabhoy, the nationalist and social reformer, proposed to start a farm in the Bombay suburban district. He wanted Jabir to be his farm advisor (consultant). At that time Jal had just got married to a very good-looking Maharashtrian girl Malati [Paranjape], and they intended to live on this farm for which land was purchased at Deonar. Jal Naoroji was full of ideas for the farm, and he also had the finances required. For Jabir it was the ideal opportunity to turn his own dreams into reality. It was to be a farm producing fresh vegetables, fruit, and flowers for the city markets, particularly the Taj Hotel of which Jal was the General Manager. Work at the farm started at a brisk pace and then tragedy struck: Jal fell seriously ill, and had a tumour in his abdomen, which must have been a cancer. Within a few months he passed away. Malati bravely decided to carry on the farm but now finances were limited. Jabir of course was in full charge of the farm, but he had to make many sacrifices for the sake of his dead friend.

Malati and Safia became very close friends, and remained so till Safia's death in 1961. Malati had a large circle of friends in Bombay, people from different communities and different professions. Safia was aways happy to meet new people, and Malati was a great source for finding new and interesting friends. Among them were the mother of Captain Lakshmi of the Indian National Army, and Achyut Patwardhan, the Socialist leader. The younger sister of Malati was Anasuya, who had married F. G. Pearce, the educationist, an Englishman who had been greatly influenced by the teachings of Gautama Buddha and Mahatma Gandhi.

Jabir and Safia were in sympathy with Mr Pearce's thinking, and two years later when they felt that it was time for Amir to go to a big boys' school, they sent him to the Scindia School at Gwalior. Mr Pearce was not only Principal of the Scindia School; the school was built up by him according to his educational philosophy which in turn was influenced by Gandhiji's Nai Talim, e.g., whereas students in many public schools spoke in English, at Scindia they were expected to speak in Hindustani, and 'Jana Gana Mana' was the morning assembly song. All this happened in 1939. Between 1936 and 1939 other important events took place.

After two years at the Chembur Catholic School, Safia and Jabir felt unhappy that their son was only learning English. The school hardly taught anything except English and a little arithmetic. Amir's parents were anxious that he should learn to speak Urdu correctly—Safia had begun to teach him a little, but it was necessary to have a proper language teacher. So Abdul Samad Ansari, a teacher in the Anglo-Urdu school at Kurla, came to teach and later to live at Chabootra. He was a very young man from a little village in Gorakhpur district of UP, intelligent, hardworking, eager to progress in life. His relationship with Safia and her family was one of the highlights of Safia's life. In later years she almost regarded him as an elder son. For thirty-five years he lived as a member of the family, helping Jabir with the farm work, and spending an hour or so every day reading Urdu literature with amma (as he called Safia). Jabir became Babajan.

As a result of his staying at Chabootra, several farm workers were brought there from Gorakhpur, and lived in Deonar for many years. In some cases their sons also found work at Chabootra Farm. Ustad Sahib (as Samad Sahib was called by everyone in Safia's family, though she called him Samad) himself made good progress in life. He had only passed his Matriculation exam when he came to stay at Chabootra. After reading with Safia books like *Aab-i-Hayat, Fasan e Azad,* Premchand's stories, and most of the important Urdu poets, he was able to appear for the Aligarh Intermediate, late BA, and finally MA in Urdu. He also passed exams in Hindi, and was able to get a teacher's job at one the best schools in Bombay—the Alexandra Girls' School. Consequently Samad sahib's family also began to go up in life. His sons received a fairly good education, and were able to earn a good living. His two younger brothers also were placed in comfortable jobs.

In 1937 the Congress Party decided to fight the elections held to form governments in the different states of India. Congress came to power in Bombay, and elected Shri B. G. Kher as its leader and Chief Minister. Kher was Jabir's close friend and was very keen that Jabir should join the government as Minister for Agriculture. Jabir did not feel he could function as a Minister, and kept out of the government, though he was a frequent visitor to the Chief Minister's office, and Jabir and Safia often visited Kher Sahib at his family home in Khar. Safia had great admiration for Kher Sahib, who remained simple and friendly in spite of his position. Although Jabir refused to join the Ministry he did take up another political post as a Congress Party member. He became President of the Bombay Suburban District Board (now Zilla Parishad). He felt that on the District Board he could do more work in the villages, and get to know their problems better, while in the ministry there would be much office work which he did not like.

Anyway, Jabir was now able to take charge of his own farm. Samad Sahib was a great support, and Safia was able to devote herself to things which interested her the most, reading, Urdu and English literature, needlework, some gardening. She had a collection of hybrid roses and other garden plants around the house, and she took a lot of interest in their cultivation.

Now Amir had completed nearly three years at the Chembur Catholic school. After that children had to go to a bigger school. Amir was very keen to go to St Xaviers, as most members of the Tyabji clan had passed through that school. Jabir and Safia wanted him to go to a school in Dadar or Byculla, as that would mean less travelling. Finally Amir had his way. One year at St Xaviers was enough to convince everyone that it was not the best choice. It took one and a half hours to reach the school, so three hours were spent in travelling every day. There was no time for sports, or anything except classwork and homework. Amir's health began to suffer.

It was decided that a boarding school would be a good solution to this problem, so in the first week of July 1939 Safia and Amir travelled on the Punjab Mail to Gwalior. The train was six hours late due to a derailment between Bhopal and Jhansi, but Mr Pearce had come himself to meet them at Gwalior station. This was the sort of friendly relationship he maintained until his death in 1960. Two or three days later Safia left for Aligarh and Mussoorie to spend a few days with close relations. When leaving Gwalior it must have been a tremendous effort for her to keep her emotions in control, otherwise Amir would have broken down completely. She did manage this. She had to go through this after every vacation for the next six years and she must have possessed great strength of character to do it every time. In fact it must have been a great effort to send her only child to a boarding school 1000 kilometres away. But she must have felt happy that her son was happier than he could be at St Xaviers, and his health improved tremendously.

During the period that Amir was at Scindia, came World War II, then the Quit India movement in which Jabir was again involved in many ways. The Chabootra Farm and Malati Naoroji's Deonar Farm were meeting places for leaders who had gone 'underground'. Some of these leaders in disguise lived for several days at a time at Chabootra. Safia, not directly involved in the political activities, had to take care of the leaders who needed food or a place to rest at odd hours. She also knew that if the police were able to find this place of hiding, the family giving them shelter would be in trouble. This knowledge did not bother her. Her husband supported these leaders, and she fully supported him.

Amir completed his studies at Scindia School in 1945. By then the war in Europe was nearly over. Gandhiji was released from prison a few months later. A new chapter was to begin in the life of the nation, and also in the life of Jabir and Safia, but she herself has written about that.

Since about 1924, Jabir Ali had become a devoted follower of Gandhiji, specially in the political and economic fields. Non-violence, as preached by the Mahatma, was the basis of his religious thought. It was the only method by which India could become a free country. The improvement in the general economic conditions should also be based on spinning and village handicrafts. Jabir himself did regular *charka* spinning and sale of khadi cloth till 1936 or so. In 1937 when Congress ministries were formed in many important provinces, Jabir stood for election to the Bombay Suburban District Local Board (the modem Zilla Parishad). He was elected President and remained in that post till 1940 when Congress resigned from ministries as it was opposed to joining the war as British allies. In his work as President of the local Board he had to tour all over Trombay and Salsette island, visiting villages in Dahisar, Vasi, and Virar as well as Trombay. He began to feel that for rapid development of these rural areas some industrialization and use of machines was necessary. He joined with some of his political friends to start a small industrial unit for producing straw board.

This unit, started in 1940, was situated between Panvel and Pen, on the banks of the river Patalganga, and a turbine was fitted on the river to provide energy for the factory. This was a definite step away from Gandhian economics. At this time his political views were strongly influenced by some of his young nephews (for instance Nazar Futehally, Saad Ali) who were socialists, followers of Jayaprakash Narayan, Achyut Patwardhan and others. Also there was the influence of S. M. Joshi who had spent a couple of years in gaol with him. All these socialist party members (the Congress Socialist Party was a party within the Indian National Congress) accepted Gandhiji as the supreme leader of the freedom movement, but did not accept the non-violence philosophy fully. So in 1942, when Congress and Gandhiji gave the 'Quit India' call, the Socialists went underground, and begun to indulge in violent acts such as blowing up power lines, uprooting rail tracks, doing all sorts of things that interfered with the war effort.

Jabir's farm and nursery was a very good hiding place for all these underground leaders. Nearby was Malati Naoroji's farm where Jabir was the adviser. Malatibai and Achyut Partwardhan were old friends, so the two farms could both be used as hiding places where secret meetings were held, plans were made for storing explosives, and sending them out where required. Jabir was actively employed in all this activity, but the police never found out. Or perhaps the police knew, but their sympathy was with the Freedom Fighters. At this stage it has to be said that Jabir was not a full and complete Gandhian. He began to believe that some violence would be needed to achieve independence. It is also a fact that none of the top Congress leaders could be called complete Gandhians. For them Non-violence was a good method to fight an Empire. That was all.

III

Safia took up her diary again after a lapse of about fifteen years. Much had changed in the meanwhile, but her zest for life was as boundless as before.

On 22 September 1942 she began:

My beloved son, light of my life, may you live long! What an age has passed since I wrote those few pages, with such joy and passion. In those days Oh! Youth itself was so intoxicating that even water tasted like wine!

But we feel our dear son's health and education are of paramount importance, and we bear up with fortitude. And we hope we shall be rewarded by seeing the fruits of our endeavours in ample measure. When this book was started we had no child—indeed, we'd borne the grief of losing two children, and resigned ourselves to God not wishing to bless us with children. Yet in spite of this deep sorrow that lay hidden in our hearts, we were so happy together that life held much joy for us. For me, to have such a good, amiable, eager man for a husband, one who was so loved by all, was cause enough for happiness, and one to thank God in his goodness for. In addition, to have such loving and concerned brothers and sisters and other relations, and friends, whose kindness is beyond description. May God reward them all for their goodness. Whenever I was in trouble or need, they would appear like angels sent from heaven to comfort and help me, and at times of happiness they would be there to increase it manifold. When we had this lovely son born to us, everyone was so happy for us, and so anxious that he should be a strong and healthy baby. [Badr and Sakina Lukmani, Faiz and Salima Tyabji, amongst others, were very supportive at this period].… Soon after Amir was born, we'd have lots of young people visiting us, especially in the first couple of years, on weekends. That was in 1925.

Shammoo bhai [Shumsuddin, eldest son of Abbas and Amina Tyabji of Baroda] also often joined these groups… Generally one or two of them would spend a couple of days here, and we'd have a great time with them. We'd go out with them, work in the garden, climb the hills, wander in the jungles,—oh, what fun we'd have and how carefree we were. Sometimes one or the other of my brothers and sisters would be good enough to come for the day, and we'd play cards in the afternoons, or read something interesting together; or those who lived outside Bombay would come to visit. One year in May, when we only had the downstairs *jhonpra* (shack), perhaps it was in 1926, we had 20 people staying with us: Bhai Hasham and his wife Dilbar and all their children …

Shammoo bhai often came to spend a couple of days with us, often with Hamida or Mukhlis [his children]… What wonderful company Shammoo bhai was: what a fine singer; and what enthusiasm for everything! He was always the life and soul of the party; he'd make everyone join in the choruses; he'd sing himself, and thoroughly enjoy playing all kinds of games. He was fond of plays, and make others enjoy them too.… In many ways, he was a very remarkable man. He'd become a child himself when he was with younger people, and they'd be absolutely at ease with him, teasing him and joking with him. He'd be very keen on rehearsing his part for the Shakespeare readings, and make others come well-prepared too. He'd be so much fun at picnics, outings, shikar—and he'd always make others join him, and make them have such fun. It's difficult to forget him! Just before he went on the shoot where he was mauled and killed by the tiger, he spent three or four days with us, and we so enjoyed it. We'd go for a walk in the evenings, and he'd take potshots with his gun. How tragic that he died at such a young age, leaving behind children who'd already suffered the loss of their mother … Seizing this opportunity, I'm starting to write again, although I have very little time today, as I'm expecting guests shortly. It's nine o'clock now. The back veranda has been swept and cleaned, and Sattar, our old servant, is still pottering about there, filling flowers and so on. We don't leave any covering on the floors during the monsoon, but today we have put down a *durree* which'll be removed again in the evening. This year, the rains have been so heavy that it's become a misery now. It started in mid-June, and since then it's been pouring incessantly without a day's break—we must have had 90 inches by now.... I'd got that far yesterday when my guests came—Sarhan and Najma [Latif] at about 9.30 a.m. They stayed till 4.30 in the afternoon. We sat in the veranda at the table and talked, and Jabir joined us an hour later. We have at the moment a lot of *chacch*, as both our buffalo and cow have just calved, and we get eleven *seers* of milk a day. We'll try to sell off half the milk, keeping the rest for ourselves—that'll be plenty. For the moment, we're making *makhan* and *ghee*.

Sarhan Mian has bought a beautiful house in Matheran, and absolutely insists that we visit him there. They're going to spend a month there now, and we plan to go in October, inshallah. After our guests left, Jabir went to the farm, and after some time I went there too, and walked a bit. Ustad Sahib joined me. Today, he went to Bombay directly after coming back from school to fetch the STC certificate, for which he'd sat some months ago. Jabir went to the farm at 8 this morning, came back at 9.30 and went to Bombay, where he had a lot of work. He went straight back to the farm from there, but returns at 6.30, when we'll go for a drive in our *tanga*.... My day passed in this way: after breakfast, I spent 1 1/2 hours in the dining room, getting the food cupboard cleaned out by Sattar, and then making ghee from the butter, which we put into a jar, while I sat with my sewing, or rather knitting (I'm making a coverlet for Amir, which may one day be completed). Then Jabir came back, and there was the bustle of his setting off for Bombay. I made some phone calls, saw to the servants' work, gave out the day's provisions to the cook, who'd come from the bazaar with the newspaper, and then went to bathe at 11. Washed my hair, aired it with incense *(bukhur)*, had lunch at 12.45, and while I was still at the table, Samad came back from school, and joined me at lunch after a wash. After lunch, he spent about half an hour reading aloud from the *Humayun*, the journal, and then went to Bombay, and I went upstairs to rest. Tea was at 4 p.m., downstairs, and then I read the papers till Jabir returned. I had *limoon ka sherbet* ready for him, and after about half an hour, spent talking about Bombay and other matters, he went to the farm, and I sat down to write this! In the evenings, after a walk, or visiting, we sit out in the garden till dinner, if it's not raining. We eat at 8 p.m., and immediately after dinner; sit down to cards, usually Cut Throat, as there are three of us, or otherwise, as today there are only two, we'll play something else. At 9 o'clock, there's news on the radio, and then after a bit more time at cards, we go to bed at ten. Of course, when there are guests, we don't follow this routine.

Now, let me turn to our household staff. At the moment we have our faithful Sattar with us, who lives in a hut close by with his wife Mariam and son Ibrahim. His actual work is cleaning the house and washing the dishes, making the beds, arranging the flowers, dusting the books, polishing the brass. There is also the cook, at the moment someone new, called Abdullah from Bangalore. Our old cook, Hyder, whom we were very happy with, has gone away, and we don't know when if ever he will return. The present man is a nice person but no great shakes as a cook.

We're not using the car at present, on account of petrol shortages, but we have a driver for it, a *bhayya* [man from UP] called Ram Prasad— who's gone to his *gaon* for a couple of months—who also looked after the buffalo and cow, and drove the *tonga*. His place has been taken by a man who works in the garden called Mahmud.

A couple of years ago, we got an excellent *mali* called *Rafoo*, and may he live long! And stay with us! We also have a couple of women workers, one of whom also fills up the water. She's called Kishti, and she's only worked for us for about two years, but her sister, Sukkoo, worked for eight or nine years for us, and only left to get married! Sadly, she got attached to someone who already had a wife and children. She defied everyone, her mother and sisters, to get married to this chap, and hardly sees her family anymore. She had a child last year who died, and she barely survived herself. I do hope she'll be happy in her new life. She certainly makes out that she is. I've been to her *jhonpri* and sampled her *rotis* and *salan*.

Today we have a new man, called Soma, for the horse and carriage, and also to work in the garden. We pay these servants the following: the cook, Rs 23 a month, Sattar Rs 20 with food and a house, Mahmud, Rs 16, the *mali*, Rs 22, without food but with a house, one *malan*, Rs 11, the other (daily wages) Rs 12, the *mehtar* gets Rs 5 for cleaning once a day, Rs 5 for the *dhobi* for four washes a month.

Of all these, Abdul Sattar's history is the most interesting. When Jabir went to Burma in 1914? and settled in Tavoy, Sattar, then a boy of 14 or 15, went with him. He was completely raw and untrained, but very willing to learn, and very strong and hard-working. Jabir taught him how to cook a bit, with others' help, and also taught him how to read and write. He's from Chatgaon, and the way he talks still makes me laugh. He says 'ch' for 'j', and says 'babasti' for *bawarchi*'. And lots of other such pronunciations which it's sometimes quite difficult to follow.

When I went to Tavoy as a bride, Sattar was established as an old experienced servant. He'd been with Jabir for three years, and knew every need of his master's, and everything about the house. There were three of us in the house, including Salim, who had joined Jabir a little while earlier: In those days, these people had a hardware business, there was a lot of wolfram near Tavoy, and very few ironware shops, of which J. Ali Brothers was one. How this was started and how it prospered, and how the integrity of the Ali Brothers was established and earned its own rewards, and how the elder brother, Jabir, in particular, did so much for the community by founding a club where people of different kinds could meet, and for their education and upbringing—of all this, I'm the witness!

When I arrived in Tavoy it was as the wife of a poor man—not that we didn't have enough to eat, but an income of Rs 300 a month was hardly wealth in an expensive place like Tavoy, but this man had gained such a position for himself in Indian and English circles, that the Indians (including the Burmese), regarded him as their leader, and the English had great respect for him. And I got the fruit of all this—Mrs Jabir Ali lived in a small house, but was treated with such honour that she could hold her nose in the air! The Muslim community there, and the other Indians, Chinese, etc., welcomed me very warmly, but as I spoke no Burmese or Chinese, it was difficult to make friends at first. But I used to go to the dinners held by the Muslims, and was on very affectionate terms with many of the women. Their men spoke Hindustani, and the youngsters English, so one was able to establish some contact with them, and there were also magazines and books to look at.

2 September: It's Monday today, but the *dhobi's* turned up, although he's supposed to come on Saturdays, and does too, but he's not been well this last month or so, and has been very irregular. We used to wonder otherwise how on earth, in this terrific downpour, this continuous rain, he could get clothes to dry! and turn up every Saturday, he and his brothers have been working for us now for four or five years, and he has

on the whole been very good, he's polite and respectful, and we've had no problem of any kind.

At present, I've had to oversee the running of the house more than usual, there've been no proper arrangements for the buffalo or the cow and the milking. We have a new man for the horse, but have to keep an eye on him all the time. Sattar is away on leave, and there's not a single servant in the house save the cook, and Kishti who does the floors. There's a dinner at Badr Bagh every day now it's Ramzan, but we can't really go every day all the way from here. On Wednesday, there's the dinner in memory of Bhai Ibrahim [Ahmedi] and on Wednesday the one for dear Uncle Amiruddin. We'll certainly go to both those.

The Tavoy Club, 1916. Safia seated right, on floor. Jabir behind her, third from left. Gandhi seated, second row left, Mrs Gandhi on Jabir's right.

At last we've come to the end of the month, and thank goodness, have had some glimpses of the sun. It'll rain again of course, and at times it's so terribly sultry that we know it's going to pour soon. This evening I'm going to Bombay with dear Badr Bhai [Lukmani] and Jamila [Mamoon Lukmani]. We'll set out at 4 p.m., and go first to Somerset [Lodge] to meet Bhai Faiz [Tyabji], and then to Badr Bagh. Bhai Faiz has just come back from a long two-month stay in Kashmir, where he had a legal appointment. Sadly, he overtired himself, either at work or physically, and fell ill. At first it was feared it was a heart problem but fortunately it's not that, but caused by very low blood pressure. The doctors have prescribed rest, and he's not even allowed many visitors, as it tires him. But he's better, there's no doubt, and pray god he recovers completely soon.

A telephone's a great convenience of course, but what a nuisance it can be. The whole morning has been disturbed—I can't sit down to anything because the damn thing rings, and then whoever's rung talks for a long time, and there you are, fretting about your own tasks.

As I was writing this, there was a call from Amte Salaam.[3] Just imagine, she's come all the way to Chembur, and doesn't even bother to let one know earlier, only rings when she gets to Badr Bhai [Lukmani]. It's not easy going there by bus, and they run every 11/2 hours, so we can't get to meet each other: It's such a shame, but also one feels a bit sad that she shouldn't have let me know earlier, and just come and gone. She's working for Hindu-Muslim unity or trying to, and has moved to Madanpura for that reason. And as it is now Gandhi Jayanti, and all the more reason for a big effort to be made, she's keen on my going to live in Madanpura for this but I'm not keen at all.

3 October: It's hot again, but the mornings are delightful. There's such a delightful sweet cool breeze till 11 or 12 in the mornings that one's entranced by it. If the world was a better place, if this terrible war was over, if the poor weren't so oppressed, and there wasn't such sadness and misery everywhere, then really on a morning like this one could fancy one was in Paradise. Dear Amir, there are many things I want you to know about, about which one is that I want to make three family trees, from which you can learn which lines you have descended from. One is that of Dadasaheb Tayyebali [Tayyebjee Bhoymeeah] from whom the Tyabji family has descended, then that of your Nana [maternal grandfather], who was in his time, and is now too, well-known throughout the country and that is Badruddin Tyabji. And then your Dada [paternal grandfather] that is Muizuddin Jiwabhai Abdul Ali, from whom you got your name 'Ali'. But making them will take a little time and effort, and I never seem to have both at the same time: I'm either too rushed or feel too lazy! Now I must go as I have to go to Woodlands to dine with Khalajan [Sakina Lukmani]. It's now half-past six, and I have to meet

your father at the Govindi Ridge from where we'll go on together in the tonga. Today Kamran bhai [Latif], Nasreen, and Faiz bhai [Salman Tyabji] are coming too.

5 October It's eleven o'clock in the morning. I'm writing this with your pen, my dear Amir, the one your father gave you, but since you've left it behind, we're making good use of it. I'm sitting on the *takht* writing this while Mahmud's churning the butter, and people are busy about their work. Your father's gone to Bombay and Samad is at school. I'm waiting for the *dhobi*, but he mightn't turn up, and in that case I'll have plenty of time to write. I've already spent an hour getting the store room cleaned and tidied up and it's still very pleasantly cool. Early in the morning it was quite chilly and there was also quite a mist.

21 October … This afternoon we had lunch at Bibi's. The reason for this was that Bibi has been wanting to hear Jabir's views on a number of issues for some time, and there was never the time for him to talk them over with her. So today Jabir had promised a two- or three-hour session with her … and from 11 o'clock, Jabir talked away.

I suppose I can't really be impartial about it, but I did think he spoke very well indeed. He talked about religion, and after comparing different ones, gave his opinion that each had a very important message to give, and that in essence, each had the same one, but because of variations in time, and of people and cultures, each emphasized a somewhat different aspect of this same message. A study of the history of the religion would indicate the reasons for such differences. And after taking these things into account, one realizes that one shouldn't, on account of one's ignorance, condemn other religions.

And the same applies to human beings. We're so ready to condemn others without knowing anything about them. But if we take the trouble to find out, we'd realize that if we'd been in the same situation and faced the same problems, we might well have acted in the same way. So we should never be contemptuous of anyone.

Thirdly, if because of circumstances, a person (or people) have developed certain characteristics or weaknesses, this doesn't mean that they are ingrained in them. If they were given a chance, and had a leader (guide), they would change totally. No-one should think himself a failure, or inferior that's merely a superficial aspect. Everyone can, with determination, change himself—and he gave instances of this.

Fourthly, Indians have been subjugated for centuries, and this has had a dreadful effect on them. Only after independence has been gained can the ill-effects of slavery be totally eliminated. People who think the opposite are obviously wrong, and ill informed.

Fifth, we have a slave mentality, having been ruled over by foreigners for so long—and this shows up constantly. We can't differentiate between good and bad—anything, any object, or custom—that came from Europe is prized, and our own things treated with contempt. This attitude has been deliberately bred in us—and it's that which makes us continue to be enslaved.

What is the true aim and goal of human beings? What should a human being aim to become to achieve his fullest potential? In which direction should we endeavour to find ourselves? How I wish we could meet like this, and talk over such things oftener, and ponder deeply over the matters that life confronts us with. Jabir says that the book, Man the Unknown, which he enormously enjoyed reading, has had such an effect on him that it's more or less his Quran! ...

It's amazing that, in spite of having had to endure so many pregnancies, and given birth to so many children, Mother so enjoyed life till the end. She loved meeting people, having them over, giving parties, and taking part in social activities. And in addition, she used to read so much, and write and correspond so much. When I was a child, my elder brothers and sisters had grown up, and were working, and the girls had married and left home, but I remember so clearly how she'd sit on the *takht* and write to all the children who were in distant places; and how she'd read with great attention the Gujarati papers; how interested she was in Urdu books, and the Arabic works of Maulana Shibli, *Al-Mamoon* and *Al Farooq*. She'd listen enthusiastically to Bhai Badr reciting certain Urdu verses and couplets, and hear him speak about them with such joy; and she'd always ask him to sing Urdu *ghazals*. She enjoyed fine *ragas* and always listened to Indian songs with keen attention and appreciation.

When my elder sisters were growing up, they learned to play Western musical instruments and sing Western songs, and my elder sister Surayya in particular was considered a fine pianist. I remember hearing her practise for hours on end at Somerset House, in the grand Hall, on the fine piano, or hearing her play for people. But she'd sing mainly Indian (Hindi) songs, usually *ghazals,* sometimes something else. She had a fine voice too—very melodious and strong. Most of my sisters sang, and at family gatherings they were expected to perform. At home, and especially at Matheran and Mahabaleshwar, we were all supposed to entertain, men and women alike, either by singing or reciting, and this included us children too, and we'd all sing or recite something or the other.

Those days, a great deal of Urdu and Farsi *ghazals* were sung or recited: Hafiz, Saadi, Shums Tabrizi, Amir Khusro, and so on. Bhai Badr introduced us to Ghalib, Zauq, Insha, Atish, Mir, Sauda, etc.... all the old poets and their work. Sometimes, to make us laugh, he'd sing songs from *nataks* as well. And also the love songs of Jurat, Faghan, Dagh, etc. Hearing all these being sung over and over again, I got to learn masses of *ghazals* myself, and I would sing them too. Hannoo Bahen made up a beautiful book of these *ghazals* as a present to me when she went to Japan, she sent copies of them to us two or three younger sisters which I treasure still. Dear Amir, I hope you will value and treasure it as greatly. It was ornamented with little roses(?)by a Japanese lady.

I remember so clearly what great interest dearest Mother took in our Urdu lessons too. When I was five or six, we began to have lessons from Ustad Amir Ali, and also to read the Quran. Our *namaz* we learnt from Bibi. All of us younger ones (six or seven of us) would read the evening and *isha* prayers together, taking turns to recite them aloud. Haffoo and I were the youngest, and we were terribly keen on the *namaz*, and would read them with great fervour... and sometimes, in the last *sijda,* when doing our *dua,* we'd fall asleep!

As for Laila-ul Qadar, it was a great thing to stay up at night, but we'd be packed off to bed at midnight or soon thereafter. Haffoo and I used to love wearing short *lehengas* for our prayers—as we rose and knelt, the *lehengas* would flutter up and down, and make a lovely frrr frrr sound! The other thing we enjoyed doing in our *lehengas* was running madly up and down the steps! The other vivid recollection is of all of us little ones sitting with Bahen Sakina to read the Quran-e Sharif. We'd all sit around the large round table, and read whatever had been fixed for the day. It was like having a little school at home! And there were so many companions at home, within the family, that there was no need for anyone else. Yes, when we were a little older, and began to make friends with our cousins, or people outside the family, I well remember what fun it was when these friends came over to the house, and how tearful we'd be when they had to leave!

I remember reading *Mirut ul Urus,* sitting with my mother—and how she'd make us write to our older brothers and sisters, it was good practice writing Urdu, and also a very good habit to get into at that early age, so that later on, letter-writing was never a chore, rather a pleasure. I enjoy it now too—it's a wonderful recreation when one is at home—but I seldom have the leisure now to write a letter every day, as I used to at one time. Except of course to Amir at school.

I was thirteen when my loved father died, in August 1906, of a heart attack, our dear mother had been snatched away from us a year earlier, leaving us desolate and our poor father unable to cope. The loss of his dear wife and life's companion affected him very deeply, and he was advised to travel abroad for his health. He was in London when he suffered a sudden heart failure, and was taken to his fathers. I will tell you of that grief later—today I want to tell you of the enchanted childhood I had, my dear Amir, of which I have such vivid memories still, and there will be some sadness, and some joyful moments.

Although my father lived in I think three houses after he got married—first in Khetwadi, and then Mazagaon, where the family was for several years, I only knew Somerset House, where I was born, and from where we moved when our father died. Dear son, this Somerset House is now Sophia College, and very greatly changed, but even so you can get some idea of how grand and extensive a house and grounds they were. There were no other houses there—it was all open jungle and utterly peaceful. It would be wonderfully green and full of little streams and flowing water in the monsoon. When I was born, my father's property included Somerset House and Somerset Cottage and very extensive grounds (for Bombay). There was a very beautiful garden in front of the house, which was blooming with roses and all kinds of seasonal flowers, which were rather special in those days, and were got from abroad.

Then there was a separate part of the garden that was called the Gymkhana, where there were two badminton courts, a tennis court, a lawn for croquet, and then a place for open-air plays *(tamasha),* where there was a sandy pit and garden seats and benches all around. And huge shady trees, under which one could spend the whole day! Then there was a large nursery—and several ferneries—and an orchard—and then, on one side, a little hill, or rather two hills—one big and one small, the small one was just enchanting and while one got marvellous views from both these hillocks, of the sea and the area around, what made the little hill so special was a little *baradari*, what the English call a summer house—oh heavens, what wonderful times we've had on that little hill! What happiness—but my eyes are moist with tears. What loved faces—and what heavenly times are recalled by these memories. And to remember me as a happy carefree child feels so strange. When we were little, we'd play and jump about and go running all over these hills.

Today I have a little more time and so I'm going to pluck up my courage, dear Amir, and write a bit about Dada Sahib Tyab Ali's fifth son, my respected father, and your grandfather [Badruddin Tyabji]. I do hope you'll read his biography and his speeches and be proud of your grandfather and like him, serve your countrymen.

Now listen. Briefly: he was born in A. D. 1844, and he died on 19 August 1906. He was married quite young. Your grandmother was known as Motibai and she truly was a pearl in her gentleness, her *namkin* (soft) glow. Then your grandfather named her Rahat ul Nafs (the joy of one's soul) and she was truly that for him. Ammajan was born on 4 December 1855, and she died on the 21st of May 1904. They had eighteen children.... [List of children with dates of birth and death]

It's amazing that every one of those children was perfectly sound and in good health. I've heard from the elders that Mrs Phipson, who used to attend on Mother at her confinements, used to be most impressed, and say that in all her years of practising as a gynaecologist, she had never known of such a case, and attributed it to my parents' virtuous and simple way of life that they had such healthy children.

One day [while staying at Sarhan Latif's] Hannoo bahen and I went to Olympia [Badruddin's house in Matheran, later a hotel], where Rashid bhai [Futehally] and Hannoo bahen used to spend three months at a time for two years. And several members of the family stayed with them then and wandered about in dear Matheran. We used to have breakfast at a different point every day, some nearby, others distant. We had some wonderful trips to Matheran during those two years.

When father had time, he'd play with us a great deal—he'd be *baag* and run after us and catch us. We'd be completely at ease with him at such times. During the vacations, when we were in Matheran or

Mahabaleshwar, he'd have a lot more time, and always be with us on our walks and excursions, and at home join us in our games as well. He was very fond of whist; I myself learnt to play it at an early age, and watched very attentively when the elders played.

I also learned to play badminton very early on. There were three courts at Somerset, and at least one in everyone's home. There used to be family badminton tournaments, and the first time I took part, I had Hattoo bhai [Hatim] as partner We didn't win that time, but later, whenever I played with Jabir we aways won! Isn't that odd!

Sundays, the whole family was together at Somerset. All the married sons and daughters would come with their children to spend the day there. Special friends would also come. At one time, Jabir would also turn up every Sunday—so he was called Haazir (Present), and everyone would laugh and try and tease me. But I was pretty cunning too—I'd pretend I knew nothing about it all. Although Hattoo bhai, who shared secrets with me, and who was always horribly interested in this kind of affair, would tell me confidentially that 'Jabir Mian has said this', or that 'He's said that', or sent this message, and that kind of thing. Goodness knows how much of it was his imagination, and how much of it true. But it did all gradually have an effect on me! I was about ten or eleven at that time, and Sharoo bibi [Sharifa Hamid Ali], would tease and call me Masooma (innocent), and not understanding why, I'd get badly teased and irritated at this silly name. (But I'll tell this story later.)

Hattoo bhai's friends, who'd formed a 'Tyabi club', would come to play cricket matches. Jabir, Aamir bhai [Ali], Hasan Faiz ul Husain, Tyab Mian, Abu Mian, Sarhan Mian, and many others formed part of this group. Jabir was a fine cricketer too. Hattoo bhai would pour out accounts of his exploits to me. Once, when Jabir had made 100 runs, there was no end to Hattoo bhai's joyful exclamations. He recounted every stroke and run in the minutest detail to everyone around. Hattoo bhai was a member of the Islam Gymkhana, and would be full of stories of the happenings there.

In those days we'd be a real nuisance to the butler—we'd eat such huge quantities of biscuits and butter that the grown-ups just couldn't believe it. Hattoo bhai would drink up gallons of *limoon ka sherbet,* and press us younger sisters to join in!

On Sunday evenings when there'd be a family gathering we'd play *ata-pata, bhirokho,* and other games. The leaders in these games were Bhai

Ali [son of Najmuddin Tyabji], Bhai Mirza Aqa and Bhai Aga Koochik [sons of Camruddin Tyabji], Bhai Faiz [Badruddin]. We'd play with great enthusiasm—the young women and children (like us) would also be included, and we'd have a lot of fun. Sometimes these leaders would organize competitions, and there'd be prizes too. Once there was a competition for the servants: there were about forty servants at Somerset and several of them had been with us for many years, and they would then go on to stay with one or the other child, or retire and go back to their villages. Croquet was popular too. In my elder brothers and sisters' time, tennis was played a lot, but with us it was badminton, and tennis was only played in the clubs.

One of the games I remember from my childhood was one where one person was the (old man or woman) and had a stick, the others would stand around him/her and say *'Buddhi, buddhi,* where are you going?' She'd say 'To pick unripe *ber.*' 'Oh *buddhi,* can we come with you?' 'You'll get tired.' Children: 'No, we'll climb on to you/ride piggy back.' At which the *buddhi* would run after them, and the one caught would become the *buddhi.* We'd play Blind Man's Buff too. Then we'd play 'Puss in the Corner', on the roof, running barefoot. When it rained, we'd have a wonderful time: we'd dance and jump about in the puddles and sail paper boats down the little rivulets, racing them. Because Somerset was at a height the water would really race down. Raffoo bahen and I loved pressing flowers: we'd pick wild flowers in Matheran or, in Bombay, flowers from the garden. We'd planned to have a magnificent collection of these pressed flowers and present them to Father, but alas, it was not to be. I also never learned to cycle. Hattoo bhai had begun to teach me, but soon after we had to leave Somerset, and then it all stopped. How useful that skill would have been now!

In Matheran, we'd walk a lot. I developed my passion for walking in those days, especially in the jungle, on hills or through fields. When we went on picnics some distance away, the grown-ups would do their best to persuade me to go part of the way at least on horseback, or in a carriage, but I'd resist to the utmost, and somehow or the other make my way on my own! I felt the same about wearing woollens, and refused to put them on! I hated having a warm covering at night, too. When the Somerset House Annexe was built, I used to sleep on the third floor, in the veranda, and however much it rained or stormed, used only a soft light covering. I had a constant struggle with my aya Fitun over this. She was petrified that I'd catch cold or fall ill, especially since the rain would spray the veranda too, but I wouldn't have any of it. I'd insist on sleeping out there and thoroughly enjoyed being sprayed with the rain and the gusts of wind. I'd have the same struggle over bath water—I liked cold water but Fitun had got it into her head that hot water was better, so we'd have a running battle over that. Needless to say, I got my way! I gave her a really bad time, but she bore it all very good-humouredly, and we were really very fond of each other.

Whenever she had to go back to her home, even for a few days, I'd be terribly upset, and cry like anything. She'd do the same, and say she didn't want to go at all. When we began to learn English, we were really horrid to her. We'd tease her by speaking to her in English, but also tell her to repeat what we said, for instance: 'Bring me some water.' This sentence seems very simple and easy, but my poor Fitu could never get it out correctly. We'd double up with laughter, and made up a little song for her: 'Fitukary, Pitankary has flown up into the sky.' And we'd all laugh and laugh at it!

We'd all be given a glassful of milk every morning, and evening, freshly milked, which Fitun would bring up in a pot with glasses, to give every child. I loved milk, and sometimes I'd forget that I'd already had a cupful, and insist on being given another. We'd also be given *mosambis,* and sometimes I'd have four in one go! When I was small, I was so fat and pink-and-white, that an aya once exclaimed, 'Dear me, she's like a little cannon ball. Whoever will be able to carry her about!' So I was a healthy little child, and never missed school, certainly when we were at Somerset. I never had coughs or colds or a temperature.

Dear Amir, there are so many things I remember about my parents. But it's difficult to write about them. I can see them in front of me, I remember clearly what they said and did, but it's not so easy to write it all down. My dear Amir, I was 13 or 14 when we left Somerset, but even in those days, there were constant changes. I was a child of three or four, but between then and the time I reached twelve, things changed a lot. The family grew, new children were born. I remember faintly when the new Annexe was built, but very little before that. I do remember that in Somerset House itself, I used to sleep with Bibi [Sakina], and when she got married, and was going away to Sind, I was asked whether I'd like to go with her. And I said 'No', perhaps because Fitu and the others had told me what to say. I don't know whether they'd really wanted to take me, or whether it was just something to say. I was only two years old then, just a baby. The Annexe had six proper bedrooms, in which there was one for Bhai Mohsin, one for Bahen Sakina, one each for Bhai Husain and Bhai Faiz, one for the children, and the last was the guest room. Eventually, two of the downstairs rooms were made guest rooms, and we girls would sleep upstairs, on the third floor. At one point, Nassoo bahen [Nasima], Hannoo bahen [Hanifa], Raffoo bahen [Rafia] and I were there. Hannoo bahen would quite often be out of Bombay as she had a delicate constitution. Quite often she'd go away with Ammajan in the rains to Baroda, or some other place.

There was another room for the children downstairs, where children who were suffering from some infectious disease, whooping cough, measles, etc., could be kept in quarantine. The guest rooms were used by those married children who had their own homes, but came to spend some time with their parents at home, for instance, Bhai Mohsin, Bahen Ameena, Surayya, Jamila, and Halima, and soon others got married and went away, but would come back to stay with their parents. Then, our nieces and nephews began to fill the house. Bahen Ameena's two children, Sharifa and Salah, were much older than me, Sharifa about ten years older, and Salah about seven or eight! Then there was Fatima, Bahen Surayya's daughter, who's only about three years younger than me, and Amin, Asaf, Farid, and Salim were four or five years younger. And then, my goodness, the way my father's grandchildren appeared, one after the other.... Now, of course, there are so very many of them that it's quite difficult to count them—bless them—because it's not only their own children, but their children's children who form our group. Many years ago when we counted ourselves, there were no fewer than 60 or 70! Now, if we can find the time and energy, we must do a count again.

Yet when I remember my earliest days, there were only Sharoo and Salah. I seem to remember Bhai Husain's return from England—I had a pretty rainbow-coloured dress for the occasion, and I still remember it had pearls sewn on it, and because I had plump little arms, it'd be short-sleeved, and every one would tease me about my arms and embarrass me very much. I was probably about five years old then.

We weren't taken to [Husain and Mahmuda Nazar Futehally's] wedding, but I remember how impatiently we all waited for the bride and

bridegroom to arrive, and how they came in their carriage. How well I remember making friends with my new sister-in-law Mahmuda, who so
loved and spoilt all three of us little ones, Hattoo, Haffoo and me. We'd go
and sit beside her and she'd tell us stories, I think Cinderella, and '*Chira
che bacche*' were repeated every day, and we'd be thrilled every time!
She'd make amusing things out of paper, and there were many other delightful pastimes she introduced us to, we were all absolutely devoted to
her. As for Hattoo, he announced, 'When I get married, I'll have a girl just
like her!'

Mahmuda, c. 1900.

She was so sweet to all of us—we have such memories of a very dear
sister-in-law. Then I recall the Bandra house where they lived for a short
while before going to Zanzibar, in Africa. When they returned, how
Farid would boast of all the things he'd seen and done there! We'd all
sit or loll on the *takht*, big and little ones, surrounding him, and he'd
boast away, really impressing us. How Farid could talk in those days,
and his manner was just like that of a grown-up, probably imitating his
father....

Dear Amir, this isn't a connected account or tale—I write about whatever I feel like. So today I feel like telling you about your aunts Rafia and Akhtar. They were both the same age, that is, they were both about three years older than me, your aunt Rafia, whom I call Raffoo, was my close companion and friend, Hattoo came between us. When Haffoo and I were small, this same Raffoo would teach or explain a poem to us, and I remember a couple: 'The Child's First Grief', and 'May Queen', the sort of poems one would learn in the first or second class. Then, in those days, with Bhai Badr, there was a great interest in Urdu poetry, and he'd read it out to us all, children and grown-ups together. Raffoo Khala would listen, and then repeat and explain it to us, I remember a couplet she'd learnt from Bhai Badr, Your cheeks would make a blooming flower pale, your tresses are like flowing water.

When we went to Matheran we'd have to take a *palki* or ride on horseback from Neral. The children would go in pairs in *palkis,* and I usually went with Raffoo, when we were very small, we'd be with a grown-up. That'd be the time when the *harfarauri* would have fruited in the Bombay garden, and we'd fill our pockets with them to enjoy on our way up from Neral! Raffoo bahen and I would pick flowers. She was very good at sports, very light on her feet and very graceful, and the champion badminton player of the girls.

She was extraordinarily agile—she'd climb up trees and jump from branch to branch so lightly that the grown-ups called her Miss Monkey. A game we played in Matheran—on trees, was Catch and Raffoo bahen would really lead everyone a dance! When Haffoo and I were very small, Raffoo bahen and Hattoo bhai would help us climb up trees, and if we protested and were too frightened to climb up, they'd chant 'Coward, coward', and really jeer at us. Raffoo bahen had great charm, she was small but slight, and very graceful and light in her movements. Her eyes were sparkling and black, and she had an extraordinarily sweet face. She was aways smiling, and she had such lovely sparkling teeth. I used to think that my sister was very pretty. She was very popular. She read aloud very well—for one thing she looked so charming, for another she did read well. We used to make her recite Wordsworth's 'Daffodils' and some pieces of Shakespeare, and 'Aunt Tabitha'. She was very gentle and peace-loving, never did she lose her temper or raise her voice, ever.

In Matheran, there'd be the sports in May, and everyone in our family took part. There'd be four to six of us in each event! Someone from each age group, girls and boys! And we were all good at sports and physical activities, and the hall table would be full of prizes on Prize Day. Apart from the children, there'd often be guests who'd take part in the sports and win a prize or two. Each of us would get three or four prizes for races like the egg-and-spoon, horse racing, etc. Raffoo bahen was of course very good at all this. She was engaged when she was very young to Hasan Latif. I remember when he'd come to the house and how quickly and easily they made friends because there was such an age difference, and Raffoo bahen didn't realize what this friendship was leading to! Once they were engaged and Hasan Bhai left for England Raffoo bahen would sit down to write to him. And how would she do it? She'd start off by writing 'My very dear … ' and then if any of us younger brothers or sisters turned up to tease her, she'd quickly fill in someone else's name and show it to us. She was very conscious that one shouldn't screw up one's face when one cried, and so if she ever cried, she'd manage to keep her face absolutely straight, with tears dropping down her cheeks!

Apart from us brothers and sisters, she had two friends in particular, I won't mention her school friends, but those within the family—they were Akhtar bahen and Bahen Saddoo (who married Salman bhai). These three were great friends, and when the others came to spend the day or came to stay with us at Matheran, they'd go into a quiet corner and share secrets. We'd creep up on them from time to time, and see them completely absorbed, talking away, giggling, and laughing away—goodness knows what they were talking about that it wasn't right for us little ones to hear! One thing I know about is that Akhtar bahen was a great mimic, and she'd mimic the elders, sending the other two into gales of laughter! Of course, mimicking the elders in front of us would have made us very cheeky and bold. So, these were Raffoo bahen's two great friends, and they'd both come very often to the house. They were both engaged to people in my own family—Saddoo to Salman bhai, and Akhtar to Salah Mian. Raffoo bahen played a great part in all this—she was extremely useful as a go-between.

We'd love singing when the entire family was gathered together, but even amongst us sisters, we'd enjoy doing it. Amma encouraged us a lot.

It was fun, and also a good way of learning the words. There used to be an Indian music teacher for Raffoo, Hannoo, and Nassoo, and we'd pick up the *ragas* by listening to them. In the evenings, Ammajan would generally make them sing, of the elder sisters, Surayya and Jamila sang very well, and they had sweet voices too. Hattoo bhai also had a very good ear and sweet voice, and he loved to sing. As a child, there were some things he sang very well, such as *Srishti karat rab ke siwa kaun hai, kaho to sahi'* [Who is there except the absolute, the creator of this universe], and then from Sadi:

> He attained exaltation by his perfection.
> He dispelled darkness by his beauty.
> Beauteous are all his qualities,
> Benediction be on him and on his family.[4]

Like the music teachers, he'd sit cross-legged, and tap the beat on his legs, and sing full-throatedly. It's a great shame that he didn't keep up his singing. Raffoo bahen didn't sing particularly well, but Hannoo bahen had a musical voice and a good ear. She was married young, into a family where her music was not appreciated, and so her singing stopped too. But her daughter Rabia inherited these talents, and her singing and piano playing gave us all great pleasure. She died tragically young at 17.

[My youngest sister Haffoo and I] used to be taught Urdu by Ustad Ameer Ali. We'd also go to school together. The first school we went to was the Mission school in Panchgani, where the two of us had gone with our mother for a few months. I was seven then and Haffoo five. When we came back to Bombay we were sent to the Mission school in Girgaon, now known as Queen Mary's, where our elder sisters Nasima, Hanifa, and Rafia went too, as did Akhtar and Camoo. Camoo, Haffoo and I were put in the same class, and Camoo and I stayed together right through school. Haffoo was with us till the 4th standard, and then in the rains she went to Devlali [and died there of a typhus infection got from pilgrims at Nasik], aged five.

This happened in 1904. And in May 1905, Raffoo bahen and Nassoo bahen went to England, in the company of Bhai Camruddin and Bahen Vazir, who were to be their parents-in-law, to improve their education.

Left to right: Nasima, Safia (standing), Hanifa and Rafia. Bombay, 1905.

It was a dreadful loss for us, especially after Haffoo's death.... They all left Matheran on about 15 May, but you can imagine how sadly we said good bye! And if we had known what was in store for us we'd have been even more grief-stricken. Our mother fell ill soon after; she had severe pains in the abdomen and she was brought to Bombay. A very well-known doctor diagnosed a tumour, and operated on her; the operation appeared to have gone well, but on the third day, the 5th of June 1905, she died. Now when I think back on it, I feel I just hadn't grasped that a mother could die. What a great loss had taken place, I simply couldn't take it in. I'd had such a wonderful childhood, brought up in such luxury and ease, coddled and loved by everyone; how could I possibly understand that much of that love had, in one moment, been snatched away? I was quite numbed. I remember in those days I'd write long letters to Raffoo bahen and Nassoo bahen. This was my great solace and occupation, especially writing to Raffoo Bahen. My father was absolutely shattered by our mother's dreadful death. I shall never forget his sad anxious look and how he'd worry about us, and keep on asking whether we were all right. The least little thing that he'd never bothered about earlier would upset him. Eventually, the doctors advised him to go abroad for a change, and just before he left, Hannoo bahen's wedding was fixed.

How one's mind strays! I started off yesterday planning to write about Ahsan and Saeeda's wedding—and what a sad period I've reached. In fact, the years 1904–06 were terrible years for us, when we lost four most loved people—Haffoo, then Ammajan, then my dear sister Jamila, who was married to Bhai Agha Koochik, and then in August, Father. After that, it seemed that my childhood, with its carefree happy days was over—one chapter of the book of life had ended. The years that followed were full of troubles, and sad memories of the dear ones lost—the house, the garden, the servants, all had gone, and a new chapter of the book of life had begun.

Of course, there were many happy times as well, and loving and kind people around me, but the shock of that loss was difficult to bear. I really can't bear even now to write about it, and bring back those memories so full that pain—but, if I have the courage later on, I'll do so later.... In 1905 Raffoo went to England, and so when Father went, he found four of his children there. For some time, there was Bhai Husain with him, and then he came back and Faiz bhai took his place, as it was thought necessary that Father should have someone with him, and Salman Bhai was at Cooper Hill college, studying engineering. Nassoo and Raffoo were in school in Surrey, and so was Tehmina [Latif]. Father bought a car there, a large one, with plenty of room for luggage, and they drove all over England in the car and had a great time. This car was to have been brought to India, but it was sold after Father's death. Bhai Mohsin, Bahen Tahera, and Amin were also in England, perhaps in 1908, and it was lovely for my brother and sisters to visit them there, especially in the holidays.

Nassoo Bahen had been engaged to Alma bhai [Latifi], and because both our parents were no longer with us, we had had lost our home, and Bhai Camruddin and his family were in England, and so was Nassoo and Bhai Mohsin, Alma Bhai suggested that they get married in London. We weren't too happy about that, but eventually agreed, and they got married in August 1908. There were a lot of family people there at the wedding, which was reported in the British and the French press.

The same year, perhaps October, Bhai Mohsin and his family returned with Raffoo bahen. She'd gone when she was still a child, her father, her mother, they were all there, and Somerset was there, and what splendour and loveliness was there! And, when she returned it was all gone! All those brothers and sisters, who lived in one family, were all now scattered in separate little flats or houses. What a tragic, dismal scene. Anyhow, when she returned, I cannot tell you what it meant to me. I was with Bhai Badr and Bibi in a house called 'Retreat' in Mazagon, close to the Victoria Gardens. Raffoo Bahen came there. Mamoon and Afzal were small children then. The day Raffoo bahen returned we slept together that night. I remember how she wouldn't let go my hand. She held it all the time.

We'd gone to the harbour to meet her off the boat, and oh God, how impatiently we waited for her to come! We didn't know when the steamer would dock, but Rashid bhai [Futehally], as usual, came to the rescue. He told us when it was expected to berth, and we all went to his office and waited there, while he'd phone the docks every so often. At last, when we knew the time, we all went to the pier, and we saw Raffoo Bahen from a distance straight away! She looked so very pretty in a pale pink *orhni* with a sparkling silver border, which looked so lovely on her charming pink-and-white smiling face. We were all entranced by her! Then she came down and we all hugged her, and took her home. What a happy time that was!

She was an ideal for me, and truly during her lifetime, her sweetness and affectionate manner, her enthusiasm, never once failed me. Never did she ever hurt me, or fail to shower love and affection on me. She was an extraordinary person, sparkling, joyful, bringing happiness to everyone. May God shower her with mercies and blessings. Her passing away was an unbearable grief to me and to all of us, no-one could ever take the place of such a loving sister. Anyway, those days we spent together, I was able to unburden myself of all the fears and grief I was oppressed by; her coming back brought back, if only momentarily, the happiness we had known at Somerset. Being so far away, she hadn't felt it as deeply as those of us who loved her, she had grown up, and the ordeal of the loss of both parents hadn't had the same shattering effect on her as on me, we recalled the old times together, and for me to have someone of my age to face the harshness of the present times—how can I explain what it meant?

She found me very greatly changed, when she'd left, three years earlier, I was a carefree, frolicking, unthinking child. Now I had become a sad, frightened girl; I would, for no reason at all, burst into tears—not the tears of a child, but one that contained all the poignancy of the sorrows I had endured. People couldn't understand why, at the slightest thing, I'd burst into tears. Dear Amir, as I write, the memory of the childhood grief quite overwhelms me, and I am flooded with tears. May God protect you, my darling child, from having to suffer as I did as a child.

First, such a happy childhood, surrounded by my brothers and sisters. And then the fearful shock of the sudden separation! Oh, the contrast between that large mansion, full of life, by the sea, from where you could see the sun rise, and in the evening the sun set; all nature's bounties spread out before one; great spaces, gardens, flowers! Leaves, trees—so many playmates, amongst my own brothers and sisters, and loving parents and elder brothers and sisters! And then, that pokey little house in Mazagon, with only four people in it—Bhai Badr, Bibi, Mamoon, and Afzal.

I don't think anyone who hasn't suffered this trauma can possibly understand what I went through. A person's life changing gradually—that's something else. But all of a sudden! At one stroke, out of the blue! Never had I known earlier what it was to be alone—and then suddenly to have to face it! How can I explain the things I yearned for, and how I despaired over them! And I couldn't talk to anyone about it—poor Bhai Badr, good man, and my loving Bibi—how hard they tried to make me feel at home. But how can a bulbul, a songbird, who flew free, ever thrive in a cage? However clean, however full of flowers, of food and water? And so I was trapped. And with no one to whom I could talk of my misery.

In those days, Chacha Sahib Amiruddin's house was paradise for me. When I went there, to see all those brothers and sisters of my age, running about, playing so happily, I could pretend for some time that our dear Somerset was not gone after all. It was not grand like Somerset, there wasn't the lovely large garden, the flowers, the servants, but the most important thing was the cheerful laughing children, in whose company I could forget myself. And I was so fortunate that these children were fond of me, so fond that after some time I felt that they had taken the place of my own family. We are starved for love, we hunt for it and find it somehow, somewhere, without it life is impossible. All my own brothers and sisters had separated, bearing with them the grief of the loss of their parents and their old home. And they all became a little different, estranged, aloof. They had lost something of the old affectionate manner, and when I went to visit them, I'd feel even more upset and grieved. So

Chacha Sahib's home, the cheerful household where life was a pleasant game, provided balm to my child's soul, even if it was only for a short time.

Yesterday, after having written all this, I was quite worn out. Truly few people can have been blessed with such a happy childhood, nor many had it snatched away at the age of thirteen or fourteen. Even now, forty years later, I tremble all over at the memories of that time. Well, I'll continue with my account of Raffoo bahen. She was not changed at all, if anything, she was even more loving and so was greatly loved by all of us. She had all the old Somerset zest for life, the gaiety, the warm-heartedness, she brought a ray of hope and life into my lifeless heart, and I became a little more like myself.

Soon after her return, Salman bhai and Saddoo bahen [Najmuddin Tyabji] got married, and Faiz bhai then invited all of us brothers and sisters to Latifia [the Latif family house] in Kihim for a few days in December [about 15–20 people]. Perhaps there were also others who came and went for a day or so whom I can't remember. We spent ten or twelve days having great fun, with much merriment. Not since Somerset went, a couple of years earlier, had all of us met and had fun together like this. I think it was in December 1908 that I went to Kihim for the first time. Just imagine, Amir, to be fourteen or fifteen years old, and never having seen Kihim! There are some things I remember very clearly about the visit: one was getting up early every day, and going down to the sea with Raffoo bahen, dancing and jumping about in the sea, and then her teaching me to dance on the sand! Oh, how wonderful it was, after all those years to have her back, to sing with her, to chat!

Hussoo bhai used to read out from the Iliad to us, we'd sit out under the trees, and we'd enjoy it very much and listened with great interest. But poor Hasan bhai (Latif) got very fed up with all these hours and hours spent listening to the Iliad. Especially because it left him no time to spend with Raffoo bahen [to whom he was engaged]. Eventually he got very angry, and was very rude one day, so Hussoo bhai decided to resolve the issue by holding a sacrifice in the Greek fashion. He made Hasan bhai buy a goat, *bakra,* and then, in the garb of Greek gods and goddesses, we all gathered on the sand, and made a great fire, and then performed all the sacrificial rituals that the Greeks did. Raffoo bahen played an important part—and Hasan bhai was the sinner, who performed the sacrifice.

Ritual penance being enacted on the sands outside the Latif family house
Latifia in Kihim, 1908.
Faiz (Hussoo) standing, extreme left, Hasan seated extreme right.

Hussoo bhai himself was Jupiter, and all of us were the vestal virgins! It
was enormous fun. And Hasan bhai's rudeness was transformed into an
amusing event. But perhaps he also managed to get something out of it,
and got more time to spend as he wished!... Bhai Badr would tell us about
the stars, and delighted us with his singing. Then we would join in the
singing and enjoy ourselves very much ...

Now comes an account by Abdus Samad, Amir's teacher, of how he entered the family at Deonar. The language is a pure Urdu, different in style
and tone to Safia's in its grave simplicity and elegance of diction, also its
humour.

*(in Safia's hand) My story in my own words Abdus Samad Ansari
(no date)*

Before I start writing about how it was that I came to be in this *mu-
barak* house and into one of India's finest families, perhaps I should say
something about who I am, where I am from, and how it came about that
I reached here.

I am a humble Muslim belonging to a poor family whose occupation
has been tilling the soil, and it is a very noble occupation. I am from the
zilla of Gorakhpur in the United Provinces of Agra and Awadh. The village

is called Babanowli and the complete address is District Gorakhpur, P.O. Hanpar, village Babanowli.

My parents were very keen on my being educated; my mother made enormous sacrifices, and sold her jewellery so I could get to college. But unfortunately by the time I got to the Intermediate class, there was nothing left in the house of any value which could pay for my continuing my education. So there was no way out; I had to turn my back on college, and face the anxieties and problems of trying to find a job. But the unemployment in India is well-known. How do you imagine that a poor man's son could possibly compete with rich men's sons in getting a job? Eventually, I found my way to Bombay, that refuge of the poor; and I found the job that had for me since childhood been a vocation, that is the noble profession of a school teacher.

I teach at the Kurla Municipal Anglo-Urdu School. I got the job on the twenty-third of June 1934. I didn't keep well—the air didn't suit me, and I was constantly falling ill. As fate would have it, a Muslim gentleman from Chembur visited the school, met the Headmaster and explained that he wanted a teacher who was well-versed in Urdu. Fate smiled again, and the Headmaster then sent for me, and at twelve that morning, I accompanied the gentleman to Deonar farm. There I met Jabir Ali Sahib, and we sat under the shade of a huge mango tree, and had a talk.

Whenever I go to the farm now, I always make a little pilgrimage to the tree. It is just next to a field of pineapples, and it had good red earth piled high all around its roots. It was under that tree that the decision was made for me to become a tutor of Amir Jabir Ali, or rather, it was there that a new chapter in my life began.

I came to give Amir his first lesson on 12 April 1937. My first impression of Amir was a strange one: curly hair, a beautiful and innocent face, and all he could say was 'Umm', 'Yes'. At first I really couldn't believe that this was a Muslim child, and also, to tell you the truth, whether this child was a boy or a girl. But when he sat down at his desk, and told me his name, I realized he was a boy, but an extremely shy and diffident child. Then, ten days later, my school closed for the summer holidays, and I went home myself. In those ten days, I realized that the boy was extremely bright, and extremely well brought up. He hardly speaks, and fobs one off with his 'Umm' and 'Yes', but when he writes, he writes very well, tries to use appropriate terms, and is good at it, and is very familiar with mathematics.

Amiruddin with Ustad Sahib, at Chabootra, Chembur, c. 1938.

I had not at that time met his mother, who is now also my true mother. Yes, I'd met his father, Jabir Ali Sahib, and often been taken to Chembur station in their tanga, and we'd have a chance to talk then. I understood from his conversation that the family I found myself in the midst of was no ordinary family, but part of the Tyabji family, and that the child I was teaching was no ordinary child, but the grandson of one of India's greatest and most honoured sons, Badruddin Tyabji, and, that on his father's side, he was related to the great patriot, Abbas Tyabji, and an heir to his great tradition, in that his grandmother was the beloved sister of Abbas Tyabji.

I cannot describe my state of mind when I discovered all this—for me it was a miracle, and in fact what greater miracle could there have been than for someone like me, whom the great and wealthy would never let approach them, for whom poverty was a sin, a fault that was so great that they wouldn't even talk to one, and for whom social differences were crucial, well, for a humble man like that to find himself in the midst of a family whose name was known to all, great and small if that wasn't a miracle, what was? In Islam, great importance is attached to virtue and historians have acknowledged that the spread of Islam was due to this quality, and if they should wish to see a living example of such virtue, they have only to turn to the Tyabji family, where every child is a shining example of it. I am of course using the name Tyabji in its widest possible sense to mean both those who carry the name, and all their relations.

To continue, after the summer holidays in 1937, I came back and started lessons with Amir. I'd come every day except Sunday. I'd get off at Govindi station, and turn up panting. I'd teach for an hour, and then make my way back. Never did I miss a day's lesson—I'd appear like some misfortune dropping from the skies, and I began to realize that we'd both got very attached to each other; and that he truly enjoyed being with me and our lessons together. I was myself a young man of 23, full of hopes and desires. We got on so well together, and kept on at the work too. Then, it was God's will that in July I fell very ill with diarrhoea, and had to stay in bed. I was absolutely alone—I knew no one, had no friends or acquaintances who might help. I lay alone in that dark room. When I hadn't turned up for ten or twelve days, Jabir Ali sahib thought, what can the matter be that Ustad Sahib, who never misses a day, should have been absent for so long? So he came to Kurla to find out what was wrong, and saw the state of affairs. Well then, what happened—what does an honourable and *sharif* man do?

This is true prayer; this is devotion to God and goodness
That man should help man. [Hali]

He immediately sent for a doctor, and then suggested I go home with him. It was enormously kind of him, but I had now to face great challenges. For one thing, I was just as shy and diffident as Amir. And then, I had never in my life sat at a table and eaten with a knife and fork. I was completely ignorant of all these niceties, nor had I even for one moment thought I might encounter such a situation. But what could I say

Look, what gifts God showers on the humble.

So, I put on my shirt, and wrapped my muffler round my neck, and that too a shirt with shiny stripes—you know of course that people of my standing and class love showy shiny clothes, and especially the Muslims. But then I saw that these clothes weren't too appreciated by the family, so I put them away, and got into the habit of wearing simple, clean clothes. And now I'm very clean. If I don't change my clothes at least every other day, then Ammajan, that is Safia Bibi Sahib, who is truly my mother now, gets very cross, and she remembers exactly when I should have changed. And it is truly wonderful the difference it makes to get into fresh clean clothes. But I must admit that as far as this matter's concerned, I'm rather miserly—I hate using up beautifully ironed and folded clothes, I'd much rather, especially with clothes that I particularly like, leave them neatly folded and preserved in the almirah and admire them sitting there, and feel happy that way.

But look where I've got to. I came to this strange house ill, and was put into the guest room. Then it was lunch time, and I was summoned to the dining table. I asked to be excused for the first few days, and ate alone in my room, with the excuse of being unwell. But how long could this go on? Someday I would have to join my hosts. So I did, and ate with my fingers. Now, from the next day, as my condition improved, I went to Ammajan, and very shyly, very diffidently, sat by her and read something from the *Diwan-i Ghalib*. It has now become a routine for us to read something every day. By reading and teaching, I became a little more at ease. Then they started showing me how to use a knife and fork. This training lasted a whole two months, and I passed the test successfully. We went to Woodlands [Sakina Lukmani], Somerset Lodge [Faiz Tyabji], to Rashid sahib [Futehally], to Camoo bibi sahib's, to Hamida bibi's, to Mukhlis sahib's, to Daulatabad, 'Farhat Afza'. Actually, I'm doing quite well as far as table manners go. Oh yes, and we went to Maltibai Saheba's farm as well.

So July passed, and then all fit and well, I went back to Kurla, and re-sumed the daily trip to Deonar for Amir's lessons. As it happened, Amir had got so attached to me in the course of this month, that he missed me very much, and didn't know how to get through the day on his own. Then it was October, and people began to leave for Kihim, to Retreat, Sakina bibi Saheb's house there. I was invited too. Jabir Ali sahib left after five days, but Ammajan, Amir and I stayed for twenty, and we had a lot of fun there. Since we were together all the time, it was a good way of getting to know and really test each other, and in this we all passed. I was very happy with them, and they thought I was okay.

November came, and we'd resumed the routine of my coming every day to teach Amir. Towards the end of November, Amir said to me one day, 'Ustad sahib, do you know?' and then he began to smile all over his face. 'What?' I said, but he couldn't contain himself, he kept on smiling and laughing. At last he said, 'Well, last night Father and Mother were talking amongst themselves, and saying, Suppose we invite Ustad sahib to stay? Then they asked me what I thought, and I said, it would be wonderful, do let's ask him to stay here. So everything's settled, and it's for you to decide.' The next day, Jabir Ali sahib broached the subject with me: Now who could resist such an invitation and from such people?

They made a comfortable shack for me, near the well, under the shade of a huge mango tree, and they said to me, 'Come and make yourself at home.' So on Monday 6 December 1937, that is 2 Shawwal 1356, I moved in. I took the 4.10 from Kurla, and found Amir with his small cycle waiting at Chembur station, with Babajan's larger cycle for me.

When we started off on our cycles, the first thing that Amir said to me was, 'Ustad Sahib, it was Id yesterday, but we didn't have *sevaiyan* simply because you were coming today, and so we thought we'd have them together. Abdul had made them today.' What affection and what genuineness! Only those who have been separated from their family, and found such affection and support from strangers can begin to understand what it meant to me. Anyway, we got there and met them, and then all four of us had dinner together. And at ten o'clock I went to my shack and lay down. I thought of those lines:

A great mercy to be granted some moments of peace.

The *jhonpra* was only used to sleep in, as all day I'd be either teaching here or at Kurla. After a month or so we had become so friendly here that a bed was put for me in the room on the ground floor, and that's where

I would sleep, and Amir and I shared a bathroom. And Amir's cupboard was divided into two, and we each had an equal number of shelves for our clothes. Now that he is away in Gwalior School, the entire cupboard is mine. When I moved in here permanently, I began to get to know Amir's family slowly, all his father's side of the family, and his mother's, all of them were people whom I would meet and talk to, except for his Hyderabadi chachi [Dilbar] who is in purdah, but otherwise I got to know the entire family.

Of the elders whom I had a chance to meet and get to know quite well, there were Dr Badruddin Lukmani, Mr Faiz B. Tyabji, and Mr Rashid Futehally. I must especially mention the beloved late Mr Futehally was a remarkable man: he was full of life and laughter; whoever met him would come back cheered and laughing, he was a very amiable man. Money would flow from him as if it were water, and he loved going out and enjoying himself. 'A generous man's wealth is never diminished.' It was at his very generous invitation to the famous hill resort of Bombay, Matheran, that I spent ten days as his guest, and enjoyed myself and made many excursions. I went two or three times to Mr Faiz B. Tyabji at Somerset. He was most generous and hospitable, and friendly. I would often sit with him and read Urdu poetry out aloud. He speaks beautifully. His son Saif is passionately concerned about the education of Muslim children—quite obsessed with it. He is still a young man, or let me say rather he only has two young children as yet, and he is active and fit—may God make him the Sir Syed of our times. Oh, there's one thing I completely forgot to mention, and that is that I almost went to Kashmir as a companion to Mr Faiz Tyabji who had kindly invited me to go with him, but unfortunately I couldn't get leave from school. Perhaps fate had decided that I was not to see this earthly paradise, so how could I go?

Has a leaf ever stirred without god's will?

As for our Doctor Sahib [Badruddin Lukmani], I will write later.

The young people who I became friends with, or rather met and talked to a lot were Afzal Lukmani, Mukhlis Tyabji [Abbas Tyabji's grandson], Saad Ali. I'll write more about Afzal Sahib when I talk about his family. As for Mukhlis Sahib and Saad Sahib, I didn't really have many opportunities of meeting and talking to Mukhlis Sahib, but when I do, I feel so completely at ease with him, and I really like him, I really can't say why. If we had been a little closer, you can be sure that if he had agreed I would have spent a lot of time with him. I feel this way both about him and his sister Hamida Khatoon, I feel very drawn to them. I admire Hamida Khatoon's steadfast determination very much—having decided which way she's going, she holds fast to it. And this quality in women is something that has been celebrated from the first day. Whenever I think of her life and the decision she made about it [marrying a young Gujarati in the teeth of family opposition, as well as that of Gandhiji and Panditji, but with Maulana Azad's support] I cannot help but applaud her.

Poor Saad Ali sahib is at the moment a guest of the government [arrested and gaoled in Yerawada for his part in the Quit India Movement]. He has a quiet simplicity that appeals very much to me. And to sit smoking away, and be committed to the welfare of workers is something I like very much. Yes, but he never smokes in front of Amma. And in these progressive days, let alone cigarettes, I've seen people smoke cigars in front of Amma. Such courtesy is a token of our earlier culture.

By this time, when I'd got to know quite a lot of people in the family quite well and they me, Amir would often call out to me in his sweet little voice 'Oh U-s-tad Sa-hi-b,' ... And he'd say, 'Now listen carefully', and recite the following couplet of Iqbal, slightly changed

You were nothing till Amir came along

And in a way, it's true, because if I hadn't come to teach Amir, I would never have had a chance to meet these remarkable people. My own mother had died—where would I have found a mother who would care for me so lovingly? If I was irritable and cross, she'd calm me down, if I'm depressed she cheers me up. Like Amir, she knows everything about me, and if I go wrong somewhere I'm pulled back and given a scolding. She showers me with loving motherly advice, provides everything I need. In this household, I am everything, and everything is mine.

[pp. 100–108 left blank]

Safia continues

Yesterday there was a meeting at Blavatsky Lodge for women at 4 p.m., or rather, it was supposed to be at 4 but goodness knows when it actually started.

We were very disappointed at first to see how empty the hall was but eventually it became about two-thirds full—there were about 300 women there. Most of the family women were there, and a few from the *jamaat*, and there were Hindu and Parsi women too. The organizers were Fatima Ismail, Mrs Sayani [Kulsum],[5] Sultana Fyzee, and goodness knows who else. The speakers included from amongst us, Sakina (Bibi), Sultana Fyzee, Laeeq [Futehally], and me, at the end, Vazir [Tyabji], Sultana Fyzee and Fatima [Ismail?] sang the national song. Hamida (Probodh) had been asked to but declined on account of ill health. Madam Sofia Wadia [later president of the Theosophical Society] spoke in English, a speech that was enthusiastically applauded, some others too spoke extremely well while others were rather lifeless and dull! Mrs Brelvi and Kulsum (Abdullah) also spoke, and so did a number of Hindu ladies who spoke in good Hindustani and said heart-warming things.

Malti, who'd come with us, thought the meeting passed off very well—and praised my speech to the skies! A number of other people also seem to have liked it—after all, how can one speak of Gandhiji and not speak from the heart? And, after all, what is speaking compared to action? One should do much more for his cause—it is only one's own frailty that prevents one from real sacrifice—so the least I can do is speak with my heart and soul.

Dear Amir, perhaps you will never have the chance of hearing your mother speak—time diminishes everything. Who knows how long my voice will last. Perhaps it will give you some pleasure to know that your mother spoke on two occasions, when Mrs Naidu was presiding, and both times, she spoke so encouragingly to me, and said how much she'd liked them. And once, by chance, when she was there at a women's meeting, I read Hafiz Jalandhari's *Salaam,* and that time too, she came up to me and said, 'How well you've read it!' That's not something I shall easily forget! Dear Amir, I shall keep this speech for you, you might be interested. I've found two other things I'd written, one after the trip to Europe, which I'd read to a group in Rangoon, and the other I'd read to a meeting of the Akhde Surayya organized in the *jamaat* after the Allahabad Conference [AICC Conference, 1932]. Read these my dear son, and learn about your mother's views! I shall keep them carefully for you.

Mrs Sayani has just come back from Delhi, where she'd gone for the Conference meeting held for Gandhiji and attended by people from all over India... She said it was very well attended and that rousing and fiery speeches were made at it. But we're not so good at action. Our leaders are mostly in gaol—who is there to guide us into action? Perhaps a new leader will appear among us. For how long can our energy and enthusiasm be suppressed? Never...

Dear Amir, when I was tidying up the cupboards, I came across a letter your father had written to me in 1905. And this is something I've been wanting to write about for a long time. As the poet says:

> Rejoice and be happy in your youth
> Make the most of these days of happiness and joy
> Because when the Angel of Death comes
> You will be silenced for ever.

Because I used to long so to know more about my parents, I feel that perhaps you will also have the same feelings and desires, so I'm going to tell you about how and when your father and I first got to know each other. We were so closely related—his mother was my first cousin Zeenuth, and his father was my first cousin Muiz. We'd known each other since we were small, but because he was more than five years older than me it wasn't until I was eight or ten that there was anything special between us. The first thing that I remember is that he was my brother Hattoo's great friend—or rather his hero, and there was a time when I was ten or so when Hattoo was constantly talking about Jabir and what he'd said and done—that he'd made a century at cricket, and so on and so forth. And of course, all this had its effect on me! All these boys had formed a cricket club and they all went to the same school, St Xavier's, and then, in the afternoons, they go and eat *dal* and *puris* and *bhajias* and that sort of stuff, and we'd hear all about it from your father. So naturally, I began to think like my dear brother Hattoo, that there was no-one to compare with Jabir. He was the King, the leader! I didn't notice or pay any attention to any of the others!

We were of course on friendly terms with all the other boys in Hattoo's group, but Jabir was someone special. Slowly my dear Hattoo bhai started talking to me about other things too—not just games. And Jabir began to come more frequently, often on his own, without the others. And Hattoo bhai would tell me confidentially that Jabir liked me a lot, that he'd said this or that. I'd be secretly thrilled, but terrified in case anyone got to know, so I'd keep up a great pretence of being quite indifferent to Jabir in front of others and quarrel and fight with him, pull his hair (which was very curly), pinch him, smear his face or nose with soap-all that kind of thing. Then he came and spent the summer with us in Matheran. We'd be together all day, and keep on teasing each other.

I'd begun to guess from Jabir's manner—his expression, how he'd begun to feel about me, but I didn't question my own feelings about him. I was after all, only ten or eleven, and I didn't want to think about such deep feelings, such responsibilities. I was too carefree and happy a child to want it otherwise. People would tease me about Jabir, and I'd pretend I didn't know what they were talking about, so everyone called me 'Masoom'! And they truly thought I was so! It wasn't so, of course, I was well aware of Jabir's feelings, but I never let on to him either that I knew how he felt! I felt dreadfully shy. Some people used to call him Haazir. And life went on, full of fun and happiness, sheer paradise. And then, one day, after we'd spent a whole June together in Matheran, I was called out of class one day by Miss Wilson, our Principal, and given a letter in a hand I couldn't recognize, because the address on the letter was in a disguised hand. But when I opened it, I found a letter from Jabir! I was so disturbed, I quickly closed the letter and put it away.

When I got home, I found a quiet corner, and read it carefully. In it Jabir said he loved me and that he hoped I liked him and so on and so forth. I have the letter with me now, and I'm keeping it for you, Amir. When I read it now, I feel like laughing, remembering the terrifying effect it had on me then, and I'm also very surprised at this, because actually it was only the letter of an innocent 'good' boy, but at that time I thought, oh heavens, my childhood is over! Life and all its responsibilities are now upon me—I was quite absurdly affected by that letter. I was quite distraught, in fact, and wept and wept. Then I quietly showed it to Hannoo a few hours later, and asked her what I should do.

I was twelve years old at that time and Hannoo herself wasn't married till a few months later, Raffoo and Nassoo bahen were in England. I wrote a very strange reply, and sent it to Jabir through Hattoo bhai, who was taking a lively interest in this affair! Jabir was very disappointed at my reply, so Hattoo bhai said teasingly to him, 'Oh, Saffoo has shown your letter to everyone, and everyone is terribly angry with you.' Jabir got very alarmed, and actually contemplated suicide!! But when Hattoo bhai heard of this, he went and explained that it was all a joke, no-one had seen the letter, no-one is angry and then everything was all right, thank goodness Jabir believed him, and stayed alive! After this, I became extremely self-conscious whenever I met Jabir, and it was very difficult keeping up a pretence of ignorance and innocence, but I persevered, and outwardly remained the same carefree tomboy, loved, spoilt, till the fates, mysterious and hidden, overwhelmed us with dreadful events, and sorrow followed sorrow. I will write some other time.

On Sundays, the entire family came to dinner at Somerset, and our close friends and relations also spent the day here. Our married sisters who were still in Bombay, like Bahen Surayya at Najmuddin's, Bahen Jamila (from Khetwadi, Camruddin Tyabji's house), Bahen Halima (Mazagon, at Bahen Amirunissa), would always come with their families. In the evening we'd play badminton a bit, but it'd be so breezy generally in the evenings that we couldn't play much, and we'd play in the mornings before breakfast. On Sundays we'd play *ata-pata*, *bhirokho*, and games like that, and everyone, including the children, would take part. Bhai Ali, Akoochik bhai and his other brothers, and our own brothers would be there. Jabir was a wonderful sportsman from childhood, at every kind of game, and most especially at badminton, he was very strong and fit; dear Amir, unlike you, but perhaps you will slowly begin to resemble your father? I've always been a very healthy child, and thank goodness, kept fit all my life. I'm now 50, and beginning to feel my age, but I don't have any illness, though I've had my share of sorrows, and troubles. Thank God, thank God for health! Of course, if a boy is exceptionally good at sports, then any girl would be drawn to him, and of course, I was! And he was very good looking—he had curly hair, an athlete's body, and finely drawn features—quite heart-compelling!

Jabir Ali c. 1908, Cambridge.

When we were engaged and Jabir was in England, I must have been twelve or so—I told Bibi that I thought he was a model of manly beauty, i.e., an absolute Apollo! Bibi was terribly amused and she'd always tease me about it. However that may be, I certainly thought your father, as a young man, and for many years thereafter, was really a very handsome man. He broke his nose when he fell into the well; his skin got blotched and leathery and tanned being out in the sun; he had marvellous hair, most of which he's now lost, his teeth have fallen out, well, after all that, what can you expect?! Anyway, we carried on meeting in this fashion.

I only found out years later that Chacha Sahib Amiruddin had broached the subject with Jabir, and Jabir had said he'd be happy to marry me; he'd then spoken to my parents and asked for my hand, and they'd both said they liked Jabir and would be very pleased if our engagement took place. But since I was only 10 or 11 years old, they thought they shouldn't speak to me about it just then, but that Jabir was welcome to come to Somerset whenever he wanted, and if all went well, and I liked him, then perhaps in a couple of years, if I agreed, the engagement could take place. That is why Jabir had been invited to Matheran, but I hadn't realized this—I thought that he'd come as a special friend of Hattoo bhai's. I think it's a very good thing I hadn't known about what the elders had agreed on, so I could naturally and spontaneously make up my mind. That's how we got to know each other, and that was when Jabir wrote me that letter. And then my mother died in June 1905, but Jabir's visits to Somerset continued unchanged. And he came to Matheran in 1906 as well, although at that time my father was away, in England.

The shock of my mother's death had affected him very deeply, and his health broke down. The doctors advised him to go to England, and so he went. For the first few months, Bhai Husain accompanied him, and then Bhai Faiz. At the same time, arrangements were made for your father, Jabir, to go to England—his own parents had died at an early age, leaving the whole family penniless. It was Chacha Sahib Amiruddin who brought them up. So my father agreed that Jabir should take a loan and travel to England to study for the Forest Service Exam. I hadn't then been asked whether I'd agree to get engaged to Jabir, but I think the elders had guessed from my behaviour that I would! So preparations for Jabir's going were afoot, but nothing had been decided between us. Father was in England and wrote to my elder brothers and sisters that they should make sure of my being agreeable to it before doing anything about an engagement.

It was decided that we'd have the formal engagement ceremony before Jabir left for England on 15 September [1906], by which time Father would also be back. Jabir and I then began to meet on our own occasionally, because the time for his departure was drawing near. And then I began to get notes from him, which I still have, that we should have a chance to say goodbye in absolute privacy before he left. He also wanted to give me a ring, and begged me to find a way of being able to meet alone. I was by then, partly perhaps because of the loss of my mother, and partly because of growing up, not quite as green and innocent a child as earlier, and I was quite willing for the engagement to be made formal. In the midst of all this, we got the stunning news of my father's sudden death, just when we were getting ready to welcome him back. The house had just been painted, and people had been hard at work to make it look splendid for him. And then this fearful news. Amir, you will never be able to understand what a tremendous effect our Father's death had on us. God, our lives changed instantly! Our dear mother's death had affected us all deeply—and now, before we had recovered, another staggering blow shattered us still further. My clothes for the engagement were being made, and I was just waiting for Father's return to be able to wear them! I still have that jora, or rather, the remnants of it, but I didn't wear it for our engagement.

Jabir was to leave on the 15th, as I'd mentioned earlier, and before he went, we met privately twice. And when we did, I wasn't the same shy girl as before... We used to meet on the little hillock at Somerset, which I've mentioned earlier. Imagine the little hill on Sathwain Pahar [a series of seven hills rising steeply behind the farm at Deonar, that was a favourite evening or early morning walk] if it was in our compound? And it had a little summer-house on it—it would have been like that. This little summer-house had seen a lot of romances beginning to bloom. If anyone was suspected of being in love, everyone would leave that little summer·house for them! And it would be their special place!

Jabir and I have spent some wonderfully happy times there. There were very few occasions that we met before he left for England, but I still remember that first meeting. I also remember what we were wearing:

I had just started wearing a lehenga, I'd been wearing frocks till Babajan's death—a black and white jora. I was just thirteen, and had planned to get into lehengas anyway, and had had some made, so I used to wear those. Jabir liked [some kind of embroidery] very much and I had a jora which had just been made. I remember all the things that happened that day that I can't write about here! Jabir gave me the sweetest ring—a band with forget·me-nots enamelled on it. I felt too shy to wear it to school, so I kept it locked up in a cupboard. It was such a blow, but it got stolen one day—a great loss for me. I tried very hard to get one made like it when we went to Paris, and I don't remember why it didn't work out. I do remember, as we said goodbye, Jabir's sighs and the look in his eyes. And how hard he gripped my hand, quite unconsciously, and I just couldn't say that he was hurting me, and he didn't let go, and I didn't want him to. And how he begged me to let him kiss me, and how happily I consented. Although I'd been happy to get engaged to him, after that meeting I was completely his, and so I have remained, his devoted loving faithful wife. When he returned from England after four years away, he went to Burma, and he was in Tavoy, Rangoon, etc. During all those long absences never once did I look at another man, or even dream of it, never

did I feel any kind of attraction. It wasn't that there weren't many opportunities. Jabir used to be away at work for long hours, and I'd be left alone.
I used to be on good terms with his male friends, I travelled on my own
from time to time, and had a lot to do with male workmen. But I was so
tightly knit by this bond that never did I feel any kind of test or challenge.
I always considered Jabir to be supreme, and still think so.

Being my father's daughter, for me Jabir was a comparatively poor
man—he couldn't offer me the kind of worldly comforts or luxury that
I had grown up with. And might have expected. But his honesty and no-
bility of mind, his concern for others, his deep commitment and sense
of duty towards others, and his conviction that true happiness arose
from such selfless service, that this was service to God, this was the true
meaning of religion.... His friendliness, his good humour, his desire to
part with everything he had to give others, and his feelings towards the
community and the country, his self-sacrifice, his selflessness, all this
made a deep impression on my mind, so that never did I for one instant
regret that I was not married to a man who could have given me a life of
ease and luxury, who would have provided me with the pleasures of the
world, to travel, and to enjoy all the delights possible! No, no, I am constantly aware of my great good fortune to have a husband like this, whom
I can with my whole heart and soul love and admire so totally, for whom
I have such tremendous regard, that I feel privileged and joyful that I can
give the world a son in whose veins runs his blood. Who will inherit his
father's qualities, his generosity of heart and soul!

Dear Amir, think of what you have inherited as a priceless gift from
God, and make good use of the bounty you have been given. This is not
your dessert, it is God's blessing on you, and it is for you to make good use
of it—God will undoubtedly ask you what you have done with what he
has blessed you with ...

... Dear Amir, as Iqbal says,

There are many thousands of devotees of God
Who wander about in the wilderness, possessed [with love for him]
But I will devote myself only to him who cares for God's people.

Having written this, I sobbed and sobbed. My eyes ached... I will
go and have a little walk and compose myself, and be calmed and

refreshed by the cool hill air—and perhaps I shall meet Babajan on the way back.

Safia and Jabir after their wedding, probably taken at Amiruddin Tyabji's home, Bombay 1915.

4 March Thank God, Gandhiji's fast is over, and he is safe. The whole country can breathe again: its anguished prayers have been answered. As the poet said:

Heave fiery sighs from your battered and burning heart. They will ensure that you will receive something from Merciful God.

My dear Amir, I have so very many things to tell you about, thoughts keep on tumbling into my mind that I want you to know of. I don't know whether they will please you, what you will make of them, but a mother's heart longs to share them with you.

I won't be able to write down all that I'd like you to know, but I'll do as much as I can. So I'll pick up the threads of what I was telling you a few days ago, about your father and me. I'd reached the point when his departure for England was nearing and we'd begun to meet alone. I'd started going to Chacha Sahib Amiruddin's myself, and we'd meet there. Jabir's family was terribly upset at the thought of his leaving, especially his sisters Farhat and Akhtar. I can't forget the way Akhtar bahen would go about singing 'God be with you till we meet again', with tears streaming down her cheeks all the while. For myself, I was still so overwhelmed by the loss of my parents, and losing our childhood home that I can't really say that Jabir's going away had much effect on me. In fact, it was the realization that a new friendship, new sources of affection and love were developing, that sustained me—the fact of separation didn't really trouble me. It didn't seem to matter compared to the other losses I had suffered. This new friendship was for me a source of hope and stability in a world that was otherwise shattered. We became closer together, and I began to realize that this new friendship would replace the part my parents had played in my life. He would be my refuge and hope.

Jabir left for England on 15 September [1906]. We began to write to each other, and our feelings for each other grew very rapidly! Jabir had of course long had these feelings for me, as for me, I had been too much of a child to be aware of more than friendship and liking. But now, all of a sudden, I felt I had become a woman, with a woman's capacity to love and I knew that I was madly in love with him. We'd write very frankly to each other and discuss all kinds of things, and in this way we got to know each other very well. I'd write every day to Jabir telling him about what I'd done every day, what I'd read, and what I'd been thinking about. I don't think there was anything that happened to me that I didn't write to him about, and to this day there's nothing that I'd wish to hide from him. The mail would go every week, and every week there'd be a letter from him. And four years passed in this way, and never did we miss a single week. Occasionally the letter would arrive late, but that would be on account of the post or some such thing. Our letters would be fifty, sometimes even a hundred pages long, and I lived for them.

Jabir left in September 1906, and the very same year we had to leave our beloved Somerset. Dear Amir, the memories of that separation still bring tears to my eyes. It's not that I haven't been very happy here, but oh, that house, and my wonderful childhood there... It was absolute anguish. [Parents, brothers, sisters, carefree, no responsibilities] It seems now like a beautiful dream—such a paradise for a child. Dear Amir, will you also think of your childhood in this way? If not quite as much? But may God make both your childhood and old age one of happiness and cheer and satisfaction and may you achieve all you wish for. Amen.

I had kept all the letters we wrote to each other from England and then Burma—mountains of them. Jabir would say 'What on earth are you keeping them for? Bum them for heaven's sake—bum them all!' Well, I took them to Burma and then back to Chembur, but when eventually I realized that I would never ever have the time to read all these letters, I finally took Jabir's advice, and burnt a whole lot of them—not just Jabir's and mine, but a whole lot of others. I did keep a few, which my dear Amir, will come to you all. I do hope you will read them some time because I fear that after us, they will not mean anything to anyone else.

7 March. It's now 1 p.m. I've just had lunch, and am waiting to give a new servant of ours, who's come from Daulatabad, his Urdu lesson! Till then, as if it were an issue of *Ismat,* I'll carry on with my tale.

… Anyway, to carry on; Jabir stayed in England for four years, September 1906 till July 1910.[6] I still have all his letters. Read them if you can. [Now destroyed] I was at school. We had left Somerset and were living at Retreat in Mazagon, near the Victoria Gardens, in a flat taken by Bhai Badr and Bahen Sakina. It was all right, but, after Somerset—oh God, how could we bear the dingy, dark rooms, the fumes. We could hardly endure it. I could only think of what had been, and couldn't control my tears and despair. What would I have done without school and my friends there? And, although Jabir wasn't there, there was a place for him in my heart—and then, there were his brothers and sisters, Chacha Sahib Amiruddin, his home. I got very close to them, and we would always spend Friday evening at his home, and stay on for dinner.… In April and May we would be his guests at Deonar, in the very place that we live in now.…

[Moved back to Somerset House for a few months] The house was a bit dilapidated but oh, how enchantingly beautiful it was. In those days, there were hardly any houses around, and there was a marvellous view of the sea. Oh, the garden and the spaciousness! The lovely air, and watching the sun rise and set would ravish one's soul. To see the earth stretched out before one, and the wide expanse of sky released one of a burden! It was lovely to be in dear Somerset again.… Such a strange coincidence that Shamima [Sakina Lukmani's daughter] was expected the very day Jabir's steamer was to arrive. I went to Chacha Sahib Amiruddin at nine that morning, to wait for Jabir's arrival. Bibi had got the most beautiful *jora* ready for me to wear that day, on which she had herself crocheted the border. The steamer was continually delayed and I began to get very depressed, when all of a sudden, there was Jabir. I was beside myself with joy—how would he look? How would he be after all those years away? We'd been writing regularly to each other, and our hearts were joined to each other, but how would it be now? Would we not be disappointed in the reality? How would he react to me, behave towards me? My heart was beating wildly. At last we met, our eyes met, and we felt at peace, reassured—no disappointment, just awfully awfully happy! Jabir seized me and kissed me in front of everyone, Chachanisahiba too. I wasn't prepared for this, but everyone was so excited and thrilled no one paid any attention.

And the evening was sheer paradise—everyone came to meet Jabir, and there was a dinner for him. But I could see only him! All I could think of was that after all these years, Jabir was back with me. And even now, when I think back to that time, that's all I can think of! Everyone else left after some time, but I stayed on for dinner, and when I went home to Somerset, Shamima had been born.... And then Jabir and I were together all the time. He usually came over, or sometimes I went. We were very very happy, we felt that no-one else ever had loved or could love as deeply and truly as we did. We hardly ever quarrelled or argued about anything—sometimes I'd get upset if Jabir didn't come when he'd said he would, and waiting for him I'd get cross but we'd make up very soon as it would be so clear that the delay wasn't caused by thoughtlessness.

We used to go to Malabar Hill or down to the sea, or sometimes on to the Tekri. I was a fourteen-year old, in the flower of youth, as they say, and Jabir was a 23-year-old, strong, fit, handsome, full of ardent longings and desires. His stay in England had made him eager for freedom, independence, but the West had not made him lose his own culture, his *sharafat*, his feeling for his homeland. Rather it had intensified these feelings, as happens when we encounter other free societies.

Jabir had not been able to find a job. He had wanted to farm, and applied to government for some land, but that was not an easy thing to do. He had a good diploma from Cambridge in agricultural research. And that was what he'd wanted to carry on with. He had no money—what could he do? Had Father been alive, he would of course have helped out, bought some land, but now, who was there to do so? Jabir had a debt to pay back—he struggled for months, quite fruitlessly!

Soon after Jabir came back from Cambridge, perhaps about a month later, Chachanisaheba Hamida died very suddenly. Chacha Sahib's cheerful household was also sunk in gloom. There were so many tiny children in the house whom Chacha Sahib was bringing up like his own. They felt that they had lost a loving mother! Farhat bahen was the eldest of the girls—Ashraf bahen had been married for some time. Farhat bahen had to look after the entire household. It had been decided when Chachanisaheba was alive that both Farhat and Akhtar's weddings would take place in 1911, and so would Hameed bhai's [Contractor]. They were all three married in March 1911.

And Jabir was vainly looking for a job till then, going from place to place. Thousands of applications were written, but there was no reply, no success! I was in the Matric at that point, and I suppose that after Jabir came back, I'd just lost interest in my school work. Till then, I'd almost always come first in my class, and had any number of prizes—I'd usually get three or four books as prizes, but I won't go into that now. Our Matric exams were to be in December 1910, but although I took the school exam preceding them I didn't sit for the Matric as I fell ill, with measles or something. I didn't mind too much about this as I hadn't planned to go to College, but my teachers were disappointed as they thought I'd do well. Miss Wilson tried to persuade me to take the exams next year, but I just didn't want to! Camoo Phupi sat for them and was very successful.

Bhai Badr and Bibi were able to stay at Somerset till November or December 1910. Then they gave up the Mazagon house Retreat and moved to Mr Welankar's house at Chowpatty, Ratan House, where they took the first floor on rent. This was a lovely new house, sparkling clean, in every way a change for the better. But when we first moved in, since it had just been built, there was a terrific smell of paint. Shamima was an infant and the smell affected her badly. At that time Bhai Faiz [Tyabji] and Bhabi Salima were living in her father Camruddin Latif's house in Chowpatty. It was a pretty spacious house, so they asked us all to move in with them. Ratan House and this Chowpatty house both became homes for Jabir, and they were both close to Khetwadi. So it was much easier for us to meet. We often went to what is now named the Pherozeshah Mehta Garden in the mornings and evenings, sometimes taking breakfast with us. What a lovely time that was, full of romance!

Oh, how divine is *the intoxication of youth! When even water becomes wine!*

What an enchanting period youth is! And especially if one can find one's dear love then! But I must confess that now I'm 50, I'm still a very happy woman. A lot of the passions and emotions of youth have gone, but just think, dear Amir, with what contentment and peace I am sitting here and writing all this to you. I don't in the least envy any young person, nor do I even want my youth back. I look back with pleasure, and ardent gratitude to God for all he has given me. Such a happy life I have had—and that the husband I was blessed with is still beside me, and our affection has continued unabated. It's no longer what it was in our youth, it's true, but there are other things mingled with it, which there were not before: to have lived together for so many years, to have loved each other for so many years, the companionship, the closeness—all these are very profound and important things, and only achieved through being together all one's life. Who else knows me so well, every impulse and thought of mine, as your father? Who else would care for me so greatly, offer me such comfort and support as your father? And then, dear Amir, we have you, the fruit of our lives together! May you be happy and prosperous, and may God guard you, and may you be the blessing of our lives.

I have been blest by God in this quiet existence of mine by another son—Samad. He has provided me with the boon of companionship when I've been alone and lonely. [Hopes for Amir's own bride and married life.] So at the moment anyway, I don't recall the past happiness of my youth with sadness, I recall it with joy that I had such happiness showered on me.

In December [1910] I went for a month to Punjab, to Kaithal, to visit Alma Mian and Nassoo bahen where he was posted. They had no children then. It was very difficult for Jabir and me to be parted for so long.

When I came back, Jabir had a dinner for me—the table was beautifully adorned with roses, and the dinner itself was very grand. School was over for me, and Jabir hadn't got a job, so we had plenty of time to meet! Jabir was usually at Ratan House all afternoon, and also in the evening if I wasn't going out with Bibi, which I often had to. Or I would go over to see him. We also played a lot of badminton, which was very popular with women at the gymkhana, and Jabir himself was an absolute master of it, beating everyone in sight! Parsi ladies would be dying to partner 'Ali'. He won a lot of cups too. At home in Khetwadi, badminton was usually played every day, and everyone played very well. His sisters Farhat, Akhtar and Camoo loved badminton, as did his brother Aamir, and many others. Jabir became quite celebrated for his playing. Of the Fyzee family, Azhar Fyzee was in Bombay then, and he and Jabir often played together; and trounced all their opponents.... We couldn't contain ourselves.

Your father's long series of successes at badminton are a saga in themselves, which I will recount to you some other time.... So time passed in this pleasant way. Now aged 14, I had recovered somewhat from the shock of my parents' death and was leading a happy life again.

After Farhat bahen and Akhtar bahen's marriage, Akhtar bahen went to Rangoon with Salah Mian [son of Abbas Tyabji]. It was now a question of Jabir having to earn his living, and so Salah Mian took him along to see what fortune had in store for him there. He spent some time with Salah Mian in Rangoon where he became a canvasser, doing all kinds of things, after which he went to Tavoy, to work in wolfram mining, and started a company of which Jabir was the manager. In spite of all the potential and hopes of success, there were all kinds of problems which arose which made the company fail.

To get the financing, etc. for the company Jabir came to Bombay in August or September 1912 for some months and we were able to meet again. Of course we'd been writing regularly to each other, not for a single day did I miss writing to him and he wrote frequently too. The letters would go by [weekly] mail, but we would write every day. For me, Jabir's being back was a golden moment. The wolfram company failed too, and then Jabir started his shop, with about Rs 150 left of his salary. With that he bought his goods. People had absolute trust in his integrity and honesty, and so his business grew very fast. This shop was started perhaps in 1914, and soon he was doing so well that he was determined to get married, and we did get married on 1 January 1915! [Practically the whole family was there for the wedding.]

During the wedding, Raihana [Abbas Tyabji's youngest daughter], who had an incomparable voice, Maryam [Hydari] whose voice was also very fine, Suhaila, Sharoo bibi [Abbas Tyabji's daughters], all of them sang. Raihana would delight us by singing all day. Maryam had specially written down the *Ameen*, and brought it from Hyderabad, and learnt how to sing it from her *ustad*. There was a dinner at Badr Bagh [Sulaymani community centre], and a party at Chacha Sahib Amiruddin's. Also an At

Home at the Princess Victoria Mary Gymkhana, the ladies' gymkhana, and Lady Jahangir helped a lot in arranging for the refreshments there. Just imagine, she had wonderful cakes made by her own staff, and helped Bibi in many other ways.

As for my trousseau, of course it was Bibi who did the most, and on whose shoulders all the efforts and responsibility lay, but I'd also done a lot of sewing, and then Bhabi Salima, who was at that point in Madras (Hussoo bhai was a judge there) well, she'd made all my underclothes and the household linen—teapoy covers, sheets, quilts, light coverings, etc., and also a lot of other useful little garments like a dressing gown, and so on, all very delicate and exquisite, trimmed and made gay with ribbon. Several of these things she'd made herself. I'll never forget the day when a huge wooden trunk arrived, full of all these things! I was quite overwhelmed with delight! I immediately sent a message to Camoo to say Come straight away, come and share in the excitement and joy! She came and we went into ecstasies over the exquisitely delicate and beautiful things together. I still have some of them and would have had many more if the moves to Rangoon, Tavoy, and then Chembur had not taken its toll of them. And then a lot of things got stolen when we'd gone to Europe and left our belongings in Rangoon.

After the wedding, there were lots of parties for us. We had only twelve days before we had to leave for Rangoon and Jabir himself had arrived only two weeks before the wedding. We were to leave for Calcutta on 12 January. We spent some days at Chacha Sahib Amiruddin's after our wedding, and we had the same room where Jabir and others had been born! After Zeenuth Chachanijan died, this was the room used by Camoo, Akhtar, and Farhat bahen, and where their friends came and stayed. So in fact I'd stayed in that room quite often even before my wedding. The wedding took place in an atmosphere of such love and happiness and gaiety. The affection showered on us was quite overwhelming. The last few nights before the wedding I slept with Bibi, and all my other sisters were especially loving and concerned. But most particularly Raffoo, who spent a lot to time with me, telling me about marriage and what it entailed, and also gave me some books to read about it all. We got some lovely presents at our wedding from the family—useful gifts or otherwise money. Bhai Mohsin, Bhai Faiz, Bahen Nassoo, each gave me cheques for Rs 200 [roughly Rs 60,000 in 2000]. With Bhai Faiz's present we bought a lot of books of Everyman's Library, with Bhai Mohsin's we bought a beautiful cabinet in Rangoon, and with Bahen Nassoo's an almirah and other useful household furniture. We got cheques from others too, with which we set up our household in Tavoy. Raffoo bahen gave us a sewing machine, Hannoo and Rashid Bhai a very expensive leather bag which is awfully useful. From Salman bhai we got a tea and coffee set; Hattoo bhai was in England, and we felt his absence very much. He'd very lovingly sent us an adjustable table which I still have. [From Jabir's side of the family] we got silver and so on! Farhat bahen and her husband gave us a picnic basket, and from the others we got silver or pieces of jewellery and so on. The Begum of Bhopal and her son Hamidullah gave us magnificent presents. (Now I'm tired, I'll stop here).

4 March: I was about to sit down to write again when Samad turned up, after a month away in his *mulk*. So then of course the writing was abandoned, and I listened to his account of what was happening then [in Bihar], did some unpacking, and now he's gone off to have a bath and get dressed and so I'm sitting down again to write. And I have to write to Amir too. The house feels full of life and cheerfulness with Samad's return. Now the house will resound with his guffaws and jokes, and then I'll get upset with him about something and he'll sulk, or he'll get upset with me—in fact, when he's around, I forget to be my staid and sober self!

I'm reading *Communal Triangle* with great interest.[7] It's a very good book, with a very clear and sympathetic account of the last 100 years' thinking, and the causes for the changes.[8] Amir, I hope you'll read this. Before this, I was reading Lin Yutang's *Leaf in a Storm*. The account of the civil wars in China is deeply affecting, and it's very thought-provoking. In Urdu, I've been studying Josh and Jigar's poems, and then there's an Urdu translation of Byron's play [which one?] of which I found the ending particularly good.

I'm not going to the wedding [Hatim to Maryam, daughter of Akbar Hydari]. I was terribly keen to go at one time, and Hattoo bhai and Maryam's invitations were so pressing, and so loving that we had to be very hard hearted to refuse them. But Jabir can't stir out at all, and then the state of the country and the war has deadened our hearts. How can we then take part in the happiness of the wedding party? We thought we would go together for a longer time after the wedding. So, in spite of Hattoo bhai's telegram 'Your presence is indispensable, you must come', we're not going, however hard it is to say no. [This sort of affection—how special it is].

When does one get this sort of loving demand? Alas! Well, all we could do was give our blessings and prayers for the wedding, and our fervent hopes that the bride and groom would find happiness in each other.

We spent a few days with Bibi before leaving for Rangoon—she'd taken an extra room for us at Ratan House from Mr Velankar. So far as I remember, it was on 12 January that we set out for Calcutta, from Bori Bunder [Victoria Terminus]. Acchoo bhai [Aga Koochik] had reserved for us, with a lot of effort, a first class coupe, though our tickets were for second class. So we had absolute privacy all through the journey, and very pleasant it was too! Practically the entire family came to see us off at the station, and the platform was full of them! The whole compartment and bathroom too was filled with the flowers and garlands they'd brought for us, and it was clear to everyone that it was a newly-married couple that was setting off on a journey! It was the first time I was to be separated from my family for such a long time, and I couldn't control my sobs—I wept and wept. But mixed with this sadness there was the joy of setting off with Jabir for our new life together. And when the moment of parting was over and the train drew out, I sobbed some more, and then Jabir wiped my tears away and I forgot my grief or rather my grief was transformed into joy. This is the secret of life, by which we are bound... Joy and grief are inextricably tied.

On the way we ran into a problem; we'd got something like Rs 1000 as presents which Jabir had wanted us to carry with us, tucked into our pockets! Fortunately Acchoo bhai who was much wiser and more experienced, persuaded him to put it all in the bank, save for Rs 250 which we took with us for expenses in his pocket book, which he kept in his breast pocket. And, this was stolen by some clever pickpocket at Bori Bunder. We hunted and hunted for it, but it couldn't be found—what on earth were we to do? We had no money at all! And on such a long journey, for food and drink, for everything, we needed money! And not a pie on us! Very luckily we found an old bag of mine, which for some reason had been packed in a suitcase or some baggage which was with us in the compartment, and when we opened it, we found Rs 18-0-0 inside! Goodness, how relieved we were. And with that money we got quite comfortably to Calcutta.

But there of course we needed more money. We telegraphed Acchoo bhai and got some money sent us, but the clerk objected and said he needed proof that Jabir was indeed the person who'd sent the telegram. Jabir of course got terribly anxious, and then, as in the course of the conversation, which turned to our family, Jabir mentioned that I was Badruddin Tyabji's daughter. So the clerk said 'Indeed? Then bring her here! And I'll see whether your claim is true.' So Jabir came to the hotel and took me along, and introduced me to the clerk, who took one look at me and decided I was indeed the daughter of the distinguished man. Amazing, and for me, a cause for such pride! That there should be some mark, some resemblance to my father so clearly marked in me! So clearly marked that just on seeing me a total stranger would be convinced that I was truly his daughter! ... Well, let me continue with my account of my life. So much time has passed since our marriage, that only if I have the time to think back can I summon up memories of what it was like, and then those memories come rushing back to me very vividly. Mind you, it's difficult to write about them, but I can say this, that I do hope dear Amir that you yourself find the kind of happiness with your bride that I did with your father. When you grow up, you will yourself realize what ecstasy it was for me to travel with your father, for the first time on our own. I cannot possibly describe it to you. All we wanted was to be together—so we didn't go to see anyone, though we did of course go out in the mornings and evenings to the gardens and exhibitions the city was full of, and which we visited, but we didn't call on a single soul.

After a week in Calcutta, we boarded a steamer for Rangoon. Oh, what an enchanting journey that was. The sea was beautifully calm at that time of year, and it was so wonderful to stroll on the deck in the evenings and later at night, and look at the sea—truly paradise! It was a wonderful voyage. And at Rangoon, there was Salah bhai at the dock to meet us, and we went home with him, where warm-hearted and enthusiastic Akhtar bahen was waiting to receive us. She hadn't been able to come to our wedding, so it was our first meeting with her as brother and sister-in-law! We spent about a week or ten days in Rangoon, and there was much entertainment and coming and going, and we were feted and made much of by all Salah bhai and Akhtar bahen's friends. I remember very well how Akhtar bahen would insist on my being all dressed up and loaded with jewellery when we were invited out, and there I'd be, a proper *dulhan!*

From Rangoon, we had to take a steamer to Tavoy, and then a launch. Salim [Ali] was in Tavoy, where he'd joined Jabir a few months earlier. He was then about 18 or 19, and came to stay with us. The little house Jabir took me to had been built by him, and he'd described it to me in his letters. It was the first home we had, and I was deeply attached to it. But I must admit, initially, I was rather disappointed with it! And it hadn't been properly set up. And then, it was a completely strange place, with strange unknown people. The next day, after breakfast at 8 or half past, Jabir and Salim went off to work leaving me absolutely on my own. Sattar of course was there, but at that time he too was a stranger to me, and there I was all alone. I did feel very very depressed and wept like anything!

Of course, there was the house to attend to, and I started on that, but the newness and strangeness of it all was very alarming. That my old home was thousands and thousands of miles away—oh God!

So the first weeks were rather unhappy ones, missing my family and home, though of course in the evenings when Jabir was back, it was quite different. But it was during the day, when I was alone, and saw nothing familiar around me at all, that I found very difficult to bear. Slowly I got accustomed to the house, the surroundings, the people, made friends, took an interest in the house, but I still missed Bombay very very much, and it took me a long time to settle down. This may be difficult for a man to understand, but I think most women would immediately feel for me.

Unfortunately, I didn't know the language and it was a great mistake and sheer laziness on my part not to learn it. I did try half-heartedly to learn it with some lady or the other, but it didn't work out. Had I kept a proper teacher and learnt in the correct way, I'd have found it much more interesting, and would have got on better.

I must admit, it's a terrible thing to be homesick in a distant land! Whatever beautiful things I saw or fun I had, would immediately make me miss them. It must have been very difficult for Jabir, but, dear Amir, do remember, when you yourself get married, it will be very hard for your bride to forget her own home and her family for a long time. This is a natural, normal reaction—you should not get angry or impatient. It all passes with time, and this strange new life itself changes and becomes one's routine life. Even if the romance dies out, the reassurance and ease increases, and those are the important things in life, outweighing all others.

It's all such a very long time ago now, it's difficult for me to say much more, except that after some time I began to enjoy life in Tavoy very much. People were very different from the ones I knew in Bombay, much less educated and cultured, very very different in every way—it took a long time to get used to them. At first I didn't think there was a soul with whom I could make a real friend of, who would understand me and my thoughts.

Of all our acquaintances, there was hardly anyone who could speak English or Hindustani, and if there were it was very limited. Our lives had been so different that it was very difficult for me to share in theirs, or they in mine, or indeed to sympathize with me. Nor did I understand their language or be able to speak it, or share their interests.

Of course, we were all interested in our homes and children, to a different extent. For one thing, I didn't cook myself, nor did I have children, so it was really difficult to get close to anyone. Nevertheless, these women were extremely warm in their behaviour, and certainly realized how alone I was. They'd ask me over to their homes, but because their lifestyles were so different, I didn't feel at ease, and never stayed long—two or three hours would be enough, especially since I couldn't talk to them. What a problem it was—how long could we sit gazing at each other's faces! I enjoyed their food, and would go happily to parties I was invited to, and was touched by their affectionate manner; but friendship was difficult.

The men however generally knew some English or Hindustani, so I was able to get to know some of them, and they would drop in quite often. There was one family I got to know quite well, and that was Dr Rao's who was in the Civil Service. His daughter, Amena Bai, was extremely friendly from the beginning. She'd drop in practically every day, and it was with her that I began to learn Burmese. They would insist on our going over every evening to play badminton, and as they were so close by, we'd go over, and enjoy ourselves. Then they'd give us tea and biscuits. There were several other young men and women from the Rao family who'd join us for the badminton, and there'd be a couple of others too. Gradually because of us, other Indians also began to play there. We remained good friends with them all the time we were in Tavoy, especially with Amena Bai. She missed me very much when we left, and I still remember her with great fondness.

… Yesterday Sarhan [Latif] and Najma made us very happy by admiring the house so much. They admired the guest room enormously! And it was clear, they were so happy and relaxed, they weren't just being polite! They were really very sincere. People have said that this place is like Matheran, some enthusiastic visitor said it was just like Switzerland! It was during the monsoon, everything was green, and there was water, hills, everything one could desire. A poetic soul has even called it 'Heaven'. And it's true, when I'm feeling happy, and in tune with nature, and our souls are in harmony, the strings plucked are so ravishing, so sweet, that it does indeed feel like 'Jannath'. What more can anyone want—provided that is what one wants and needs.…

I think I last wrote about our first few months in Tavoy, and our friendship with the Roy family—Dr Roy, his two wives, two daughters, son and various young cousins [kept up with them in Bombay, now living in Dadar]. Then there were some *zerbadi* families (half Burmese half Indian Muslim) whom we were very friendly with. The young people would often visit us, and Jabir would take a great interest in them and do everything to encourage them as far as education and knowledge went. Several of them were very likeable, and some of these were very keen on activities for the Jamaat. So they had founded a Madrasa Islamiya, and when I'd first gone to Tavoy I took a special interest in the girls' education there.

At one point in Tavoy we had a horse carriage—such a lovely carriage, drawn by a beautiful horse—it was great fun. Jabir and Salim had ordinary cycles at first, and then later they got motorcycles with a sidecar. On Sundays we'd usually take a picnic with us and go off somewhere twelve or fifteen miles away, into the jungle, sometimes taking books with us, sometimes with friends who'd make a big group. Tavoy is situated in very beautiful country—rivers, forests, hills, bamboo and other trees, made it enchantingly pretty. It was always lush and green, and there was constant rainfall from May till December, though the heaviest rainfall was from June till September. The average rainfall is 250 inches. There are beautiful gardens, and large rubber plantations.…

We got to know the owners of some of these plantations quite well, and Jabir had in fact stayed there several times. Jabir would go to Tavoy on his motorbike. I would of course be alone all day. There was a place by the sea called Maomagnon, that was very beautiful, very like Kihim with the same broad white sandy beach and hills around. The houses were of course in the Bunmese style. We went to stay there several times in the houses of friends, and had a very good time. Once or twice Akhtar bahen came to stay with us, and once Nadir [Tyabji], a three- or four-year-old boy, also came. She added enormously to the fun and gaiety, and then of course I wasn't left on my own when Jabir and Salim went to the office. She's such a cheerful and lively person and so enjoys things and cheers everyone up with her high spirits and gaiety. We did all the things one does by the sea—we bathed, played on the beach, went for walks—we did all that. We were after all young, and eager to enjoy ourselves. I don't need to explain—those who are young will understand what I mean! And those who have passed their youth will recollect the joys of it all!

Akhtar Bahen and Salah Mian came several times to Tavoy, and Akhtar Bahen spent a month or so with us, though Salah Mian couldn't spare more than a couple of days or so. … Akhtar bahen would teach our Tavoy friends all kinds of games, and establish very close friendships with them all. Jabir and some other young people got together to form a club, where people played badminton, and also ping pong and bridge. There would be some illustrated magazines and papers. Later on, the club was able to buy some land and build its own clubhouse, with a tennis court and several badminton courts. Unfortunately by then we'd had to move to Rangoon.

Of the Zerbadi community we were very close to Mohammad Salah and Ghani. There was also a boy from Madras, a Chillya, called Shamsi Tambi whom Jabir was especially fond of, and a Burmese barrister Maong Maongji, another close friend. We were also very friendly with a number of Chinese, in particular with a magistrate Khyan Byang and his sons.

The war had created a great demand for wolfram—the government was doing its utmost to make merchants and traders start mining it, as part of the war effort. As a result, Tavoy expanded very fast, and very wealthy people came and settled there. Trade flourished, lots of shops opened, large houses were built. There were also a number of English people who were very friendly to Jabir as far as business went, but would not come to the house, and we ourselves drew away when we realized this. After this, I never wanted to have anything to do with the English in India, although admittedly there were a couple of people who were very nice to Jabir. But that was before we'd got married. They knew he was going to marry, and said all sorts of things about what we'd do together, but that was all. We on our part did all that courtesy required, we went and called on them, but most of them didn't even bother to return our calls, and if we met them somewhere, they'd be full of apologies and excuses, which initially we were taken in by, but as time passed, and there were no invitations or calls from them, it got beyond bearing, and we were deeply wounded by this insulting and petty behaviour. And they kept up this pretence all through—till the end. The only description for it is contempt/scorn.

It took me a very long time to get over the hurt and humiliation caused by this sort of behaviour. In a strange country, making all those offers to help, then just to ignore a newcomer, to leave her to struggle on her own—what heartless inhuman behaviour. Not once did any of those ladies ask me how I felt in this strange place, in this new country, whether they could help in any way, or keep me company [and help me over my bouts of homesickness]. It's beyond belief. And then they think themselves so great and cultured and educated! Far more civilized were the *zerbadis* and other uneducated people who showed such concern and sympathy for us. They'd come and visit us, ready to help us in every way. To hell with these people's education and culture! ...

In the evening there was a function organized by Atiya Begum [Fyzee] at the Anjuman. I went with Bibi. There were samples of embroidery and needlework, a girl inaugurated it by singing a *nath*, others read or sang *ghazals,* and one lady recited her own poem, Sakina [Ilyas Muizuddin] had also brought some pieces of her own furniture. At the last meeting, we'd been told what colours and what scents one should wear in April, and what songs were appropriate, a number of people spoke about this, but there was nothing much to it. Atiya Begum spoke well, and pointed out that we must observe the colours that appear in nature at this time, and what colours does one feel like wearing in the heat—white, and pale colours, which feel cooler. And in nature too, there are at this time white blossoms, such as the *chambeli, jasmine, mogra, jooee* [varieties of jasmine]. And their enchanting smells are wafted in the air—and so it is those scents that one feels like wearing. She sang a *ghazal* by Malnya as an example of the kind of music that is appropriate. After that, a lady called Nadir Jahan suggested that people talk of their experiences, and Bahen Nazli [then Begum of Janjira] spoke about the Begum of Bhopal, and how wonderfully she made use of her time, from morning till night, and how pious she was—the truly Islamic spirit in which it was all done. Her simplicity, her knowledge, her simple way of life, saying her prayers, her conduct of state affairs, and so on. After this Atiya Begum also spoke about the same lady. But the less said about that the better.

Some time ago there was an exhibition of handicrafts at which prizes were awarded. A lady had brought along some work for which she'd been given the first prize. An amazing piece of versatility—she'd used hair to draw a portrait of her own family, an astonishing piece of skill and so unusual. The tea was served in a different room, and we got tea and some *bhajias* for four annas!

Yesterday before the *mushaira* we celebrated Iqbal Day, and that was followed by the *mushaira*. Dr Sufi Hafiz and Mahir also spoke about Iqbal's poetry, and compared him with Tagore, concluding that Iqbal was the greater poet, especially in view of the fact that Tagore's work is full of peace and repose, whereas Iqbal's arouses one, attempts to awake the sleepers. I know Iqbal's work very well, and have greatly enjoyed it, so obviously I would agree with all this. Of course, Iqbal is a wonderful poet. Hafiz also read out a comparison of Iqbal and Tagore, that was very fine. He also read a *ghazal,* and finally, from the Shahnama-i-Islam he read the portion relating the Battle of Badr, to alert and arouse us. He reprimanded the audience for their unruliness and endeavoured to maintain the decorum appropriate for a literary gathering. We were all commanded to wait for the last item, the *fatiha* for Iqbal's soul.... The *fatiha* was recited by a Maulvi sahib, as was the reading from the Quran with which the function began.

Although we liked Hafiz' reading very very much, and one cannot really find fault with the things he chose to recite, the trouble was that his wonderful moving eloquent recital left no room for any criticism at that time. But today, thinking about it, I feel that the poems he chose to recite were ones that my feelings for this country are at variance with—because I do feel that at this moment in our country's history, when unity is the need of the hour, not to mention the freedom struggle, to ignore the condition of this country was a serious shortcoming. True enough, the state of Islam, the constant focusing on the Prophet [have their own importance] but what we need badly now is unity, to forge unity at this time of subjugation, to fight for independence, and this is a matter that overshadows everything else and one really cannot take pleasure in anything where this all-important matter is ignored. So, when the memory of his magical eloquence dimmed somewhat today, I felt this lack even more strongly—if there had been a couple of poems relating to these issues, what a difference it would have made....

Mushaira at Kihim [in Amir's hand]

There was an Urdu *mushaira* some days ago in Bombay, and that set off a great deal of interest in the family, and led to Camoo Phupijan's deciding to have a *mushaira* in Kihim. It was to be on Saturday 5 May, so that those who were working in Bombay over the week could also take part. It was held in front of Camoo Phupi's house and everyone sat on the sand, while the poets came up on to the veranda and read from there. Badr Mamoo [Lukmani] presided over the *mushaira*. He read some verses from Ghalib, Zauq, and Insha. Asaf bhai [Fyzee] conducted the proceedings, called out each poet by name, and gave them a *takhallus* as well, such as Amiruddin Devnari, Iqbal Gwaliyari, Zafar *paondhujavi*, and so on. First of all Camoo Phupi read a short poem which everyone liked very much and applauded loudly. The first poets to read were the children: Waseem [Muizuddin] read a short poem which took everyone by surprise, and he got hearty applause for his effort. Then it was Amiruddin's turn, and he too was warmly applauded. Then it was Shums' turn, and he read something that was a take-off of Mahir Alqadri. Iqbal also had a humorous poem, and then when Aamir bhai [Ali] read his, there were such guffaws people couldn't stop laughing, especially the children. Both the Urdu and his metaphors were terrific, it was quite something. When Rafique bhai's name was called out, he chose to read with the older people, and his imitation of Mahir Alqadri was very good. Fehmida read a very strange poem which made everyone's head spin. Jamila read a poem written by Abu bhai [Futehally], which was also humorous.

Then it was the turn of the elders. Badr bhai [Tyabji] read a comic poem which had everyone in splits. It was very oddly composed but he read it in such a way that it all sounded right. Zafar bhai [Futehally] read a poem quite marvellously well in which food *(bakra khori, aam khori)* occurs often, and in the end, everyone goes home after a good *hawa khori* (outing). Shahinda Bahen [nee Fyzee] read out a letter to a friend. Sultana Bahen [Fyzee] read a poem, and very well. Her *takhallus* is Zafar; and she is of course a real poet. Asaf Bhai [Fyzee] read out a poem which starts 'I remember those days long past', very well composed, telling us about all the faults that have crept into our family. He recounted how nowadays people don't even want to walk at all, and when they're playing games, they're more concerned about their clothes than anything else. Halloo Khala read a poem, and Mother sang a poem she had composed herself, which everyone liked very much. Husain Mamoo's poem wasn't that great, Hannoo Khala had written a short little one, while Ilyas Bhai's poem was very fine. In it he described the beauty of Kihim, and what joy it was to leave Bombay and the drudgery of work there and get to Kihim. Sakina Khalajan also read a poem, and then, because Badi Phupijan [Faizunissa, then nearing 100] couldn't be present, Abu Bhai read out her poem.

In Tyaba Khala and Shujoo Bhai's poems the constant refrain was 'All this is God's Glory'. They were both good, especially Shujoo Phupa's. Nazir [Latif] Bhai's poem, which everyone liked very much, had a hilarious line which went:

Thinking poetry was grass, all the donkeys started grazing on it. Which was very clever, although not his own. The last poem was Rahat Khala's which she read very fast, and then Adnan Bhai read one of his compositions, a mixture of Urdu and English which made everyone laugh heartily. When the reading was over, Camoo Phupi gave us *am ras,* and some *channe* which were very delicious, and also some *chikki,* and it all went very well. The poems were far better than we'd expected, especially Waseem's (who's only seven years old) which really surprised people. When it was all over, people thanked Camoo Phupi, and made their way home.

Janab Mahir Alqadri 29 *May 1943*

This year in Kihim there was a real craze for *shairi.* There was a poet who had taken part in the Bombay *mushaira,* and it was Zeenuth Khala's idea that we should invite him to Kihim, and let him read to us. This was Mahir. He arrived in Kihim on the 13th of May in the evening. We all gathered at Zeenuth Bahen's at 9.30 that evening. Mahir Sahib has a fine voice, and everyone enjoyed the first poem he read. He is a young, tall man, with long hair. He was wearing a *churidar pyjama* and *sherwani,* and he carried a stick. Shujoo Phupa kept on calling out, '*Wah wah'* or '*Khoob, khoob'.* At eleven pm we had a short break, and we were served *sharbat* and *bhajias,* and people went and talked to him.

The poems people liked were '*Subah Baharen',* '*Ganga ka Kinara',* '*Jumna ka Kinara'.* Then he read some more. There was a very fine poem titled '*Naujawan Bewa',* which everyone liked very much. His '*Salaam'* was also quite good. In one poem it is recounted what happened to a young man from the village who went to the town. First, he used to talk to his mother; and that is described, and then what he sees when he gets to the town. He has a fight with the police, and ends up in gaol, and what that did to his mother, and her tragic end. It got pretty late, so everyone was keen to get home and to bed. Badr bhai thanked Mahir Sahib, and made a short speech, and then we all went home. . . .

Safia writes:

There has been such inflation that it's difficult to know what one can eat—thank goodness for the mangoes from the garden. For example, rice has gone up from 6 to 7 annas a *paoli* to Re 1.8 annas. The same for wheat, *bajra, jowar,* for meat and vegetables... apart from which there's such great scarcity there is hardly any stock in the shops. And as for the government shops, after waiting for hours one gets 1 *paoli*. . .

Amiruddin writes (19 June 1943):

Amma's written at such length about the Akhde Surayya that there's not much left for me to say; but I'll start off by recording those present at the meeting [account of those present]. Altogether there were [blank] people.

This is what I said in my speech:

'Madam chairman, ladies and gentlemen. I would like to say a few words about the belief that the "Good Old Days were the Best". In those days there were no trains, and certainly no big ships of the kind there are now. If one was travelling a long way, it was difficult to take much with one, and even if one went to Agra one would have been certainly looted by dacoits. Even if one reached one's destination, it would take a long time, as even getting to Poona used in those days to take a week, whereas now one can reach it by Deccan Queen in two or three hours, or even less if one goes by air. Now it's no effort to transport goods. In the old days, there were small boats which sailed from one country to the next, and they would frequently sink if there was a storm, and all the goods would be lost. Agriculture has also become much easier, there are pumps attached to wells, and even small cheap pumps can pump up three or four times more water. Earlier the farmer was dependent on the rains, and now that is not necessary.

'In the same way, we can heat our homes in the cold weather, and cool them when it's hot with fans and air-conditioners. Cinemas now have cooling systems, and so do lots of trains. It makes travelling much more comfortable.

'One great improvement is that in the old days teachers would scold and punish their students a lot, and now school boys have become so bold that the teachers don't dare to punish or scold them. Science has made such progress that even the most dreaded disease can be treated: earlier there was no cure for snake bite, and now there is proper treatment for people who would earlier have died.

*'For all these reasons, in the old days, the state of the world was [as the poet
    said]: Culture had no place in his heart
There was not a sign of progress in his steps....'*

Safia writes:
A lot of people would say how remarkable it was that in spite of mother having so many children, they were all so healthy [and well-formed]. This, the doctors would say, was on account of my parents' sober and virtuous life. On one occasion, a very wealthy zamindar from one of the states, perhaps Udaipur, whose children had all died in childbirth or infancy, went to the extent of asking for a silk handkerchief, as a kind of auspicious token, and when the next child was born, he was wrapped up in this! And he survived! When he grew up, he came to sit at my mother's feet in gratitude, and the handkerchief had been carefully preserved as *tabarruk!*

In those days, Father was known as a very gifted and competent barrister all over India. He would travel to distant places on cases, and come back loaded with praise and honours. He was also well-known in Hyderabad Deccan and was acquainted with the nawabs there. One gets a glimpse of this from the Somerset *akhbar* books, in which Ammajan and her children would write and record events. I've looked at these *akhbars,* and found some passages extraordinarily moving. Ammajan's entries are so very interesting and show such strength of mind and character. I've heard that Ustad Amir Ali used to be full of praise for her handwriting. Her sweetness of nature, her calmness—all this can be made out from her hand. Although she had so many pregnancies, her interest in and knowledge of current affairs, to make the time to read so much, and so on and so on.

All my sisters, youngest to eldest, all had such a beautiful hand—when I showed this to Samad, he exclaimed and said this was truly a copybook hand! No one nowadays writes like that. Apart from that, it's amazing to read about what those people did and enjoyed—for instance, Bahen Surayya, who must have been a 15- or 16-year-old then, went to a party and gave a very detailed account of it all. It was a grand affair, at which the wives of the Governors of Bombay and Madras were present. She recounts her conversations with those ladies. She even played the piano at that reception.

At other places, there are reference to their playing badminton or tennis, and riding, to meetings in Bombay, and going to *madrassas,* to concern for the country and its progress. And their excellent Urdu—no one nowadays speaks or writes like that, nowhere near. The trouble is that there's such a fashion for learning English nowadays, that no one has the time for Urdu, and children are left completely ignorant of their mother tongue. Fortunately people are becoming aware of this gap, and teaching their children Urdu again ...

Oh heavens above, what a narrow escape we've had! Had an awfully anxious morning yesterday, but now I'm calm again. What happened was that yesterday at about 11 in the morning I was sitting sewing near the *takht* and humming a *ghazal* of Mahir's 'On the banks of the Jumna', enjoying myself, with the picture of a lovely Indian girl before me when all of a sudden I heard a voice saying 'Is Mr Jabir Ali in?' And I saw there were three or four people there. At first, I said he wasn't, but then something about them, their expressions, made me very uneasy, so I went out to the steps and asked them what the matter was. And then they told me they'd been instructed by their superiors to get this house vacated. I don't know what else they said, but I was so very upset that I shouted out, 'My god, if you drive us out it will be terrible for us. We have spent our entire lives here! Where will we go? And what will happen to our garden, to everything? And then, look at the condition of the house—it's no palace, it's a good solidly made house. What good is it to you? And just think what it'll do to us. There's so much land around—why can't you occupy that, and build suitable housing for yourselves there? Especially homes like ours? Please please do spare us and find some other place for yourselves!'

Collier, who was in charge asked, 'How long have you been here? How long has this land been in your family?' And so on. Then he asked whether he could look at the property, but it seems my outpouring affected him so deeply that he went away without looking at anything. No sooner had he gone than I burst into tears and wept and wept. The house and garden had become so very very dear that leaving them would be an insupportable grief.

Chabootra, Deonar, c. 1940.

When I told Bibi about this, she and Muzaffar and Iqbal came over straight away, and spent about three-quarters of an hour with me, and tried very hard to persuade me to go back with them. I didn't do that, but we all had dinner together that night. All evening we were waiting tensely for the officials to return—to meet Jabir and perhaps to give us official notice to vacate! When they didn't come that evening, nor the next day, we began to relax a little bit. Jabir then went to meet Mr Collier at army headquarters the next day, and was very courteously received. Collier said, 'Yes, we have indeed got orders to requisition your place, but when I met your wife, and heard what it would mean to you, I instructed my officers that we were not to act on those orders.' May God bless him. May this misfortune never fall on us! Amen. . . .

I'd reached the stage of telling you about Tavoy quite a long time ago. I don't know, dear Amir, if it conveys anything to you. We had a small house in Tavoy, made of wood. The rooms were upstairs as was common in Burma, there was a veranda in front, which we made into a very nice one, and which looked onto the street, and towards delicate groves of bamboo, fields, and hills in the distance—a lovely view.

Leading off the veranda on one side was our room, and the sitting room which led into the dining room. Salim's room was opposite ours, and the dining room was next to the kitchen—Sattar's kingdom. He was with us all through our stay in Burma, as our cook. When he came back to Bombay with us I took him to a lot of people to learn how to cook other dishes. Ashraf bahen for one took a lot of trouble over him. Whatever his shortcomings, as they now appear, his loyalty to us was unwavering, and never once did he refuse to do any job, or let us down when we were in a crisis. Apart from cooking, he looked after the horse, did all kinds of things for the baby, even washing dirty clothes, nursed your father through his illness, worked in the garden, did everything there was to do in the house, and also cheerful. I do get irritated with him now and then, but when I think back to all he has done for us, my irritation subsides, and you too, dear Amir, must not forget to do all you can for him and for the other servants who have done so much for us, help them and their relations to get jobs, and whatever else they need.

This house in Tavoy had been built by your father when we were getting married, on land that belonged to a friend, Tajammul Husain, but the house was your father's! We bought the furniture with the money we got at our wedding, as there were only a few pieces there earlier. We had Sattar as our faithful servant, but did have a lot of trouble with the second servant, couldn't find anyone suitable till just before we left, when we had an excellent boy called Athar Ali whom we left with Salim and Tehmina when we went to Rangoon.

I've spoken about our friends the Raos in Tavoy, and there were several other *zerbadi* friends whose names I won't give here. Of our Indian friends, the closest was [Nagardas] Gandhi, who'd come to work for the Tatas in 1916, and came to stay with us by chance. In fact we had Bhai Abbas [Tyabji], Salah Mian and this gentleman together. Bhai Abbas and Salah Mian spent about ten days with us, but Gandhi was our guest for over a month. I must say something about Bhai Abbas' visit—we had a wonderful time with him, we took him to all the beautiful spots around us, we had picnics and introduced him to all sorts of people and there were parties held for him. So it was all very nice.

Safia and Mrs Nagardas Gandhi, Tavoy, c. 1916.

As for Gandhi, we took to him straight away, and by the end of the month we'd become very close friends, and still are, although alas it's not too easy to meet nowadays. You know, dear Amir, that this book was a gift from him, and he gave your father another one like this. And when you were born, they gave you a gold chain which I still have with me. We once spent about a week with them in Banaras, and they continue to press us to visit them again. We often went to stay with them in Tavoy, and once I think we must have spent a month there, they just wouldn't let us go. We had a problem at that time, as we had no servants—Sattar must have been on leave. Gandhi had a car, and they wouldn't stir out without us in the evenings. They would just insist that we join them, so we'd go out for a drive with them. He had arrived on his own, and his wife and son Inder joined him a few weeks later. At that point his wife was quite unacquainted with English manners and customs, in fact she was rather simple and orthodox in her ways.

But Gandhi had lived in England, and although he was very much a nationalist and patriot, he had no prejudices or communal feelings, and he was very keen on establishing close relations with Muslims. He became a very very intimate friend of ours, and his wife and child also—so much so that in 1917 they sent their son Inder with me to Bombay, and he spent about six months with Bhai Badr and Bibi and went to school with Shamima. His wife and I became very close friends—there was hardly a day when we didn't meet. In fact we both travelled to Bombay together in 1917, and she spent a few days with Badr and Sakina, and although she'd been brought up in such a conservative Hindu household, she adjusted very quickly to new ways—for instance, sitting at a table on a chair, speaking a little English, not too much. With me, she'd carry on a conversation in broken Hindustani, otherwise the only language she knew was Gujarati.

I've mentioned our veranda, well, we'd sit and have tea there every day. Your father and Salim Chacha would go to their shop (ironmongers) at about 7.30 every morning, and occasionally come back for lunch, otherwise it'd be sent to them. They'd either cycle down or go on the motorbike. They'd come back at five when we'd have tea together, and then go to the Club where we'd play badminton and then have a game of bridge, and get back home for dinner.

One day as we were having tea and Gandhi was with us, we noticed that there was a tall well set-up young man, dressed in Western clothes, who'd pass by there every day. There was very little traffic on the road, so we'd notice whoever was passing by. After a few days, your father and Salim Chacha said to Gandhi, 'Why don't you go down and bring him here? Poor chap, all alone in this tiny place.' Immediately, Gandhi was on his feet and went down, and soon brought this person up to us. It turned out to be a Parsi named Manekjee who worked for the Burma Trading Corporation. His manner and appearance were very pleasing and polite. So then every evening as he passed by he'd look up, and if we waved to him he'd come up and spend the evening with us, and it then became a habit for all five of us to be together. Before the Club started we used to go to Dr Rao's to play badminton, and we'd usually ask them to stay on for a meal, and sometimes we'd join them for dinner.

At Manekjee's we'd have delicious Western food, and with Gandhi, after his wife had arrived, the food would sometimes be a bit like ours and sometimes pure Gujarati. After some time, another Parsi called Hirjee came to Tavoy, whom we got to know quite well through Manekjee, and we'd meet him every day as we did the others. But he was quite different from Manekjee, and none of us liked him much. Then another Parsi called Sohrab (Tata) came to work for the Tatas, under Manekjee, who we also got to know very well, and who were pleasant people, and since there was no one else, no other relation, we became each others', and shared our happiness and our sorrows with each other.

There was a Pathan, Yusuf Khan, young, good-looking, with pleasant manners, gentlemanly, we liked him very much. Your father set up a business with him in Rangoon. Young as he was he had developed a heart problem, we accompanied him to England but tragically he died there. And that ended your father's business relations with him, because his brother, who had earlier been so very good to us, changed completely, and it was impossible for us to carry on working with him. At first, your father was doing well in Burma, and had a good reputation with many of the firms there. But as a result of working with Masti Khan, things reached such a pass that we had to leave Burma. You can hear more about it from your father.

You can see that in Tavoy we had some wonderful friends—real ones, and we spent that year very happily on that account. It's not that one didn't miss home, one did, but much less than one would have otherwise. If, my darling son, I had had you, or some other child, then I wouldn't have felt the pangs of separation from my family so much. I'd be left alone for the greater part of the day while your father was at work, and I'd have had the child for company! You can imagine how we feel, after so many years of childlessness, to have you! …

On Sunday, I finally got down to doing something I should have done ages ago. Fatima, Farid Tyabji's wife, had given me the journal she'd kept in gaol, to read through, and correct the Urdu whenever I felt it needed to be done. (Who was I to do such a thing—I feel quite embarrassed even mentioning it). Anyway, this time in Andheri my sister-in-law Mahmuda [Husain Tyabji] asked me whether I'd finished reading it. I felt very ashamed of myself, and started on it straight away, as soon as we got home. And whatever I felt needed correction (in my humble opinion) I changed. I found it very interesting—the way Fatima used her time in gaol—it was admirable. She taught some women Urdu, learnt Gujarati and Marathi from others, showed others how to sew and knit, and did a lot of other things too, I've no doubt. In any case, she got on very well with the other inmates, and was missed by them all when she left. Good for her—*shadbash!* ... [On a visit to elder sister Nasima Latifi, on Malabar Hill] went to call on Nazli Begum, at her Ridge Road house, where I'd not been before. The house is small, but built in a modern style, with a lovely view, and the bathrooms etc. are quite luxurious. We stayed and chatted for a long time, and then, I don't know what possessed me, but I invited myself over to lunch on Friday, and they were very hospitable about it. But the next day, when I went to Bhai Faiz, I learnt that Atiya Begum had behaved very rudely to Saif. And Bhai Faiz said to me that he wouldn't suggest that I should accept an invitation to a meal there. So then I felt obliged to cancel the lunch with Bahen Nazli, on the excuse that Nassoo Bahen was unwell. But I think Nazli suspected there was some other reason behind it, and she certainly was very cold to me at Badr Bagh the other day. Jabir said to me that I should have gone to lunch, that I shouldn't get embroiled in other people's quarrels, and next time I'll be more careful. That time I was certainly in a very difficult position. I hope now it'll be a long time before I run into Atiya or Nazli again. That evening when we'd gone, Atiya Begum had been very nice to me, and talked, as usual, a lot about herself. Heaven knows how much of it is true, and how much made up! ...

Asaf [Fyzee's] talk was of a new and different kind: he'd studied the old *Akhbar ki kitabs* [now housed in the Bombay University library], and talked about certain passages in them, and read them out. Since we were all descendants of Bade Dadasahib Tyabali [Tyabjee Bhoymeeah], he started off by saying a few words about him, and then read out the family tree. What a story—from such pitifully poor beginnings, to have educated himself, and then to have risen so high that his was a name respected and known in England and France!

Dadasahib wrote an autobiography in one of the *akhbar* books which is a most amazing piece. I've read it, and find it deeply moving. Asaf said he was planning to have it published. He told us about Dadasahib's children—six sons and four daughters, and what we now call the *khandaan* [family], are all descendants of those... The fifth, Badruddin, to quote, was actually the full moon which shone brightly in the sky. He'd been a very bright boy from his childhood, and did very well in school and college. Asaf read out some portions of the *Akhbar* regarding him: he was seventeen years old when he was sent to England, his elder brothers were anxious that he might be tempted to forget his own religion while he was in England, so he was made to write a statement, which is in the *akhbar* books—and which Asaf read out to the audience, in which he states that he will not give up the religion he had been born into, and various other promises.

In his school in England, he had very soon shown promise, and Chacha Sahib Camruddin very proudly stuck in the *akhbar* book a cutting from the London *Times* about a function at the Highbury Park College where the students had put on a show that a number of distinguished parents had attended. The show included a passage from Julius Caesar in English, something in French from Moliere, something in Latin, and finally another language that I can't remember [Greek?] In each of these, the report stated, 'An Indian boy, Badruddin Tyabji, took the leading part and to everyone's amazement, it was this Indian boy who was the most proficient in these languages.' And he was given a special prize in addition to all the normal ones—which is still there.

And the account of all the functions held when Father was appointed judge was written by Zeenuth (your grandmother, dear Amir) and this was read out too. Then there was an account written by Father on Urdu, or rather some portions from which it appears that although people had officially given up Gujarati and started speaking Urdu as their mother tongue, our family really had no knowledge of Urdu. So that when Father went to London as a lad of 17 or 18, he asked Munshi Nausher Ali, who had been the scholar/adviser to the King of Awadh, whom he had got to know quite well, whether he could study Arabic and Persian with him at which Nausher Ali smiled and said, 'Suppose you get down to your Urdu first!' Father said, 'But that's my mother tongue, I don't need to learn that', to which the reply was, 'What you speak is a mixture of Gujarati and Marathi, it's not Urdu. Urdu is the language of Delhi and Lucknow, and it has its own grammar, its idioms, it is a different language.'

So then Father started lessons with him, and every sentence of his had four or five mistakes! By the time he returned to India, he'd learnt this Delhi/Lucknow language from Munshi Nausher Ali Khan, and he then tried to correct and improve the family's Urdu, and told them too that it wasn't Urdu they were speaking but a *khichri* of Marathi and Gujarati!

Asaf read out to us the piece written by Father pointing out our most common faults and also setting out some rules.

He also read out some of these comically written passages from the *akhbar* books, especially the Amiri volume, which is full of them. Of Chacha Sahib Amir, he said his language was very faulty and an absolute '*khichra*' but very humorous. He read out some passages which had people rocking with laughter. Honestly, the words used! And the expressions! There were some of Zeenuth's teasing remarks, and also the account by Chacha Sahib Camruddin of '*Boobre Kan*' and '*Boobre Zubaan*' which was very amusing. It's true that two of his sons, Mirza Aqa (Akoochik) and Mirza Jan [mispronounced certain sounds] a lot. They must have gone to play with their cousins, Ameena, Sakina, Hafiza, who must have teased them and said they couldn't understand what they said. So then the youngest, Mirza Jan, went to his mother who was from Iran, and said, 'Mother they're *boobre* if they can't understand what we're saying!' At which there was much laughter, and Uncle Amir liked the word so much that he constantly used it!

From the *akhbars* he's looked at, Asaf thinks that Father's use of Urdu was by far the most correct, while Uncle Najmuddin's was scholarly and full of Arabic, and Chacha Sahib Amiruddin's full of mistakes, but very lively and humorous. Unfortunately, because we'd started late, at 7 p.m. instead of 6 [on account of a funeral at Badr Bagh] by 8.30 p.m. many people had gone, and we had to stop. There were many other interesting things to discuss, but I hope we can do that some other time.

Asaf hasn't seen the Somerset and Chowk Hall and Mahabaleshwar books—he'd have found many remarkable things in them. For one thing, one feels very proud of the way Father's young daughters and sons wrote—a most beautiful hand, and no wonder, considering Father's concern with correct writing and speech. And the way Mother wrote—it's such a great pleasure to read her pieces, and one is overcome with gratitude at having had such wonderful, such talented, such good people as parents....

Yes, in those days [1919] we'd really enjoy going to the club. We had made lots of friends by then, and I didn't feel as homesick as I used to at first. There were the Gandhis, the Manekjees, Sohrabji, Hirjee, Chinese and Japanese, and half Burmese friends. They were really like one's relations. In the morning, on Sundays, we'd take our breakfast and go for a picnic, on a motorbike, and then in our pony carriage. We had a very nice horse and a little carriage—tum-tum—which became quite a passion with us. It was really lovely. We'd take something along for the horse, such as sugarcane, and really loved feeding him with it. Tavoy was an exceptionally beautiful place—there were hills, greenery, water, very interesting surroundings; how I'd love to see it once more! But of course that's impossible. However we have our wonderful memories Jabir was really the moving spirit behind founding the club in Tavoy. And it was running very well. By the end, we'd bought some land and built a clubhouse there, there was a tennis and badminton court, and we'd play there every day. We'd have a game of bridge after the badminton, and then look at the illustrated papers. There'd be parties and discussions too. It was a very happy time, but I can't say I miss it, because I so love our life here in Chembur.

Of course, in those days we had all the vigour and freshness of youth, but many of the blessings and joys that we have now didn't exist then. For instance, Amir and Samad—where were they? And then, we have all our relations and this beloved country. I really couldn't live anywhere else. Now, I don't have that longing, no what I pray for is that I should never have to move from this beloved house till my dying day! More, I would so love to be buried here, under that shade of some tree that we have nurtured so lovingly!

In Tavoy, apart from the Club, there was also the Islamic Madrassa, in the founding of which also your father played a large part. When I first came out after my marriage, I took a great interest in this school—and would go to teach the children, and instruct them in hygiene and things like that, sewing and mending. Jabir has always felt very strongly that life was something given in trust to us, and it was our highest duty to serve our fellowmen. And my feelings have been influenced by all this. Keeping house and offering hospitality are of course a woman's main responsibilities and occupations, but at a time like this, when you consider the state of the nation, both men and women have to see it as their chief responsibility and duty to help the less fortunate, uneducated, or impoverished fellow-countrymen.

A man is not to be judged by whether he lives in a grand imposing splendid house, regardless of how elegantly it is furnished, how well-dressed he is, how many servants he has, how well it is run, no, it is by how much time, money, and energy he spends on such work. And I my-self feel that this is the touchstone of a fine man—everything else is of little value. Also, whatever we know of our country's history is from the books that our rulers have written and taught us to read—Jabir told me that I should acquaint myself with the thinking of all our leaders, and so I have bought a whole lot of books published by Natesan, and am reading them one by one. So I am slowly getting acquainted with the leaders of the Congress, their views, their speeches, and am deeply moved and influ-enced by them, so that I am now firmly with the Congress, and to see the nation free and have Indians freed from slavery is something I too have begun to long for.

When in 1920 Gandhiji had started his 'Turk Mawalat' [Khilafat] movement, and his *Young India* had begun to draw so many people to it, we ourselves, though we were in Burma, were not unaware of it. Our friend Nagar Gandhi had spent a month, perhaps more with us in Tavoy, and that was when we formed a very close friendship with him. He and Jabir would sit and discuss all kinds of things, and I'd join in too. It was then that he made us promise to take *Young India* for a year, and read it carefully. So we did just that, and were deeply influenced by Gandhiji's views. And this gradually led to the point when, in 1931, Jabir also be-came a *satyagrahi*, and joined in the ahimsa struggle. We felt at that time that if a person like Jabir did not join in the struggle, who was fit to? As for me, I had this house, and enough for Amir and me to live on, and so I supported Jabir wholeheartedly and said I would do my bit to share in his sacrifice for the nation....

Now back to my account of Tavoy. Jabir had made many friends amongst the young Musulmans there, and did his best to make them realize the importance of education and culture. Most of them had fin-ished their education and were anxiously looking for jobs, but Jabir tried to instil in them a love of learning, and lent them his books, and made them understand the importance of educating their children. Of course, the result was that a lot of our nicest books disappeared. These people were very good to us, and in times of need they were like one's close family, we shared all our joys and pleasures with them. In all my time there, although we would occasionally get bad news from Bombay, there was no really serious illness or blow to us. It was after we'd left that

Aamir bhai's death occurred, and of course my two little daughters were born in Rangoon.

Salim came to Bombay at the beginning of 1918, wanting to study at college. Jabir felt he was quite right, and since the shop was doing quite well, he agreed that Salim should go to Bombay for a couple of years or so and go to College. He'd also been keen on his getting engaged to someone while he was in Bombay, so he could get married a few years later. Salim joined the Commercial College and got engaged to Tehmina, Camruddin Latif's daughter. But when it was time for him to return to Rangoon, he insisted on getting married first. So he got married in December 1918, and then came with his wife to Tavoy in 1919. Aamir bhai, who had got married a few months earlier, came with them. He was employed in the Police in Hyderabad, but took a couple of years' leave to try things out in Burma with J. Ali and Brothers. He spent about ten days with us in Tavoy, after which we left for Rangoon, leaving Aamir bhai and Salim to run the company in Tavoy.

In Rangoon, Jabir was appointed manager of Masti Khan's firm, at a salary of Rs 500 a month. We'd planned to go to India after leaving Tavoy, as Jabir had not really had a break since, and we wanted to spend two or three months travelling and meeting our relations …

I must write about a very interesting evening we spent yesterday in the middle of our humdrum life. Asaf and Sultana [Fyzee] have founded a circle or group of Urdu lovers to give them a chance to meet and discuss Urdu writing. It will meet once a month, and one person will talk about a book, and this will be followed by a discussion. They intend to have about twelve or thirteen members, who will have to speak on a book once a year. Only members' spouses will attend—no-one else will be allowed.

Yesterday we had our first meeting at Asaf's, at Ahmed Manor, Warden Road. There were, apart from Asaf and Sultana, Mahir Alqadri [the poet], Professor Nadvi, Agha Kashmiri [playwright] and Khurshid [his wife], Mrs [Camar] Ahmed, Sajjad Zaheer and his wife, Shahab Sahib,[9] Jafri Sahib, Kaifi [Azmi], and a few others whose names I'm not familiar with. It was decided we should meet on the last Saturday of each month. Shahab Sahib spoke wonderfully on the biography of Maulana Abdullah Sindhi, by Professor Almohammad Sarwar. After giving a brief account of his life, he discussed his views which are presented in the book, quite beautifully. Unfortunately, we ran short of time so there wasn't much time for a discussion. We should have left at 7.30 to get our bus from Sion, but Samad couldn't bear to leave, so we stayed on till 8. We left with Nadvi sahib and greatly enjoyed his company, and then thank goodness, got a bus at Sion station so we were home by 9.15. It would be wonderful if this circle really gets properly established—I'd enjoy it so very much....

We went to Rangoon in June 1919. We first lived in [blank] which was owned by an Anglo widow. She lived on the ground floor, and we were on top. It was a lovely spacious house, a little off the main road. It had a pleasant garden, there were two large bedrooms with bathrooms, and a separate dining and sitting room, with a small veranda in front and at the back. We stayed in Rangoon till 1924, and I made several trips to India during that time, as well as one to Europe, I never stayed long in Rangoon at one time, and never really enjoyed it, for various reasons. We were very happy in Tavoy, but in Rangoon over five or six years we were visited by one disaster after another which quite broke my heart. If it had not been for Jabir, I would never have survived—life would have been one of hopeless despair....

Gandhiji was released from prison on the [blank]. He is now living in Juhu. He is better but not well. Who knows whether his efforts [barkat] will bring any relief to this nation.

Amir writes:

19 June 1944 I got back for the summer holidays on 24 April. It was decided about then that we would have a *mushaira* here on 4 June, and Amma and Ustad Sahib had planned and made a lot of preparations for it. For each person they'd chosen a certain poem or ghazal, and the person was to act the part of the poet who'd written it. Before the *mushaira* we'd gone to Kihim and had a lot of fun there too. I was there from the 5th, Amma came on the 15th, and we went back to Bombay on the 27th.

Father also came for a couple of days. One of the amusing things that happened was a play based on Shaukat Thanavi's 'Allahabad ke amrood'. It was very funny, and people laughed and laughed. I was Shaukat. Rafiq bhai made a long speech in the beginning, and praised our company to the skies. Not that he's a great one for self-advertisement, but he was really terrific that day, and then each one of the players was so good, that everyone in the audience was really astounded. And lots of them just rolled about on the sand with laugher! Before the play there was lots to eat—now let me think what there was: there was *sharbat* and *biryani,* and we had lots of fun.

Well, we got back from Kihim, and then the preparations for the *mushaira* were in full swing again. How many people would there be? What would we offer them to eat? Everything was debated carefully. Ustad Sahib, who had been away for the vacation, came back on 31 May, Amma wasn't feeling well, she had a temperature, so Camoo Phupi came with the others on Saturday evening to help out, and did a lot, and [other relations] also came and helped in various ways. All the arrangements had been made for the seating and other things. And then we got a number of phone calls from people to say they couldn't make it, and we wondered for some time whether to cancel the whole thing, but eventually decided to go ahead with it. Amma was much better, and Mukhlis bhai and Aziza Apa came and helped out. So everything was organized, and what organization!

When the *mushaira* was to start only five or six people had arrived, so we had to wait. Well, that sort of thing was only to be expected. But slowly people trickled in in the way the tide flows in. [Some others] had come early to help out. By a quarter past six, a lot of people had gathered, and Amma had also come down. It started with Asaf bhai, who was the Master of Ceremonies as well as Iqbal, reading a portion from the 'Falsifa-i gham.' He read in a clear loud voice, very slowly, like a stream which had come down from the mountains, and was slowly trickling down into the plains. Ustad Sahib described his dream, which is to say, all the poets in the *mushaira* are long dead, and wondering what on earth is happening here. Really, if only one could have such dreams every day! Abu bhai hadn't yet come, so Badr bhai, that is Mir Taqi Mir, read his *ghazal.* At first we couldn't make out what had happened to his voice, and then we saw that he was halfway between reading and singing the poem. Iqbal who was Nazir Akbarabadi read out a poem with great feeling. Sometimes he'd leap into the air, and sometimes he'd wave his hands about, and sometimes very softly, sometimes shouting out aloud, anyway he read with great passion. By then Shujoo bhai had arrived, and he read something of Sauda's. Mukhlis bhai was Nasikh and absolutely the epitome, the soul of Nasikh, with a huge beard and absolutely the right style and behaviour. He made us laugh till the tears streamed down our cheeks, and our

tummies ached. Haloo Khala was Mir Dard, she read out a poem which
we could barely hear.

After that the lamp was placed in front of Ustad Sahib, or rather
Chakbast, who wasn't slow to praise himself. He made us all laugh like
anything, and made it clear that Chakbast was the only poet of any note.
Next came Zauq, in the shape of Mohsin bhai [Tyabji], and read some
of his poems to us. The same work of which it has been said 'Such lofty
thoughts that they seem to be plucked from the heavens.' Then the same
Mohsin bhai assumed the garb of a Lucknowi poet and became Hasrat
Mohani, and it was said that 'Oh, he's changed his caste' [i.e. from Delhi
to Lucknow].

Then came Ghalib, that is Sakina Khala, the poet of whom it has been
said [by Iqbal]:

*Through your poetry you showed us how high the bird of imagination
can soar.*

Khalajan's voice is no longer very strong, but she read well, and people
were moved by it. Amma read sitting down, but read very well, and in a
very moving way. Momin was Ilyas bhai, and he was really every inch of
him Momin—down to the hair, the moustaches. The children couldn't
contain their laughter, and the elders too were very amused, as if Shoukat
Thanavai's.... was being read. He was wagging his head, and singing away
as if to outdo Tansen! Nassoo Khala read a poem of Jigar Muradabadi,
but sitting down. Zafar bhai had chosen his own poem and he was Akbar
ilahabadi.... He read it very well. Then Babajan read that very famous
poem of Insha's 'Kamar bandhey ho'. He'd tried very hard to find appropriate clothes but hadn't been able to get either the *joothis* or the *sadri* or
the right kind of *pagree* [shoes, jacket, turban], or anything. But anyway,
he read well. 'Kamar bandhey huwe' was a... ghazal. Then came Nasreen
bahen, who sang Anees' 'Subah ka Sama'. She'd said she didn't want to
read a *marsia* and sadden us, because after all we were in a heavenly place,
and so she read this out.

Zeenuth bahen, who read something of Hali's, started laughing
and couldn't control herself but anyway read well. Nafisa came next, as
Anand Narain Mulla, and read a very passionate and moving poem very
well. Sultana bahen was Dagh, and very appropriately dressed in black

sherwani, with a black cap, everything just right, she read a *ghazal* beautifully. Shahinda Khala read out a poem of her own, which she sang very beautifully, and people applauded and encored it. Rahat Khala was Surwar Jahanabadi, and read at the speed of the Deccan Queen. When Asghar Govindvi was called out, people started laughing, and so did Hannoo Khala, who was Asghar. She didn't make too many gestures, but she read well. But when Vazir bahen got up, and it was commented that 'Hafiz Jalandhari used to be thinner', she got very embarrassed, and didn't read well after that.

Then I came on as Josh, and read '*Kisan.*' I had learnt it by heart, but kept the paper in front of me when I read it out. Rafiq bhai was Ahsan Danish. He was a bit nervous because the written version of the poem he was going to read was with Zeenuth bahen, and she'd come late, so Rafiq bhai read very fast, but well.... Ustad sahib read the Hamd of Naseem, and said he'd come now as a Kashmiri Pandit. Then what do we see but Salim Phupa as Nasir Bumbavi, and he then read a poem which was full of English words, which everyone enjoyed very much, and he was made to read a lot of it all over again. There were lots of words that he found difficult to pronounce but it all added to the fun, as it was that kind of poem.

Oh yes! I haven't written at all about the children's *mushaira,* which went off very well. It was held before the adults', Shums read out the Hamd, quite confidently, and everyone was quite pleased. Mian Farhan when he entered the field was so nervous that for a good five minutes he fidgeted about, pulling at his pyjamas, and then when he started, my goodness, it was like a mail train shooting through a tunnel. Not many of us could understand what he was saying, but we all laughed a lot. Rashiduk was also very frightened but he gave us all a lot of pleasure and read something or the other. Hasan and Fari presented a dialogue which was also quite good. Hasan was a star and Fari a child. Rabbi read 'Our Country' very well, in fact as well as Shums, Sadiq and Waseem did the conversation between the fox and the crow quite well, except that poor Sadiq kept on forgetting his words, and having to look at his paper which was quite difficult to do. Jamila read Iqbal's *Noya shuala* very well, but she had a bit of an argument with Hali (Zeenuth) over which passages she should stand up to read out. Then Rummana and Razia had a dialogue which was also quite good.

So the *mushaira* was really quite a success—there were sixty people present, and they were all quite happy over it. We gave people mangoes which had been kept in ice, and they all enjoyed themselves. Hasan had 13 mangoes! They left about 9 o'clock. ...

On the 17th, that is Saturday, there was a Fancy Dress party at Somerset Lodge, and by that time we'd had the good news that Aamir bhai had got a First in the BA, and come first in English. The fancy dress was fun, except that no one knew quite who the others were. So there were some problems. ... Some people had taken a lot of trouble: Sultana bahen was a balloon seller, and had such a wonderful mask that people were very amused by it. Surayya bahen was a scarecrow, and a very lifelike one. Rafiq bhai came as a sadhu, Muqbil bhai as a bearer (?), Adnan bhai as a Parsi, and they were all very well got up. So was Mohsin bhai, and Ilyas bhai as Jahangir. I was Don Bradman. It started at 9.30 and went on till 12, and we really didn't know that the time had passed.

Safia continues:

These days I can think of nothing but my parents. And, as the poet said, 'Your face, your smile, your way of talking, your graciousness, munificence'—are always before me. I have been reading their letters to each other, and their biography, and whatever I'm doing I'm wrapped up in their world, and my heart is full of my love for them, and my adoration. For me, they are not less than gods, I would say they were God if it were not for fear of the Shariat.

Yesterday, 23 November, the function to commemorate Shibli was held in the Anjuman-i-Islam, organized by the Anjuman-e-Taraqqi Urdu. It was presided over by Bazlur Rehman, and the programme began with a speech by Zakir Husain, oh, first of all, Shahab Sahib read some *aiyats* from the Quran, and then Atiya Begum was invited to speak, as she was so close to him, had known him so well, all I can say about her talk was that it was indescribably awful—we were all embarrassed beyond belief, as she was just so full of herself. Saghir Nizami recited a very passionate poem of Shibli's *'Mareez e Europ, Turki'*, to a *raag*. Shahab Sahib's talk was also very good; [a lot of people from the family attended, including Faiz Tyabji's entire family-all three sons and two daughters-in-law, Asaf and Sultana Fyzee and the rest]... Oh, Somerset House! Come, dear Amir, let me attempt to describe to you the greatly loved, the beautiful, and I think quite incomparable house of my childhood. Oh, just the mention of it sends me into transports. I'm no longer in this world, it seems to be paradise itself—Really, one thinks of the saying 'This is Paradise, this is Paradise, this is it!' But this kind of poetic emotional language, if I give it rein, what will it convey to you?

If you were to see my father through my eyes, then you will see a man who was peerless, quite like an angel. My mother; his 'Exquisite Pearl', how pious and meek, so competent, an incomparable wife and mother! In this magical place my brothers and sisters were like happy fairies. This is truly how I think of my childhood. Gracious and loving parents, who showered on us all that we wanted—not a wish that was left unfulfilled—a lovely home, with a wonderful spacious garden, with so many brothers and sisters of my age to play with, whatever we wanted to eat, lots of lovely clothes, what more can a child want? Worry or anxiety was unknown to us, there were servants galore, horses and a carriage, faithful retainers, who were loving and loyal to us—well, anyway, now I'll talk matter-of-factly, without any poetic exaggeration.

Somerset House was a very large grand mansion in the old style. It had an imposing and beautiful staircase, it was very spacious, with long wide verandas, and marble floors. In the front veranda, on one side as one came up the stairs, there was a large *takht*, and a large round table, on which were ornamental objects, vases and so on. In another area there were sofas, chairs, tables, etc. Ammajan used to spend most of her day here, and so did Babajan when he was free. This is where the children gathered too, whenever they could, and visitors were received. There would be the papers, and other books, and we'd do all our sewing and mending sitting here. This veranda led on to the drawing and dining rooms. I'll do a little plan of the veranda and these rooms: [Blank] Above this there was a large room that was Ammajan's, this had its own bathroom and veranda. Father's room had a large terrace in front of it, and his own bathroom and dressing rooms.

Adjoining Ammajan's room there was another large room where first Bibi lived, and then it was used by Surayya Bahen and her children. There were two bathrooms, and then another room on the other side of Mother's, which opened on to a gallery which led into two rooms, one above the other, which were for ages used by the younger brothers such as Hattoo bhai. Upstairs too, there were verandas on all sides, and there were several other rooms below, which were used as guest rooms.

On the ground floors, there was a big room near where the big *takht* was—and a staircase led up from there. Adjoining this there was another room which at one point was the bagatelle room and off this there was yet another office room which Bibi used a lot, and which was both our library and the office. It contained a couple of large tables. Passing through that one reached Father's office room, and beyond that there was another room which was for ages Salman bhai's. Each of these rooms had its own bathroom. Goodness knows how many bathrooms there were! Countless! The back veranda looked on to a garden, not that great, which had different kinds of crotons, and some fruit trees and creepers.

Next to the kitchen there was a quarter for the *darzi* where our Nanhoo *darzi* worked day and night at producing all our clothes. He was lame, but a very very skilled tailor. Next to his quarter, separated by some open ground, were the stables, and quarters for the coachmen and syces and so on. Goodness knows how many there were, because they all lived there with their families, and there were ten or twelve of these people! And then the stables—there were usually eight horses there—one pair that was for Father's own use, one for Mother. What I remember is that it was a pair of chestnuts, with a splendid harness *(ban-than kiye)*, very handsome, very fast, that were Father's, mother had a black pair, Duldul and Ilmas, and there was one big Australian pair. As one horse began to age, he'd be replaced by another.

Anyway, when we were very little, meaning about four or five [c. 1899] Somerset Annexe was built. This was very like Somerset Lodge, and this is where we children moved to. There were six bedrooms, with bathrooms and verandas. From what I remember, one room was occupied by Bibi and Bhai Badr (and their children); one by Bhai Husain and his family; the third by Bhai Faiz, Bahen Salima and Saif (but only for a short time); the fourth, on the second floor, was for me and my small sisters, Nassoo, Hannoo, Raffoo, and when Nassoo and Raffoo went away to England, there were only Hannoo and me, and when Hannoo got married, then Fittoo, Surayya bahen's daughter, moved in to sleep with me. The other two rooms were guest rooms, and there was always someone or the other there—never were they empty: Bhai Mohsin and his wife, Jamila bahen, and Halloo bahen with their husbands and children were constantly coming to stay. Other relations would come and stay too, your own grandmother, Amir, [Zeenuth] spent several months here and in Matheran and Mahabaleshwar with Salim.

In front there was a very large *chaman* [flower garden] laid out very beautifully with flower beds, in which all kinds of flowers bloomed, and the most wonderful seasonal flowers, which were very rare in Bombay in those days, and which were ordered from abroad. And of course, there were roses and dahlias and flowers of that kind. Fine sand and gravel was spread all over—it would come in cartloads. And whenever there was a pile of fine soft sand left lying somewhere, we'd have a wonderful time playing, sliding about in it. All around this garden, there was a circular drive, which then led up to the stables. On one side of the flower garden there was the gymkhana, which was like a park, with huge trees, and benches and chairs under them, and sanded paths, there were two badminton courts, and a croquet course, grass slides, of the kind there are at Camoo Phupi's, but much much longer, on which we used to slide a lot, because it was on Somerset Tekri. Well below the badminton court was the tennis court, with steps leading down to it.

This gymkhana was itself one terrace lower than the house, and the tennis court was two terraces down. From there, a path led to the Tekri, which we called the Big Tekri, and then, following paths like those on the hills, we emerged on to the Chhoti Tekri, where there was a little pavilion, such a sweet little pavilion! Between the two *tekris* there were all kinds of things—an orchard, a fernery, a rock garden—Jabir says that the Somerset House garden would have been about seven acres, and then of course where there is now Somerset Cottage and Somerset Lodge—well it was all Grandfather's, and the houses he had made. I remember very well the bit where Somerset Lodge now stands—they used to grow cucumbers and maize there, and there was the well, and the *dhobi ghat.*

One *dhobi* wasn't enough for the household-just think how many people there were living there. Let me try to count: first, there were Father and Mother and all their children; if the children were married, then their husbands or wives and children! Farid bhai and Salim bhai were six or so when they left Somerset House; and Fittoo was much older. Salah Mian was also here for many years, on account of school; Sharoo bibi would often come, and then of course there were the guests! There were forty servants—just imagine—about eight *malis,* probably about as many coachmen and syces, about six *mashawls,* goodness knows how many mamas—each one of us had their own! And then there was the cook—and the two or three kitchen boys working under him, the butler, and those serving at table, all these were house servants. Then there was Father's old Munshi Hari Rai who served Father for many many years, and then the official *chapprassis (chobdars)* who were attached to him, perhaps four of them, and they'd be in red coats, and one or two *pattewalas* (peons) and the other boys. I remember Bhao and Pandu.

Ustad Amir Ali would live with us, and give us lessons every day. He had his own room. What I remember of my childhood is being taught my *alif bey pey* by Ustad Sahib, and then when I began to learn English, Bibi would look at our lessons every day and help us. All of us had our desks in the big front veranda where we kept our books.

We'd play badminton before breakfast, and then after breakfast, we'd do our school work sitting at these desks in the veranda. The carriage would take us and bring us back from school every morning and afternoon. When my sisters had all gone away, and only Fittoo and I were left going to school, we'd give lifts to other children who lived nearby, which they still remember even now. Dhunbai and her sister Shirin were among that group, and then we'd have great fun playing together in the evenings.

At one time, there was a music teacher for Nassoo, Hannoo, and Raffoo bahen. Fittoo and I would watch and listen to them, and pick up a lot of the songs. Ammajan was very fond of music, and would teach us a lot of poems and make us sing them. Then, when we began to read we would all of us take a book each and go and sit in the garden with it. When I started going to school, I think Mother was probably anxious that we shouldn't forget our Urdu, and so she'd make us sit by her and make us read delightful stories aloud to her, and so that we shouldn't forget how to write, we had to write to our brothers and sisters. And when Father was away in England, we would write to him every week.

We also first learnt to sew from our mother—I remember so well sitting by her and making pretty little bags. We'd have to do a bit of sewing every holiday to keep in practice. In the holidays, we'd have a lot of fun, but we were always told, 'Enjoy yourselves, but do a bit of work too!' Father didn't have the time to supervise our homework every day, but he liked us to go in from time to time and ask his help. And if ever we did, he'd explain things so beautifully, that it would forever be engrained in our minds. Never did he speak harshly to us little ones–he was extraordinarily gentle and kind to us. Of course he inspired great awe in all of us—and there was no question of our disobeying his slightest command. We believed firmly that whatever he said was for our benefit, there was no question at all of his ever being unfair or unjust. We were all deeply imbued with and influenced by his character and values—for us, there was no one in the world like our Father. Our Mother's character and personality was also so clearly stamped by our Father's, that I always thought of them as one! I'd never for instance seen any sign of disagreement or quarrelling between them (although I imagine there must have been) but, because we never saw it ourselves we felt—Oh, these people are one! The same tastes, the same values and absolutely an instance of [Persian couplet] 'You are me and I am you.'

One year, perhaps 1904 or 1905, when we were in Matheran, Father gave us a lecture on Urdu grammar. Every morning, after our walk, we'd be asked to gather in the sitting room, and he'd explain the basic principles of grammar to us, and tell us about our most common mistakes, and how we must now correct them. So we got into the habit of pouncing on each other, and we had a lot of fun doing that, and we did improve the way we spoke a great deal. There were some Gujarati words in particular that had crept into our language. He was very particular that these should not be used—one of these words was 'apan'. Father told us that if ever he was caught using the word, he'd pay a fine of five rupees—and three for other mistakes. One afternoon in Matheran, when he was playing whist, they had a splendid win, and he turned thrilled to his partner and said, 'Well, haven't we *(apan)* done well!' Or something like that. I pounced on him (I was watching the game which I'd loved since my childhood) and said, You've used the word 'apan'! I still remember the way he smiled at that (what beautiful lips and teeth he had) and acknowledged his fault, and I got my five rupees, which I wrapped up carefully in a cloth and put away, but somehow it got lost. What a victory that was for me! ...

10 December: Yesterday, 9 December, was a very auspicious and also successful day, we celebrated Badruddin Tyabji Day, and remembered our dear Father and Mother, and recollected all their wonderful qualities and prayed that all their descendants should act according to their sincerity and integrity and their love of the community and nation, by their virtuous and noble lives.

The morning of the ninth, Vazir and Shafiqa and I were hard at work from 11 am onwards to make the downstairs room [at Somerset Lodge] ready for the function. Both my dear nieces worked so willingly, within hours the room had been fittingly prepared: in front, there were carpets spread out, and two large imposing chairs for the President (Alma bhai) and the speaker (Bhai Husain), and there were stools next to them, and I sat on one of them, as if I were the organizer of it all. Everyone had been told to come early, so we were able to start punctually, on the dot of six. We had placed all kinds of things on the dining table, all the scrolls of tributes with their silver or sandalwood boxes, the letter from the Sultan of Turkey Abdul Hamid, in Turkish, together with a letter in Arabic, and a gold medal with *tughras* [finely calligraphed inscriptions].

Then there was the tie he had last worn—he had of course died in England—and his glasses, the collar Mother had crocheted for him which he used to wear with his judge's robes, and for which she'd won a prize, the *akhbar* books, and all sorts of other things. People looked at all these things with great interest, but in particular Nadvi Sahib and his wife were absolutely fascinated by the *akhbar* books, and are terribly keen on studying them all and writing about them.

The function in celebration of the 100th birth anniversary of Badruddin Tyabji, with Alma Latifi presiding, started with a few words from him, and then Ilyas Muizuddin recited a poem by Phupijan Faizan (over 90 years old); then various messages were read out, by Safia, from Bhai Badr and Bahen Sakina, Bhai Hamid and Sharifa, Salman, Hatim and Mariam; Badr and Surayya; Afzal and Muzaffar; then there was an announcement that Hamid bhai and Sharoo bahen were donating Rs 1,000 for a library and bathroom at Badr Bagh; then followed Safia's speech; Husain Tyabji's talk, and a short concluding speech by the President. Actually, I'd asked Asaf to read a few *ayats* from the Quran, but at the last minute he got out of it, and Raihana, who was to have ended this meeting by singing the national anthem was down with a temperature and couldn't come.

There were about 80–90 people who'd come, of the friends, there was Pakvasa [Mangaldas] (President of the Assembly); Brelvi; Wandrekar, Vaikunt Mehta [important members of the Congress Party]; Professor Nadvi and his wife; Miss [Piroja] Narielwala, Shahab Sahib, Harris,[10] and others. Of the family practically everyone had come, young and old, of my brothers and sisters we especially missed Bhai Badr, Bibi, Bhabijan Mahmuda, Halima bahen, Salman bhai, Hatim bhai, Maryam, and all the other relations who couldn't be present.

As far as time went, the function was very successful—it started on the dot of six and finished at eight. Alma bhai was quite good in the chair—might have been better. Ilyas recited the poem rather well—but, in my humble opinion, Bhai Husain could have done a better job of speaking about Father, which would have meant much more to the audience. What he did was start by recounting all his virtues, and claimed that he was one of India's great leaders. It would have been far better if he had related some of the events in Father's life, and read out portions from his speeches. And then brought in what people had said about him, and read out some of the outstanding appreciations of him. People both in India and England thought so very highly of him, that he could simply have used their words instead—how much more effective it would have been! Anyway, the concluding section was better, and the disappointing beginning was forgotten, although really I can't say it was a good talk, since we had all expected so much from him. If only he had written out this speech, then he would only have said the things that were necessary, and not left out other important things. Unfortunately, he both left out things and talked too much about less important things.

My own brief 10–12 minute talk went down so well I was quite amazed. People came and congratulated and thanked me with such warmth and sincerity I was taken aback. Practically everyone was full of praise—brothers, sisters, nephews, nieces, Nadvi sahib, Shahab sahib, said such things, that I can't possibly write them down here—Amir, you'll think I'm exaggerating! They said, in their wonderful tongue, full of exquisite phrases, 'but you have fulfilled a daughter's duty quite marvellously!' And what beautiful language and expressions. Miss Narielwala said 'What beautiful Urdu! I loved your speech!' and the children also came up and said nice things in their own way, of which Hasan's was the most touching. He came to me and holding my face in both his hands, he said, 'Safkhab, what wonderful things you told us about. I could have listened to you for hours!' I was very moved by this.

Saif came up to me and said, 'Phupijan, you've saved us Tyabjis' honour'....

Amir writes:

9 June 1945 Good heavens! What a long time has elapsed without a single thing being written in this book! And now I have to write an account of what happened during this period. Now I have to think back... On 12 March, Mother went to Andheri because Hannoo Khala wasn't feeling too well. She came back in the evening on 16 March, and that very day I started working in Nazar bhai [Futehally]'s factory.[11] I started off by learning how to do basic carpentry. I came back on the 17th. We then decided that I should go every Monday morning, stay there till Wednesday evening, return on Thursday morning and stay in Andheri till Friday evening. On Saturday evening Hasan [Tyabji] came over, and Abdullah and Adam were also here. We played cricket and then we decided to have a proper match the next day. On Sunday Rabbi, Rashidak and Farhan came to spend the day. We made boats, told stories, and played games. In the evening the others turned up, and we had a game of cricket. Hasan and Rabbi and Rashidak also took part and so did Nazar bhai, who'd come with Shamima bahen to fetch the children. The next day Hasan went to school and I went to Andheri.

So the time passed in this way—I'd come and go from Andheri, and we'd have cricket matches on Sundays. Oh yes, one thing I must mention is that one day Mamoon [Lukmani] took us to the place where they were shooting the film 'Humayun'. We saw the wonderful sets of the palace and the gardens, and got some idea of the tremendous hurdles that have to be overcome in the shooting of a film. It was a pity though that no-one explained to us what these things were and how they were made.

A few days later there was a meeting at Blavatsky Lodge to celebrate the centenary of Nanasaheb (Badruddin), to which most people from the family came, and there were a few outsiders as well. Mr Kher, Nagindas Master and some others spoke. Some people were quite happy with the arrangements but others were very critical and said it was very badly organized, and that there had been no publicity at all. Then one day Dr Zakir Husain came to Somerset Lodge and spoke there about the Jamia. Practically the whole family had come. He spoke so beautifully, and his language was so forceful that people were deeply impressed. I had myself never heard anyone speak so wonderfully.

Soon after that I stopped going to Dynacraft. Apart from some carpentry, I'd learnt to use the lathe, and then at least I learned how to use the *karwatr randa*, and various other tools, and got some practice using them.... When in Andheri, I used to go to Juhu with Zafar bhai for a swim—we'd cycle down and have a lot of fun. In the factory I got to know some people pretty well: there was a man called Patwardhan, and amongst the workers there was Ramnath who worked on the lathe, and the carpenter Keshav. In the afternoons I'd read, and in the evening we'd play games. So altogether it was a great time for me and we had a lot of fun.

... On the 1st of April, at Alma Mamoo's [Latifi], Sajjad Zaheer spoke about the beginnings of Urdu. He didn't speak too well, and especially after Zakir Husain's talk, it seemed pretty feeble.

Kihim is drawing near, and soon, the boys from Gwalior will also arrive. We've been to Bombay a couple of times, and visited Asaf bhai and Faiz Mamoo. The war in Europe seems to be ending, and people are talking about what will happen next. One day when we were spending the day with Mukhlis bhai, there was a rumour which turned out to be false, that the war was over. [We] plan to go to Kihim on 7 May.

Oh, I completely forgot to mention a trip to Wadowlee with Mr Reuben and his family, where we spent the whole day and had a lovely picnic in a very beautiful spot. There is a house which some cinema-owner has now bought, and we had a great time eating and drinking and playing games. On the 25th Mr Khanolkar and the Bombay group got back from Gwalior, and I went to meet them. Father has now started going to Poona to advise on some farms there, and he says it is a very beautiful place. He'd also gone to Nizamabad for a week at the beginning of April. Now everyone is setting off for Kihim and there's hardly anyone left in Bombay.

(23? June) On Saturday Daniyal bhai [Latifi] spoke to us about why he had joined the Muslim League. He spoke in English. But most people disagreed with him, and there were many things he said that he really didn't know much about, and also he had some views with which people disagreed quite violently, and thought quite wrong, such as the necessity of creating Pakistan. He said little that could justify such an act, or give good reasons for it, and as a result people became even more opposed to the idea. But there's no doubt that he didn't attack his critics, and when people attacked him, he was not at all perturbed, on the contrary, he said that on this issue, we need more light and less fury. It happened to be my birthday that day, so I got a lot of presents, and also ten rupees, my first salary, for teaching Iqbal [Lukmani] mathematics. The following day, on Sunday, there was a meeting at Dadar at which Pandit Jawaharlal Nehru spoke, to which I went with Father. It had been raining, so it ended rather late. The meeting was held to hoist the flag, and he spoke about that, and also why we refer to Bharat Mata, and he also spoke about the sacrifices people had made in the three years he'd spent in gaol, and about the courage they had shown. That evening, Sakina Khala's family had dinner with us.

[Date?] Sofia writes:

It's quite impossible writing in this book with ink. I'm going to copy out something from a book *We took to the Woods*. It's the answer to 'Is it worth while?'

'So after all, why should we bother to go outside? There would only be one reason, to see our friends, and our friends come here instead... So if they are willing to put up with my off-hand meals for the sake of lounging around in their oldest clothes and being free to do and say what they please, if they are willing to swap their own good beds for our not-so-good ones plus a lot of excellent scenery and fishing; if they want to take the long involved trips with nothing much at the end except us and the assurances that they are very much more than welcome, why, that's the way we want it, too. And that's the way we have it. ... I know that many people and perhaps most people couldn't feel that living here, they held within their fist all the best of life. So for them it wouldn't be the best. For us, it is. And that's the final answer.'

Louise Dickinson Rich

People may recount tales of bygone days,
But the days of my youth, how will they ever return?[12]

5

Letters from Europe: 1870

Amiruddin standing right, with brother-in-law Shaikh Fatehali seated
left, elder brother Najmuddin seated right, British partner in the middle.
Havre, 1870.

Amiruddin Tyabji (1848–1917) was the youngest of the six sons of
Tyabjee Bhoymeeah. Like most of his brothers, he entered into the family
business after being educated at school and university in England. He
may not have been a particularly successful partner in the family business
initially, but after his return to India became a dearly loved and extremely
responsible member of the joint family.

The Changing World of a Bombay Muslim Community, 1870–1945. Salima Tyabji, Oxford University Press.
© Nasir Tyabji 2023. DOI: 10.1093/oso/9780192869746.003.0005

Having eluded all the charming young women with whom he flirted in his early youth, he lived up to the statement he made in one of his letters home from Havre, about marrying a woman with a heart, one who understood his values. This was to his elder brother, Shumsuddin's widow, Hamida. They did not have any children, but brought up a large family of orphans, their grandnephews and nieces, among whom were the remarkable brothers Hashim, Hamid (one of the earliest members of the ICS), Jabir, the Gandhian and agriculturist, and Salim, the ornithologist. He was eager for the women in the family to come out of purdah, and in every way to encourage them. The sisters included Camrunissa (Camoo) who played a large part in the life of her sister-in-law, Safia, and was the first woman teacher in the family, earning her living by teaching before her marriage to a cousin, Hasan Aly.

In later life, while Amiruddin continued to be a friend of Nawabs and Rajas, joining them on shooting and hunting trips, he was also an active member of the Bombay Municipal Corporation. He took both his family and civic responsibilities very seriously.

These letters were written from Le Havre, France, 1870, where Amiruddin had been sent at the age of 23 in connexion with family business, representing the firm of S. Tyabji and Co., which traded extensively with France and China. After a few lonely months, Amiruddin's irrepressible good spirits and charm soon gave him a position in the society of the town—he became a sought-after young man, invited to balls and dinners, about which he writes home with great vivacity. His letters to friends in England indicate that this was nothing new to him, and give a hint as to the cause of his elder brothers' anxiety

There were however two young nephews, Abbas (Tyabji) and 'Nuzzer' (Nazar Mohammad Futehally) studying in London, who visited him in Havre. His letters to his nephew-in-law, Hassan Aly in Istamboul, were addressed to 'Hajee Hassan Hindee, Istamboul.'

The few extracts from his letters quoted below, which deal with issues of marriage, conversion, and social values in general, show a young man of extraordinary common sense and dignity. His family seemed to have thought him a frivolous, perhaps not very responsible young man, as some of the letters here indicate (and surprisingly Asaf Fyzee, another great-nephew, many years later, used rather harsh terms for him) (see Fyzee, *Tyabjee Bhoymeeah*, p. 12) but the vigour and clarity with which he writes to his many English admirers, and the humour in his retorts to his elder brothers suggest a strong and mature nature. As the letters demonstrate, in spite of having spent many formative years in England in school and then at University, he remained very firmly rooted in his own cultural values.

These letters were written in English. At one level this reflects the extent of anglicization of the men in the family—a trend that was noticeable as early as the 1880s, when the men's Urdu entries in the *akhbar* books were markedly more stilted than the women's, but their English correspondingly fluent. At another level, the writer's use of this language enables him to turn the view outward—it is the natural medium for one writing from Europe. It makes him open to the world in a way the use of Urdu would have perhaps inhibited. The choice of medium would of course depend largely also on the recipient's knowledge of the language.

For Amiruddin Tyabji, in 1870, English was the natural language of communication when writing to his family, sometimes including his niece Amirunissa (he normally wrote in Urdu to his sisters and other female relations). His joyful, insatiable desire to explore and discover is also a forerunner to the other family documentation of itself and its beliefs.

I Extracts from Letters relating to Religion, Marriage, and Happiness

Letter to 'Alice', 17 May (1870). This is in response to the qualms expressed about a young boy who was being offered to Amiruddin as a servant, and of the influences he might be subjected to in a Muslim household.

I thought the Europeans were much more civilized, to think so much, what religion a boy as a servant would be allowed to follow! I am surprised at this very uncivilized questions [sic] for I never thought for a moment on the subject. Don't be vexed if I say something on the boasting of the great [sic] civilization of Europe, but in reality they are just as bad, as any nation on the earth. Really I am astonished at this.

Again if I am bound to keep the boy until he can get his own living. O! that's very fine, that is to say I must take the trouble to bring him up, and when he is old enough I am to leave him and all my troubles with him are thrown away—is that it?

The worst of me is that I get in love with my servants, and if they leave me, I nearly break my heart—so I must have a boy whom I would not be obliged to leave him when he is old.

To 'Mrs Eliane' (Twymann) 28 May Whom to Marry?

When I wrote you to find me a beautiful lady I [did] not mean only beautiful but also all that is required in a lady. I don't much care for money as God has given enough to have a piece of bread and cold water and what I want is Love, and I know well that happiness is not bought by beauty. But do you think the English ladies have any love. I find very hard to believe it.

To Mrs Twymann, 4 June

If you knew anything about my religion (Mohomanedism), you will never say that we are not allowed to marry a Christian lady. We are so free from bigotry that we laugh, when we hear anything of this sort from the civilized people (as the English consider themselves to be). What has the 'awful' difference in religions has [sic] to do with Love. I am not going to marry such a lady, that will never be happy unless I embrace Christianity. I will marry one, who will love me as I am. You make me laugh, why should I be offended, what have you done to me? On the contrary, I am happy to think that I have some friends who will give their opinions freely, and I thank you very much for them.

II Comments on Relationships within the Family

To Hasan Aly Fyzee, Istanbul

Writes that Abdul Husain, who is Amiruddin's 'major-domo', is now working under 'Bhai Badr' [Tyabji], and 'he knows well the tiger he has to deal with. I am rather glad, for he will soon improve under him don't you think so?'

Hasan Aly offers him a 'PAREE' (fairy) in Istanbul, but he won't be tempted, asks nervously whether a lot of *jahez* is offered together with the bride, that he's a simple, poor man, etc.

To Badruddin Tyabji, Bombay

Havre 10 June 1870
My dear Brother Budroodeen

Many thanks for your few lines of the 14th inst. It is not from brothers nowadays to expect long letters. I did not know it was so hot as to prevent you from writing a few lines more.

I suppose it will be still hotter so I had better not bother you, with a long letter; so I would just say a few words more.

I hope you have by this time received the accessories of your sewing machine which I left in Liverpool, while I was there to be sent to Bombay as soon as possible.

I beg of you once more and I hope for the last time to pay Nazroo Bibi, one hundred rupees, if you have not done so before. I dislike that sum being unpaid, I am sorry to hear about its being unpaid by every mail, and really I feel it very much.

What do you think! If you were to write a few copy books to improve your Handwriting not that your write bad, but altogether illegible.

Now I wish you goodbye with best love and Salaams, to yourself and all
Yours affly

To Elder Brother, Shumsuddin, July 1870 (then in Karachi) about two of their nephews, Abbas (Later Chief Justice of Baroda, and later still an ardent Gandhian), and Nazar Mohammed Futehally, founder of the Trading Firm N. Futehally and Co

Nuzzer is more gay and amusing and also a 'coquet'. Abbas is very grave and weak, but a little taller than Nizzer (about 1/4 inch) they are both drowned in studies and are very good boys.

From Nephew 'Nuzzer', the 'Coquet'

Letterhead
S. Tyabji and Co.
Havre Kurrachee Bombay
Havre 6 September 1870
Tuesday afternoon
Ameeroodeen Tyabjee Esq.

My dear Uncle Ameer

I bind myself as a gentleman to give you a nice present according to my position at that time, and the present must be given within one year. If you marry any other lady but Miss Clara Harvey, or will never marry.

Nuzzer Futehally

Or in other words you will marry Miss Clara, or if you do not I lose the bet.

To Elder Brother Camruddin, 3 November 1870

My Dear Brother

I must thank the hours of the 1st Oct. for driving away for a time your peculiarity never to write and allow your thoughts to set on paper.

I must thank you the more for it must have cost you a deal of exertion to perform a brotherly duty. So I thank you most sincerely.

Really it is very flattering, and I am so glad, you have also found my likeness to be all humbug, so of course it is. I did not like to praise myself, but now I suppose I must tell you, that many have told me the same thing over and over again viz. 'your portrait is all humbug, you are much better looking, the artist has not done you justice.' But the poor artist, dare he compare his art with the perfection of reality? No! Saying so I generously forgive him, and hope you will do this also. [Regarding order for a gun] buy the best and that you find the cheapest....

[With reference to a girl] Of course I take in her as much interest as I did before, and why not? ...

To his Brothers, November 1870

Gentlemen

We have been favoured with your letters of the 15th... last, through our friend Mr. Lazare. We are sorry that our letters did not reach you at the proper time, but we can very well account for its being a week later. We are in France, and have French Post Masters, who know no more about their business than I do mine. Mr Najmoodeen and myself went to enquire about our sending the letters and when are we to post them, but the man who came out to answer our questions proved as good a Post Master as the French have proved themselves soldiers. Had we gone on asking him more questions about the route through which we could send our letters, perhaps he would have put to us a question also, asking us, 'Pardon messieurs, mais ou est L'lndes? [Excuse me, sirs, but where is India?]' So we did not drive him to that extremity....

Ameeroodeen

Conclusion

By the 1880s, the descendants of Tyabjee Bhoymeeah had clearly aligned themselves with the forces of social reform, and politically, with the Indian National Congress. Their stand was made clear when Camruddin, Bhoymeeah's third son, together with other progressive Bombay leaders such as Pherozeshah Mehta, became an active member of the movement to appeal to the Privy Council against the High Court judgement in the Rakhmabai case;[1] and when Badruddin, Bhoymeeah's fourth son, agreed to chair the third session of the Indian National Congress in 1887.

Badruddin faced the virulent hostility not only of Sayyed Ahmed Khan and his supporters, who advocated an exclusively Muslim movement to secure political and educational rights for the Mussulmans, but initially the scepticism if not open hostility of the Muslim elite of Calcutta and Madras. Furthermore, opposition on his own home ground, within the Anjuman-i-Islam, as well as the Bombay Muslim communities, eventually led to his retiring from active politics.[2]

The support from his own clan, loosely termed 'Tyabji family', or as they referred to themselves, the Khandaan, remained undiminished, and the views which had led to Badruddin adopting the 'nationalist' approach, continued to be held for several generations thereafter, by a family which regarded itself as Muslim, observed the prayers, the fasts, and performed the pilgrimage enjoined to believers in Islam.

Theirs was not a narrowly exclusivist belief in Islam; it was one that made them regard themselves as part of a highly heterogenous society, within which they maintained their own identity.

Part of the reason for this open-mindedness may have been the highly varied nature of Bombay society; it was impossible to function within the modernizing spheres provided by missionary schools and colleges, or at the Bar, without encountering fellow citizens who were Marathi-Gujarati, Konkani, or English speakers, and their cultures, without being prised open, so to speak.

The Changing World of a Bombay Muslim Community, 1870–1945. Salima Tyabji, Oxford University Press.
© Nasir Tyabji 2023. DOI: 10.1093/oso/9780192869746.003.0006

Part of it was perhaps due to the nature of the Bombay Muslim elite: ship owners, merchants and professional men, largely self-made men, as was Bhoymeeah himself, so that the essentially conservative nature of the aristocratic land owning classes that constituted Muslim leadership in the UP and Bengal was not a liability for them in relation to social and political change. They were not beneficiaries of, or particularly affected by a sense of loyalty to, the old Mughal order which made the Muslim upper classes so resistant to change from the West, or so fearful of competition from better educated Hindus.

However, it was largely I suspect due to the extraordinary personality and character of Bhoymeeah himself.[3] All his sons, and several of his daughters, inherited from him an openness and self confidence which propelled them into taking stands that were far in advance of the society of that time: These were all outstanding pioneers in different areas.[4]

It is not surprising, given the family's strongly nationalist consciousness[5] that at Partition, only the Fyzee sisters, who had associated closely with the North Indian elite (more so than with their own *khandaan)* and were on familiar terms with Iqbal and Jinnah, should have migrated to Pakistan.[6] The other significant exceptions were some of Camruddin's descendants.[7]

The importance of the writings examined here is that they flesh out these facts, and make us aware, through this group's own words how this standpoint, this mentality was arrived at, what the questioning was that lay behind it, what options were explored in informal ways, to what extent the women followed the leadership of the men, how much they were able to modify it. The *khandaan* has left behind treasures of self revelation—diaries, account books, letters of a very personal nature, letters relating to issues of Muslim law—most of this material unknown and unexplored so far. This work is a very modest attempt at bringing these sources to light.

APPENDIX

A Twentieth-Century View of Europe

Safia Jabir Ali's elder brother, Faiz, to whom she was greatly attached, partly because of the literary tastes they had in common, was in the early years of the Badruddin books responsible for making the journals as full as persuasion or bullying could achieve. In later years, he was principally responsible for the full accounts kept up in the Tyabji-Latif family home at Kihim, called Latifia. In this he had an energetic supporter in his eldest son, Saif. Consequently the Latifia *akhbar ki kitab* is packed with lively accounts of activities during the long summer vacations of the clan in the 1920s and '30s.

Saif became a successful lawyer. He was also passionately involved in promoting girls' education among the poorer Muslims (as 'Ustad Sahib' notes in Safia's Memoir). Later in life he was able to turn to his true vocation, mathematics. He spent five years in Cambridge working on problems in Quantum Mechanics, under P. M. Dirac, for a research degree. Such commitments left him with little time for two of the earlier passions of his life, an interest in painting, both of the Indian miniature school and European, and in Western classical music, as the letters quoted below demonstrate.

The self-confidence in one's own cultural roots that is marked in the earlier nineteenth-century *akhbar* entries, and is a characteristic of Safia's personality, re-appears here too. There is a very strong sense of rootedness in his own culture. His encounters with Shaw, or Lawrence Binyon, or friendships with great musicians like Wellecz, or great art collectors like Werner Reinhart, were based on the assured con-fidence in the worth of his own civilization, about which he was deeply knowledge-able. Hence he was at ease with those belonging to another culture, who were equally deeply rooted in theirs.

He was writing back to a family that was as interested in the music, the architecture, the paintings, even the business methods he encountered as he himself—it was an in-formed family that waited for his letters.

The zest with which many of these experiences are related, the spontaneity of his comments, make this a remarkable record of high culture in the Europe of the late 1920s. It's also a record of low culture, for some of the most fascinating passages dwell on the details of cheap living, of eating and travelling in the Europe of the time. The letters written from Vienna, Berlin, and also from Florence are full of graphic ac-counts of discussions with leading musicians, art historians and painters—an unusual and insightful account of the musical and artistic life of those cities. Of interest as well are the writer's reflections and comments on the development of his own musical knowledge and taste, and equally his reactions to the great painters of the European pantheon.

The easy conversational tone of the social encounters he had with students, intel-lectuals, established musicians, and the intellectual and social elite of these European cities gives the material a charm, spontaneity, and genuineness that would be hard to capture in a different genre.

It's a pity that there is absolutely no comment on the great social and political up-heaval taking place in Europe at that time. One would also have liked to have known what Saif Tyabji's encounters with his Jewish friends and discussions on Zionism led to for him.

Ultimately of course, one realizes that these letters, with all their spontaneity and charm, with all their seriousness, were meant for public consumption—and perhaps that, as well as lack of time, inhibited him from expressing his views on such poten-tially controversial issues.

Accounts of the ballets, plays, concerts he went to in the course of a very rushed week, however bare, are of interest on their own, yet others, setting out the timetables for complicated journeys by train in the Midlands, for instance, show the immense care with which his time and money was used, so not a single hour or penny should go wasted.

Similarly, comments and asides to the immediate family, of no interest to the ge-neral reader, nevertheless provide the meatier passages with some context, they are as it were the juice in which the meat is stewing, and provide some indication of the writer's personal preoccupations in the midst of high culture and drama. These pas-sages are italicized and in smaller type so that one may easily ignore them. The spon-taneity of the letters is sometimes conveyed by odd spellings or a hurried misuse of language, which I have occasionally preserved, but at other times in the interest of readability corrected. For the same reason I have retained the beginning of the first letter, which was conscientiously repeated in each following one, as it makes clear that the letter was addressed to the entire family. However rushed Saif might have been when writing his weekly letter home which contain mere listings, he never failed to mention each member of the family by name. Other briefer passages which have no relevance for the reader have been omitted. I haven't marked these gaps as they are not significant.

I Aden to England

June 1929

10th June 1929 8 hours distance from Aden
My dear Father, Mother, Badr, Haffoo, Vazir, Mohsin and Kamila
When I was an articled clerk one day we had to take the opinion of B. J. Desai [distin-guished lawyer, nationalist, 1877–1946] on a certain matter. Merwanji was attending to the matter and I went with Merwanji to Desai's chambers. I had always thought Merwanji extremely lucid in his presentation of facts, and in this case, which was a complicated one, I thought Merwanji did very well. But when he finished Desai said 'I think Merwanji the facts of the case are these', and then he stated the facts so ex-tremely clearly that I was left wondering whether I had considerably overrated Merwanji's power.

The moral of this long story is this. I afterwards carefully considered Desai's state-ment of the facts to find out why it was so clear and I discovered that the sole reason was that he had stuck closely to the chronological order of events in his relating them. Well then:

6th After having finished waving you goodbye I went down with Salim Khaloo and Tehmi Khala [*the ornithologist Salim Ali and his wife Tehmina, Saif Tyabji's maternal aunt*] to their cabin. We then all of us went to the purser to whom we gave all our money. I have now got only 2 pounds and the Indian money about Rs 5. By the time this was finished we were opposite the Gateway of India. I met Humayun Mirza [*a distant relation, son of Iskander Mirza, first President of Pakistan, 1956–58*] standing on deck and he after declaring that he was feeling sick went down into his cabin to come again after 3 days.

But I am losing my chronological order. Salim Khaloo and I then walked about the deck for some time. Salim K. had obtained an introduction from Dr Joti Sircar—you know Sarhan M's great friend and now Sir J. C. Bose's [botanist] assistant and right hand man to a Prof. Dr Hans Molisch who is also on board. He is travelling 2nd because, as we subsequently learned, he could not get into the 1st class. As Salim K. and I walked up and down we decided on trying to find out this Dr Molisch. Of course we did not know him and we had to look for likely old men and accost. After a couple of turns we saw an old man with a good forehead, a ruddy skin and grey hair sitting on a deck chair in front on the saloon. We both immediately thought that this must be Dr Molisch and as we walked past him the old man gave to Salim Kh (as S. K. says) the glad eye. S. K. promptly sat down by his side and said 'Good morning'. I sat down on a deck chair on the other side and said 'Good morning'. The old man turned to S. K. and replied too 'Good morning'. Immediately he opened his mouth we knew that we had made a mistake. For there in the centre of his mouth a huge front tooth was missing in his upper jaw, and as he talked you caught glimpses of the upper surface of his tongue. S. K. winked 'No luck' to me and after a few minutes of difficultly sustained conversation we told him we had work to do in our cabins and rose. We had of course no work to do in our cabins. What we really wanted to do was to walk about and look around. This now became most difficult for the toothless old gentleman got up and took his position in the open part of the deck between the 1st and 2nd saloons and we had to walk about furtively and take advantage of every inch of cover lest the toothless o.g. should see us and get offended at our having told him a lie.

By this time it was time for lunch, 12.30, and I went down. My cabin companions were already in their places. I had tried to get a place next to Dr Molisch but I had been too late and the places had already all been allotted. My cabin companions are now next to me. They are: 1) Dr Sathe, a civil surgeon from Dhulia who was with Salman Chacha [*paternal uncle, senior engineer*] and takes pork and whisky in moderate quantities. A very pleasant man. Going on a pleasure trip to Vienna, Milan, England etc., and says he wants to look at the latest methods in surgery. Don't believe him in this last statement. 2) Something Pershad Mathur, who appeared for I. C. S. last January, rank 24, obtained a place in the U.P. Provincial Service and has got special leave to go to England where he will make an attempt in the July I. C. S. Thorough Indian, does not know how to eat or behave or do anything. Has no pyjamas. Extremely pleasant fellow. I teach him how to hold his fork. 3) Hazare, Bombay Maratha going to London for a few days and then going to stay 2 years in Berlin for business. A B. Com. and was one year behind Afzal [Lukmani] whom he knows well. Admires me greatly.

By the time we were seated down for lunch we had got quite out of the harbour and the sea was getting rough and I was feeling not quite comfortable. However I got through the greater part of lunch all right. The I. C. S. man was next to me and he was performing regular Cheiro tricks with his spoon and fork. At the moment of which I am writing he was on his soup. He turned round to me to complain that it was 'not nice' and then in the same movement he suddenly turned round and got sick with greater force than I could have believed it before possible. This completely put me off and I immediately came up on deck and then on deck I remained for the next two days. Immediately I went down I felt rotten and terribly sick. On deck with the fresh air it was all right. I had no dinner and I slept the greater part of the night on my deck chair.

7th The sea was very bad. By far the greater number of people were not visible and of the few of us remaining none could brave the dining saloon. We only went down when it was absolutely necessary. It was terribly hot in the cabins. The stewards were extremely nice and they brought us something to eat on deck although there are a dozen notices all over the place saying that meals will be served in the saloon only.

I noticed a fine old gentleman with quite a sunburned skin sitting very near the place where we had accosted the toothless o.g. I went up to the Chief Steward who was standing near and asked him if this was Dr Molisch. He said, 'I think so'. I accordingly went up and Dr Molisch was extremely pleased to talk to someone. The whole of the 6th and the 7th till the time that I started speaking to him he had spent lying in his deck chair either with his head thrown back and mouth open and eyes closed or reading 'Unhappy India'. He was however one of the two or three people who always went down for his meals and I believe he made quite hearty meals. I had a long and interesting talk with him. He is now 72 years old. He was Prof at Vienna of Plant Physiology and for the last year he was the Rector of the University. A very big gun therefore. He had come to India on the invitation of Sir J. C. Bose and was now returning after having worked in Calcutta for about six months. He told me all about his three years stay in Japan some six years ago when he had been invited by the Imperial University to organize its Department of Plant Physiology. He had been very pleased with Japan and with the reception that he had had there. Now he has retired from the University and will stop working regularly. He however intends on returning home to write a small book on India chiefly scientific but also containing some general observations. Hence the reading of 'Unhappy India'. He saw on his way back from Calcutta, Delhi, Agra, Ajmer, and some other places and he has been particularly impressed by 'Muhammadan Architecture'. He is extremely bitter against the English and all the nations who were the enemies of Austria during the war and this is not surprising if the hardships which he suffered during the war and immediately after it and which he described to me are considered. His dress was of course quite professorial and I wonder how we did not spot him from the first as Dr Molisch. He had been sitting quite close to the toothless o.g. when S. K. and I had made our first unsuccessful attempt at discovering him.

By the way I quite forgot to write that on the 6th almost immediately after our fiasco of the toothless O.G. I had another fiasco. I was walking along the deck and I met Mr Billimoria (the second juniormost partner in Merwanji who is going to Europe for four months with his wife and daughter) walking along with a lady. I bowed very politely but when the lady began to stare at me with some surprise I got a little confused and said 'Mrs Billimoria, I think', in as ingratiating a tone as I could summon at the moment's notice. The lady however walked off—I did not catch what she said and then Mr Billimoria informed me that she was the daughter of Prof Vaccha of the Berlin University going to see her father.

I later became quite friendly with the toothless O. G. whose name is Mr Eames. He belongs to the Excise C. P. and is on leave preparatory to retirement. He is just now going to England with his two fairly pretty daughters (whom we had previously seen walking on deck and who, Tehmi Khala thought, were twins. I have not yet been able to ascertain whether they are or are not twins). These twins Mr Eames informed me he was going to leave in London for a commercial training. Mr Eames himself will return in about six months to his wife and younger child whom he has left in Nagpur. When I heard this I thoughtlessly remarked 'I suppose they (the twins) will get married and will settle in England'. I think this remark must have somehow displeased Mr Eames for although subsequently I was frequently near him and his daughters he has not introduced me to them although he must have seen it in my eye that I want to be introduced to them. One day however when the sea was very bad and the ship very unsteady I gave my arm to one of them and helped her to the dining saloon. Except in this matter of his daughters, Mr Eames and I get on very well. As a matter of fact through him I have come to know most of the English people here whom it would have been difficult to get to otherwise as they are all very stand-offish.

Dr Sathe introduced me to another gentleman who I think together with Dr Molisch forms the cream of the 2nd class. This is Mr Gilbert, the Conservator of Forests, Central Div., B'bay Presidency. He is an extremely nice man and with a most beautiful sense of humour. He has got deep blue twinkling eyes and he is 200 lbs all muscle. It is wonderful how his Forest Service has trained him for though (as he says) his eyes are slightly short-sighted he has seen more things than anyone else on board. He first observed a flying fish, a stormy petrel, and other birds flying over the sea. Yesterday however he made his greatest discovery. He saw something yellow floating in the sea and then he saw such yellow things again and again. Finally when one such yellow thing came nearer the ship he was able to identify it as a mass of dead locusts. We steamed through such dead locusts for four hours yesterday evening. There must have literally been millions and billions. They were probably migrating from Arabia where they breed to India and they must have met some adverse wind and perished. This morning Mr Gilbert found a live locust and brought it to me and asked me to take it to S. K. (yes I forgot to say that I introduced S. K. to Mr Gilbert.) S. K. was tremendously pleased with the locust and there will probably be a note in the next journal of the Natural Hist. Society on this incident.

We are to get to Aden today sometime in the afternoon. I do not think that I shall go ashore. Dr Sathe is going ashore and I am asking him to post my letters. Tehmi Khala is keen on landing but I do not know what her idea is exactly, We shall not have sufficient time to go to the tanks which are I believe the only things of interest at Aden. Well, we shall see what happens.

Father, in my copy of Tyabji, Muhammadan Law lying I think in my study, I have made a note in the inside of the back cover of a Prof of Muhammadan Law at Marseilles and of a society which published texts of Muhammadan Law Will you kindly send me this reference?

I am getting on with my German but not to my satisfaction. With love and *salaams* and *adaabs* to all

Lloyd Triestino 10th June 1929
Between Bombay and Aden
To Alma Latifi, I. C. S., on his way to attend the first Round Table Conference, 1930.
Maternal uncle
Many thanks for your letter of the 16th which I received just the day before I embarked. Many thanks also for your kind letter of introduction to Sir Atul [High Commissioner in London]. As you say it will be a little difficult to get firms in England to entrust work to a young and inexperienced man, but as you say again there is no harm in trying. Besides I am going to harp on the point that the present system—viz. rushing to a solicitor when matters have already gone very far—is all quite wrong, and that the right system is to have a permanent legal agent who would continuously keep in touch with correspondents in India and let the European firms know from time to time not only such facts as to the financial position of the Indian Dealers as he can get hold of but also such bazaar rumours as he may think relevant. You will see that the idea at the back of my head is to act almost as [much as] a commercial agent as a Legal agent, and I have hopes that I shall be able to make many people see the advantage of having their commercial agent a solicitor. Of course in England and in Europe I must be very careful as to what promises I make because I do not know how much of such really commercial information I, a young solicitor with naturally limited opportunities of getting at information because I shall be doing no business on my account, shall be able to get.

We have had a very bad sea the last few days, and you will also I am afraid experience it. I hope that the Red Sea will not be very bad.

We were all very anxious to learn whether you had been confirmed a Commissioner. Father could only tell us that you were going back to Ambala.

London The American Express, Visitors Writing Room 27.6.29

I have left my letter writing to the very last moment and so you will not get anything much this time. Precedent Hattoo chacha [youngest paternal uncle].

We had a very comfortable voyage after Aden. The Red Sea was delightfully cool. Tehmi Khala, Salim K., a Mr Chopra (facetiously referred to by Salim K. as the kitab) and I got out at Port Said where we got about 3 days after leaving Aden at 6 in the evening. Before dinner (7.30) we went out for a walk along the banks of the canal up to de Lesseps' statue and had coffee in the Casino, very near to the pier. After dinner we got into a carriage and drove about the town. I purchased a copy of 'Italian in 3 months', Hugo, at a price which I later on discovered was 50% too much.

We landed in Venice on Friday the 22nd at 6 a.m. Getting through the Customs was a job and especially so because the scout (Did I write to you about the fellow named Thakkur who is going to join the Scout Jamboree and who knows very little English) had been given into my charge, and after seeing to my own luggage I went and saw to his. Well, we rushed from the quay to the station—on foot because we thought that would be quicker—to catch the 9.25 to Paris. We got to the station at 9.26 but only to be greeted by the happy news that there was no express at 9.25, but one at 11. So we started off. Four Indians in my compartment. We did not sleep very much. Next morning at ? we were in Paris and we changed stations to Paris Nord to get the Boulogne-Paris Express. At the station we found that there was no room in the 2nd class and were starting to feel depressed when Grindlays interpreter came up and told me that if I paid the chief officer there something 'leetle' he would put us in the 1st class. Well we did give him the something 'leetle' and the result was that we travelled from Boulogne to Folkestone 1st and some 1st class passengers also travelled 1st but travelled sitting on their suitcases in the corridor. By the way, the something 'leetle' was 10 francs which would be about a Re for the *four* of us. France is cheap.

I had written to Mrs Binney (I think I had told you about Mrs Binney whom I had met in Hanumkonda) [former Hyderabad State, now in Andhra] and she has asked me to lunch with her on Monday when she is coming down to London for a day from the country. But this is a digression.

What wonderfully fast boats the Boulogne-Folkestone boats are. At Folkestone I got separated from the rest of the party. In the train I was sitting next to an old gentleman from Liverpool who had taken his son for a week to see Paris. The son would be about 20. From Venice I had wired Saeed bhai [Dr Saeed Mohamedi, relation through Saif's father] to meet me. When I reached London I found a gentleman named Dr Tripathi who told me that Saeed Bhai had gone on a holiday to the Isle of Wight and that the wire had been opened by Shakir Bhai. Shakir Bhai [Dr Shakir Mohamedi, younger brother of Saeed] in his turn had been busy that evening and had asked him (Dr T.) to meet me.

Well time is over. I shall continue the narrative next week.

II London and the South

30th June 1929

I am commencing this letter very much before time. Today is only Sunday and the mail has to be ready by Thursday

Before I proceed further I would like to say two things which will help Badr [younger brother] when he leaves for England.

(1) A couple of shirts *with* collars, i.e. tennis shirts are very handy. Most of the people on the boat are in a shirt and a short. It would hardly be worthwhile taking a shorts along merely for the voyage. But the shirts would come in handy.
(2) A dressing gown is an absolute necessity. It was very awkward for me on the boat because everybody had one and immediately I arrived here I got one. I could not do here either without one.
(3) Badr should get one of these new kind of suitcases which have room for hanging the coat and trousers as in a wardrobe. A fellow who was in my cabin (Hazare) had one like that and it was most convenient. You do not have to fold your coast (an infernal nuisance) and as a matter of fact a coat folded and tightly packed gets crumpled however carefully folded it may be.

By the way, the smaller of my two suitcases is quite gone. On the voyage the porter broke the two straps and the handle and today I broke the key. In any case I would not have been able to get in all my clothes (with the new additions) into the old suitcase and I intend to purchase another suitcase—a suitcase of the kind that I have just described. I saw some nice ones at Hope Bros. for about 2 pounds, but I think I shall go to Selfridges as this will also give me an opportunity of seeing Selfridges.

Some other things for Badr: a) A small towel in the suitcase is a great convenience when travelling. The towels in the trains and waiting rooms are of very doubtful appearance. b) Something like the collapsible glass I have got is a great convenience. Otherwise you would not know how to wash your head whilst having a bath. The only way would be to hold your nose and dive—an awkward operation at best.

I think in my last letter I had come to the time when I arrived in London. As I think I have written, Saeed Bhai was not in London and my wire from Venice was opened by Shakir Bhai, who asked a certain Mr Tripathi to meet me. Dr Tripathi brought me to Saeed Bhai's where Shakir Bhai was busy with some patients. I had tea there and met a certain Mrs Mansfield who was an intimate friend of Mrs Mahomedi's. At about 5.30 I left for 102 Gower Street ... there was a hotel much patronized by Indians. Shakir Bhai had asked a friend to arrange for a room for me there, but as a matter of fact no arrangement had been made and I spent the night with 2 others in the same room. Both of these 2 others had been on the same steamer and one was a cabin companion of mine. For 3 days afterwards we were 2 in the room and I remained 2 more days in the same hotel.

This morning I transferred [to] these lodgings, no 5 Oakley Street near Regents Park. These lodgings are at least as comfortable as my room in the hotel and I pay here 23/6 sh (1 sh 6d for a bath every day) for bed and breakfast against the 28 sh I paid there when we were more than one in a room and 35 sh when I had a room to myself.

The next day after my arrival here was a Sunday, In the morning I visited Nasoo Phoophee [Alma Latifi's wife]. She has got a very nice room in quite a fashionable locality. She was looking very well. Nasreen was not looking so well. Jami and Qamran and Daniyal [Latifi children] were at their respective schools. I had lunch with her and after lunch I went to Hyde Park to meet Shaker Bhai there. Shakir Bhai brought along with him a certain Dr Khan who has married a Swiss lady. I had to meet Shakir Bhai at 3 at the Marble Arch entrance of Hyde Park but they did not come till nearly 4. I had tea with them and

[A]t 5 I left to keep an appointment with the Fyzees at 5.30. However I had not yet got accustomed to the time travelling takes in London. I did not get to their place till nearly 6. With Athur Bhai and Azhar Bhai [*the two youngest Fyzee sons, amongst the first Indians to play at Wimbledon*] I found Rahamin [*husband of Atiya Fyzee, and a noted painter in his day*]. Azhar Bhai went away after a short time and the three of us and their housekeeper had supper together. I cannot say that I enjoyed myself very much as almost all the talking was done by Rahamin. If anybody else tried to say anything Rahamin put on a very glum expression and looked at the ceiling. Athur Bhai agreed with Rahamin in everything that he said. However I did some business. I got the name of a good tailor, information as to what to do to get to Wimbledon and what clothes to have made. The next day I went to Pooles (the tailor recommended by them and not the great Poole) and had a suit of 8/8 sh made. The material is very nice and I think you will like it. I also ordered evening clothes at Hope Bros and got the shirts and collars necessary.

In the evening I went to Covent Garden Opera and saw 'La Boheme'. It was very good but still I was disappointed. The chief tenor was an Englishman, Nash, who was really very good. The evening however made me decide that I shall not go into the gallery again. At Covent Garden I shall *have* to go to the Gallery as the next higher seats are 13/6 (gallery is 3/6) but I purchased tickets for 'Marie Rose' (Barrie) and 'Exiled' (Galsworthy's new play) for the Upper Circle at 5/9. 'Marie Rose' was simply magnificent—but I am anticipating. I also purchased other tickets and I am now booked up as follows

1st July—'Young Woodley'
2nd 'La Vie Parisenne'
3rd Covent Garden (there is a Russian Ballet Co)
4th 'Tannhauser' an opera at the Lyceum Theatre
5th 'Faust' same place
On the 6th and 7th there is nothing.
On the 8th 'The First Mrs Fraser' and on the 9th 'All God's Chillun' by O'Neill.
Thursday 4th. I find that I am planning my letters on much too ambitious a scale.
I must bid good bye now.

9.7.29 From Durmast Cottage, Burley, Hants
You see that I am writing from Lady Bowen's [*widow of Sir Stanley Bowen, Editor of The Times of India, Bombay, in the 1920s*]. I am having a glorious time, but I have only a few moments to write to you. The important events of last week were firstly a visit to Mr G. B. Shaw. I had written to him asking him whether he would see [me] and he had given me an appointment on Thursday last. I was with him for about 11/2 hrs.

London, 10.7.29
We had a very interesting talk chiefly about the position of the Musulmans now. The thing was interesting but on the whole I was very much disappointed with G. B. S. himself. First of all his forehead was nothing like so high as it is drawn and secondly he *was not* in a suit of red velvet. And his method of talking was very arbitrary and very much as if he was laying down the law. He is of course a very big man but he need not have been continuously laying down the law.

Thursday evening saw 'Tannhauser'. It was very good and I had a good and very comfortable seat which I find adds greatly to one's enjoyment of anything. On Friday I left home at 5 in the morning to go to Wimbledon and sit in the queue. I got a fairly good place in the queue. There were about 100 people in front of me.

Saturday went to Wimbledon late and went into the standing enclosure which meant standing from 12 (when I reached Wimbledon) till 7 when all the matches would be finished. I however got a very good view of Borotra *vs* Cochet and Collins and Gregory *vs* Allison and Van Ryan.

Sunday stayed at home in the morning. Had supper with Nasoo phoophee.

Monday went to Lady Bowen's by 9.30 train. I have had a most enjoyable 2 days there. Yesterday (Wednesday) I left Burley by the 2 o'clock bus and got to Bournemouth at 3. 15. There I had tea with Mrs Solly and returned to London by the 6 o'clock bus which was a little late and brought me here at 10.30.

Now goodbye

12.7.29
I should feel very much obliged if you would kindly send to me a box of my visiting cards. They are in one of the drawers on the right hand side of my desk. Please also send me the refill for my pocket book which I have got in the central drawer. It is wrapped up I think in a piece of brown paper.

16th I saw Wagner's 'Valkyrie' last Sunday. It was very good indeed. I got a very good seat. Father I think that your advice of going into the pit is quite wrong. For a seat in the pit in the opera you pay about 3 sh. To this you must add 6d for the stool if you want anything like a decent seat and go a couple of hours before the show commences. Against this the lowest reservable seat is 4/9—not so very much more expensive. Besides you can then go at the proper time and sit on a velvet padded seat instead of on a most uncomfortable wooden bench. And this is a great point I think when there is a question of spending 3 hours regularly in the theatre every day in the week.

On Saturday I did not do anything in particular in the morning. In the afternoon I went to see an air force display at Hindon which was really a most impressive affair. You no doubt saw pictures and accounts of it in the papers.

In the evening I went out in search of new lodgings. 5 Oakley Sq where I was was managed by an Italian and was quite a dirty place. Finally last Sunday the geyser got out of order which meant that you could not have any bath. This did not really matter so much as I was away at Lady Bowen's for a part of the week but I could not go on staying there. Well at about 10 in the evening I found a nice place at 43 Oxford Terraces within 5 minutes' walk of Hyde Park and I have taken a room for 30/- sh a week.

18th Thursday has arrived and my letter is as it was. I shall therefore only give you a summary of what I did reserving comments for some later occasion.

Sunday morning High Mass at Westminster Cathedral (not Abbey) magnificent music.

Lunch with Aly Hydari who was in the nursing home and has been there for the last 3 months. Was looking terribly thin but otherwise healthy. Had had an operation of 40 minutes 3 days before. Bone below the knee had to be scraped because of some pus or something. Will write a long letter in re this to the Nawab Sahib for purposes of working into his favour. As a matter of fact I haven't thanked him and the Begum Saheba yet for the wire of send-off. Afternoon Service at St Paul's. Good music again.

Monday morning did a number of business calls. Evening Serge Diaghaleff Russian Ballet—music dancing—mag.

Tuesday morning saw Mr Mott again in his office. He was very apologetic that he could not yet invite me to his place but he has been having lots of trouble with his servants.

Wednesday British Museum—almost completed the Indian paintings. There are about 5 vols left which I shall look at today. Evening Russian Ballet mag. again.

News of future shall probably be 3 days at Stratford in Avon for the Shakespeare festival. Tomorrow I am going to see the illuminated manuscripts and paintings in the India Office. I have obtained a reader's ticket through Lawrence Binyon. Going to purchase some second-hand books today.... I must thank Haffoo and Badr for their letters.

18.7.29

My dear Badr

Just a line to thank you for your letter but really to say that I am sorry that your I. C. S. thing fell through. Not very sorry though, for I never liked your getting in on the strength of your backward classedness. Now you must work like the deuce and really do well next time. As I have frequently told you undergo a few months of torture now for eternal bliss and happiness afterwards. Yrs affly

20.7.29

From the 15th of September or so please address my letters *c/o* American Express Co. 11 Rue Scribe Paris

I have been spending some busy days: 5th.7.29 (Thursday) [FBT] By the way I do not remember Father whether I had asked you to send to Dr Hans Molisch, Wien VIII, Zeltgasse 2, Austria, a copy of the Nehru Report. I had promised to give him a copy and I should feel very much obliged if you would kindly send him one.

My week's programme has been as follows:

Friday 19th Completed seeing the pictures in the British Museum and in the evening went to see 'Siegfried', the third part of Wagner's Ring

Saturday I cannot recall what I did in the morning. However in the evening I saw Gounod's 'Faust'. It is really a beautiful opera but after 'Siegfried' it struck me as just a light opera with its choruses and solos.

Sunday In the morning I washed some clothes and made up my programme for the next two months. I had written to Sagheer Bhai [third Mohamedi brother, living in Paris] and I have received a very nice and very prompt reply from him. He strongly advises me not to come to Paris till the 15th October and I think that I shall not go there till then. In the meantime: August 11th, 12th, and 13th at Cambridge. Mr W. Stanley and his family are living there. I am of course in communication with them and I shall probably lunch with them when there.

August 23rd, 24th and 25th Leave London finally and stay in Oxford.

26th Leave for Stratford on Avon in the afternoon and get there by evening. There is the Shakespeare festival going on there and I have taken tickets for

Monday August 26th Hamlet

Tuesday 27—Romeo and Juliet

Wed. matinee Twelfth Night

evening—Macbeth

August 29th I leave for Birmingham. After this I am not quite sure as to what I shall do but roughly I have planned to get to Chester by the 30th. I shall make Chester my headquarters of going about in N. Wales where I want to spend a week. I therefore return to Chester by the 7th Sept., and then go to Manchester. After staying a couple of days there I spend three days in the Lake Dist. And then to Glasgow to which I have allotted a week. Not to Glasgow itself of course but to the excursions from Glasgow. I then go to Edinburgh and after staying there a couple of days I cross to Hamburg about the 1st of October. On Sunday evening I went to see Nassoo Phoophi. She is leaving for Paris tomorrow and I shall probably not see her again as she will return to London when I get to Paris.

Monday I went to the India Office Library. Evening Covent Garden Opera where there is the Russian Ballet Co.

Tuesday Business calls Evening 'Bitter Sweet', an operetta by Noel Coward. Quite good. *Wed* Business calls. Evening Covent Garden Russian Ballet

This Russian Ballet Co.—the Serge Diaghileff Co. is the Ballet Co. Stravinsky the Russian composer is attached to them and the Ballets that I saw were by him, Tchaikovsky and???. Stravinsky is really most wonderful. There does not at first seem to be any tune (melody) at all and yet the music is very satisfying.

Well goodbye now. I saw N. Phupi again yesterday.

28.7.29

Today is Sunday but I am going to write off my letter to you today. I have got tickets for the theatre for every night next week and when there is wandering about to be done the

whole day and the theatre at night I find that there is not much time for letter writing. The real reason for my not writing to you that one mail was that after leaving Aden there was really not much to write except to go on giving further details of my cabin companions who were really quite ordinary people. Besides I was busy preparing my programme for London and this I found no easy or short job. There was yet another reason for not writing. I wanted to bring Vazir [fiancee] into the limelight as it were. As you know besides this joint letter I write an exclusive letter to Vazir every week and that week I wrote the exclusive letter but left out the joint one. As it happens Vazir says the exclusive letter got lost. Well! Well!

I enclose [a] letter to Auckland Jute.

I wrote to Mrs Flora Sassoon the last week, getting her address from the telephone book. She has replied saying that she is just going out of London and will be glad to see me in September. Of course in Sept I will not be here. In any case Father you do not enclose the card for her which in your letter you say you will do. You remember lecturing to me on a similar occasion. Thank you very much for sending me that analysis of Badr's marks. As a matter of fact I had seen the official results before we reached Aden (you remember that I. C. S. candidate in my cabin—Mathur) but I had only just glanced at it.

I had not intended calling on Mrs Percival at all—I am rather pressed for time—but she wrote to me last Thursday asking me to dine with her on Friday. This letter I received on Saturday. This morning I telephoned to her and she has asked me to tea today. She invited me to dine but I said that I had no evening free till next Sunday. You do not in your letter say who Mr Charles H. Roberts is, and I had to tear the envelope of the letter of introduction to find out. Now I have not got another envelope of that size to put the letter in and this difficulty may be the cause of my not calling on him. You remember Mrs Binney of whom I have already written to you. She was in the country and she had written to me saying that she would be in London for a week from the 26th. This morning I telephoned to her and she again wanted me to dine with her. But I have brought her down to a lunch. In compensation I want to ask her to dine with me and then go to the theatre. I am wondering if this is too ambitious. I have to spend 23 pounds per month. This month I have managed to keep in this limit. But with the travelling about etc. next month I do not know whether I shall be able to do so. Of course next month the daily theatre will go off.

The most important event since last Thursday has been my going down to the shooting grounds last Friday and getting my gun fitted. I do not remember whether I wrote to you that I had purchased a most glorious pair of Holland and Holland 'Royal' guns. Their price when new must be in the neighbourhood of 200 pounds. Some Lord or the other who wanted a new pair for the season which will soon commence and was in need of a little pocket money immediately wanted to get rid of them quickly. I saw them after a great deal of wandering about at a certain Watson Bros, a small but very old-established gunmakers at Bond Street. The pair was offered at 35 pounds including a magnificent leather case. As a matter of fact I had almost decided on purchasing another; a second-hand 'Pudey' for about 30 pounds and I passed Watson Bros on my way home and just called in to see what they had got. I asked for 12 hours to think it over and then agreed to take the two guns with two simple leather cases instead of the double case. One gun is for myself, the other for Badr when he gets into the I. C. S. or married, whichever is earlier. If he does neither I shall sell it and then my Holland Royal will have cost me about Rs 200.

Well, last Friday I went to the shooting grounds. What wonderful people these shooting instructors are. In a moment he had my gun adjusted for me and then I found that it was really difficult to miss. I was of course quite out of practice and I had only my low-powered glasses on. On the other hand the 'birds' came more or less regularly. But as I said with the gun adjusted I found it difficult to miss. I think my gun will be a great success.

You will be interested to hear that yesterday in the morning I went to the Indian Section of the Victoria and Albert Museum and saw the curator and tackled him in the same manner as I tackled Mr Lawrence Binyon, viz., pretended to know a great deal about Mogul art, Persian influences, Ajanta technique, etc. I was similarly successful. More successful in fact because Mr Stanley Clark was not going off to Japan as Mr Binyon is doing and he had accordingly more time to spare. He has very cordially invited me to his room next Monday when he will take me through those paintings which are not ordinarily exhibited and he wants my help in deciphering an inscription at which Sir Thomas Arnold has tried his hand I wish I knew a little Persian!

It is very unfortunate that Sir Thomas Arnold is not in London now. I wanted to see him very much. Binyon spoke about me to Sir Thomas just when he was leaving London and I was flattered to learn that Sir Thomas would have liked to meet me.

You would be astonished, were you to see me with these great people, at the capabilities of your son.??? when in London was nothing compared to me. I make full use of all my connections and relations. The fact that I am the son and the grandson of High Court judges is always looming in the background like the lower note in a Wagnerian harmony. My I. C. S. connections are mentioned sometimes, at others the Finance Member of Hyderabad [Akbar Hydari] becomes a near uncle. I find that a self-deprecatory remark judiciously dropped in now and then is of much help. Altogether the work is not half as difficult as one may suppose.

I have had a very hectic time with my business calls. I have as yet made about 50 calls on Chambers of Commerce, secretaries of the societies of manufactures and merchants. I do not know what the results will be.

I went to the aero show at Olympia last Friday. As the visit was sandwiched between an organ recital at Westminster Cathedral (which immediately followed the visit to the shooting grounds) and the opera at 8 in the evening I had not very much time. One loses such a lot of time in traveling about here and then one has to waste time for meals. I had however a good look at the aero engines which interested me most.

This morning I am doing nothing except just writing this letter. I shall then have my bath and after having lunch I shall go to the Victoria and A. Museum and stay there till it is time to go to Mrs Percival's at 4.30. I have to dine with Shakir Bhai.

I think I shall postpone going to Paris till November and spend October in Germany and visit Berlin Dresden Leipzig and Frankfurt in addition to Hamburg. This resolution is due very considerably to my discovery that in Germany one can stay terrifically cheaply in the Jugendherbergen (shelters for wanderers in German). I must therefore now hurry up with my German. I have accordingly now got a Hugo's 'German in Three Months' and carry it about with me.

The day before yesterday I went to see 'Merry Wives of Windsor' in modem dress. I enclose a cutting from the Times and you will see that it has been most terribly criticized. As it was I thoroughly enjoyed it. The play was not Shakespeare's at all. There were whole passages and even incidents inserted but as a comedy I thought it very good indeed. Of course this reduced the thing from a highly scholarly experiment which it was supposed to be at first to just an adaptation for drawing theatre audiences. As a matter of fact though I was there on the 2nd day of performance there was a very thin house indeed. Yesterday I saw Galsworthy's 'Skin Game' which has been revived. I had read the play in Bombay but on the stage there was really first-class acting as it was at the Wyndham theatre where I had already seen Galsworthy's new play 'Exiled' it was terrible and reduced half the audience to tears. I find I have not kept the copy of the Times containing its criticism but it had been eulogized in a way that I had not seen anything done since my arrival here.

[Received 18th August]

8.8.1929 [in FBT's hand] During the last week as I think I wrote before I had a ticket for the theatre every night. On Friday I saw 'The Matriarch' by G. B. Stern, and on Saturday 'Bill of Divorcement' by Clemence Dane. Both of these were really splendid, especially the 'Bill of Divorcement' which is a play to show the muddle to which this last bill making divorce so extremely easy has reduced society to.

I have just written off for particulars of the Malvern Festival which is to be a festival of Shaw's plays. Malvern is a little out of the way but I would like to see Shaw played and from Stratford-on-Avon after the dose of Shakespeare I might see how Shaw tastes. *Thursday was the 1st of this month and almost the whole of the day I spent in 'business'. I had to get money from the American Express as I had only about 5 sh left and I was almost on the point of borrowing money from somebody or the other. This was because I had spent all the money I had brought with me from Bombay and all the 1st month's instalments in clothes (about 20 pounds) the guns (35 pounds) and books (20 pounds) and the American Express refused to give me any more money before the 1st. Except for this minor difference, my finances are by the grace of god in a sound condition. I am to spend 23 pounds per month and during the last month I spent 22 Pounds. I hope I have not written all this to you before (I have a suspicion that I have) or you may think I am becoming Aminesque.*

By the way I prepared a letter for Amin Bhai too, on board, asking him how he was and what his programme was and hoping that he was well. I received a reply after some time and he says that he and Sultana are coming to England and visiting Holland in September. I shall of course visit Zurich but I suppose I shall miss them here. I am now expecting Azeem [Tyabji, close relation and friend] daily, I hope that he will get in touch with me immediately he comes for I think I can now with my fresh experiences help him greatly in settling down. You will be interested to hear of my latest plans formed as a matter of fact only last night:
August

11 go to Cambridge-spend afternoon with Cockroft on whom Asaf B. has given me an intro.

12th 4.30 P.M. tea with Nicholson

13th 11 a.m., lunch with Wentworth Stanleys who I believe I wrote to you are in Cambridge. Evening, return to London.

14th evening Bach and Handel concert

15th

16th Beethoven concert, concerts by Sir Henry Wood's orchestra in Queen's Hall

17th and
18th nothing
19th Wagner concert
20th Mozart concert
21st and
22nd nothing. 23rd leave London by bus at 9 in the morning get to Oxford at 12
26th Leave Oxford at 12 get to Stratford on Avon at 4.12 Evening 'Hamlet' at the
Shakes. Mem. Theatre
27th evening 'Romeo and Juliet'
28th afternoon 'Twelfth Night' evening 'Macbeth'
29th Leave Stratford 1.30 Birmingham 3. 15

I have taken my bus tickets up to Birmingham. By booking through (I am allowed to break my journeys provided I give the dates), I get a ticket from Lond. to Birm for 12 sh instead of sh 21 which it would otherwise cost me. Train would cost me about 30 sh.

Before I leave London I have still got to do 1) visit Windsor 2) Hampton Ct Palace 3) Tower 4) docks 5) complete inspection of India Office pictures and further visits to Tate and British Museum. Although I have been to the British Museum a dozen times I haven't yet seen the Elgin Marbles!

Mr Stanley Clarke the head of the Indian Section of the Victoria and Albert Museum lunched with me today. I was with him from 12–4.30. Today he showed me after lunch all the workshops of the Museum where they do all the repairing and mounting etc. It was really most interesting. Codrington, an assistant in the same department who knows Mahomedi Mamoo [*Sir Akbar Hydari, Prime Minister of Hyderabad under the Nizam*] well has asked me to lunch with him on Wednesday next but I shall I think tell him that I really cannot afford an afternoon and that I would much rather spend the evening with him. I have got no theatres etc this week except that I am going to see the 'Sacred Flame' by Somerset Maugham tomorrow in which Gladys Cooper is acting.

After I leave London, i.e. from Birmingham I go to a place Llangollen in North Wales (recommended by Codrington) and walk for 3 days. I then go to 1) Liverpool 2) Manchester 3) Bradford 4) Leeds 5) Sheffield and again walk in the Lake District for 3 days. I then go to Glasgow I would like to spend three days in the Scotch Highlands but I do not know whether I shall do so. You see I want to cross to Hamburg and go to Cologne and up the Rhine to Margence before it is too late for the Rhine. I get to Paris about Oct 15th and remain there till December 1st. Now comes the important change. I go straight from Paris to Vienna and make Vienna my headquarters till the end of February, spend March in Italy and catch the Aquileia on March 30th at Naples and get to Bombay on April 15th.

To continue my account of what I did last week. I did a lot of sight seeing on Monday. On Tuesday I made an awful hash. I wanted to go down by steamer to Tilbury and the steamers leave at nine in the morning. I got to the pier at 9.10. Phut went 10 d in train fares and one hour of good English time. Tomorrow I shall make another attempt at getting to Tiibury. I want to do the docks at the same time. I shall come home dead tired and probably fall asleep in the theatre in the evening. But I have got quite accustomed to going to bed at 1 and getting up at 8.30. What a terribly late city London is. When I return from the theatre at about 12.30 the streets are still crowded. If however tomorrow is as rainy as it is today I shall finish the India Office instead. The India Office library is really magnificent.

Please send the enclosed to Fitoo Bahen [Fatima, Mrs Tahir Mohamedi]. I do not know her address. I have not received any letters by this mail. Did you miss it?

I think, Father, that my letters after the 1st week of September should be addressed to me c/o American Express Co., 11 rue Scribe Paris. These instructions cancel previous instructions.

I wrote to Mrs Sassoon and got a visiting card back saying that Mrs Sassoon is leaving London but will be pleased to see me when she returns. I shall of course not be here. I have not tried to see Lady Beg. I had tea with Mrs Percival and she asked [me] to go again and see her. I called on Polak last Sunday but he did not keep me to lunch though I was there till pretty near lunch time. He was otherwise very nice and kind. I just had a glimpse of his son who had got out of bed at 11 A.M. because it was a Sunday I find that that I have lost my muffler [after all]! Well! And a winter in Vienna to come.

11.8.29 [letterhead] Livingstone Hotel Petty Cury, Cambridge

You see from the address that I am at Cambridge. But to commence from where I ended my last letter.

On Thursday I went to the docks and Tilbury. I spent a most interesting time. I left from the Tower Pier just under the Tower of London by a steamer at 9 in the morning. We got to Tilbury at about 12. How terribly dirty and crowded and rich East London is. I saw Jews and warehouses and cranes and shipping till I was sick. I think I must have walked 10 miles. King George's Dock alone is 1 ¼ miles long. And I went round Tilbury Docks, Victoria Docks, and King George's Docks. I had a long conversation with the man in charge of the grain elevator and he explained to me the whole mechanism. It was most interesting. However there were no really big boats in the docks. All the big boats I suppose go to Southampton or Liverpool. The largest was in Tilbury Docks, about 25,000 tons I think.

On Friday I went to the India Office Library and finished looking at the pictures of the Johnson Collection. These last pictures were specially interesting as for the first time I saw complete sets of *rags* and *raginis* and I was able to make a full list of them i.e. of the *ragas* and the respective picture which represented it.

I do not think that I wrote to you that last Wednesday Mr Stanley Clark, the Curator of the Indian Section of the Victoria and Albert Museum, lunched with me. I gave him a good lunch and incidentally this was the second decent meal which I have had at my own expense in England, the first being the lunch which I gave to Mr Gain and Mr Brett of the firm of Gain and Brett (Mr Gain has done a lot for me in the way of introducing me to trade associations). My usual meals are at Lyons and cost between 4 d and 1 sh 1 d. The menu is steak and kidney pie (7 d), a dish which I have found the most filling of the cheaper dishes, roll (1 d), and butter (1 d). I then have to decide between a lemonade and a pudding. If I am very hungry and more solid is necessary to fill up great gaps I have to decide for the pudding. If I am not very hungry and feel that I can indulge in a little useless luxury I have the lemonade. The lemonade is really real '*limoon ka sherbet*' and Lyons give it to you first class—in fact, it is like Leila Mumani's [aunt and future mother-inlaw]. You will say that the butter is a luxury and might be dispensed with. But it is not so. With this masalaless food it is impossible to eat the bread with the meat and you require the butter to—so to say—grease the bread.

The other day when Mrs Binney and I were walking through Hyde Park after I had had lunch with her she began to say how much she would like to be very rich and asked me whether I did not feel the same. I said that I had no objection to being rich but I could not see what more I could do if I was rich than I am doing now (Father please note). She said that she would go into the most expensive restaurants and eat only the most expensive dishes and tip lavishly. On this I could sincerely disagree with her. If I had a few thousands more to spend during my trip to Europe I would probably purchase a 70 pound gun instead of a 35 pound gun but I would still go to Lyons and have steak and kidney pie. I might possibly go into the stalls instead of in the Upper Circle but of this I am not sure. I would however drink lemonade in the theatre in the intervals. It is frightfully expensive.

On Friday evening I went to Saeed Bhai's *and met Azeem there. Mrs Saeed was going off for the weekend to Saklatwalla's (ex M.P.s) place* and I met the old communist [Saklatwalla] there. What a hopeless person he is. He would not speak at first but after some encouragement and a little carefully directed flattery he poured his political opinions at me in a steady stream for 15 minutes. In spite of your frequent observation regarding him, Father, I had always felt angry at Punch's and the other English papers going for Saklatwalla in the way they did. Now I almost feel that they are justified and identify him as a cross between a Hyde Park orator and a fanatical mulla.

I brought Azeem back with me and on the way I gave him a dinner which differed from my ordinary ones in this that there were both the lemonade and the pudding *and* there was *also* mixed salad. I unloaded on him all the guides and things which I had collected and also a great deal of verbal information. I especially impressed on him that he should never go in the pit or gallery in the theatre but always to the cheapest reservable seats which are usually the upper gallery at 5 sh 9 d. The experience gained from some of the most intense theatre-going ever done by a person in my position and financial circumstances speak decisively for this plan. *Finally I made an appointment with Azeem to take him to Watson Bros the next morning to show him my guns. The appointment was to meet in the Piccadilly Underground Station near the clock showing the times in different parts of the world at 9.45 A.M. The next morning at about 9.35 I was at the station and I remained there till 10.30 but Azeem did not turn up. I do not yet know why he was not able to keep the apptmt. Possibly he came over here—to Cambridge—early in the morning as Paranjape whom he had seen the day before had advised him to run down and make a personal attempt to get into the University.*

However I left Piccadilly and rushed off to catch the steamer starting from Westminster Pier and going up the river to Hampton Court.

I got to Hampton Court at 12.45 after a really most enjoyable 3 hours on the river. After having something to eat I went round the palace. Really Tudor architecture is a magnificent architecture. I wish I could see the place as Henry VIII left it or at least before the place had been changed by Wren. You remember Father that from the Versailles-like area from where you can see only Wren's work it is quite nice and even impressive but where the two architectures are juxtaposed you wonder what had happened to Wren.

I left Hampton Court at 6. And then another thing happened which adds further proof to my theory that it is impossible to lose anything in London. The day before when Azeem and I were leaving the Lyons after dinner I suddenly missed my umbrella. I distinctly remembered leaving it on the sofa at Saeed Bhai's and so I thought I must have forgotten it there, so when I got to Waterloo Station (I returned from Hampton by train) I telephoned to Saeed Bhai to ask him whether it was really there before going there to fetch it. My horror was extreme when he said that it was not. I gave up my umbrella for lost and made up my mind to call at the lost property office of the tube railways and the trains (you have to go by train to get to Saeed Bhai's). On my way home I called at the same Lyons to which we had gone the preceding night to get some sandwiches to be eaten as lunch the next day on the way to Cambridge. And as I was standing waiting for them I asked the waitress whether any umbrella had been found there. I thought this a very hopeless enquiry because Azeem was quite sure (and Azeem I have always believed to be a particularly clear-headed and non-forgetful person) that I did not have it with me when we got to the Lyons. Well anyway it was here and at present the umbrella is lying on the mantel shelf in my room.

This morning I started for Cambridge by the 10 a.m. bus. What magnificent buses run from London to here. They are more comfortable than 1st class compartments. The only difficulty is about the luggage. The railways for one shilling take your baggage from your place and deliver it at the other end. This is for me such a convenience that when my bus tickets are exhausted (I have purchased tickets from London-Oxford, Oxford-Stratford, and Stratford-Birmingham) I do not think I shall do any more travelling by bus. (You must be wondering why I have purchased all these tickets so early. It is because I have now got my tickets from London to Birmingham for the total cost of 12 sh. If I had purchased them separately later the aggregate cost would have been about 1 pound.)

On my arrival here (I have put up at a fairly decent hotel as I shall have to give my address to Mr Wentworth Stanley), I rang up Cockroft, a Fellow of St John's [*Sir John Cockroft, Head of the Atomic Energy project at Harwell, Nobel Laureate with Rutherford, 1951*] on whom Asaf Bhai had given me an introduction. Cockroft had replied to my letter from London and invited me to tea. I told him on the phone that I would leave the hotel at about 2.30 p.m. and after walking down the Backs get to his place at about 3.15. Walking down the Backs was a tougher job than I had thought and Cockroft's place was further away than I expected and I was not able to get there till 3.45. However I spent a most enjoyable evening and I was with Cockroft till nearly seven. He has promised to take me through the Cavendish lab tomorrow.

Tomorrow at 4.30 I have tea with Prof. Nicholson [authority on Persian art] and then at 7.30 dine with Cockroft in the hall at St John's.

I must say I am very much disappointed with Cambridge. There is no—at least now in the long vacations there is none of that 'atmosphere' of which I had hoped to have a breath. The river is good, but it is swarming with boats either with GIRLS or chubby undergraduates reclining in them, and on the stretch of river between Trinity and St John's there were two gramophones playing jazz music. Then again I had always thought that the buildings were very soul-raising. But the great court of King's College has a magnificent Gothic chapel on one side, fairly good gothic buildings on two others, and a wing in French Renaissance on the 4th. I could not imagine a more jarring combination. The back facing the river was almost worse. There was of course the French Renaissance bldg facing the river and on either side projections of the two Gothic wings. But one of the wings had a quite recent extension and this is a kind of Stripped gothic style with all the beautiful mouldings and ornamentation taken off, presumably in order to make the building easier to clean. In this respect St John's is I think the least offending.

Well it's 11.30 now and I must go to bed.

12th Today's doings have been fairly interesting. In the morning I had an aptmt with Cockroft in the Cavendish Lab., and he took me round the whole place. This was my first glimpse of a Research lab. in Physics and it was certainly very impressive. Places were pointed out to you, here Sir Earnest Rutherford works and this is Sir J. J. Thomson's table. In this room [ ] first detected isotopes. I found it extraordinarily thrilling. From the laboratory I went to the Fitzwilliam Museum and went up to the director and asked for 'Indian Paintings'. They have very few there. I identified some of the *Ragini pictures* with the *Rags* with the help of the notes I had made in the India Office, and the Director thanked me profusely for this. I hope the identifications are correct!

I next went to Kings College chapel which was locked yesterday and went up to the roof from which there is an extensive view. I next went to the University Library and asked again for 'Indian Paintings'. To get into the Library it is necessary that you should be accompanied by a graduate but the two above words in inverted commas did the trick again and I was taken to a Mr Thomas who is in charge of the Oriental part of the library. Mr Thomas lent me his copy of *Brown's Catalogue of Persian Mss* in the library and took me into the Mss room and I enjoyed myself there thoroughly for a couple of hours.

At 4.30 I had to be at Prof. Nicholson's for tea. I was there at the tick and had a very sumptuous tea with Mr and Mrs Nicholson. Prof. Nicholson was extremely nice and kind and he showed me round his library and the photographic copies of the *Musnavi* on which he is working. I was with him till 6.30. By the way he told me that some days before he had considerable difficulty in taking a friend into the University Library to see a Mss as the Librarian is extremely strict and he was very much surprised to hear how easily I was able to penetrate to the holy of holies: the MSS room.

In the evening I dined in the Hall of St John's with the Profs and Fellows as Cockroft's guest. The Profs and Fellows certainly do themselves well and I have had a splendid dinner. (I had as much *limoon ka sherbet* as I could decently drink both openly and surreptitiously.) I had asked Cockroft to introduce me to Prof Rapson, the Editor of the Cambridge History of India, and I sat at table between Cockroft and Prof Rapson. Prof Rapson is a small fattish man, very nice and pleasant and very much like a grocer except in this that he has a fine head. He is really Prof of Sanskrit but he has been entrusted with the work of editing the first two volumes of the *Cambridge History*, a work that he does not like at all. After dinner, we went up to the drawing room or I don't know what it's called and had coffee and I continued to talk with Prof Rapson. At about 8.45 Cockroft and I left and I walked down with Cockroft in the direction of his house (which is some way out of Cambridge) till it became quite dark (at about 9.30) and then I returned to the hotel. It is now just 10.30 and I shall end for today.

13th Today I enjoyed myself but not as much as yesterday. I left the hotel at about 9 and went down to have a look at Newton's statue in Trinity which I had somehow missed during my previous visit. I then took a punt and spent nearly 2 1/2 [hours] drifting about on the river. I enjoyed it but I would have liked some person to do the paddling while I lay on my back imbibing the Cambridge atmosphere. I had a fairly large punt—a four-seater—and I must have looked a little lonely in it. From the river I returned to the hotel to have a wash before walking down to the Stanleys' for lunch. I found that they were further away than I had imagined and it was fortunate that I had left the hotel half an hour before lunch. As it was I got there punctually to the tick. Mr Stanley's father is a knight—this I only discovered when yesterday I rang them up and the voice at the other end said, 'I am Lady Stanley, Mr Stanley's mother'. I still do not know what the name of Lady Stanley's husband is, and I had to call him respectfully just 'sir'. They have a very fine house situated in quite large grounds. Lady Stanley was something like Lady Bowen—energetic and social leaderistic. This after-noon she was organizing a cricket match and a dinner and a tea party. Sir Stanley is something like Sir John Bowen, downtrodden and of no moment in the house, only to twice the extent that Sir John Bowen is. The ratio Sir John Bowen/Sir Stanley is practically = Lady Bowen/Lady Stanley = 1/2 as regards niceness and pleasantness. However Lady Bowen and Sir John were so extremely good that Sir Stanley and Lady Stanley are not bad. Sir Stanley had a terrible cast in the eye.

This I was fool enough not to perceive immediately with the result that *twice* I thought he was addressing me and made an attempt at a reply when he was really addressing Mrs Stanley. Mr and Mrs Stanley were extremely nice. They have no house of their own as yet ready to receive them and are therefore living with Sir St. They have just purchased a house near London of which they showed me photographs. It has got a very nice garden and very fine timber (30 acres in extent) but it has no electric lights or central heating nor a sufficient number of rooms and baths. They are going to have a new dining room too and while all these alterations and additions are being done they will go into a fur-nished house or flat in London. After lunch when Sir St. and Lady St. left (they motored down to London) we all went down on our knees on the drawing room carpet round the plans of the house and did some house planning in a very similar manner and style to what Sarhan M. [*maternal uncle, Sarhan Latif*] used to do when in Bombay—and with similar results. The porch gave us most trouble. As it was quite impossible—we were all agreed on that—and it had to be altered. We were also more or less agreed as to the form of the new porch, I however requiring some persuasion before I came to this agreement. But the size and especially the form of the cornice troubled us. Mr Stanley had prepared a suggested section of the cornice out of a huge piece of cardboard. Mrs Stanley thought this too heavy. My opinion was that it was not really heavy but that it looked heavy be-cause of an optical illusion caused by the misdrawing by Mr Stanley of a well-known geometrical figure, viz., the arc of a circle. To this opinion I after some time succeeded in convincing Mrs Stanley. Later in the argument I won much admiration both from Mr Stanley and Mrs Stanley by demonstrating that method of drawing a circle through three given points. Next time that anybody asks me the use of 5th standard geometry I shall quote this as a relevant instance.

After this, Mr Stanley took me round the garden and presented me with a scarlet rose, a violet sweet pea and another violet flower with a beautiful scent of which I do not remember the name. The rose I presented to Mrs Stanley with the appropriate remark that it 'would go well with the colour of her dress' and the sweet pea and the other flower I later on dropped into the dustbin at the station. For the sweet pea and the other flower—Sic Omnia transit Gloria, or whatever it is.

Mr Stanley dropped me at the station in his car and I took the 3.35 train for Ely. I got to the Cathedral at 4 and had a very interesting time till about 6, going through the Norman, Romanesque, Transitional, Gothic, Early English or Lancet and Gothic Decorated, Geometrical and flowing styles of architecture with the help of good Baedeker. I do not know Father whether you visited Ely but the Cathedral is supposed to be remarkable in having all these styles distributed in different parts. I returned to Cambridge by the 6.30 train, and had roast beef, two helpings of raspberry and Bird's custard and 2 cups of coffee for dinner or supper as it is here called. *There is not much more news of today to be given. I have given instructions that I should be called at 7 tomorrow and that my breakfast should be ready at 7.30 so that I may be in good time for my bus at 8.30. After dinner, I wrote a letter to Sir Arnold White. Did I write to you that I had enquired for him at the India Office but they would not give me his address as they said this would be against their rules. They suggested that I should write to him but this for some reason or the other got left till today. I hope he is in London and that I shall be able to see him. I have asked for an apptmt. I gave the letter to the head waiter and asked him to have it posted at once. He said he would run down himself. He is appallingly obliging. I wonder whether he is expecting a big tip.*

Good night all. It is only 10 by my watch but you must all be dead asleep at 2 or so in the morning.

15th I have arrived in London and my letters will become short again. When there is no theatre I have nothing to do in the long evenings but write—so that by feeling the weight of the letter you will be able to say whether I have been going to the theatre or not. *I left Cambridge yesterday by the 8.30 bus and got to London by 11. I had not kept on my room here but I had left one of my suitcases here and it was understood that I was coming back. I then visited the American Express and got a whole heap of letters and pamphlets especially pamphlets. I received two letters from Somerset—of the 26th and 27th. They contain the 'dhumkies' for short letters which I was very much afraid that they would contain.*

By the way I was rather disappointed with the way my visit to G. B. S. has been taken by you all and especially Badr. I had no intention of doing what young and fervent ladies of 35 do, viz., look and admire and collect autographs. I wanted to make friends if possible and get to know something of the high-brow socialist circle. My plan was to see both Bernard Shaw and Sydney Webb and trade especially on Raffoo Phoophee [paternal aunt] having stayed with Ramsay Macdonald. *However I soon found that I really had no time for any such thing and above all the Season soon ended and everybody left London for the holidays. As a matter of fact I did not even write to Sydney Webb. I had intended asking Bernard Shaw to lunch with me but he was soon leaving London and as I would not see him again it was not much use spending a pound or so on a lunch.*

As a matter of fact the best friend that I have made here is Codrington, an archaeologist and in the Victoria and Albert Museum. I lunched with him yesterday in the afternoon. He is quite young but he struck me as a clever and singularly forceful person and I am sure that he will go far. He knows Mahomedi Mamoo well. He has been in India quite long and he will come again in a year or so. I have invited him to stay with us when in Bombay. The rest of yesterday I spent looking at those 10 cartoons in the V. and A. Museum and at Westminster Abbey. In the evening there was a Bach and Handel concert given in the Queen's Hall by Sir T. Beecham's orchestra.

17.8.29

I am now in London and so my letters will again be very short. My doings since last Thursday have been Thursday I returned from Cambridge to the same lodgings, 43 Oxford Terrace. To the North—about 5 minutes walk of Marble Arch. I was taken up to the same room too but then the house keeper came running up saying that I would get another room as they were going to put a double bed in that room. So, I went up to the second floor where there was to all appearances an even finer room. But appearances *were* deceptive. The room faced the street and as you know there is no time in the 24 hours when London traffic ceases and all through the night I kept waking up as each lorry trundled past. So I changed into my present room which is right at the top and though small, very quiet. When I first came here it was I think shown to me as a 27/6 sh room but the other day when I asked Mr Mawley he said it was 30/-. Well we shall see whether a little diplomacy won't do. Mrs Mawley has a housekeeper (he is either a bachelor or a widower) and it was this housekeeper who had told me it was 27/6 sh. I shall go up and pay the housekeeper. Well, to continue my story. On Thursday in the morning I went again to the British Museum to see the Greek sculptors and the few Persian Paintings that they have got. It is funny that they should have such a fine collection of Indian Miniatures and I believe of Japanese and Chinese Paintings and have so little of Persian Painting. Those Greek Sculptures of course are very fine. I left the B.M. at about 5.30 and after having fish, roll and butter at Lyons just in front of the Museum I went down to Crystal Palace where there are fireworks every Thursday evening.

The fireworks were really splendid and I thoroughly enjoyed myself. I did not purchase a ticket for a seat but just lay on the grass on the slopes of the gardens. There were hundreds of people sitting on the grass. There was just next to me a very amusing Scot who had been settled for a long time in London. I had quite a good deal of conversation with him.

On Friday I visited the Tower. In the afternoon I had tea at Saeed Bhai's where there were also a Mrs Abdul Rehman and a Major and Mrs Pershad. The only interesting thing about them was that Mrs Pershad was rather good-looking.

On Saturday in the morning I went to the National Gallery. In the afternoon I went to the Crystal Palace again and at 3.30 there was dirt track racing. Dirt track racing is very thrilling. In an oval the long diameter of which must be about 250 yards or so speeds of 45 miles or so are attained. The Crystal Palace record as a matter of fact is 45.93 m.p.h. and clouds of 'dirt' (really cinders) are thrown up where there is more curve in the track. However after a short time I left as it gets rather tedious. You can't go on being thrilled for very long. I also went up to the High Tower there. What a magnificent view there is from the top. I had only a very little time for the exhibition inside the Crystal Palace. I believe the original sculptures in the Palace are not very good but there are plaster casts of all the famous pieces in the world and it would therefore be a very nice place to do some studying, especially as I found the Crystal Palace one of the few places in London which is not crowded. I had to come back for the concert at 8 at Queen's Hall. On Saturday it was a mixed programme: there was Purcell (English XVII century). They are boosting English composers terribly now. (The Queen's Hall concerts have been arranged by the British Broadcasting Co), Weber (Invitation to the Waltz, a nice light piece), the flower song from Carmen, the Prelude of 'L'Apres Midi d'un Faune', the ballet by Debussy, one of the most famous of the modem pieces of music. I had seen 'L' Apres Midi d'un Faune' at the Covent Garden when I went to see the Serge Diaghileff Russian Ballet Co. The Ballet was written for Serge Diaghileff by Debussy who would I suppose correspond in the musical world to Bernard Shaw in the literary. From the different reviews I gather that Stravinsky and Tchaikovsky are supposed to be more popular but Debussy is the height of Modern Music. However I think I shall stop describing the concert. I have kept all the descriptive programmes which are very interesting.

On Sunday in the morning I went to St Paul's for the service. The music was magnificent. I am very sorry that I did not go there oftener. I had been to St Paul's in the afternoon before but the afternoon music is nothing like so good as the morning music. It was really glorious. From St Paul's I had to rush off to see Sir Thomas Arnold who had asked me to go and see him at 2. It was something of a rush because I had to have my lunch in between and Sir Thomas was right at the end of London near Kensington High Street and he was not near the station either. However I got there 10 minutes before the appted time and had to wait at the gate before knocking. I spent a very interesting time with Sir Thomas indeed, nearly 2 hours I think. I am sorry that I have not been able to meet Sir Thomas more. As the chief person here working on Indian miniatures he was extremely interesting to me.

And he was very nice because he knows so much of our family. You will no doubt remember that he was the guardian of Saleh Bhai [Hydari, Sir Akbar Hydari's eldest son, and the first governor of Assam after Independence] when he was here. He said that he was responsible for Saleh Bhai's marriage which I thought was claiming rather too much when I learnt that all he had done was to send Saleh Bhai to Grenoble to learn French and that S. B. had first met his future wife there.

I felt inclined after discussing with him his latest book on a mss of the *Hamzah* and a list of Akbar's court painters that he is preparing, to think that Sir Thomas generally does believe that he is responsible for more than he actually is. Did I write to you that Mr Stanley Clarke told me that he thinks Sir Thomas does not know Persian well. This I think is going rather too far, though I do not know Persian myself and have therefore no means of testing Sir Thomas' knowledge.

On Sunday morning I returned home and had a bath after 2 days—don't be aghast. I am usually cleaner in fact a bath a day and did some domestic work i.e. repairing socks, sewing on buttons, etc. What an amount of time this takes but I think I turned out fairly decent work. And then washing was a big item. Now I have decided that I shall give more things to the laundry. I find that I can afford it.

On Monday I went down to Windsor in the morning. What a magnificent place it is. Worthy of the King of England and of the Emperor of the British Empire I thought. The afternoon I spent in the India Office Library looking through the works of M. Blochet of the Bibliotheque Nationale of Paris. When I went to see Sir Thomas I discovered what a great mistake it was to go and see a person without having first read all his works. With Sir Thomas I had a ready answer viz. that I am not interested in Persian history or miniatures. (Sir Thomas has hardly published anything on Indian dittos yet.) But I shall have to be more careful with Blochet. First of all because everybody tells me that he is particularly fierce and secondly because he calls all Indian paintings 'Persian' of the Indian school.

In the evening there was a Wagner concert. I enjoyed it but not as much as I had hoped. I think Wagner suffers very much if pieces are cut out from his 'music dramas' and separately performed. I had heard as I wrote to you 'Tannhauser' twice and though the overture of 'Tannhauser' as performed in the Queen's Hall was very much better done than at the Carl Rosa Opera yet I think it suffered greatly not being followed up immediately by the rest of the opera where all the themes and whole thesis so to say of the overture was developed, I enjoyed the overtures of 'Tristan and Isolde' and 'Parsifal' (which I have not heard yet) much more. The 'Rienzi' prelude was also performed.

Well, I must end for today. I don't think I shall be able to write much more. I leave for Oxford on the 23rd and from there you will get a longer letter for Oxford I suppose is a place similar to Cambridge at least so far as evening engagements are concerned.

23rd The mail day has arrived without my being able to write much more and so I shall end this letter rather abruptly.

20th Tuesday In the morning I went to the India Office Library and I was there almost till 2.30 when I went to get some lunch. I always find that these late lunches do me a great deal of harm. They sort of make me extremely tired and then after lunch I [am] not good for anything. However,

After lunch I went down to Kew and did not enjoy it half as much as I would have done if I were not feeling so disgusted with the world—all the effects of the late lunch. I sometimes at places like Kew feel the need for a companion. What is the good of seeing a beautiful dahlia when you cannot tell your companion 'What a beautiful thing it is.' In the evening there was a Mozart and Schubert concert. There were three symphonies of Mozart, a concerto of his and a symphony by Schubert which is I believe the longest symphony in existence. Hard work it was going through such an amount of difficult music. I *was* tired by the time I got home. 21st Wednesday *Morning I went and called on Leviticus of Leviticus and Co again. He asked me to come and have tea with him at 3.30. I then called on Gain of Gain, Brett, and ... He was very busy and so I just said goodbye to him. The rest of the day*

Till 3.30 I wasted aimlessly wandering about. In my wandering I spent 10 shillings purchasing 1) Otto's German Grammar (the big one) and 2) two maps of Wales of the parts where I am going to do my walking tour. In the evening I had tea with Saeed Bhai and then a Brahms' concert—2 symphonies, an overture and 6 songs. There was some miscellaneous music by Grieg and others coming after the interval but I came away.

24th Oxford

I have now left London for good and so it is time to give you a general survey of my doings there. But before I begin that:

Thursday 22nd Morning went down to the Tate Gallery. This visit was especially made for the purpose of hunting out the Rahamin pictures. (I could not find them during my previous visits. I had been on Sundays and Saturday afternoons and the director not being then in the office no body could give me any information of them.) Well, I sent up my card and a Mr Ede met me. Unfortunately I could not see the pictures themselves as they had been sent to the workshop for framing. If I had pressed I could no doubt have seen them in the workshop but I did not think it worthwhile. As to the history, they were presented, one by Sir Victor Sassoon and the other by the Maharaja of Baroda (or was it Kapurthala. Yes, I don't think it was Baroda. It was some minor chief). Mr Ede did not like them at all but I am afraid that Mr Ede (as you will see later) is not quite to be trusted. There is no doubt that the Trustees accepted the paintings with great delight and that they are much appreciated. I learnt later that

Rahamin had called at the Tate only a few days before to try and persuade the authorities to hang them in a conspicuous place no doubt as a preparation for the exhibition of his pictures which he is going to hold in December.

Well, to drop Rahamin, I found Mr Ede a most interesting person. He is 35 years old, a modern artist, and a very modern thinker in artistic matters. We became immediate friends. He was interested in Ajanta and I told him about its present condition, etc. He asked me when I was going and I told him that it was the next day. He then said that it was [a] pity that people came to the Tate only just before going away. So I asked him whether he was free in the evening and on hearing that he was promptly asked him to dine with me. This had the effect of his asking me to dine with him. He added 'I have got rather a beautiful house which I would like to show to you'. Well it was decided that I should go down to Hampstead after the matinee for which I had a ticket was over. I left Ede, had lunch and went to Piccadilly to see 'The Father' by Strindberg. This was preceded by 'Barbara's Wedding' by Barrie, a jewel of a piece in one act. 'The Father' was a very depressing and highly exaggerated account of a father and mother who both want to control the education of their daughter and in this combat the mother so goes after the father that the father falls into a faint and before he comes out of the faint and it becomes certain whether he has become mad or remained sane (the doctor who is in attendance says that he cannot give a definite opinion till the patient recovers) the curtain finally falls.

Well I left the theatre and took the tube to Hampstead. I had no difficulty finding Ede's place. There was a nice little garden in front with a lawn and a few roses and anemones. Ede came to the door himself—he saw me entering the gate through the window—and after I had placed my hat, umbrella and otto on the table in the hall, he took [me] round the house. In the hall there were a number of water colours in slightly later than post-cubist style. During our round of the house I was at first not quite certain whether the Edes had just come into the house and their furniture had not till then arrived or whether they were going to leave and their furniture had already been sent away. However I knew my host already sufficiently well not to make any indiscreet inquiries. Later on I learnt that as furniture always kills the artistic spirit of the room and spoils its proportions they had taken away all the furniture that they possibly could to have as much bareness as possible. The house was apparently partly Tudor and very nice and quaint. We finally settled down before a round [table] where Ede had already been sitting sticking in into a manuscript the reproductions which were to form the illustrations. The book was on a French painter and sculptor who had been killed in the war. We soon settled down into a sort of argumentative conversation. It wasn't very much argument, though. We sort of each made a series of statements, the series of the one being so to say punctuated by the series of the other. The argument went something like this: Note: Except for the words, this is exactly what was said.

Self Yes, this is a nice house. I like this sideboard here.

Ede This was originally the kitchen and this (the sideboard) was the dresser. We have made the dresser into a sideboard.

Self I have been having a very interesting time looking at the pictures in the Tate. I confess that I am not able to understand the latest paintings. I can enjoy a Manet or a Pissarro and the work of the Impressionists but I cannot understand what the post Impressionists, cubists, etc. are driving at. Now this picture over there (pointing to a very 'late' landscape hanging just opposite to me). What does it represent? Has it got a story to tell? Or is it merely a decorative piece?

Ede Well it is a decorative piece. Modern art is really decorative only.

Self But then modern art has fallen pretty low if all that it claims to do is to be decorative though I suppose decoration is no easy thing to do.

Ede Well, the real aim of modern art is to do away with all clogging details, get to the real spirit of the model. This picture for instance I think is good because it shows the inner lights and colours which constitute the beauty of the landscape.

Self I see, so the modern art does tell you some story. In the present case for instance it tells you what constitutes the true beauty of the landscape.

Ede No, when you asked me whether modern art tells a story I thought you meant stories such as those painted by Hogarth in the Mariage a la Mode. Such stories do not concern modem art.

Self No, what I meant by story was not this. I call a story anything which a picture tells me and which a competent observer looking at the object would not be able to find out for himself. For instance a picture may represent a mountain and may further say that the mountain was made by god and tell you this or say that the mountain was not made by god and was made by some other … or made itself or was never made at all and tell you that. I take it that no person however competent could merely by looking at the mountain be able to say whether the mountain was made by god or not. In such a case, I would call the picture a story-telling picture and I think that the more a picture is a story-telling picture the higher it is as a piece of art.

Ede Well modern art does not attempt to do anything of this kind. It takes upon itself the work of analysing the beauty of the thing it represents.

Self Then I must say that I have not much desire to know modern art. I would much rather look myself at the object represented and do the analysing for myself. It seems to me that modem art is now doing exactly what all these keys and guides and summaries are supposed to do—sort of extract all the beauty and goodness from a piece of work and place it before you in a compact mass. I would much rather wade through the 6 or 7 vols. of Gibbon myself and see the beauty of his historical representation than have somebody tell it to me in a few pages. It is quite possible that the artist is very much more clever in seeing the points of beauty in a landscape for instance and that through his representation of the landscape can tell the person looking at the picture many things which such [a] person may not have been able to see for himself. But then such a person who has not been able to see for himself would probably not understand those things when he is being told them by the picture.

Ede Ah but in saying this you touch a great truth which I do not know you realize it [sic]. All art should be for the artist himself and no art should be painted with the idea that anybody else will look at it.

I find that I always make my speeches twice as long and much more convincing than Ede's. Of course our conversation was much more broken and wandered off the point much more especially when Ede spoke. He said later on when he learnt that I was a lawyer; 'Ah, that is why you stick to the point so much'. I told him that if I did stick to the point it was probably because I was a mathematician and after hearing this he would frequently repeat, 'Yes, mathematics and art go together'. I informed him that Einstein was a very good violinist.

As to the rest of our very long conversation I shall tell it to you when I return to Bombay. What I have written is only a small fragment. I of course disagreed with Ede on the point that an artist should not paint for anybody else to look at.

By this time it was getting quite late. I could not stay very late because I was leaving London early next morning and I had still to do all my packing. So we started cooking dinner—that is, he started doing so. Mrs Ede was in Edinburgh with her father and so he was quite alone by himself. I must say he gave me a splendid dinner: There was very good soup and omelette and potatoes and peas and melon and custard for sweet. I left him at about 8.30 and got home about 9.15 and had my cases ready for travelling by about 10.

23rd I had given instructions that my breakfast should be brought up at 7.45. I was ready for it and I then asked the maid to get a taxi. I find that it is impossible to do without a taxi. When I had come to Cambridge I had taken only one suitcase and I had got quite killed in carrying it from my lodgings to the tube station and from the tube station to the place where the buses started from. For my two cases two porters would be necessary and their charges would come up to at least a shilling. Besides there would be the tube fare and a taxi would not be so very much more expensive and as a matter of fact it came to only 3 shillings. On the other hand I was saved much worry and trouble.

I got a very good seat—a double seat all to myself—and I had a very comfortable run to Oxford, where we got about 11.30. I let the cases be in the bus (which was going on to Birmingham at 12) and told the driver that I was going to look for lodgings. The bus driver said that if I did not return till 12 he would leave the cases in charge of the car park attendant.

I started looking for the lodging but I found that this was no easy matter. The post office could not tell me anything and the policemen could not tell me anything. I at last got out an address from my bus guide. This place was on the High Street and so probably expensive. On calling the lady told me that her rooms were 7/6 but she would charge me 6 sh p. day. I said I wanted something not more than 5 sh for bed and breakfast. I asked her if she knew of any such place but she did not. So I walked along and enquired at the next shop, and so after two or three inquiries I came to this place where there was only one room vacant, a very nice room on the top floor. Price 6/6. By this time I was feeling so tired and hungry that I hadn't even the patience to go back to the first place and took the room and this is from where I am writing. By this time it was past 12.45 and so I hurried back to the place where the bus had stopped. The bus was of course not here but my cases were not there either. I cross-questioned the attendant in the car park so much that I made him quite angry. But all that I could get out of him was the address of Samuelsons (the owners of the bus) agents—a music store. There my story was heard by two plump attendants who after listening to it with great attention rushed off to fetch another plump person—a gentleman—who was presumably the proprietor. Toothpicks or something like that. Mr Toothpick was very nice. He looked up the time table and found that this bus would get to Birmingham at 3.30 and leave again for London at 5.45 and reach Oxford at 8.30, the same driver driving. He suggested that the whole story should be telephoned to the office of Samuelsons at Birmingham. I thought this a good idea and then he informed me that I would have to pay him 2 sh, being the cost of a call to Birmingham. On hearing this I made a suitable protest, said that it was not my fault that the cases were carried to Birmingham, assuming that they were carried there, etc. Well it was finally agreed that if it was discovered to be my fault I should of course bear the loss of the 2 sh but that if it was the driver's fault he should pay the 2 sh. And Birmingham was telephoned to.

I left the office very much upset. By this time it must have been much past 2 and as I was feeling very hungry I went into the first restaurant that did not look very expensive. There as I found that all the meat dishes were over a shilling I had a cup of coffee and 3 buns with butter apres le methode Mohsin [younger brother]. The three buns I found very filling indeed and I had quite a good meal for 8 d. This month I have spent a great deal [of] money and so I must be very careful now. Even as it is I shall probably pass my allowance of 23 pounds p. mensem.

I returned to my lodgings and taking my Baedeker marched off to the Bodley. I had written to the librarian from London on the suggestion of Sir Thomas Arnold and had got a very nice letter saying that I would find the reading room very uncomfortable as repairs and cleaning were going on, but that they would be pleased to show me anything that I wanted to see. I must say that they have been extremely good. The gentleman whom the librarian had suggested that I should see—a Mr Parry—was unfortunately away for the week end. A Mr Needham attended to me. Some of the albums and pictures had got under other boxes and beams and he got men to take them out. I was in the Bodley till 5 when they closed and then I went into the Radcliffe Camera, the reading room of the Bodley (which Father you no doubt remember—it is double asterisked in Baedeker. It is a beautiful Italian Renaissance building) which is open till 10 p.m., to look up Fox-Strangways' 'Music of Hindustan' who has compiled a very complete list of the *rag*, giving the names of the provinces in which they are chiefly current. It is of course very useful when looking at *rag* and *Ragini* pictures. I used the book a good deal in the India Office Library too when looking at the Johnson Collection. I have been making a list of the *rag* pictures and the way they are represented. Sir Thomas Arnold was very much pleased at this. There is at present no such list and nobody seems to quite know how to identify any picture with a particular *rag*. Unfortunately very few pictures have anything written on them. Some of the pictures are easy to identify such for instance as Todi who is always represented playing the *been* with black buck listening and similarly Asavari and Bhairavi and Bhairav and Khamaj. As Haffoo will no doubt tell you there are in the classical arrangement 6 *raags*: Bhairav, Malkaus, Dipak, Sri, Meegh Malhar and Hindol, and each of these has 5 *ragnis*. But besides these there are hosts of other *rags* such as Kalyan and Bhopali etc. (Fox-Strangways gives 70) and these are represented in pictures which are painted in the province in which that particular *rag* is especially popular. So that if we can identify the *rag* not only do we make this much progress but we can also say where the picture was probably painted. It is a very interesting study indeed.

Goodbye for tonight

27th Stratford on Avon

I am afraid that this will be another letter begun on too ambitious a scale and which then peters out. I had intended bringing the narrative up-to-date and then writing to you an a/c of my business doings. But I have got into the midst of theatres again. However.

To continue the a/c of the day of my arrival at Oxford. I left the Radcliffe Camera at 8 and went down again to the place the buses stop. The suitcases did arrive. I believe that the driver had forgotten to drop them but he of course made all kinds of excuses which by the way changed their form and substance quite a number of times during our short colloquy. I of course made no attempt to recover the 2 sh but I persuaded him to drop my suitcases within a few yards of the place where I had taken my lodgings thus saving 1/6 for taxi hire. I have written I think that I have found that it is impossible to do without a taxi.

24th Saturday In the morning I left home at about 9—as the Bodley would not be open till 10 I went down to Christ Church. What a magnificent college it is. There is no doubt that Oxford is a much finer university than Cambridge so far as the buildings and scenery is concerned and if it was not for the traditions of Cambridge in Maths and Physics I would now give my vote for Oxford without hesitation. For one thing I have found that here they do not have three or four styles of architecture grouped round the same quad which as I wrote to you I found so jarring at Cambridge. And the gardens here I thought much finer.

On Saturday I had only time to see Christ Church—and of that only a part before it was time to go to the Bodley. I was at the Bodley till 11.30. Mr Needham was again very kind. I have been told that in Germany too all the curators and Profs are very good but that in Paris they are particularly bad. Well, let us see what happens to me. I had to leave at 11.30 because I had to lunch with Prof Margoliouth. I had written from London to him and he had replied very nicely in a letter which I enclose because I think that the reference in it to our 'name' will appeal to all at Somerset Lodge. Yes, and on my arrival at Oxford I had telephoned to Prof Gilbert Murray and he had asked me to go and see him at 4 the same day (Saturday). Before going to Prof Margoliouth's I purchased a copy of Bridges' poems. You see both Dr Bridges and Prof Murray live at Boar's Hill about 2 miles from Oxford and I intended calling on Dr Bridges after leaving Prof Murray—for Badr's sake. I confess that I fell so low as to get a copy of *Oedipus* too—for Prof Murray to sign on. I thought of purchasing a copy of Margoliouth's '*Mahomedanism*' too but I thought there had been already sufficient indulgence of the lower appetites and did not spend any more money. As a matter of fact the expenditure of this 6/6 on books has hit the budget of this month hard and now there is no chance of keeping within the 23 pounds.

Prof and Mrs Margoliouth were very nice indeed and they gave me a very good vegetarian lunch. It was in his library that I for the first time learnt that Prof Margoliouth had published such a number of vols. in the Gibbs Memorial series, which I thought rather shameful. He has got a very fine library of Arabic books. He was in India only last year and delivered the Wilson Philological lectures. How extraordinary that I never knew of it. I suppose I was so sort of upset with no work to do that I missed the notices announcing them. Dr Margoliouth drove me back to the High Street as he had himself to go there. I have never in my life seen such a bad driver and I don't think I shall ever see [one] again. Mrs Margoliouth told me that last summer they had done a motoring tour to the North. I wonder they manage it. Possibly they had somebody else with them who drove. I wish I had asked.

Oh yes, during lunch Prof Margoliouth suddenly asked me whether I had been to Cambridge. I said yes. Then he asked me whether I had met Prof Nicholson. I said yes, I had had tea with him. Then P.M. said that he was asking me these questions because I had addressed 'the lady opposite' (Mrs Margoliouth) as Mrs Nicholson. I was very profuse in my apologies and took care not to made such a mistake again.

I took a bus from the High Street for Boar's Hill and got there in about 15 minutes. I was dropped almost at Prof Murray's door and as it was only about 3.30 I walked up and down the road till 4 which was the appointed time. I was taken to the study by the maid but Prof Murray had me sent down to the drawing room. On the staircase I met

Mrs Murray who came up to me with a very cordial 'How do you do' She is thin and rimless pince-nezed and she reminded me of both Lady Bowen and Lady Stanley for she was active and talkative and quite nice. She spoke much more than Prof Murray. There were in the drawing room besides us another old gentleman who 30 years ago retired from the I. Forest Service (Bombay). He asked me whether I was a Parsi and a young lady who was either a daughter or daughter-in-law of Prof Murray. Tea was soon announced and we adjourned into the dining room where we were joined by a nurse with a one-year-old grandchild of Prof Murray. It was a treat to watch Prof Murray play with this rather stolid child who smiled slowly and carefully every time the Prof rapped on the table and bent his magnificent forehead over the child. After helping myself to a considerable amount of bread and butter, I said 'I did not quite re-alize that I was inviting myself to tea when I said I would come at 4.' Prof Murray said, 'It was I who said you should come at 4, wasn't it?' I did not clear the matter up.

After tea we again went into the drawing room and I produced the 'Oedipus' and Prof Murray signed on it. He seemed to be genuinely pleased when I told him how much we had enjoyed reading it.

I had to soon leave as I wanted to get that autograph of Dr Bridges. Dr Bridges was a good distance away, I found, almost a mile. Well he was in due course tackled and his autograph is at present in my suitcase. Mrs Bridges I found again active talkative, nice. The only person whom I have as yet met and who was not active, talkative and nice was Mrs Nicholson who was only nice.

25th Sunday In the morning I went down to Christ Church Cathedral which is also the college chapel for service.

I can't say that I enjoyed it very much. I then went round all the colleges systematically.

Unfortunately it being a Sunday no admission could be had to a number of places. Balliol was altogether closed. However I still did do a lot of seeing. Magdalene is simply magnificent I think. In the evening I took a canoe and went up the river to-wards Shipley (I think) which Baedeker says is a favourite boating excursion. But I was very much disappointed. The banks are not at all pretty being for a long distance lined with boat houses. Then we have a series of regularly placed camping tents all of the same size and dirty yellow colours with young men in very camping attire lolling in front of them. But this was not all. Each of the little camps had a name and this name was written on a large board and fixed facing the river: One was 'the Wrecker's Rest', then 'the Dewdrop Inn', then 'Du Bud Bil' (evidently the first syllables of the names of the occupants), etc. I felt that if I was working for an examination and sud-denly read all this I would not be able to do any more work for a week.

26th Monday In the morning before going down to the Bodley I went to St John's, a college which I had seen closed on Sunday. I then passed Balliol and seeing a gate open I went in though I knew that the college was closed for cleaning. An attendant of course soon came up and told me what I already knew and I apologized profusely but I had already had a good look at the college bldgs at least from the outside. I must say that although Balliol is very big the buildings are not impressive.

I went in to the Bodleyan and just finished all their pictures and had a little time for revision when it was time for me to leave. My bus started at 12. I arrived at Stratford at 2.30 as the bus was a little late. I have got a very nice room in a little house here. *Cont on 28th* It is however rather far from the centre (that is, about 1 mile) of Stratford. The name of the landlady is Mrs Barnard. The information directory had given me the names of a number of places in Stratford and I had written to about 7 or 8. They all replied saying that they charged from 7/6 upwards for bed and breakfast. Mrs Barnard to whom I had not written and who got my name from a friend of hers to whom I *had* written and who had no room said that she wanted 3 sh for the room without breakfast and 5 sh with b. Well, I came up to her and told her I was a 'student' (a very true thing) and said that I had no more to spend and asked her whether she would give me break-fast of 1 sh. I would not want eggs or anything expensive, just toast and butter and coffee. She is evidently a very nice person and was deeply impressed by my story—so much so that she asked me whether I was an orphan! I said no, but this statement did me no harm for I elaborated on my loneliness here and how much I would like to have friends and entreated her to treat me as a member of the family. Well all the things were nicely arranged. I was introduced to her 2 dtrs (she is a widow) who work in a book making and illuminations factory here and who now and then have small parts in the plays. She now also gives me a nice supper. She had in correspondence threat-ened to charge me 6 d per bath but now I shall have to pay her 15/- for supper, bath and all for 3 days. My budget is I think almost as extraordinary as that of the Govt of India. They spend 55% of the revenue on the army (Is it so much though? I always say it is whenever any talk of India rises). I spend an almost equally high percentage of my income on theatres. I have I find got very good seats in the theatre.

I left this place and walked down to the Shakespeare 'Birth place' at about 3.30. You no doubt remember the house quite distinctly Father. I spent about a couple of hours there and then on the way home had a peep into 'New Place' and its gardens and the Town Hall with its paintings of Garrick and Shakespeare. I got home at about 6.30. After having a bath I came down for supper. But there had been some misunder-standing. Mrs Barnard had thought I would not require anything that day. Well, it was something of a rush. She produced a piece of bony but rather nice meat, bread and butter and jam and 3 cups of tea which all I gobbled down. But I got to the theatre in plenty of time, almost a quarter of an hour before the curtain rose.

Hamlet himself was I thought very good but some of the minor parts (especially the ghost) were rather jarring. In the end I came away with the impression that the wording of the play was better than the acting. I had a very pleasant walk home in the cool moonlight.

Tuesday 27th I had the whole day free and as you see I wrote a portion of this letter. I left this place at about 11 and went down to the station to make some inquiries about my going from here to Malvern. I then went down to the church where Shakespeare is buried and from there walked down to Anne Hathaway's cottage about 2 miles away. Then I came home for a few minutes and then had another very pleasant walk to Luddington where Shakespeare is supposed to have been married. There are no ancient remains there, the church having been entirely rebuilt but it was a very nice walk. Counting the walk later in the evening to the theatre and back I must have done yesterday at least 12 miles. After I returned home at 11.45 I sat down to think.

The problem was this: should I go to Evesham or not the next morning (i.e. today). *Pros* This was a well known fruit-growing district and fruit was said to be cheap. (2) I must during this trip to Europe go at least once to some orchard in the country and have a good feed. (3) If I did not take this opportunity I do not know when an-other would come for it will soon be winter. Before that I may not be in another fruit growing district. (4) I had nothing to do in the morning till 2.30 when the Matinee performance of Twelfth Night commenced.

Cons (1) Evesham was by no means near as it took 55 minutes by bus to get there. (2) There were really no suitable buses as the first left at 8 in the morning (too early) and then there was no bus till 12. (3) It would be a pretty expensive thing to do for as the place was far the fare would be at least 2 sh and then however cheap the fruit was it would cost 2 sh or half a crown. (4) I was going to do a good amount of going about and such other opportunities would be sure to come. I had certainly a great deal to do in the morning for I have any number of letters to write. Well, the cons won, so here I am finishing this letter.

Goodbye for now I am afraid that the a/c of my 'business' doings in London will have to stand over. I have no time to read so mistakes will please be excused.

P. S. I have quite forgotten to acknowledge your letters, father d/d 30 July and 9th Aug. Mother 2 Aug and 9 Aug. Badr d/d 3 Aug. Haffoo d/d 2nd Aug and 8 Aug., the last from Andheri.

I am afraid Badr I got Ahmed's address a little too late. In any case I doubt whether I would have gone and seen him. I knew him very cursorily you must remember.

Haffoo's letter of the 2nd Aug contains a piece that is delicious. She writes:

Thanks for putting my name also in father's and mother's letters. We got it at lunch time when we were eating a delicious Cabal (with a capital C). If all this delicate irony and humour are intentional, Haffoo, I am prouder of you than I have ever been before.

I am afraid that I had never seriously intended calling on Miss Gardiner so it did not matter that I got the letter too late.

Regarding our old friends, father, I had thought that as I had so little time I had better concentrate on the Motts, especially as I already knew Eric. But I must say that they rather disappointed [me]. I of course wrote to Mr Mott and he asked me to call at his office and then took me out to lunch. I went to their office twice again. The first time I met Mr Mott he told me that could not ask me to come down immediately as they were having some trouble with their servants. Then Mrs Mott was going away to Cornwall and finally they were all going to Cornwall. The result was that I never saw their house. I must say that I felt rather sick especially because for a number of days I made no engagements for myself as I was expecting an invitation any moment.

I am sorry that I did not go to Mrs Venables before and see more of her.

My programme stands except for some minor alterations of which you will hear from time to time.

28.8.29

P. S. No 2 I enclose a p.c. from Prof Molisch in which the sentence commencing 'perhaps you are interested' will interest you too. Does this mean that we are going to have a handsomer Salim Khaloo. I was wondering whether I should have my nose operated on too in Vienna. People object to its being so pointed. Have you heard anything in India about this operation?

I am writing the p. s. at 1.45. I spent the morning walking along the banks of the Avon and dreaming and reading from 'Macbeth'. We have 'Macbeth' this evening and I find that you enjoy your play much more if you have just read it. It is otherwise sometimes rather difficult to catch the words. In Macbeth I have got a seat in the balcony which though very good so far as the view of the stage is concerned is just a little far.

I hope that that copy of the Nehru Report has been sent to Dr Molisch. I am sorry that I am giving you all this trouble but I believe that Dr Molisch is a kind of man with [whom] it would be very nice if I could get friendly. He has a very cultured family and I understand that till that terrible crash just after the war came they were very rich.

III The Midlands, Wales, Scotland

3.9.29

Birmingham
Hen and Chickens Hotel [letterhead with a print of the façade]
I have just received my Indian mail from the Post Office and I shall acknowledge all the letters in order.
Father d/d 15th Aug. (mail of 17th Aug.)
Mother 16th "
Badr 16th "
Haffoo "
I am very much afraid that this is again going to be an unsatisfying letter. I have been very busy indeed and I am getting more and more busy. To give you a summary of what has happened since last Wednesday.
Wed 28th. Stratford on Avon There was a matinee at 2.30 'Twelfth Night' which was really quite good and would have been better if it had not been so cut up. It is a pity that even at Stratford in the Shakespeare festivals they find it so necessary to cut the play. In the evening we had 'Macbeth'. It is a wonderful play. I was very much impressed indeed and I think I saw things in it which I would never have seen however many times I read it.

Thursday I had arranged that my luggage should be taken by the Railway people from my lodgings and sent off to the place where I had arranged for a room at Malvern. So I was quite free. I left very early at about 7.30 (which was very early after the theatre) and took the bus to Warwick. There I got another bus to Kenilworth which I reached at about 9. I spent a couple of hours going round the ruins. Once more I repeat—loudly, hear who may—Gothic architecture is a magnificent architecture. I wonder father whether you remember the banqueting hall at Kenilworth. All that remains are the walls and those soul stirring windows. I spent most of my time there contemplating those windows. There was an American pair at Kenilworth going round at the same time that I was. They had rolled up in a magnificent double six Daimler and a guide was taking them round. The man was tall and thin and looked very much like Henry Ford. I wonder whether it was really Ford come to see Kenilworth incognito, possibly with the idea of buying it up and carrying the whole over to one of the suburbs of Detroit.

I left Kenilworth and came back to Warwick. Then I had a look at the Cathedral church which has got a fine Gothic Perpendicular chapel and above all at Warwick

Castle which is said to have one of the finest parks in England. They did not let you see very much of the Park, however, so most of the paths had 'Private' boards across them and the grass all round had been made 'Private'. I returned to Stratford at about 3.15 and at about 4 I got a train which brought me into Malvern at 6.50.

I went up to the place where I had taken a room (bed and breakfast 5 sh) which I found quite a dirty one. However it was considerably cheaper that any other so one had to lump the dirt. I left the place in what I thought was good time for the theatre which I thought commenced at 8. When I got there I saw crowds of people coming out of the theatre. I wondered whether there was a matinee. But I had merely given another demonstration of the fact that I am a great fool. The theatre did not commence at 8 but at 6. On Thursday and Friday they were doing 2 parts each day of 'Back to Methusaleh' and so they commenced at 6 and had an interval from 7.45 to 8.30 for supper. Well the result is that I have missed Adam and Eve and Cain and all that. I of course saw the 2nd part.

Friday I spent the morning in first of all writing off some urgent letters and then went up the Malvern hills. Very beautiful, these, but hardly to be compared with our Ghats. Evening 3rd and 4th parts of 'Back to Methusaleh'.

Saturday In the morning I went down to Worcester to contemplate further Gothic architecture in the Cathedral. I am becoming quite a devotee of Gothic and I can now tell at sight whether a specimen is Early English or Decorated Geometric or Decorated Flowing or Perpendicular or Tudor. I like Tudor best I think. In the afternoon there was a matinee of the 'Apple Cart' and in the evening the last part of 'Back to Methusaleh'.

Sunday I took a return ticket to Monmouth on the Wye Valley. I got there at 11 and then I started out to hunt for a bicycle. At about 12 when I had quite given up hopes and had decided to get to Tintern by bus I got a Sunbeam, 3 speed gears and all. The cycle was however not so comfortable as I had hoped because the seat was rather small and hard and I was pretty sore by the evening. Well, I started at 11.50 I think, and got down to Tintern (12 miles) along the most wonderfully beautiful road skirting the banks of the Wye which father I have no doubt you know quite well. I do not think I have ever seen such glorious green scenery. I qualify my ecstasies because I am still of the opinion that the most wonderful thing in the world is the moonlight shining on the wet sands at Kihim in front of Latifia when the tide is out. The sunlight on the Wye added to the effect of the green banks was a pretty near approach to Kihim but I think that Kihim still leads.

I went down 2 1/2 miles further from Tintern to Wyndcliff which 'commands' (to quote Baedeker) 'one of the finest views of river scenery in Europe, remarkable for the beauty and variety of the foliage'. All very well but in soul-stirring value the sands of Latifia stand higher. I was pretty tired when I got back to Monmouth at about 5.15. You know we had got rather soft on our m/cycles and suddenly going off about 28 miles in a very hilly district was I found no joke. Hunt, the man who hired the cycle to me, was very nice. He gave me a first-class tea and above all an opportunity for having a good wash. Of course there was not much time for I had to catch my train at 5.47. I got into Malvern at about 7.40, picked up my luggage from a porter in whose charge I had left it and got into Birmingham at about 10 p.m.

I am as you see staying in a hotel and paying 8/6 for a very indifferent room. On Monday I left the hotel early, purchased a newspaper, looked up the 'apartment' adverts and started a search for lodgings. But I walked from 9 to 11 and found none. The places were either too expensive or if they were near 5 sh (which is the figure I aim at) they were full up. Well, I swore and returned to the hotel.

As after this it is all business I shall just copy out the relevant pages from my notebook.
Birmingham Programme

1. *Wolsely Motors (I had to sell them that invention of Ottman's of Hanumkonda of which I think I spoke to you in Bombay and also an invention of my own)*
2. *Birmingham Jewellers and Silversmiths Association*
3. *Brass and Copper Tube Ass*
4. *Brass Wire Ass*
5. *British Tube Ass*
6. *Brazed Brass Tube Ass*
7. *E. Camps (on whom Camar Bhai had given me a letter)*
8. *Chamber of Comm*
9. *Major C. R. Dobbin of the Federation of British Industries on whom Mr Gain had given me a letter*
10. *Visit Wolverhampton Chambers of Commerce*
11. *Coventry ditto*

Results
Monday
Wolselys telephoned to. I had written to them (and to a number of others) from London. Wolselys had sent me the most encouraging reply. Appointment given at 2.30
Called on Chamber of Commerce. Secretary busy. Asked to call at 4.
Called on Major Dobbin. Major away on holiday. Saw his Secretary and explained my schemes to him.
Received favourably. To write from India.
Called on no 5 above told Sec was away. Might get an apptmt for Wed.
Called on no 6 above. Sec out. Appointment at 5.
Called on no 3 above. Offices locked. Was informed that they would reopen after lunch.
Went down to have lunch at Lyons (who have got branches here) Hurried to Wolseleys. Got there much too early. Saw their Chief Designer as their Managing Director was very busy. Before we commenced discussing the invention (yes, only singular. I have decided to try and sell my own on the Continent) it was agreed that Wolselys should not make use of the idea if they did not purchase it for 6 months provided that there was nobody working in their offices on a similar invention. I was to have an assurance from the Managing Director to this effect. You will no doubt think that if it comes to the crunch this assurance won't be worth much. But I am afraid that we shall have to be satisfied with it. You see Ottman had patented his invention and I had made inquiries in London at the Patent Office and found that the patent had expired and that it would require about 10 pounds and any amount of time to get it renewed if it was renewed at all. Came back to the city and saw the Sec Chamb of Com at 4. Good reception, to write from India.
Called on 3. Sec away on holiday, to write from India
Called on 6 Good reception. To write from India. Introduced by him to Mr Mullins of Cold Rolled Brass and Copper Association. Called on Mullins. Good reception, to write from India.

By this time it was 6.45. Went into Lyons again and after fried fish roll, and butter had the luxury of stewed plums and cream (5 d). Returned to hotel to work out the time table for the next fortnight. I have been very lazy in not writing and making appointments beforehand. But you can imagine that it is no easy thing making appointments distributed between Birkenhead and Liverpool, Manchester, Bolton, Sheffield, Leeds, Bradford, Nottingham, and Leicester and all within about 10 days—from Tuesday the 10th 11.54 to Friday the 20th 5.17 p.m. to be precise. Then I leave for the Lake Dist.

Tuesday (today) I went to Coventry in the morning and saw the Sec Chamb of Comm. Afternoon Wolverhampton and ditto. Since return to Birmingham I have had dinner and have been writing this letter. I have now got some urgent letters to write and so I end. If I get any more time I shall write to you my opinion of Birmingham which I leave tomorrow 4. 15 p.m. If not, goodbye. P.T.O. I have not replied to your letters. I don't think father there is anything in yours requiring reply. Yes, there is one important thing. I should feel very much obliged if you would let me know whether I am doing right in pushing my 'schemes' on in this way. I believe that the 'Law Council' in England would be down on me if I was a member of the Law Society. How do I stand in India? I forgot to look up the point in Bombay because it never occurred to me. But Mr Mott pointed it out. By the time I get your reply I shall have already done all that I intend to do. Still however I would like to have your opinion after consultation of the authorities if there are any decisions or rulings on this point.

Mother Nothing to reply to.

Badr If you get married or pass you can get the gun. I think I shall be able to discharge all my obligations. Haffoo Thanks for long and interesting letter. I think the letter looks nice typed closely as you have done this one. You have made very few mistakes. Shabaash!

10.9.29 Liverpool

I have not yet got my mail from India. It must be waiting for me at Manchester. My arrangements were I am afraid not quite good for I shall be for nearly 4 days without letters. But it is difficult to arrange to get letters very punctually. One is so afraid of letters getting stranded.

I think my last letter ended with an account of what I did on Tuesday 3rd. On Wednesday morning a letter was handed to me by the hotel office and on opening it I found it to be a letter from Wolseleys. They thanked me for having so kindly given them an opportunity of considering Ottman's silencer but they were sorry that it would be of no use to them. They repeated their assurance that they would not make any use of it for 6 months. Well I had breakfast over this and then telephoned to Nortons whose reply to my letter from London was the next best. The Managing Director would see me at 2.30. I had not much time because at 4. 15 I was to take the train to Llangollen. I then went down to the shop where I had purchased this fountain pen to finally have the nib changed to the present one.

You of course know that I have got a new fountain pen. I justify this investment in the following manner. First of all that Blackbird really did not write properly. You probably noticed while reading my letters the number of times that the flow stopped.

Secondly it was a terrible nuisance filling it as it was not self-filling—and I had to fill it a number of times. Thirdly it did look queer when a gentleman dressed in an 8-guinea suit worn over silk underwear pulled out a real morocco pocket book and started writing in it with a 'Blackbird' with a tiny clip. Fourthly I have got this pen for about 3/4tr of what it would cost me in India and as it is going to last me my life time it is a good investment. Well.

Well, I had telephoned to Cambs (of Hercules Cycle Co. on whom Camar Bhai had given me a letter) the day before. He had just left for India and his partner had asked me to come down to their works (which I later on learnt were the largest in England) on Wednesday between 10 and 11. So I started off. I was received very nicely and was shown round their works which were very interesting. The only bit of business done was that I asked the director who first saw me to have 3 copies of a letter from the Sec of the Indian Merchants Chamber of Com. introducing me to the Sec. of the Manchester Chamber made for me and he in fact had 4 copies made.

Well, the going round the works took a good deal of time and I could just get back to Lyons in the city, have a cottage pie, and start off for Nortons.

[At Nortons] though the apptmt was for 2.30 I was kept waiting till almost 2.45. I started negotiations by saying that before I said anything more I would like to have an assurance that if the invention was not purchased they would not make use of it for 6 months. Reply: 'Alright.' I: 'I should feel obliged if you would make a note of this'. And then we started a most curious discussion. The Managing Director with whom I was having the interview was prepared to give me a verbal assurance but he would not make a note of it nor would he write a letter to me containing such an assurance. I said I could not see what objection there was in writing down anything that had been said in such an interview. He drew long rigmarole pictures of how written document could be mutilated or misinterpreted. I said that I was afraid that I was in that case wasting his time. He then became very nice and said that he hoped that I did not think that I was being badly treated. I said that I could quite understand an attitude (taken up by many manufacturers) that they would rather not see an invention which was not protected but that I could not quite see why this assurance could be given verbally but not in writing. The M. Director: 'Well then our position too is in effect that we would rather not see an invention that is not protected.' This ended the business part of the interview.

I then said that I too was a Norton owner (not a quite accurate statement as you know) and that I would very much like to see the Norton works. The M. Director became quite chatty and we talked over Nortons in the colonies, of the chances of a Norton winning in the next T.T. races etc. He then went into an adjacent room to fetch somebody to show me round the works and returned with Jimmy Simpson, a famous T.T. rider who was till recently an A.J.S. man but has now come to Nortons and whom Badr knows well. He was limping badly from an accident in last year's T.T. but he said that he was told that he would be quite alright by Christmas. Well he took me round and I saw the 1930 models which are already in production. The Norton works are as different from the Hercules works as they can be. Whilst in the cycle factory everything was as modern as it could be, in the Norton works I saw the men fitting crankshafts and connecting rods with large files in their hands. I remarked on this and Simpson said, 'Yes, but this is the better method'. I also went into the racing shop where machines were being prepared for the next racing season. By this time it was almost 3.30 and I told Simpson that I must be going. He was himself returning to the city and he offered to drive me there. He could drive quite alright in spite of his leg and he was as different a driver from Prof. Margoliouth as the Hercules works were from the Norton's works. He did not drive very fast and his only peculiarity which can be easily described was that he changed down to second immediately the car slowed down to less than 20 m.p.h.

I got to the hotel in good time, took my luggage in a taxi and got to the station. At 6.35 p.m. I got into Llangollen in N. Wales on the banks of the Dee.

One of my cases I sent down immediately to Bonnewydd still further west and then leaving the other in charge of the porter I started out to look for a room. About ten feet from the station entrance I saw the 'Green Field Hostel' (I think this was the name) and on my enquiring found that I could get a nice room and breakfast for 5/6. I went down to the platform and got my suitcase.

There was still plenty of light and opening my Baedeker I saw that a hill within about a mile of the town was marked with a single asterisk. There was an old castle called Dinas Braen at the top, at one time, the residence of the kings of Northern Wales. I started for this but did not get to the top as I was feeling very tired with the day's rushing about. So after passing a pair who were so engrossed in each other that they hardly noticed me I sat down to admire the view which was very fine indeed.

As you know, my plan was to start off the next day very early in the morning, walk along the Berwyn Mountains towards the West on Thursday, Friday and Saturday and get to Dolgelly within a few miles of the coast by Saturday evening. But beastly Birmingham had so tired me out that as I sat there the following discussion and decision took place:

Saif no. 1: (to Saif no. 2) You are feeling terribly tired and tomorrow you have got to get up early in the morning, pack and carry down the suitcase to the station and send it off. Don't you think that it is better to stay on in Llangolen tomorrow.

S. no. 2: I am tired but what about all the very elaborate plans which I have formed for this walking tour. I have spent about 6 shillings on maps alone.

S. no. 1: As to your plans though you have certainly spent a lot of time in forming them they are very hazy indeed. Even now you haven't quite fixed all the paths that you are going to follow. Besides in your plans you have allotted to each day a walk far too long for you to be able to do in a day. You must remember that the maps merely show flat distances and not distances up the hills and down the valleys, and this country is certainly very hilly.

S. no. 2: But I want to do this walk very much.

S. no. 1: You merely want to do it in order to be able to boast of it. The scenery round about here can hardly be improved and there is no meaning in going further afield. And remember how tired you are. Besides here you have got a nice place to live in, not too expensive, and you haven't the faintest idea as to where you will sleep if you go on this silly walking tour. Finally you don't know what kind of weather you will get. May I ask what will become of your walking tour if it starts raining?

I am afraid that the argument which should have had least weight (viz. the one that I was feeling very tired) had in fact the most and the walking tour was dropped. I returned to my hotel and went to bed at the phenomenally early time of 10.45.

Thursday I was down and having my breakfast by 9.30. There were only two others staying in the hotel—a grocer and his wife from a seaside place near Liverpool. The landlady had spoken of them the evening before and called them 'nice business people'. Relying on this description I sat down on the same table as they and later apologizing (there is nothing as safe as an apology) started a pleasant conversation. They were evidently quite well-to-do and we talked of all things from the price of milk to the good work that Philip Hayden was doing at the Hague. They were certainly very nice if not very much educated. They were most interesting and for the first time I realized how true Bernard Shaw's description of the terrible power of the press was on those who 'knew how to read and knew nothing else'. Mr Ryder's morning mind was created entirely by his morning paper and as he very kindly lent to me his 'Liverpool Echo' after he had done with it I could cheque [sic] this fact with great accuracy.

At about 10.30 I started off for the Elwyseg Rocks (one asterisk in Baedeker) by a walk which I had planned on my map, about 8 miles round I thought. Oh, by the way, I have forgotten to write that the day before in Birmingham I had got 2 one-shilling boxes of sandwiches from Lyons (I had used these and the 1-shilling lunch boxes a good deal in London. I do not remember whether I wrote to you about them. The sandwiches are neatly packed but rather expensive as they do not amount to much). One of these boxes was intended for the evening meal on Wednesday and the other for breakfast on Thursday when, as I have already written I had intended starting very early. As a matter of fact on Wednesday I had found the sandwiches so insufficient for dinner that I had had a plateful of bread and butter and a teapotful of tea at about 9.30. Well, the other box of sandwiches remained and this I took along with me. (I must say I am getting a little tired of this fried fish punctuated with sandwiches or bread and butter and tea and I am looking forward to a quiet and comfortable time in Vienna where I want to get into some cultured family on terms of fullboard and lodging. I am relying on Dr Molisch for this).

I climbed up to the rocks and got into the moors at the top. And there for the first time I saw the heather. It was intensely purple and except for a few patches of brilliant green it covered the whole moor. I came suddenly upon this view and for some time my senses were sort of stunned. I could hardly realize that this extraordinarily brilliant colour was really true. There were a few pine trees scattered over the moor and as I said a few patches of green grass and also here and there some small shrubs (which I later discover were called bilberrys or winberrys which had now (it is autumn now) turned quite gold.

I was certainly not disappointed with my first view of the heather.

I sat down to my sandwiches in a suitable place but I found that I could not keep my mind on the beauty of the scenery. The colouring was so intense that I felt that I would require a week to settle down to it. As it was I merely felt stunned.

By the time I got to the other end of the moors it was quite late. There I was informed by a woodcutter whom I asked the way (rather unnecessarily for I had my map) that I had been trespassing. I had as a matter of fact raised some grouse and a hare. Well I returned home at about 6 and I felt even more tired than I did the day before. The walk must have been much more than the 8 miles which I had estimated.

Friday I started about the same time (10.30). There is not much to describe. I saw much the usual scenery. Green banks, and brooks and bubbling water and things which you would get anywhere. I should really have done the first part of my outing on a bus and then I would have been able to again get to the heather. As it was by the time I got near it I was feeling so tired that I thought it wiser to take a bus and return. On Saturday I started for Bontnewydd.

I took a return ticket from Llangollen and also at the same time purchased a ticket for Liverpool from Llangollen dated the next Tuesday

I wonder whether I ever wrote to you that from London I had written to Mrs Pughe on whom Mrs Richardson had given me an introduction. Mrs Pughe lived at Helygog near Dolgelly (nearest market town) and Bontnewydd (nearest station). She had invited me for a weekend but for a long time I did not decide whether I would accept or not. Finally when I saw that my walking tour would take me quite close to her I wrote to her that I would come down and from Birmingham I wrote to her that I would be in Helygog by Saturday evening.

I got into Bontnewydd at about 12 and the first thing to be done was to look for something to eat. If I was not such a great fool I would have looked at the map and discovered that Bontnewydd is merely a station and there is no inn for about 3 miles around where I could get the usual bread butter and tea. Well I was informed of these facts by the porter who could only suggest that I could go to the station master's house (quite close) and implore Mrs Stationmaster to give me something to eat. I carried out this suggestion and received a small packet of bread and butter. Mrs Stationmaster had no meat to make sandwiches and the fire was engaged so she could not boil eggs either. But I can hardly complain for she refused to take any money.

Well, I walked along. Mrs Pughe's place was about 1 mile by a shortcut and about 9 round by the road, but as I had written that I would not come before the evening I did not want to go there immediately. I first of all finished off the b. and b. (Mrs Stationmaster had put a little marmalade in some of the sandwiches which only made the packet sticky without much altering the taste) and then after proceeding some distance sat down to digest the meal, admire the view which was magnificent and think generally.

The first thing I thought of was this: In my programme I had allotted to Mrs Pughe the week end from Saturday evening to Tuesday morning when I intended taking the 10.55 for Liverpool—in other words 2 days and 3 nights. As I sat there digesting Mrs Stationmaster's bread and butter I suddenly began to think whether Mrs Pughe would want [to] have me for such a long time. I remembered that Lady Brown had asked me down for 2 nights and she was an old friend of the family while I had never heard of Mrs Pughe till Mr Richardson had given me that letter. After a long cogitation which made my head ache (It is bad think[ing]hard after a meal however light it may be) I decided that I would see Mrs Pughe and after feeling the atmosphere decide how long I would stay. I forgot to say that I had left my cases at the station. There were no taxis or carts available and the porter had suggested that when Mr Pughe learnt that I had two heavy cases he would come down with his pony to fetch them. On meeting Mrs Pughe therefore my first request would have to be to ask Mr Pughe to go and get my cases for me. I was therefore not too hopeful of the reception I would get.

I would like to write a long description of the delightful time that I spent eventually with Mrs Pughe (aged 60), Mr Pughe (country gentleman and sportsman aged 65) and Mrs Pughe (Snr) aged 95 and of the grouse which I shot on the Welsh moors. It is 11 now. *Tomorrow my day is very full. I shan't have a moment for letter writing. Besides Vazir's letter is not written yet.* I am afraid that the Pughes will have to wait till

I get back to Bombay for, for the next few mails each week will have its own interests and there will be no room for the Pughes.

I arrived in Liverpool this afternoon, 2.30 and am fairly comfortable in lodgings.

17.9.29 [Manchester letterhead, written from Sheffield]

I received the following letters by the last mail: *Father d/d 21st, Mother's d/d 23rd, and Haffoo's d/d 23rd.*

I have received letters by every mail. Once or twice I did not get letters but then I got two the next mail.

My heartiest congratulations at the great success of the Naidu meeting.

I am sorry that the reading of Macbeth was not as great a success as it ought to have been [play reading organized by Faiz Tyabji, an ardent Shakespearean]. The impression [of] Macbeth performed at Stratford on Avon is still fresh in my mind. That was certainly a success.

To go on with the news when I ended. I think I was at Tuesday 10th. I got into Liverpool at about 2 on Tuesday, purchased a copy of the 'Liverpool Echo' and started off to look for lodgings. I got some remarkably cheap ones but hardly comfortable ones. 2/ 6 for bed and breakfast. I would have gone further afield and looked for better ones but it was only a question of a couple of nights and I was feeling very tired. So I decided to stay there. Then I got into a silk shirt and Dias' suit and went to [see] Mr Abel J. Harley. But I think I have described all this in my last letter. Well. Wednesday On turning up my notebook I find that on the 'Liverpool' page I have the following entries:

1. *K. Harding. F. B. I. (which means Federation of British Industries) 11.30. Not in which means that I had written to him from Birmingham and had received a reply in Wales saying that he would not be in Liverpool at the time I was there. This was a pity for the district secretaries of the F.B.I. are influential people).*
2. *Abel J. Harris to call between 4 and 5 (this means as I think I wrote in my last letter that I had written to Mr Harris from Birmingham saying that I would call between 4 and 5. He had replied in a letter which I got at Mrs Pughe's which was really extraordinarily nice).*
3. *Chamber of Commerce 10.30 (the figures give the time of the appointment as allotted in my own programme. One under lining means 'written to'. Two underliniations means 'written to and reply received'*
4. *American Express to get money b) letters*
5. *J. P. Edwards*
6. *Solicitors*

I started off in the morning in good time. The 'Results Liverpool' page in my notebook says 'chamber of commerce, met Sec. by apptmt. Was very nice. I must write. Has agreed to put para in his journal'. This is all in the results page for Liverpool.

From there I went to the American Express Co and got my money for this month. I have taken some French money but they could not give me any German. I was particularly keen on getting some small change in German money. I remember when I landed at Folkestone coming from Venice to London I had to give the porter half a crown instead of 6 d because I had no change and I could not see where I could get it. I also checked the timing of the trains which I have written down in my notebook. I have got three pages of them and when you read what an amount of travelling I have done in the last few days and shall do in the next few days you will say that I must have written in a remarkably small hand to get it into 3 pages.

By this time I was feeling like having something to eat. After lunch I went to the office of Alsop Stevens and Robinson (no longer Alsop Stevens and Crookes—that was the old name, wasn't it). I told them that my father was reading in their offices and was an intimate friend of Mr Alsop. I had quite a good reception and permission to go round was easily given. An articled clerk (who by the way was just fresh from Cambridge and knew nothing at all) took me round or rather accompanied me round. Their office is a huge one and absolutely magnificent. I think an accurate description of it would be to say that it was like the Imperial Bank offices in Bombay. All old papers carefully folded up, indexed and put away in pigeon holes and closed cupboards. Of course the cost must be terrific. But the most interesting things were their system of making bills and their accounts department. They do not allow the whole matter to go on until it is finished and then when the matter has been forgotten by everybody the papers [go] to the bill department for them to make the bill chiefly out of their imaginations. But every evening every partner and managing clerk dictates his bill for the day. So that the bill grows at the same time as the matter goes on. It seems that this is the general practice in England but I had not quite realized it when I was in Mr Mott's office.

The accounts too were really well kept. They were pretty well done in Mr Mott's office but here I thought that the system of ruling the books even better. Altogether, as I said before it was a magnificent office.

As to 3) I had an apptmt with Mr Harris to go into the Liverpool Cotton Exchange and see the coming in of the telegrams giving the opening prices of the New York Exchange. I was not very lucky and the market was quiet, or to use an expression not so commerce-technical the shouting and gesticulating was only moderate. We were there in the Exchange for quite a long time—possibly for ¾ of an hour. Mr Harris had invited me to spend the evening with him chiefly because the previous day I had asked him to do so. Our arrangement was that I should go to the Cathedral to hear the evening choral service and then join him at the book stall of the station to accompany him home.

I went down to the Cathedral. This is [supposed] to be the biggest cathedral in England but as yet it is hardly half complete. Unfortunately there was for some reason no choral service that evening and I merely found an ordinary service without any music going on in the Lady Chapel. I was rather disgusted and left almost immediately but by the time I got to the station it was very nearly the time when Mr Harris was to meet me there. So if there had been a choral service I would have been sure to be late.

Mr Harris arrived punctually and going up to the booking office and purchased a 1st class return ticket for me. I of course protested loudly but he was pleasantly adamant. This by the way will be I think the only time that I shall have travelled first in England. We soon got to his house, a nice one in the suburbs. I had met the son before on the train from Folkestone to London. There were besides Mrs Harris, a brother-in-law, a sister and a daughter, fairly pretty and extremely nice. The son was 20 (he informed me later) and the daughter about the same. I had an extremely pleasant evening. I was much appreciated and they laughed at all my jokes. I had a good supper too. Nor was the evening useless to the mind, for there for the first time I enunciated in public a new theory of the most important weapon in this world, a theory that had been revolving in a nebulous state in my mind for a long time but which I had formed clearly to myself only a few days before—on, in fact, the 'precipice walk' which as I have written before is a most extraordinarily beautiful walk. As you will also probably be interested in this theory I shall give you a short account of it.

Up till recently I had believed, I think in accordance with the current opinion of philosophers, that flattery is the most powerful weapon in this world. Both the results of my own experiments and the results which I observed other people obtaining by the use of this weapon were so astounding that it hardly seemed possible that God could have created an even more powerful weapon. Yet even in those early times I had from time to time used another weapon with surprising results. I am not prepared as yet to argue that these even more astounding results are not really due to the fact that this new weapon is not so well known as the weapon of flattery and that its edge has not yet been dulled by indiscriminate overuse.

But I myself have now little doubt that the weapon of 'apology' (for it is to this weapon that I refer) is an even more powerful weapon than the weapon of flattery. I have known flattery to fail many times but I have never known apology to fail except in one instance and then both flattery and apology failed ignominiously. To myself I explain my, what would now seem extraordinary dullness, in not fully realizing all the potent forces of apology before, by the fact that up till recently I was not able to quite understand how the weapon of apology worked. Mine is essentially a logical or mathematical mind and I cannot fully even realize the effects unless I have fully understood the cause.

As I said before, for the first time I saw clearly how an apology worked on the precipice walk. As you may not have given all the time that I have to this problem and may not yet have arrived at all the results to which I have, I shall explain them to you in that most lucid of all ways of explanation: viz. by an example. Imagine that A has hurt B. Further, assume that this hurt is 1 inch in extent. Now let us first of [all] completely realize that B will think that this hurt is some amount more than 1 inch in extent. He may think that it is 1 1/2 ins or 2 ins or 5 ins or 10. My experiments have not as yet been sufficiently sustained or accurate for me to be able to discover the exact ratio: True extent of B's hurt/ Extent of the hurt as imagined by B the ratio is probably complicated and made uncertain by that most elusive of all factors—B's character. However there is not the slightest doubt that the ratio is less than 1. a matter of fact my theory of the working of the weapon of apology is not affected even if B realizes the true extent of his hurt or even if he thinks that he is hurt less than he actually is. So all this is by the way ...

Thursday 19th Bradford Burwoods Cafe
I had gone on writing till 12 the other night and written 16 pages. Now it is Thursday and I hope I shall be able to catch the mail.
Summary of news
Thursday 12th Liverpool dep. 9.40
Manchester arri. 10.25

I went to a hotel, changed into 8.g.s. (8 guinea suit)-called on 1) Federation of British Industries 2) Chamber of Commerce 3) Assoc. of Belting Manufacturers 4) Boiler Mnftrs-had a bath (which I had not had for 2 days). Comfortable hotel-fairly cheap.

Friday 13th Called on 1) Cotton Spinners Asso 2) Calico Printers) 3) Bobbin manu. 4) Leather Belting mnftrs. 5) Loom manftrs 6) Textile machinery-went to public swimming baths (ink in fountain pen finished so continuing to write standing in P.O.) was disgusted by them.

Sat did nothing in fact in the morning. Had asked Goldstein (Asaf bhai's friend) to come to my hotel at 1.30 and lunch. He arrived. We lunched. Went out with Goldstein to look for house for him-talked great deal of Zionist movement.

Sunday 8.30 left for Blackpool to spend the day with Golds. Spent terribly enjoyable day. Golds. PhD of Camb in Maths. Mrs Golds PhD of Camb in Physical Chemistry. One child. Returned 11 p.m.

Monday Manchester dep. 9.44

Sheffield arriv. 10.25

Called on 1) Sheffield Lighter Trades Assoc. 2) Messrs Slack Sellars on whom Jabir M. had given [a] letter.

3) Cham. of Commerce 4) Fed of Bri. Ind. 5) Mander Solicitors

Hotel fairly comfortable

'cheap'

Tuesday Sheffield departure 9.35 Nottingham arriv 10.20

Called on 1) Fed. of Brit. Ind. 2) Chamber of Commerce.

Nott. Dep 1.55

Leicester arr. 2.22 Called on 1) Hosiery Man. Ass. 2) Boot Assoc. 3) Chamb of Comm 4) Fed of Brit. Ind. Leicester dep 5. 11

Sheffield arriv. 6.30 Wed. Sheff. Dep. 9.12 Leeds arriv 10. 11

Called on 1) Leeds and Dist. Manu 2) Chamb of Comm 3) Fed of Brit Ind. Leeds dep 12. 12

Bradford arriv. 12.45 Called on - diverse people Brad dep 4.15

Leeds arriv 4.50

Called on Dr Berenblum-introduction from Golds. Bere govt cancer research [???] age about 30—married accomplished pianist who plays for the broadcasting cos— of course Jew and in this case Russian—one of the cleverest women I think I have met in my life. Spent terribly enjoyable evening with the pair. Returned to hotel 11.30 p.m.

Thursday (today) Leeds dep. 9. 15 Halifax arriv. 9.50

Called on Chamber of Commerce Halifax dep 10.45

Bradford arriv. 11.15

Time of writing 2.30 have called on ... people this morning. Got one other call to make in Bradford apptmnt at 3.

Future programme Brad dep 3.45 Leeds arriv 4.15

One call to make

Leeds dep 5.35

Windermere arriv 9.35 P.M.

20.9.29 9 P.M. [Letterhead] Waverley Hotel and Cafe

I missed the last mail by about 2 minutes. So by this mail you will get 2 letters.

In my last letter I brought my account down to yesterday afternoon. As you may have noticed yesterday was one of the most crowded days that I have yet spent and my personal opinion is that I have reason to be proud of having brought it (the day) to a successful conclusion. You remember that I got up yesterday at 7.30 and then every moment of mine was full till 5.35 when I got into the train to leave Leeds. The most difficult things were to allow times for walking from one place to another and secondly for changing clothes, repacking and getting from the hotel to the station. As it happened I was late nowhere and hardly a minute was wasted. After getting into the train I changed my mind as to my destination and I decided to go to Lake Side instead of to Windermere. The pros and cons were:

For Lake Side

Pros

1. *Lake Side is at the bottom of Windermere Lake while Windermere is at the middle. Therefore the next day (today) when I take the steamer from Lake Side on the lake to go North towards Ambleside and Grasmere I would travel on and see the whole length of Wind. Lake instead of only half as I would do if I went to Lake Side*
2. *Lake Side itself is a pier while Windermere is not. If I wanted to get to the Lake from Windermere I would have to go 1 1/2 miles by bus to Bowness.*

Cons

1. *I would get to Lake Side at 10.15 instead of 9.35 when I would get to Windermere and 9.35 was late enough*
2. *Lake Side had only one hotel which was rather expensive-9/6 for bed and breakfast as I afterwards discovered. At Windermere there was much more choice—at Bowness if I was prepared to go on to Bowness the same evening there was considerable choice.*

I weighed the pros and cons and found the pros more weighty. This involved an alteration of the route to be followed in the last 2 hours of my journey. For though Windermere and Lake Side are as the crow flies within 10 miles of each other you get to them by entirely different routes once you get to Cairnforth with [sic] is about 2 hours distant from them. My two cases had been labelled to Windermere and had been put into the baggage van and so I got out at Cairnforth and saw that they did not go off to Windermere. The hotel was very comfortable and it's not surprising that I found it so for this was the first time that I went into such an expensive one.

This morning in order to suit the general tone of the hotel I discarded the cotton shirt which I had worn the previous evening and donned a new silk one. It is curious what a difference a silk shirt makes in the attitude towards you of all—from the girls who then look at you long and pleasantly to the porter who asks you 'First or third, sir?' and you have to say hurriedly 'Third'. This morning on the strength of my silk shirt I carried on a long and interesting conversation with the girl in the reception office of the hotel when I went to pay my bill, during the course of which I told her all about my travels. I don't remember of ever before having told any pretty hotel attendant of my personal affairs.

As a matter of fact I found time for this conversation between breakfast and 11.20 when the boat by which I had decided to go left, because it had suddenly commenced to rain and I could not go out. It may reassure people at home if I say that I quite realize that I am in the Lake District to admire only beautiful scenery and there is, I think I can say from what I saw today, sufficient to occupy all my time. The voyage up Windermere was an entirely new and wonderful experience for me. I had not realized before how beautiful such a voyage could be. The rain had stopped and the hills were alternately lightened and darkened by the clouds driven fast by a strong breeze. A considerable amount of gold has now come into the foliage of the trees (for it is now the end of September) and this of course responded with great effect to the sunshine.

From Ambleside at the N. end of the lake I took a bus which however did not go further than Grasmere. I was told that I would get another bus for Keswick in a quarter of an hour. (I had purchased a timetable (3 d) at the pier at Ambleside but I had not yet had time to peruse it). I had not till then decided whether I would break my journey at Grasmere, spend the afternoon there and go on to Keswick in the evening or go straight off to Keswick. But I left my case with the bus man and walked into a cafe to get some lunch. While waiting for my coffee, cold beef, bread and butter and beetroot spoiled by being vinegared I turned over good Baedeker. He, I found, had hardly a single asterisk for Grasmere or its surroundings, while the surroundings of Keswick were just flooded with asterisks. I then referred to the time table and found that there was just a quarter of an hour for lunch before the bus for Keswick arrived.

Well in Keswick I arrived at about 2. On referring to Baedeker—'King's Arms, pension 10/6'. I saw the name King's Arms as we passed it in the bus. I pulled out my cases—one of which is heavy with the weight of about 15 Baedekers and innumerable maps and guides and plans, and was walking towards the King's Arms when I saw the 'Waverley' within 10 feet of where the bus had stopped. As it did not look exorbitantly expensive I went in to inquire and found it a real find. Bed and breakfast 6/6, hot and cold water laid on in every bedroom. Even in that 9/6 hotel you got your hot water in the form of a tinpotful of lukewarm liquid placed outside your door in the morning and announced with the most infernal sleep-destroying knocking on your door.

I asked the manageress where I could get a bicycle. Keswick is a place truly beloved by the Gods. For opposite the hotel was a place where I got a good bicycle, 9 d first hour, 6 d each subsequent hour. So at 3 P.M., having put my tweed cap on and set it at a suitable angle I set out to do the round of Derwentwater Lake which is about 10 miles. Keswick as you may remember is on the banks of Derwentwater.

Within half a mile of Keswick is Craig Hill which Baedeker describes as the best viewpoint of the Lake and this I can now endorse. Really the view from Craig Hill is most soul stirring. (By the way I suppose that you have by now gathered that I use the word 'soul stirring' in a purely technically descriptive sense). It must not be taken as an admission to the effect that a view is capable of stirring the soul or even as an admission as to the existence of souls.) When I got to the top, the sun was just opposite and the surface of the lake was brilliant with silver. Towards the South the hills in every shape and every shade of green looked over the water. The sky was blue—not as blue as one's is, but, yet, blue and dotted with bits of white cloud still scurrying fast. Towards the North the view was not so beautiful.

I soon remarked that of the whole view before me the most soul stirring part was the silver on the water, and this was so brilliant that one could hardly look at it. And then a statement over which I have thought more than I think I have over any other single statement came again into my mind. You will be interested to hear father that it is a statement made by you. When (I think it was in 1918) we were in Matheran for the first time, I had one day remarked before you that it was curious that the moon light was so beautiful and you had said—in effect—that the sunlight was at least as beautiful, only, our physical powers were so weak that we could not look at it when it showed itself in its full beauty and intensity. Now here, merely because he was so weak, man was not able to see anything in the sun playing on the water, and called it glare, while he went silily [sic] into ecstasies over crude blotches of colour caused by the sun when it was at its weakest, viz. at sunset time.

When I was at Berenblum's last Wednesday he made a remark which had been so long, though rather nebulously, been brewing in my mind that I immediately agreed with him. He said that a fair method of judging the progress which any science or subject has made is to see to what extent mathematics has entered into it. To clear the air of any suspicions as to the partialities of Berenblum I may repeat that he is in the Cancer Research Lab and that he frequently said that he regretted that his knowledge of Mathematics was practically nil.

You will wonder what the last para has got to do with what has gone before, but it seems to me that Mathematics is the only way of getting over the limitations of the mind. We have given plenty of attention to weapons for getting over our physical limitations and we have developed our tools from the flint hatchet to the 20-foot lathe and the Gillette blade. It is time that we now devise something which will enable us to see the beauty of the sun's glare. Even as regards the mind we are better off. For as I said before we have Mathematics. What I mean is this: my mind is strong enough to realize the conception—I admit not quite clearly—of -2. And I can also realize + 4. But the process of -2×-2 I think is too complicated for realization by a human mind. Thus with the help of Mathematics we have from one conceivable thing??? by a process which is not conceivable.

On the day that I left Sheffield to visit Nottingham and Leicester there was one of the thickest fogs that I have yet seen. As our train steamed out of the station the engine belching forth black smoke which rolled out into the clammy mist we past [sic] the gigantic works of Camel Laird? and Co. and through the mist and smoke we could see the blazing red furnaces—a most impressive sight. Opposite to me was sitting a youngish man with a forehead of sufficient sq. ins. of surface for me to credit him with considerable intelligence. To him after saluting him with 'It's a dull day', I said that so far as I had seen Sheffield was the nearest thing to Hell that we mortals had succeeded in creating on this earth and pointed to the furnaces. He replied, 'Yes, Sheffield is not exactly a beauty spot.'

I was a little annoyed at being misunderstood in this manner. I am afraid that I am a little liable to getting annoyed. I remember when I had written down all the accumulated wisdom of my twenty-five years in Vazir's autograph book and somebody had misunderstood or not understood me and said 'What a funny thing to write', I had felt considerably annoyed.

But all this is besides the point. I had of course not at all implied that Sheffield was in any way not a beautiful spot. Possibly Sheffield was rather different in appearance to say the views from the Precipice Walk at Dolgelly which had their colours etc arranged more in accordance with the current etiquette as to beauty. But I was not prepared to say that those fires glimmering through the mist and framed by the black smoke were less *interesting* than those views. Father you may remember, or literary Badr may recall the name of the person who in a letter in reply to Wordsworth's invitation to him to visit the Lake District gives a long description of the beauties of the Fog, of the dirt and of the oily Thames of London. I suppose the letter was written half in fun but I have always a little believed in it.

21.9.29 As I sat on Craig Hill a gentleman dressed in a grey flannel double-breasted suit and a lady in a frock to match came up. I looked at them and said to myself, 'Ah! Here is an opportunity to study human nature. Here are two people whose souls are absolutely irresponsive to the beauties of nature and yet they think it worth their while to spend their time and money coming here instead of remaining comfortably at home'. Soon afterwards I got up to go down and cycle off. As I was starting I heard the sounds of a baby crying just below the rock which is at the top of Craig Hill and then I heard the aforementioned woman shouting out cooing expressions evidently intending to excite the virtue of patience in the infantile mind. The shoutings were however of no effect and it was only after he of the double-breasted flannel suit had rushed down that the child quieted down. As we were now quite close I remarked 'It would have been a job rolling her up'. (The child was in a perambulator.) The gentleman replied, 'Oh, we did not roll her up. We carried her up between the two of us'. *I then realised that the lady was a miniature Leila Moomani and the gentleman was her worthy second in not allowing children's perambulators or suchlike things [to] interfere with the true course of righteous pleasure, and on such realization I humbly though silently begged their pardon for ever having thought badly of them.*

The rest of the round of Derwentwater does not call for particular remark. I got in at 6 p.m. and went up again to Craig's Hill to watch the sun set. A bitterly cold wind had started up and though I got some shelter by lying close against the rocks, I regretted not having brought my raincoat. The setting sun was producing the most wonderful effects on the grass and the browning fern and the purplish rocks and as it set behind the hills the valleys became dusky with evening mist. I was reminded of the times when at Ajanta we used to come out after having watched the sun engolden the great Bodhisattva in Cave no 1, to watch it engolden the trees on the opposite side of the valley (already autumn-tinted at the end of October) to the accompaniment of the whoop of a monkey or a dove's cooing sound. Here however the only accompaniment was the whistling of the wind which had become really very cold and very strong unless there was also the discordant sounds of some holiday-maker. I really believe that sounds so abominable as those which I have heard here cannot be made by anybody but a holiday-maker of the Lake District.

This morning (Saturday 22nd) it was raining and generally looked very unpromising. However by 11 we could see a few patches of blue in the sky and so I got the cycle again to do the Honister House round (22 m. 'one of the finest drives in the country' to quote Baedeker who awards it 2 asterisks.) I found the drive very hilly indeed and on the whole uninteresting. We could easily duplicate it in my own country and I have come here only to see such things as I cannot easily get there. The most soul stirring things were the views of Honister House itself, a huge slate crag, and of Buttermere. Buttermere is surrounded by purplish hills and its water, a scintillating grey because of the cloudy grey sky, was wonderfully set off by the colour of the hills. At first, when I got a view of the lake I felt a little disappointed that the water was not blue but then its colour so grew on me that I would not have had it changed for all the world. Returning from Buttermere via Newlands I for the first time realized what can be accomplished with browned fern, yellowing grass, and a smooth hillside. I got home at 6 having had my lunch at a farm, home-made bread, butter and cheese and coffee.

I shall post this letter tomorrow as I do not think I shall get any time to write more. This you will realize when you know all my programme for the next week.

Programme.

Sunday 22nd Morning climb Helvellyn 2.10 Leave for Patterdale by bus, arrive 3.30. Sight see and view see till 5.45 when I get a steamer going up Ullswater. Arrive Pooley Bridge at the other end of Ullswater 7. Start by bus 7.5, arrive 7.45 Penrith Station. Penrith dep. 7.55. Carlisle arrival 9. 10 Spend the night at Carlisle.

Monday Carlisle dep. 5.10 a.m. (unearthly hour, there is no other suitable train) Edinburgh arriv 7.50. Give some clothes to laundry and go to Leith for getting information as to steamer departures for Hamburg. At 2.45 leave for Mark Inch to visit Mrs O'Gilvie. Return 9. 10. At 9. 15 leave for Glasgow and arrive there 10 p.m. Tuesday Business in Glasgow

Wednesday Glasgow dep. 5.50 (unearthly hour again) arrive Mallaig 11 A.M. At 11.30 get a steamer to Kyle of Lochalsh, get there at 2. 10. Take a ferry from there to Kyleackin in the island of Skye from where I get a bus to Sligachan Hotel.

Thursday and Friday Stay at Sligachan Hotel and see Loch Scaviag (one asterisk Baedeker), Loch Sligachan and the Cuchullin Mountains (both 2 asterisks 'probably the wildest and grandest scenery in the kingdom' vide Baedeker)

Saturday Return to Mallaig in a similar manner in time to catch the 12 o'clock train. Get to Tarbet at the head of Loch Lomond. Take a steamer to Balloch at the south end of Loch Lomond. Arrive Glasgow 7.38 and Edinburgh 8.50.

[Phew!]

[Letterhead] Sligachan Hotel 24. 9.29

So here I am in Skye in the most fashionable hotel in the West Highlands.

My last letter contained the a/c till I think 19th Saturday

20th Sunday (I am not sure whether Sunday was the 20th. However I am writing an account of Sunday, my last day in the Lake District). In the morning it was pretty bad rain and I kept indoors—doing I don't remember what. Possibly writing to you, possibly looking up time tables. Looking up timetables and making programmes takes a tremendous amount of time. At about 12 I went out to Castle Head again to have a last look at Derwentwater but I was feeling depressed for some reason and it was still drizzling so I soon returned. On the way I stopped at a cafe and had rolls and coffee. I generally have lunch outside the hotel where I live for I could not very well tell my landlady that I would not want the ordinary hotel luncheon costing about 3/6 possibly and that I would want a lunch costing about 8 d or 10 d. My plan was to take the bus leaving Keswick for Patterdale at the south end of Ulswater at 2.10. I was at the bus station (only about 20 yards from the bus station [sic]) in good time and it was a really very beautiful drive from Keswick to Ulswater. But I think I have no doubt that the South end of Ulswater was the most beautiful thing I saw in the Lake District. Of course, calling anything the 'most beautiful thing' is rather unwise and might possibly even get one the reputation of being a poet. This last I say for this reason. When I was with Dr Robert Bridges he took me to a point in his garden from where you got a really fine view of the towers and spires of Oxford. Pointing to this he said 'this is the finest view in the world. The view of Florence (from such and such a place) is very fine, but this is the finer still'. I felt tempted to ask, what graduated scale or thermometer or galvanometer he used by which he could so accurately estimate the relative beauties of views. I have since come to think that a propensity to make such rash and meaningless statements is one of the unavoidable accompaniments to poeticness. I think it must be rather pitiable being a poet: you write so many truths for the benefit of other people and live yourself in such an artificial and queer darkness. Besides I imagine a poet has no time to read Mathematics. I have always thought it curious that Shakespeare who knew so much of life as I suppose any other man gave up writing poetry immediately he could afford to do so.

Well, to return. I got to Ulswater at about 3.30. I was to take the steamer on the lake going Northwards at 5.45. So I had 2 hours and a quarter to look round Patterdale. Baedeker says, 'Some prefer the scenery of Ulswater to that of Windermere and Buttermere'. I am certainly one of the some. The autumn tints have now all come and the trees have the most wonderful gold and copper hues. On the East there is a high and precipitous mountain, rocky in places, in others covered with dense foliage. This whole hill I could see reflected on the water as I stood on the west bank.

I passed a couple sitting in a car deeply engrossed in each other and oblivious to the beauty around. I realized then how absurd it is to go into the moonlight to make love. One should only make love in the most ugly places reserving the beautiful ones for saner moments when one is able to appreciate and make some use of them.

At 5.45 I got into the steamer. I have seldom enjoyed a trip on the water so much. Baedeker says that the scenery at the Northern end is rather tame. With him I entirely disagree—incidentally I think for the first time. We got to Pooley Bridge (the North end) at about 6.45 and I got into another bus for Penrith where I was to catch my train.

Sunday in England is really a most awful day. Of course all the offices and shops are closed but besides this there is no delivery of the post and the train services (except for the excursion trains which are quite a number) almost suspended. The result was that I could not get any train from Penrith to Edinburgh on Sunday evening. *I therefore decided to catch the 8. 18 train from Penrith getting into Carlisle at 9.15, spend the night there and then get the 5.25 A.M. train from Carlisle to Edinburgh on Monday.*

When we got to Penrith station (at about 7.10, the bus went right up to the station) I told the porter that I wanted to get into the 8.18 train. The porter replied, 'Why not go by the excursion train at 7.20, sir?' I replied, 'I don't think I shall be able to catch it because I have left my gloves in the bus and I must go to the garage and recover them'. (The bus had driven off immediately after dropping us.) Well, this forgetting of the gloves was a great tragedy.

For besides missing a very much earlier and a fast train, my own train was nearly an hour late. If I had got into the earlier excursion train I could have caught at Carlisle the Edinburgh Express which was late and been in Edinburgh about the same time that I got into Carlisle. Well, on Monday morning I got up at 4.30 and was in good time at the station for the 5.20 for Edinburgh where I got about 7.50.

About what my plans are after this I have already written to you, viz.: to go down to Mrs O'Gilvies (Hasan Mamoo's great friend) in the afternoon (she is about an hour and

a half's journey from Edinburgh) return in the evening and go down the same night to Glasgow. On the train from Carlisle to Edinburgh ... [Left unfinished]
[changed notepaper] Kyle of Lochalsh [Dated] 28th Saturday 6.30

Then spend the day there (Tuesday) and on Wednesday get to Skye via Loch Lomond, return the same way on Saturday and the same evening get to Edinburgh and spend the rest of my time till I get my steamer either at Leith [in Edinburgh] or at Newcastle. You are now to hear of some of the most rapid changing and rechanging of plans in history so please remember what they originally were.

I left one of my suitcases in the cloak room for I was going to take along only one with me to Skye. I then went down to the Post Office: there were no letters.

I then went to the Enquiry office at Waverley Station to inquire about the tickets and fares. You see on certain days cheap return tickets are issued and I wanted to take advantage of any such concession. There I was told that I could get a return ticket via Glasgow to Loch Lomond for 2 pounds.13.0 but that if I took the circular tourist ticket going via Perth and Inverness and return via Glasgow or vice versa it would be (as he said) pounds 2.3.0. I decided to stick to my original plans, viz. going and returning via Glasgow.

Oh I forgot to mention that while coming from Carlisle to Edinburgh in the morning I had already made one change in the programme. I had decided that instead of pushing on the same evening to Glasgow I would stay the night in Edinburgh and get to Glasgow the next day by the 9.5 train. I had accordingly arranged for a room in the hotel and left my other suitcase there.

From the railway inquiry office I went down to Leith (which has recently been made into a suburb of Edinburgh) and discovered that there was no suitable steamer. So I shall leave for Hamburg on the 3rd from Newcastle.

Coming back on the train from Leith I made a big change in my programme. I decided I would take the tourist ticket after all and instead of going to Perth direct I would go via Mark Inch (Mrs O'gilvie's) which is not very far out. That is, I would go down to Mark Inch by the same train as before, get a train at 6.49 p.m. [to] Ladybank Junction, change there for Perth and get into Perth at 10.15. I would spend the night at Perth and catch the 5.5 a.m. train for Inverness the next morning (Tuesday) and get into Skye the same evening. As you will probably like to follow my route on the map I enclose the map from my time table. My route from Perth is via Stanley Junction, Avern?, Tomatin, etc. I have marked it on the map. From Kyle of Lochalsh to Portree I go by steamer.

Well, on Tuesday evening I found myself having dinner in the Royal Hotel at Portree, sitting opposite to a very Scotch gentleman from Glasgow In the course of conversation with him I learnt that Monday the 30th inst was to be a holiday in Glasgow and this immediately involved further changes in my plans. As I told you before Sunday is an awful day for travelling in the British Isles. As a matter of fact there is no connection between Skye and the mainland on Sundays at all. I had therefore decided on leaving Skye on Saturday and getting into Glasgow the same evening, looking round Glasgow on Sunday, doing my business calls there on Monday and then returning to Edinburgh either on Monday evening or Tuesday morning. On hearing the news above stated from the Glasgow gentleman I decided to push on straight from Skye to Edinburgh via Glasgow on Saturday and make a day excursion from Edinburgh to Glasgow on Wednesday. This would involve further expense but so far as I could see it could not be helped. ...

The next morning I left Portree for Sligachan where there is just a hotel and a post office. It is the centre for rock climbing in the Coollin Hills and the nearest place (7 miles) over bog and rock to Loch Cornuish, which and the Coollin Hills are the only places in Scotland to which Baedeker awards 2 asterisks.

I got to Sligachan Hotel at 8.30 a.m. What I did there on that day and on Sunday will be described later. On Saturday I got into the bus leaving Sligachan at 8.30 a.m, to catch the steamer going from Portree to Mattaig via Broadford and Kyle of Lochalsh at Broadford if possible, otherwise at Kyle. I learnt that it was too late to get the steamer at Broadford and when the bus got to Kyleakin (on the other side of the straight [sic] to Kyle of Lochalsh where there is the steamer pier by??? ferry) I was further informed that I had missed the steamer at Kyle of Lochalsh. I should really have come down to Kyleakin by an earlier bus at 7.30 A.M. Well this of course involved a rapid change of plans. If I wanted to get to Edinburgh the same day (Saturday—today) I would have to take the 10.40 train via Inverness and Perth, in other words, the same route that I had come. The only alternative was the rest of Saturday and Sunday in Kyle.

Fortunately Kyle is a beautiful place and a nice place. Baedeker gives the names of 2 hotels, the Kyle and the Station Hotel. Of these the Kyle is the less expensive. While stumbling along towards the Kyle under the weight of my now one suitcase, I saw another hotel which has no name. (I am now writing on hotel stationery) but which has a huge sign 'Temperance Hotel' hung out. Here I am going to spend today (Saturday) and tomorrow (Sunday)

Well so much for my plans and their changes. I spent a very nice evening with the Thoms (Mrs O'Gilvie's parents with whom she is now staying). They are very Scotch and my experience up till now has been that the Scotch are not so hospitable as the English and certainly not so hospitable as the Welsh with whom it's a real pleasure to have anything to do, witness my experience with the Pughes and the Harris'. However I got a packet of sandwiches out of them besides a 'high tea' as the evening meal here is called. They have a rather large house and a nice garden—things which I was expecting from Mrs O'Gilvie's pressing invitations to 'come down and have tea with us and see my people. We are only an hour's journey from Edinburgh by a fast train.' (It was an hour and a half by the fastest train I found.).

My experience at Perth was rather amusing. I got in there quite late and went into the nearest reasonable hotel. I avoid the station hotels owned by the Rly Cos to which Baedeker invariably gives asterisks and which are rather expensive. But this hotel was full and so was the neighbouring hotel. This was rather surprising for the Scotland season is now getting over. However, I found a place, the 'Waverley Hotel' a few hundred yards further. Here I was not greeted with open arms and when the manageress learnt that I wanted to get up at 4.30 the next morning to catch the 5.5 train she repeatedly asked me to go to the Station Hotel. But I had signed my name in the register by then, the contract was completed, and I was not going to be put out. Boots I found quite a nice chap and he promised to call me up at 4.30. They had no night porter it being quite a small place. Well, my room and bed was rather nice and I was tired and I soon fell fast asleep. Fortunately I am getting accustomed to this kind of travelling and at the tick of 4.30 my eyes opened and I looked into the radium dial of my watch. I gave Boots five minutes before getting out of bed lest it should hurt his feeling to find me already up when he came to call me up. Then I hurriedly dressed and packed but there was still no sign of boots. I had quite a job finding my way down for the hotel was in utter darkness. I did not know where the switches were and I was on the second floor. When I did get to the hall it took me a good ten minutes drawing back all the numerous bolts in the front doors. As a matter of fact for a few moments I almost despaired of letting myself out in time for the train. I left 6 sh (for my room) on the hat rack and got out. Outside I met a hefty-looking man and on my asking him whether he would carry my case said he would do so for 2 d but with such a Scotch accent that though for the moment I said yes and agreed to his demand, whatever it was, it was only after we had walked a good twenty paces that I realized what he had said. At the station I found I was in fairly good time and paid the porter 2 d, the smallest amount I have given for the carriage of my case. Up to now, I invariably paid 6 d. though the man may have carried them only 6 paces. The lines

 Elastic siders
 Minus binders
 Tuppence for Tuke..Penninglow

which Mother may remember (they were in the *Boys Own Paper)* have made me afraid of going under 6 d. On the train from Perth to Inverness I made friends with a nice young chap who is just going into New College at Oxford. I have promised to look him up when I return to England. He lives in London.

 I have really had a glorious time in Sligachan. The hotel was fairly comfortable, my room was not very good as it was in the old part of the building but the common rooms were luxurious and the food quite good. The Coollins and Loch Cornuish are wonderful sights. I don't propose to go into hysterics over their natural beauty. I suppose you have already had sufficient of that kind of stuff in my last two letters. All that I shall say is that they might quite appropriately be awarded all the hysterics which the Lake District or Wales or the Wye Valley has received. The peculiar thing about them was that they constitute a kind of scenery which it would not be easy to find in or near India for I don't suppose that there are anywhere many places which have this peculiar combination of a large and deep lake surrounded by mountains 'remarkable for the number and jagged nature of their peaks' (vide Baedeker), consisting of bluish-purplish stone, shiny with moisture and patched with grass turning gold. And this fact more than reconciled me to the time, money and trouble expended in getting to Skye. At present I think that the view of Loch Cornuish and another view of one of the spires of the Cullins will take their places besides the view of the heather at Llangollen and the view of Ulswater as the European scenes which are to serve me some useful purpose amidst the din and noise of cities (I have quite forgotten Wordsworth's lines). I am afraid that the Valley of the Wye (except possibly for one scene of the sun shining on a stretch of the river and the green banks) is not likely be of much practical use of this kind. Well two such views which *will* be of such practical use are I think cheap at about 3 pounds for railway, steamers, and bus fares and another 3 pounds for hotel charges.

 There is a very rough and dirty path from the hotel to Loch Cornuish which Baedeker says can be done in 3–3.5 hours if you walked very fast (it is a job walking fast for 3 1/2 hours) and that for me at least it was practically impossible to do it in 3 hours. Along this path to Loch Cornuish I went every day during the three days (Wed., Thurs., and Fri.) that I was at Sligachan. On the first day I met not far from the hotel a gentleman who sat next to me at table, wondering how to get across the first of the 3 streams we had to cross. I was intending to do it shoes on, trousers pulled up, but he persuaded me to take off my shoes and socks too and wade barefoot. He then followed me in a similar manner and we then kept together the whole day. We returned to the hotel late in the evening, having walked practically all the time as at one point we missed the path. We however had a fairly clear day and we got some wonderful views including the view of the spurs of the Coolins above referred to, which as a matter of fact can be had from comparatively near from the hotel. The next day, my companion, Mr Combe, said he was feeling tired and so I went alone. I got quite a bad day—extremely bad so far as visibility was concerned—and though I got right over Loch Cornuish to the 'View Point' I could hardly see the water below me. In the afternoon it began to rain and blow hard and my overcoat got heavy with water in spite of such protection as I could give it with my umbrella. It was not an easy task holding my umbrella in that wind either. The last day I had a beautiful day. Mr Combe came with me again. We spent about 1 1/2 hours at view point and I got that view of Loch Cornuish also referred to above firmly imprinted in my mind. I made quite friends with him. In appearance he looks very much like Daud Bhai but he is not quite so thin. He is very taciturn but with a very charming smile when he displays an appropriate amount of rather bluish false teeth. I did not discover till the last day that he was a chemist in the war Dept. He seemed to me to be very sympathetic and understanding and I gave him some account of my troubles as to the true meaning of beauty and all that. He said that he preferred the effects of the sun and shade playing on heather-covered banks to any effects of sunlight on moist rocks which I found so satisfying and said that it was not probable that he would come to Skye again. He repeatedly said that he could not understand my trudging along the same path for three days in succession and I explained it to him that I liked looking at the same things again and again till I had got them more or less as permanancies in my mind. He was sceptical about my being able to retain any impressions for any considerable time.

These three days in Sligachan tired me more than I remember ever having been tired before, and after the first feeling of disgust was over I was quite glad that I had got stuck in Kyle in this manner. The afternoon till about 4 I spent dozing in an armchair in the dining-sitting, trying to read the *Essays of Elia* (a rotten book) and then *Kidnapped* by R. L. S. (another rotten book) both of which I had culled out from the hotel library. I would then have given a five-pound note for a volume of Barrie's plays. At four I sallied out to do a thing I had been wanting to do for some time, viz. find out the name and residence of the local minister and call on him. I did so and the results will be chronicled tomorrow as it is now 10 p.m.

[Never were].

CONT. Edinburgh 1.10.29

I find that I have got a number of letters from home not marked 'replied'. Amidst all my rushings about I forget whether I have or have not acknowledged them so at the risk of repetition, I have received:

Father's d/d 24 and 25 Aug. viz mails of 24 and 31st Aug.

Mother 's " "

Haffoo 's " " "

I post my letters at all kinds of odd times. From London I used to post them on Thursday or Friday as the post closed on Friday at 6 P.M. Since I have been travelling more I just see whether there is any chance of my getting time for writing more and if there isn't I post just what has been written on a Monday or Tuesday or any day. This letter I shall hold on [to] till the last moment as here in Edinburgh I shall have the evenings free and so I shall be able to go on adding to it. It might quite possibly become one of the longest letters I have written to you. I hope Jabir Mamoo will send me a copy of No 2 Shakespeareana. If not, please send me your copy.

I am glad that you have decided to post the mail of 4th Sept to Lond. I do not know whether you have though. I received Vazir's letter from the G. P. O. this afternoon but nothing from Somerset Lodge. Possibly those letters have gone to Paris and I won't get them till the 10th or 12th when I get there.

When I was at Cambridge the Stanleys said nothing about what happened at the Bunder and I did not ask them anything. Haffoo I note is again sarcastic: she says: 'I hear that Sulaiman Bhai has shot a very big panther ... I suppose he must be very excited about it', meaning that we others who have shot 6 (or is it 7?) panthers don't get excited over such minor things.

I am glad to hear that Saughain? has at last been brought to bay. I hope that some settlement will soon be arrived at.

I am afraid that I shall have to post this letter tomorrow and I am not feeling in the mood for letter writing now. The whole of today it was rainy and cold and very unpleasant. I made four calls and spent some time in the afternoon with the Schlepps whom I liked very much. Prof Schlepp is the father-in-law of the Ede of the Tate Gallery. He is retired from the Edinburgh University. The younger Schlepp was it turned out with Asaf Bhai at St Johns and is at present Lecturer in Maths at Edinburgh. I get my boat from Newcastle on Friday the 4th

[Letterhead] Hotel Traube Koblenz

10.10.29

I am afraid that I have missed this mail too. At least so I understand, I went to the Postamt to enquire and received a lot of information in German which my train and steamer and Kihim work on Otto's grammar not having been able to clarify I am a little hazy as to how I stand. However I shall post this letter tonight and go to bed early, and no doubt, sleep well, as I was up till late last night and got up early this morning, as you will soon hear.

This letter will be very small because I am feeling in no mood for letter writing in spite of the good stationery and a very comfortable chair and table and a beautifully got up smoking room. Well, my last letter ended on Saturday 28th Sept. afternoon at Kyle of Lochalsh so far as I remember.

28th Sept Evening spent with Mr Settle, Scottish Free church Missionary and Parish Priest at Kyle, talking religion and generally gossiping with him. Most interesting man. Enjoyed myself thoroughly. He took me to see the church ('beautiful arches'—per Mr Settle) and on my noticing a bicycle in a private room informed me that that had belonged to the previous priest. He himself used a m/cycle getting about. When bidding him goodbye I 'wondered whether he could tell me where I could hire a bicycle.' I wanted to go round the drive over Loch Gluich ('one of the most beautiful in the Highlands'—vide Baedeker—about 40 miles). He immediately offered me the cycle and I returned to the hotel to a good warm and cheap supper provided by my landlady—a combination of qualities which I had got a little unaccustomed. By the way I was living in a Temperance Hotel, 3 meals a day, and this was the last called 'high tea'

29th glorious ride round Loch Gluich. Returned about 6 P.M.

Monday 30th Kyle of Lochalsh Steamer dep. 8.30

Mallaig " arriv. 1.30

" train dep 1.45

Arrachan (at the head of Loch Lomond) train arriv 4. 15

Steamer dep. 4.45

Balloch (south end of Loch Lomond) steamer arriv. 6.45

Train dep. 7.00

Glasgow " arriv. 7.45

These times are approximate. I have thrown away my timetables so I cannot give you a more accurate a/c.

Tuesday 1st October

Called on Sec. F. B. I., Chamber of Commerce and one other Federation. The big industrial cities in Britain seem to be very bad[ly] off as regards hotels. Now that I have left England I can say that by far the best hotel in which I have stayed—cheapness, cleanliness and comfort all considered was the hotel at Keswick. As I said I got into Glasgow quite late and was walking out of the station struggling under the weight of the one suitcase, (the other as you remember had been in the left luggage office at Edinburgh) when a young man came and offered to carry it for me. He appealed so appealingly that I had not the heart to stop him from earning sixpence. There seems to be a lot of unemployment in Glasgow—yes, I remember because the shipyards have not booked many new orders, a gentleman in the train and connected with the shipping trade told me. I had found this desire to carry my cases also very rife in Manchester where there must also be a lot of unemployment.

As a matter of fact this young man turned out to be very useful. For after having been informed that two 'commercial' hotels (the names of which I had collected from a commercial gentleman on the way to Skye a week before—all those mentioned in Baedeker being very expensive) [wee full] I was thinking of going to one of Baedeker's in despair when the young man took me to another 'commercial' hotel where I got a room. This however was about the worst and noisiest room in which I have yet slept barring one bedroom at Bhandari Palace on Hindu festival days.

The next morning I found that half the hotel was empty possibly because the other rooms were also like mine. I was charged a shilling for a bath in which there was hardly sufficient water for me to immerse myself. By the 2.30 train I came to Edinburgh (arrived ?.30), and then started another hotel search—a search which lasted till 6.30.

There was not a room to be had for love or money. At last I gave up doing the round of the hotels. I had risen in my attempts to the heroic heights of preparing myself to pay 15/- for a night. At last a hotel manager gave me the name of a lady in the suburbs who might have apartments. I went there and I had luck or thought I had luck such as never fell to man before. A big room, beautiful furniture, a beautiful garden in front of the house, price 5/6 for bed and breakfast. I said that I'd take the room and that I would go to the station to fetch my cases (one from Waverley station where I had got to from Glasgow, the other from Queen St. Station where it had been lying for a week). It was a job bringing those two heavy cases in the tram, but I was not going to pay 5/- for a taxi. Fortunately the tram from Waverley passed Queen St.

When at last my cases were safely in the house where I had taken the room the land lady came to me and said that I could not have the room. It seems that the hotel manager who had sent me there had been sending other people too, and someone had in the landlady's absence come and taken the room and paid in advance to one of the maids. At least so the landlady said. However she really seemed to be—as they say— more a fool than a knave. So I started off at about 8 in search of another room. By this time it was quite dark and fright! fully cold (do you remember Hattoo chacha's fright! fully?) and raining and blowing as I hope it can rain and blow only in Edinburgh. I think that the gentleman in charge of keeping hell up-to-date might have a look at Edinburgh at one such time. I imagine that a room or two with Edinburgh rainy and blowy weather would be quite in place in hell however well-kept it was. Well, to end the story again, as they say, I got a fairly nice room about 9 or 9.30, not very far from the other place. I got my cases there—again a job for I could not get anyone to help me—had something to eat and went to sleep.

Wed. Called on 4 people. Lunch with the Schlepps.

Thurs sightseeing in Edin-too wet and cold and blowy to see anything. Had to hold on to my hat with both hands most of the time.

Friday Edinb. Dep 7.30

Newcastle arrive 10.15. Made 3 calls and forgot to CALL AT THE P. O. FOR MY LETTERS

Newcastle dept (per S.S. Dunstanburgh, 2,000 tons, carrying capacity 12 passengers—actually carried 3 passengers including myself) … 2. 15 p.m.

Saturday North Sea very bad.

Sunday 7 a.m. arrived Hamburg Persuaded much against my better judgement to go to the (oh irony) 'the Commercial Hotel' with my ship companions.

Monday Calls in Hamburg. Hamburg is really an extraordinarily beautiful city. Mr Meiningen (of Biutlac Ltd, Newcastle of whom I may write to you some day when I have time) had told me that it was a *'beautiful city'*. But Mr Meiningen was a German Naturalized British and a commercial man and I have a suspicion of a commercial Jew, and I thought any large industrial city where there was lots of money to be made would be beautiful to Mr Meiningen. But my apologies to Mr Meiningen.

Tuesday 8th Hamb., dep 8.30

Cologne arriv 3.5

Wed 9th Cologne

Thursday (today) Cologne departure (by steamer on the Rhine) 7.15 A.M.

Koblenz arriv 2.30 P.M.

And by the way as to my theatre programme:

Sunday-arrived in Hamburg, tried to get a ticket for Fidelio

(Beethoven)-State Opera House-but all reasonably priced tickets sold out.

Monday 'Schwabda' a ballet opera at Hamburg State Opera.

Tuesday 'Tales of Hoffmann' State Opera House

Cologne As you may remember I had heard this opera in London. The Hamburg version was infinitely superior. We have got a record or two from this opera.

Wed 'Don Juan' (music Gluck) and 'Der dreispig' (music da Falla) ballet operas (music da Falla) had heard in London when the Serge Diaghileff Russian Co. had performed.

As the Serge D. Co is acknowledged to be the finest in the world, London version, certainly as far as the dancing went, superior.

2.10.29

I am afraid that I shall have to post this letter tomorrow and I am not feeling in the mood for letter writing now. The whole of today it was rainy and cold and very unpleasant. I made four calls and spent some time in the afternoon with the Schlepps whom I liked very much. Prof Schlepp is the father-in-law of the Ede of the Tate Gallery. He is retired from the Edinburgh University. The younger Schlepp was it turned out with Asaf Bhai at St Johns and is at present Lecturer in Maths at Edinburgh. I get my boat from Newcastle on Friday the 4th.

IV Europe: The Rhine, Paris

[To Asif Fyzee]

I had been waiting to write to you till I had come to the Rhine, a thing which I had made up my mind to do chiefly on your recommendation. Well, just an hour ago I got out of the Rhine steamer.

But to give you first some news of how I fared in Cambridge. You must have learnt from my letter to Shahinda that I went to Cambridge and thoroughly enjoyed myself there. I had written to all the people on whom you had given me letters asking them whether they would be there when I had intended going there. As a matter of fact I went up there at rather a bad time inasmuch as it was during the vacations. However, Cockroft asked me to have tea with him on the day I arrived there and Prof Nicholson on the day after. I got to Cambridge on a Sunday and spent the whole afternoon with the Cockrofts. The next day Cockroft took me to dine in the Hall at St John's and I had before had tea with Prof Nicholson.

Cockroft I thought a remarkably capable and forceful personality. I wished I could have had an opportunity of meeting him again. As it was he seemed to be very busy— though it was the vacations—in the Cavendish Lab and I did not want to hang about him and take even more of his time than he was as it was giving me. I felt that it was men like him who were the real backbone of the Cavendish lab.

With Prof. and Mrs Nicholson I got on extraordinarily well. This was the more surprising considering what an almost taciturn couple they are and that I do not know anything about Arabic or Persian research at all. However they gave me a very good tea and afterwards Prof Nicholson took me into his library and I saw what the study of a great scholar is like.

Mrs Gray I unfortunately did not meet. She said that just at the time that I was going to Cambridge she would be having some people to stay with her and that it would not be convenient to her to have me. She subsequently wrote a very nice letter saying how sorry she was that she could not entertain one of your friends.

When I first wrote to Goldstein [an introduction from Asaf Fyzee] he was in Gottingen. By the time that I got to Wales he had come to Blackpool and used to run into Manchester to look for a house there. When I got to Manchester he had not yet got a house but I went over the next day—Sunday—and spent the whole day with them. They are both very nice but I think I preferred Mrs Goldstein to Goldstein himself and this not merely on account of her beauty!

Goldstein gave me a letter of introduction on a Dr Berenblum in Leeds whom I think you have not met. He is also quite a young man (about 30) and a Russian Jew who had first emigrated to Belgium and then come over from Belgium to England when the Germans invaded Belgium. He is now waiting for his naturalization papers. Goldstein and he it appears lived together for a year or so. Berenblum is now engaged in Cancer research. I spent an evening with him and his wife—and I think I can say without hesitation that so far as one can judge in such a short meeting he is the most strikingly intelligent man that I met in England. He has recently married an accomplished pianist and, of course, a Jewess—who plays for the broadcasting concerts sometimes. How can the Jews not produce able men. They know the principles of eugenics. One Jew, a Wrangler, marries a Jewess—a PhD of Cambridge in Physical Chemistry. Another, a research worker in Cancer, marries a gifted musician.

I crossed over from Newcastle to Hamburg on the 3rd. I was in Hamburg for a couple of days and then I came down to Cologne where I spent another two days. The slow steamer from Cologne to Koblenz had been taken off from the first of this month, so this portion I had to do in a fast steamer. At Koblenz I spent a night and the next morning at 10.30 took the slow steamer which runs from there to Mainz. You remember that from Koblenz to Bingen is the most beautiful part of the Rhine course where it flows between those high hills. I got off the steamer again at Bingen and stayed 2 days there—and from there I came here this evening. Tomorrow by the 8.30 train I go to Paris.

I had been wondering before whether it would really be worthwhile coming up the Rhine as you had suggested. But now I think that I would have missed seeing something most interesting if I had not come here. The Rhine seems to be a combination of the Tower of London and its history, the Wye Valley and its beauty and Birmingham and its industry.

Well, now I must bid you goodbye
Paris 16.10.29
I have at last arrived in Paris.

17.10.29

I have not the slightest idea when the mail goes from here. Today is Thursday evening. We had to post on Thursday evenings in London. I don't suppose it is earlier here in Paris. Anyway it can't be helped now

You will again I am afraid have reason to complain of my letters. I shall be very busy in Paris, as in London. It is only when travelling that you have long evenings when you don't know what to do, and probably you will never again get long letters from me for I shall do no more touring. You will be interested to hear that there is quite a possibility of my coming back a month earlier. I have been spending frightful amounts of money lately. During September I spent 20.10.0, i.e., 7.10.0 pounds more than I ought to have. And in October I have already spent 21.0.0 pounds. I shall then drop Italy. Though if I can do so I shall spend a week or 10 days in Milan, first of all because there is now a lot of trade between Milan and Bombay and secondly I would like to go to the Scala. I liked Hamburg so much that I think that I shall spend more time than I had at first intended in Berlin. So now my programme is something like this: Leave Paris about the middle of December (or commencement), go to Lyons, 2 days, ...??? 1 d and Geneva 2 days, then to Vienna. Stay in Vienna 1 ½ months then do [sic] to Prague, 2 days, Dresden 2 days, and Berlin. Stay in Berlin 1 month then again come south to Leipzig 2 days, Jena 2 days (for the Zeiss factory which I have always wanted to see) and Zurich (3 or 4 or 5 days, according to the warmth of the reception from Amin Bhai and his wife). And Milan. Embark from Venice or Genoa as necessary (Venice steamer leaves 15th March, Genoa steamers 1st March and 30th March). You see that I have dropped Spain out. The railway fares are prohibitive. It is they as a matter of fact which made the Sept. and Oct. expenses excessive. At Hamburg I purchased a 3rd ticket (from Hamburg to Cologne) but 5 minutes after getting into the train I paid the difference and went into the 2nd class. What fine 2nd classes they have on the German Railways. They are quite as good as the English 1st Class.

I have now got both my cases new. I think I wrote to you that soon after my arrival in London, the more doubtful of my cases sort of gave up the ghost. The other one behaved similarly at Hamburg. For the suitcases I must say that the kind of travelling that I have been doing imposes great strains on the suitcases and nothing in the composition of which cardboard enters will do. I have now got two very nice cases. The London one (42/-) is bluish-grey, extremely strong and with a convenient tray. The Cologne one (I purchased it in Cologne) is fibre and very nice (31 marks = 31 shillings)...

To give you first of all ... my diary since Coblenz, where I think I ended:

11 Friday Left Koblenz 10.15 by slow Rhine steamer. Arrived Bingen 3 in the afternoon.

12th Saturday Stayed in Bingen.

13th Sunday Bingen dept 3.9. Mainz arrival 5.33 (we were about 1 hour late).

14th Monday Mainz Depat 8.30. Paris arrival 7.30 But as Paris is West European time that is one hour later, it meant Paris 8.30, or 12 solid hours in the train. Nothing for India, but quite a long journey here. Really Paris and Mainz are not so far away but there is not a good connection between them.

Up to now I have not been feeling happy in Paris. I hope I shall soon start feeling better. Just now I keep remembering of [sic] those luscious teas which I used to have with my legs over the armrests of those comfortable cane chairs in Karachi too often. This I have come to regard as an almost as unerring a sign of my having done too much as my finger test is of the state of my bodily condition. This last by the way shows that a diet of fish, roll and butter doesn't agree with me or at least that I don't thrive on it, a conclusion which Mrs O'Gilvie when I met her, confirmed. However, the food in Paris is very good and very cheap and I shall I suppose have to take care lest I get too fat for my clothes.

Hotel de Richelieu

Rue de Moliere

Paris 22. 10.29

This morning I received a large number of letters, I had written to Mr Chavannes (an old friend of Hasan mamoo's) from Mainz. His reply I received this morning only. Though it seems to have been posted on the 14th. The postal system here seems to be about as queer as the system in our great Musulman and first native state in India [Hyderabad]. Then I received two mails from Somerset Lodge, viz., of the 29th Sept and 5th Oct. There was also a letter from Jabir??? Bhai who complains bitterly of the bad monsoon and generally of the bad way in which Bombay commerce is just now.

Before I make any further progress I shall write what I have been wanting to write to you for a long time. If you have any opportunity of meeting Major Clarke, the Indian Trade commissioner, who has his office at Ballard Estate, please hug him. He is for me a most important man. Mother I should feel very much obliged if you would kindly invite him to tea or something, but without sort of going out of your way. He it is who sends the Dept of Overseas Trade at London all their information regarding Bombay and when I return I am going to call on him and if he knows us already it will be very helpful to me.

Another man of whom if you take attention I should be very much obliged is Mehta, the Sec. of the Indian Merchants Chamber. When I had gone to see him before leaving he had been very nice and said that he knew you, father. At the moment I had pretended that I knew all about the great intimacy which existed between you and him. However, he has been tremendously helpful. His letters (I don't know whether you saw them) or rather copies of them for he had given me letters on only two or three Chambers of Commerce have been Open Sesames at all doors—and I have distributed about thirty copies of the letter on the Manchester Chamber of Commerce, and propose to distribute more. It is curious what an effect they have invariably produced.

Haffoo has been I must say very regular in her letters to me. Her last letter from Somerset Lodge was very well typed. The next letter from Hyderabad was rather difficult to read and would have been still more difficult if it had not been for father's elucidatory notes.

I am glad that the English I. C. S. results so far as they concern Badr have been satisfactory. The car in which Simpson drove me was nothing special, only the office two-seater Morris Cowley.

Badr and Haffoo will be interested to hear that Mischa Elman and Elisabeth Schumann are both in Paris and I shall try and hear them. But I shall not try very hard. I have more and more come to conclusion that it is much pleasanter hearing chamber music on the gramophone than in the concert hall. Besides my aim in coming to Europe is 'to experience sensations which I cannot experience in India' (an aim which, by the way, has as a result of some deep thinking been slightly displaced in the direction of 'to experience sensations which would change me most') and inasmuch as modern gramophone recording reproduces almost perfectly and I can therefore hear anybody in India at a much smaller cost I have no longer an overwhelming desire to hear the virtuosos. It is different with the operas. You cannot reproduce an opera and I have therefore been going to the opera regularly. Since my arrival here, I have heard 'Boris Godunov' and the 'Valkyrie' at the Opera House and 'Tristan and Isolde' at the Opera Comique. The last two are by Wagner and the first by Mussorgsky who is in many ways considered to be Wagner's equal. The singing and the mise-en-scene was simply wonderful—at a rough approximation = 100 English opera. I had heard the 'Valkyrie' in England, the other two I heard for the first time.

I took Jami [daughter of Alma Latifi] last Sunday out for the day and we went to St Germain en Laye. We spent a moderately pleasant day. There wasn't much to do there. I am just now going to meet Sagheer Bhai [Mohamedi, youngest Mohamedi brother] to purchase a pair of skates for skating on ice. I find Sagheer Bhai extraordinarily good. He seems to know all about Parisian life and to have fully entered into it, yet a more level-headed, helpful and nice person it is difficult to imagine. He seems to be an almost ideal person. He has it seems a great number of friends here and he lives certainly a very sociable life. At the same time he reads and takes an interest in music and literature and in culture generally.

I have also [in addition to learning how to skate] decided on joining a dance class. This not because I very much like the idea of dancing or because I have become immoral but because I had made up my mind to penetrate to the heart of Paris though it may be necessary for that purpose to dance in the cafes at Montparnasse every evening till 4 in the morning.

24th I have not quite made up my mind about the skating and dancing yet. I am going for the day to Chantilly next Thursday and in the cool of the atmosphere of the 'Banlieu' (environs) of Paris I shall decide. The pros and cons are as follows

Cons

1) *Rather expensive*
2) *will take lots of time*
   Pros

Everybody here seems to dance.

The unknown factor which I have not yet been able to define is what I shall get out of dancing. I want to dance in order to meet people. *The question* is whether I shall meet the kind of people I want to by dancing. Well now goodbye.

30.10 29

I can hardly realize that it is now almost 16 days that I have been in Paris. I have as yet done nothing. The vain rushing about and doing nothing which I have done is tremendous. However I had better commence with a formal a/c.

My last letter must have brought you up to—but I think I said nothing at all of what I have been doing in Paris so I shall commence from the 14th Arriv Paris

17th I spent the morning going round the Louvre. As yet I have been about 4 times to the Louvre, of which the first time I looked around the whole place, the sculpture galleries and the Salle d'Appolon, and the other three in looking at the pictures. My ideas as to what I want to look at in the picture galleries have changed a great deal since I left India. As you can well imagine, during all these three or four months that I have had nothing to do and been continuously meeting people of the kind of Ede of the Tate Gallery, I have formed quite an elaborate theory 1) of what painting and all art should aim at and secondly how it should attain this aim. Some future time you may suddenly receive a letter of 40 pages and find yourself inflicted with this whole theory. Anyway, I am now looking at the pictures from the point of view of my theory and I have to look at all schools and all periods. The plans which I had formed in India of looking only at the Raphaels, Rembrandts and Rubens I gave up after a very short trial in the National Gallery.

The second interesting piece of news which I have to give is that I have through the 'Bureau de renseignements' got into touch with a Madame Beaugrand in order to 'echanger des conversations Anglais contre Francais'. I have been to her twice now and I shall go again on Fridays. But through a lady friend of Sagheer Bhai's I have come to know of another person who is much better. He is Deliano, a Rumanian who is studying at the Ecole des Mines here. He speaks French well and we are to meet 3 times a week when we shall talk French for one hour and then English for another hour. I have just received my skates from the Galleries Lafayette which I purchased there. I shall go and see Sagheer Bhai tonight after the theatre and fix up our going to the Palais de Glace where they have skating on ice.

The day before yesterday I went down to Versailles. At first I was very much disappointed with the place but the view of the palace from the gardens—I did not go into the gardens till after having gone through the buildings—considerably lessened my disappointment. I am going to Versailles again tomorrow.

As to theatres, I have been very busy. On the 23rd I went to the Opera Comique after….—'Pelleas et Melisande'—by Debussy. 24th Theatre Gymnase, which corresponds in Paris to the Haymarket and Wyndhams in London, i.e. it is a theatre for the modern classics. I am not able to follow all that is said in the theatre [but] I can keep up with the general sense. At the Gymnase I saw 'Melo', a very good piece. On Friday, 'Vieux Colombert' which is another theatre—according to Baedeker—like the Gymnase. But the Baedeker which I have—borrowed from Jami, your copy father is 1913 edition—is 6 years old and since the Vieux Colombert had been changed into a cinema.

When I went into the theatre to purchase the tickets I did not look round and find this out! It was only when I had to pay for the ticket—12 francs for the best seat in the theatre—that the cheapness aroused my suspicions and I realized that I had purchased a cinema ticket. I tried to get a refund but without success. However the piece was quite good—the Zeppelins' tour round the world in 20 days.

5 Nov. 29 Paris

I have just received my mail—rather late, for it is Tuesday afternoon, but the American Express people here take long in redirecting.

I haven't got much to write this week. I must have ended my last letter on Thursday. On Thursday … I went to Versailles again and spent all the time in the garden. I have got into touch with a friend of Sagheer Bhai's, a Rumanian, who is studying mining here and we have agreed to meet 3 times a week to talk French for an hour and afterwords English for an hour—he wants to learn English. On Thursday I had to be at his place at 4.30. Well, I could not get there—this paper is frightful. I can't write on it all. I wonder whether you will be able to read anything—till nearly 5 and then he informed me that he could not have a lesson because he was suddenly called away. In the evening I dined with the Chavannes. I spent a very pleasant evening indeed. M. Chavannes is a great talker and has definite and well thought out opinions on most points. His wife is very charming but the husband quite eclipses her as far as interestingness is concerned.

1st Friday *In the morning I went to Mad. Beaugrand of whom I think I have already written.* I had got my skates and so [i]n the evening Sagheer Bhai and I went to the Palais de Glace where there is skating on real ice. It is quite a smart place. Father, you may possibly know it. The ice is of course artificial, a circular piece a good 50 yards in diameter. All round are tables where rich people drink coffee or tea, American visitors taking liqueurs. The place is roofed in and the walls are practically all mirrors.

Skating is difficult but not very difficult—about as difficult as cycling I imagine. I got quite tired by the time we left—we were there from 9–11.45. At first I used to just hug round the railing but towards the end I could go round a little.

3rd Saturday I went round and round the town. I purchased a new overcoat—800 francs (120 fra = 1 pound). It is really very good. My old one had got really very shabby. I started out in the morning with 1000 francs in my pocket determined to spend them. I purchased a very warm muffler also, and a couple of pairs of woollen socks....

You will be amused to hear that the muffler which Haffoo made for me I brought with me to London. There I had it packed up in the case containing the guns and the books I bought in London, together with the pullover because I thought that it would be a nuisance carrying them about. They are now all lying in a godown in London. This was a real mistake for even in September in Scotland I felt the need of warm things. However with this overcoat and muffler I can make myself as warm as I like. Paris is getting quite chilly now, especially in the mornings. I wonder what Vienna and Berlin will be like in January and February.

I have now more or less definitely made up my mind that I shall return by the boat leaving Genoa on 1st March.

4th Sunday I went to a chrysanthemum show. As a matter of fact there were roses and many kinds of vegetables and fruits displayed too. But the chrysanthemums were the chief things. They were of course magnificent. I then went to the Madeleine where there was to be an organ recital after the service. This was to commence at 12.30 and I was a little late. At three I had to go to the concert of the Conservatoire de Paris, probably the most highbrow body of its kind in the world. All the tickets are taken by subscription but the very cheap tickets are available to the public. Last Sunday Backhaus and Dolores de Silva were the guests at the conservatoire and the programme included Schumann's Symphony in D (I believe this has been recorded) and Beethoven's Concerto for Piano in A Major (Backhaus) and Handel's Largo (Dolores de Silva).

In the evening I went to the Comedie Francaise, the first state theatre, to see 'Poliche' by Henri Bataille. I am beginning to like French acting more now. 'Poliche' was really very well done, I thought.

4th Monday Morning Bois de Boulogne-very beautiful. I almost walked my legs off....

Visit to the dentist-filling had [come] off. I decided on taking prompt measures. I telephoned to Delgano asking him whether I should come. He said yes. When I went there it was 5 minutes of 4.30 when I had said I would come. Deliano was not there. Beastly nuisance.

Evening 'Valkyrie' at the Opera. This was the 4th time that I heard this opera of Wagner's—twice in London, the 3rd time at the Opera Comique in Paris (or was it at the Opera, I don't remember) and the 4th time at the Opera. 5th Tuesday....

This morning I spent in the Luxembourg, after having been finally to the dentist. At 4 I went to the Palais de Glace again—alone. I am making good progress with my skating and hope to be able to soon thoroughly enjoy it. The rink closes at 7 (to reopen again at 9) and then I returned home after dining to find the mail from home arrived.

I find that at home a good deal of fun is made of my writing 'besides the point' for 'beside the point' and 'nocking' for 'knocking'. I hope that it will be remembered that I never reread my letters for the simple reason that I go on writing till there is no more time and I then stop, fold the letter, address the envelope and send it off as I shall do now.

12.11.29

[Written to Jabir Ali and his wife Safia]
By going to the Brasserie Universelle and having their Peche Melba I have now completed the last of the instructions given by you Jabir M. to me. I must say that this last piece of advice was very much inferior in quality, I think, to the other pieces. I thought the Peche Melba a very ordinary affair indeed. I did not dine or lunch there, just went round at about 5 and asked for the thing.

I don't remember when I wrote my last letter to you but I think it was after I had visited Sheffield and before I got to Hamburg ... At both the places they remembered you quite well and at Hamburg I was asked when I said that [you] were no longer in business, whether you had made so much money that you no longer thought it worth while to work

You remember you had (continued 11.11.29) told us that there was nothing in Paris which had impressed you so much as Napoleon's tomb at the Invalides. I went over to have a look at the dome soon after I arrived here. The entrance, the height of the roof and especially the blue light inside are certainly most impressive. But I was extremely disappointed with the tomb itself. Instead of a block of marble, white and square as the emperor's forehead, there was, as you know a piece of brown marble cut into all sorts of Bourbonnic curves. One might think that the legs of some of the pieces of furniture at Versailles had been used as sort of stencils to cut the stone and that under it slept not Napoleon but Lewis [sic] XVIII. Well, I am glad that I am not Napoleon to be able to be made to suffer like this.

The French people I think in many things don't know where to stop. Take for instance the Sainte Chapelle (you remember in the Palais de Justice) which Baedeker calls a perfect gem of gothic architecture. Do you recollect it? It is a most magnificent piece but one or the other of the Bourbons went and gilded the interior. Can you imagine a gothic interior gilded? Think of a mass of Bach's being sung in the frightful atmosphere of gold and blue (for they have not contented themselves with gold). All the colour which I allow Gothic must come from the stained windows. The rest must be deep dark grey.

A propos to the Mass of Bach's, I have been hearing some really magnificent church music. It is rather difficult to get into it—for one thing they, especially the Roman

Catholics, make you get up, sit down so often during the service that you cannot pay much attention to the music. Now I take a seat in a comer and just stick tight. In the Madeleine there is every Sunday an organ recital. The organ is a grand instrument.

Well now I think I must bid goodbye. I hope you will be able to read this letter. My handwriting is really not so bad. Only this paper is very bad. I can't write on it at all.

With love to yourselves and to Amiruddin

13.11.29

I have received no letters from you this mail yet. I don't know what is the matter. It was a holiday on Monday (the 11th, Armistice Day) and so I thought that I might get my letters today (Wednesday) instead of yesterday. But I haven't got anything yet (it is 10 p.m.)

I have just returned from the restaurant where I have had my evening meal. What good food you get here. This place where I go to is a 'prix fixe' restaurant where you get a meal for 8 fr 50 cent (= 1 sh 5 d) consisting of soup or *hors d'oevres varies* (really very good), two meat dishes, including vegetables and two desserts. You could not get anything like it in England for less than 5 sh. I can't imagine how they can do it. And every one of the dishes is most beautifully cooked. For dessert you may have cheese and a sweet or if you prefer two sweets where you may choose from grapes, pears, oranges (sometimes) and about 5 or 6 different puddings and cold sweets. At first the names were quite unknown to me and every meal was an adventure. But now I know most of the commoner French dishes. Oh yes, I forgot to say that this 8 fr. 50 includes half a bottle of wine or a bottle of beer or aerated water. It is wonderful.

The place where I live I think I wrote to you is a hotel and not a pension. But if you want it they serve breakfast in your room. I used to have my breakfast here at first but I don't do so any longer as I find that in the creameries they give you a bigger cup of coffee and more bread and butter for 3 fr 50 cent than they give in the hotel for 5 fr + 10% for service. As to the much praised French rolls and butter and coffee. The rolls are so far as I can see nothing particular. Lyons rolls when fresh (and they were generally fresh) were as good as any that I have had here. Nor is the coffee anything peculiar. Here when you ask for cafe au lait they bring to you two small jugs of equal size and the same shape, one containing strong coffee, the other full of milk. You empty them both in your cup and you naturally get good coffee, and you would get good coffee if you did this, whether in France, England, India, or Timbuctoo. As a matter of fact in the place in Gower St in London where I had gone to first they used to give us exceptionally good coffee prepared, I have noticed, according to the same recipe of mixing strong coffee with plenty of milk.

I have to thank Haffoo for her good advice to me not to starve myself. I don't think I am starving myself. The difficulty arises from the fact that I have always so little time. I can't gorge myself at each meal and then spend an hour digesting it like a boa constrictor. I am afraid that there is no doubt that I have got a little thinner than what I was before but in order to get fat one must sit comfortably the whole day in an armchair and not be rushing about London or Paris or be tramping through Welsh moors or Scotch bogs.

You must be wondering what I look like now—here goes. On my head there is perched a dark grey felt hat. The hat is very good. I went into Dunns at London and purchased their most expensive model, and Dunns as you know are the biggest people in London for hats. Now it is getting cold and I usually have my overcoat on—the overcoat which I recently got. My method of purchasing it was to go to the Galleries Lafayette and purchase the most expensive thing that they had got in the colour I wanted—very deep, almost black-blue. As to my suits, you know them. On ordinary occasions I have Dias' outfit on (and it seems that it is a very effective indeed outfit as you will see later) and on special occasions I sport the London suit which is just magnificent. It takes you some time to realize all its beauties. You then acknowledge the supremacy of the London tailor. None of your thin waists and turned up shoulders which disgust you so often here in Paris. It is loose, very comfortable to wear, and yet with a cleanness of line difficult to describe.

As to my feet I have now got two pairs of English shoes, both of them by Mansfields who occupy the same position in the boot trade as Dunns do in the hat trade and both the pairs stand in the same relation in the matter of price to other shoes as my hat stands to other hats. I also flaunt socks, 27 francs the pair from the Galeries Lafayette. Altogether a very smart appearance. I wish mother could see me now. It would please her tremendously for I know that at the bottom of her heart she has always had a desire to see me smart. I am afraid that by the time I return to India I shall be a little seedy for as you know I am rather hard on clothes.

I first realized exactly how impressive my Bombay suit was in this manner. When making business calls I usually dressed in my London suit but I had had the other suit dry cleaned and pressed in Edinburgh so I put it on when I was in Newcastle. You remember I wrote to you that I had a letter of introduction from Gail on Maj. Gen. Sir something Montgomery K. C. I. E., etc., the Newcastle representative of the Federation of British Industries and, as I found, a very peculiar man. He sat in his room heated to Hannumkonda May heat by a roaring fire with his hat on. He had been in India and in Bombay 20 years ago and he immediately started asking me all about the latest news from there. He said that he would not be of much use to me and I soon found that Flattery had little or no effect on him. I would have tried Apology but I did not think it worth while. However all this is beside the point. After a little conversation, he offered to introduce me to Mr Meiningen, a naturalized German 'whose sons had fought for us in the War' and the head of one of the biggest firms in Newcastle. He wasn't sure whether Mr Meiningen would have the time to see me but he would telephone and try. Fortunately I said that I did not particularly want to see Mr Meiningen as I wanted to get into touch as a commencement with the Secs of associations and not with individuals, but that I would not mind explaining my schemes to Mr Meiningen if he thought it was any good. Well, Meiningen was telephoned to and my purpose shortly communicated to him, including my disinclination to see him. The result was that Mr Meiningen telephoned that he would be obliged if I would step into his office. The Major. Gen. something Montgomery accompanied me to the lift of Meiningen's office and there we bid each other goodbye. I went up and was shown into a luxurious waiting room and in a few moments into Meiningen's sanctum.

Sitting opposite to him on the other side of his desk I soon decided on my plan of attack. Grey's cigarettes were offered to me and I would smoke through two thirds of them very fast and then throw them away implying that I was much too rich to trouble to smoke the stump, however expensive the cigarette may be. I worked through about five or six cigarettes in this way. During our conversation I would every now and then get up saying, 'I am afraid I am wasting your time', and offer to go away. Sometimes I would get up with one hand in my trouser pocket and stalk across the magnificent carpet to flick the ash off my cigarette into the grate instead of in the ash tray which had been placed for me. There was a large mirror in the room and I could see that my suit was looking very fine. I could also see that Meiningen was saying to himself 'If this man for his informal grey suits uses such cloth as this' (you remember I had gone into the Bombay market and purchased the most expensive cloth to be had) 'what must his formal clothes be like?' Father, don't think I at all overdid it. After the experience of some 40 or 50 interviews of a similar nature I have got a fairly correct touch in these matters. And the results prove that what I did was right. Meiningen practically went down on his knees. He had very little business doing at present with India but he begged and prayed me to help him and put him into touch with some good firms in Bombay. With a wave of my cigaretted hand, I promised to do what I could for him. 'But', I said, 'Don't expect too much of me. I am a solicitor and not a businessman. I don't want you to say later "Mr Tyabji promised this and Mr Tyabji promised that and Mr Tyabji has done nothing." I want to promise little and do more ...' Meiningen smiled thankfully and his secretary who was also in the room beamed in thanks too. Well, we began talking of my tour. I told him that I was leaving for Hamburg in 2 hours. 'How?' he asked. 'By the Tyne Tees Shipping Co's boat,' I replied. 'Oh my dear sir! Oh my dear Sir! I pity you! Those are not the boats for a gentleman like you (I can almost hear him saying this) Small ones—twelve passengers. What I do is to take the 11.45 to Harwich where I get a fast boat to the Hook and from there a through saloon train takes me into Hamburg the next day at 12 [in] comfort and you save 24 hours. It costs a few pounds more but what are a few pounds to a gentleman like you?' 'Oh, I don't know about that', I modestly replied, 'Pounds are pounds to any person. But,' I regretfully continued, 'I wish I had known all this before.' I forgot to tell him that I had most carefully studied all the connections between England and Hamburg and chosen this because it was the cheapest.

Well, to give you some news of Paris.

6th *Wed.* Visited Chantilly. Evening opera I think it was 'Valkyrie'. I don't remember. In my diary there is only Opera.

7th *Thursd.* Don't remember what I did in the morning. Evening Opera Comique. 'Pelleas et Melisande' of Debussy.

8th *Frid.* Mad. Beaugrand (for exchange of French against English conversation) Evening Skating.

9th *Sat.* morning. Don't remember. Afternoon Deliano (a Romanian to whom I have been introduced through Sagheer Bhai.) We talk in French and English. He is nice and interesting. Evening *Opera* 'Faust'

10 *Sund.* Morning Armistice Commemorative Service in the Eglise St Louis in the lnvalides. Gregorian chant 'Te Deum' (magnificent, heard for the first time) Beethoven's Mass in E maj, De Profundis of Gluck. Service altogether fine. I was in the gallery above. I had paid 10 francs for the seat, and so did not get up for the service, a great thing. Afternoon, concert in the Salle Pleyel. Beethoven's Eroica symphony, Chopin's 2nd concerto for piano and orchestra. Nikolai Orloff at the piano, and 'Don Juan', Richard Strauss' symphonic poem (not Mozart's overture as at first I thought.) Evening *Opera* 'Lohengrin'. Absolutely glorious. When you go and hear Wagner you

don't come back home humming silly tunes as from a performance of 'Carmen' or 'La Tosca'. All that you can say is 'What an opera!' There are five or six themes, not more, and though you may be hearing the opera for the first time you come to know them all before the first act is one third over. After they have been once fully announced they are seldom wholly repeated, except on some especially solemn occasion. There is a flash of a note or two from one or moan from another and you know what the characters are singing about though you cannot follow the words. And then the whole music is built round the story and the words. I almost cried when Lohengrin sailed away leaving his newly wedded princess forever to the sound of the 'Lohengrin' theme which I may shortly describe in terms of which I had heard that very morning as the compression into about 6 notes of that Mass of Beethoven's and the Gregorian chant. As you may remember Lohengrin is the knight of the Holy Grail who appears in his Swan-drawn boat to clear the princess Elsa of the false charge which has been brought against her, and then marries her. I think that among what I have heard of Wagner's yet I like 'Lohengrin' most. Of course I know 'Valkyrie' much better because I have heard it now some 4 or 5 times whilst this was practically the first time I heard Lohengrin.

Mond After Delgano, Evening Comedie Francaise, 'La Belle Mariniere' (The Beautiful Sailoress) very well acted I thought and a good piece.

Tuesd Morning Went to the Embassy and called on a firm of international solrs[solicitors]—nothing doing. Evening 'La Bosoche', an opera by Messager who after Debussy is I suppose the most famous modern French composer. It was at the Opera Comique. I did not like it particularly though the *mise en scene* was good.

17.11.29

I enclose a letter for the Comm. Of Police which please send to him together with my licence after filling in the blanks. I believe that my licence is in the middle drawer of my desk. If it is not in the desk it may be in the rifle case. Badr you should also make an application for an import licence. I hope that Badr you have been continuing to send advertisement to the Times for the m'cycle. If not please do so. You can give the slip to Babuji and all [will] be done. There isn't really much to be done.

I hope you have been able to send that copy of the Nehru Report to Dr Molisch. I want to make use of him a great deal in Vienna and therefore to get in as far as possible into his good books now. I am already late in letting you know but please send letters in future— i.e. after the receipt of this letter by you to Hullo, there seems to be no branch of the Am. Exp. at Vienna. If this is true it will be a great nuisance. I shall make inquiries at their office here.

I have been having an awfully interesting and a very busy time here, making lots of new friends. One result of this is that I have no time to write to you.

I notice with pleasure that Badr's letters now contain bits of advice or bits of sarcasm. He is evidently growing fast. I remember distinctly the time when his letters used to be sentimental and I distinctly recall the shock with which I realized how young he was on reading such a sentimental letter once.

I am surprised to hear that you did not get a letter by one mail it is evidently the one written from the Lake district that has gone astray A pity, though I am not quite sure of this for it consisted of some 30 or 40 pages of philosophical reflections on nature, beauty and allied subjects. I don't mean to imply that I am so modest as to think that it would not have interested you—though possibly that is what I mean. However . . .

The most important events of the last week are my picking up 2 young American artists in a picture gallery and a young Dutch artist in the Musee Guimet. This latter was standing in a [sic] frenzied admiration before a copper casting of Nataraja. When I saw him I immediately fell in love with him for this and promptly accosted him with 'C'est joli, ca, n'est ce pas, Monsieur?' I don't know whether you know the Nataraja of which I speak. The finest are in the Madras Museum. The only one that I have ever seen except in illustrations was in the collection of Treasurywalla, . . . the founder of the Lotus Club of whom I must have written to you when you were in Karachi and we at Palli Hill. I had always tremendously admired these Natarajas as works of art and when I saw this young Dutchman who did not even know that Nataraja was Siva dancing the Tandava dance, go into such ecstasies over it you can imagine that I promptly fell in love with him. The result is that he is going to dine with me tomorrow. He can speak a little English—about as much as I can French. We can get on quite well.

I have been trying to persuade some other people here also to go and look at the 3 or 4 castings and the few fragments of Indian sculpture in the Musee Guimet. I remembered how much I liked Mr Lawrence Binyon's method of talking of Mughal miniatures, so different from that of Vincent Smith who took a photograph of a man sitting by a statue of Buddha, in the same manner, to prove apologetically that the statue was not after all very much distorted. All this seems to me so ridiculous now after having seen the work of and met some of the people whose cry may be summarized into 'Distort, distort if there is a sous' worth to be gained by it.'

I have now got into the Bibliotheque Nationale too. I spent the whole of today there.

There are some very fine and at the same time very interesting pictures and my notes are swelling rapidly. I wonder what I shall do with them. Throw them away the first time I can make up my mind to do so. I suppose the difficulty is that they are not sufficiently complete to form into a paper and yet contain too much interesting matter to be comfortably thrown away.

25.11.29   Paris

My dear Father

Hasan Mamoo has promised me a present of 5 pounds. Could you open a credit for me for this amount? I don't expect that I shall have to go outside what I have got already. Indeed I hope to bring a little back. But as this little will be very little and the margin therefore very small I should like to have so much more credit if you don't mind.

25.11.29

I have just received my mail. I cannot quite understand whether you have been getting all my letters or not. I have been writing every week or rather one letter for each week and you may get no letter one week and two the next, but you ought to get 1 letter for each mail. Now in her last letter Vazir wrote to me that there was no letter at all for one week. On the other hand father you do not say any such thing.

By this same mail I received letters from Father Heras too. It is a difficult problem to decide whether to go to Spain or not. However, to give you some news of the last week. Last week I had an appointment with those three Americans in the lobby of the Theatre Francaise, where the girl works. You remember them don't you, but I will now give you their description. First of all there is Richard Dicus. He says that he is of Greek extraction, but I would have said that he is pure Anglo-Saxon. Age about 30 1/2 an inch or so taller than me, broad and strong. Good forehead, straight nose, and strong features. Eyes more what are called 'honest' than any others that I can immediately recollect except perhaps those of that Scotch missionary priest that I had collected at Kyle of Lochalsh. Looks as little like an artist as you can imagine. To come to the more interesting part, his mind. You remember that I had met the two men in the Salon de Sur Independents. There is the Salon d'Automne which might correspond to the Academy. Then there is the 'Independents' who want to have nothing to do with academical methods. Their chief point however is that they have for their exhibitions no jury for admission but any picture offered for exhibition by one of their members is hung up. Over these are the Vrais (True) Independents. And to crown all are the Sur Independents. I had first started conversation with the other (King) when we were standing before a very worthless series of pictures (to use the expression used by Dicus later 'I would rather hang a cheap calendar in my room than those pictures'). I had not quite made up my mind about these chiefly because King seemed to like at least some of them. Soon after Dicus came along and without much hesitation delivered his opinion on the pictures, already quoted. And I said 'By Jove he has said the right thing.'

Well, we wandered about the gallery for some time. I have by this time collected a sufficient number of deep thoughts and well-turned sentences to impress anyone whether he be artist, philosopher, international lawyer or Jew exporter of piece goods to India. Of these I gave them a suitable selection and we became more or less friends. A rendezvous was made for the next day.

The next day (oh I forgot that I was giving you an account of Dicus' character, but it does not matter. One matter is interesting enough). The two, Dicus and King, turned up at my hotel at 2.15 and we walked down to the other side of the Seine to the Rue de la Seine and the Rue des Beaux Arts which run from behind the Academie Francaise. These two streets are extremely interesting and you will understand what kind of things they are if you look at the ... plan. You just go on crossing from one side of the street to the other and spend as much time as you like in the small and generally well-lighted and well-hung galleries. Well, we wandered about till about 5 and then took seats in a cafe. And then I started the discussion again—what exactly is your aim in painting. Do you want to tell a story (by story I mean anything, for instance you may tell that god exists or that God does not exist), do you want to decorate, or do you want to perform a psychological experiment as for instance was performed when the Blue Boy was painted and it was proved that you could agreeably fill a canvas with nothing but blue. Above all, have you realized that you must in being an artist try to do one of the above things or at least something supplemental to one of the above things and that you must have a clear realisation of what you are doing.

The conversation was not very interesting. Neither of them has thought more than a very little and their minds are very slowly [sic] especially slow in comprehension. Dicus is possibly slower than King. They could not either of them give me a clear account of how or why they chose the profession of an artist and what they were going to do. They were both very strong on this that they 'would paint what they like' but that was about as far as they could get.

In the conversation it appeared that Mrs Dicus worked in the Theatre Femina which has recently been taken by an American repertory company. I pricked up my ears and said that I hoped I should have an opportunity of meeting Mrs Dicus. But I was doomed to disappointment. Mrs Dicus is very pretty and very charming but she is not an actress. However, I was invited to spend the afternoon next Sunday at their place, half studio, half apartment, which were shared by 5: the Dicuses, King, and another American couple, the male part of which was studying architecture here.

Well, the next Sunday I was there. You have to go right to the south of Paris out of the city gates and then take a train for another 1/2 mile or so and then wander about a little more on foot. I found a young French girl with the 3 Americans. She could hardly speak a word of English but she told me, 'Je peux comprendre plus americain qu'anglais'. (I can understand more American than English) although how she could understand our conversation which consisted chiefly of exclamations and American argot (to lapse into French again) is more than I can understand. But there was no doubt that she seemed to be able to catch the Americans alright while she sometimes could not understand my English.

We had a very nice time. Mrs Dicus was a little shy, the French girl a little less so. There was tea and pastry and France certainly produces wonderful pastry. I thoroughly enjoyed myself and there was no discussion. King brought out his landscapes (he is chiefly doing landscapes) which were displayed in a proper manner on an improvised easel with critical remarks, artistic anecdotes and technical details as to the mixing of colours, incidence of the light and depression of the background all complete. It was, as they said, all 'student work'. One small sketch which looked rather nice at a little distance I said I rather liked and it was in the end presented to me. I don't know what I shall do with it. I think I must keep it as a memento of this evening if for nothing else.

Well after this I asked the trio to dine with me. It was arranged that I should come round to the theatre in the Champs Elysees at 6 in the evening and then we would all start. We came round here to the Palais Royal near the Louvre to the Restaurant Leon Royal where I always dine. After dinner we adjourned to a cafe not far off and chatted away till near eleven. Mrs Dicus, poor girl, had to be at her work again the next morning at 9 and she finally made us break up.

We met again on Saturday, dined at the same place, and then went to a Cinema. You see that my acquaintance with these people has not continued of [sic] any high intellectual and controversially spiced character but has become of a nice cinema variety. By the way the cinema (I mean the theatre) was very nice and I have to thank them for taking me to a Parisian 'Picture Palace' of the first class. A thing certainly to be seen and a thing which I would never have seen though I often thought of doing so. Just imagine I didn't see any of the big cinemas of London. Now I have to go down to the studio the day after tomorrow.

I wonder whether I ever wrote to you of my 'smoking life' here in Europe. As you are aware at home I didn't smoke and I used to rather look down on the people who used to smoke and spend money on cigarettes for the sole purpose of looking smart. In London too I always refused cigarettes. But one evening I went to spend the evening with the Shakir Bhai's after their marriage. Mrs Shakir, as I have already written to you is a very nice person and she pressed me very hard to smoke. 'Well,' I said, 'if you are so keen about it I shall smoke.' I estimate that I smoked some 25 cigarettes that evening. That day the cigarettes came in really useful because Mrs Shakir would also keep on pressing me to have sweets till long after I was thoroughly sick of them. If I went on smoking I could say that I was 'engaged' and so excuse myself.

But the real importance of smoking I realized when I was making my business calls. Of course wherever I went I was offered cigarettes. I already suffer from a too juvenile appearance and I did not want it to occur to people just when I was asking them to entrust me with important business that my father had told me not to smoke and that I was a good boy and did not do so. Of course it would be silly of them to allow any such thing to do me any harm but with all respect to the big English business men, it is remarkable how silly they can be in some ways—vide the German gentleman (what's his name?) of Newcastle.

Well, the net result of this was that all through my wanderings in the Midlands the fingers of my right hand used to be through smoking of a rich amber colour, of a deeper or lighter shade according to the brand of the cigarette that I had smoked during the course of the day. My best achievements were in Sheffield and Bradford where I used to be smoking from about 10 to 5.30 almost continuously.

When I left the Midlands my smoking naturally stopped as there were no more cigarettes offered to me and when I was in Sligachan and Crombie offered me cigarettes I remembered just in time that I had no cigarettes to offer him in return to say 'I don't smoke, thank you.'

Since arriving in Paris, I have started another stunt. As you are probably aware it is now some time that I have realized quite fully the tremendous power of the weapon which may be shortly called 'Pretending to be modest (and not being it).' Of course being really modest is one of the worst things in the world and the man who does really suffer from modesty had better commit suicide and have done with it immediately. Well, to come to the point, I now carry about with me Gitanes Vizir cigarettes. They are French government uncured tobacco cigarettes and so strong that they have made everyone to whom I have yet offered them cough. Well now if anybody offers me cigarettes I make a neat little speech somewhat to the following effect, 'No, thank you, I don't smoke. Or rather, I do smoke, in the sense that smoking does not make me sick, but I really don't care for ordinary cigarettes. They are too insipid. These that I have got are good but I would like to have something stronger still. Would you care to try these?' And I offer my Gitanes. Well he tries one and after one or two puffs gets a fit of coughing which he tries in vain to hide. You see what happens now? He says to himself, 'By Jove, this chap is modest. He smokes these atrocities and then he says that he "smokes in the sense that smoking does not make him sick!"'

I suppose in Germany I shall have to get accustomed to those other atrocities, the cigars, in order to impress people there.

V Bibliotheque Nationale

I have never really sent you an a/c of my doings in the Bib. Nat, and as it's not likely that there are any further developments coming, I had better now give you a connected a/c from the earliest time.

When I was in London I never missed an opportunity of asking people what there was to see in Paris and Vienna. In Vienna I knew that the Imperial Library, now the Bibliothek National, contained a magnificent edition of the Hamzeh (which has as a matter of fact been recently edited and the illustrations published by Prof. Gluck whom I hope to meet in Vienna) and also some parts of Shah Jehan's album. I also knew that there were some very fine things in Paris, but I did not know where they were. Baedeker gave no indications. He could not as a matter of fact be expected to. Lawrence Binyon was vague. Codrington seemed to be more helpful and he told me to go to the Musee Guimet and was very insistent that I should write to Hachard, the curator, beforehand as 'you will never find them in their offices.' Stanley Clarke, although he takes a great deal of interest in these miniatures, was a blank. It was only from Sir Thomas Arnold that I got some helpful information. He showed me Blochet's Inventory and Description of Oriental Miniatures in the Bib. Nat. and also Blochet's book on Persian miniatures, both of them rare works, though the last was published only some 10 years ago. 'But he is a very difficult man', said Sir Thomas of Blochet and then he recounted to me his and Mr Percy Brown's experiences in the Bib. Nat. Percy Brown was in Paris collecting materials for his 'Mughal Paintings'. He did not know French very well and as he could not get what he wanted to appealed to Sir Thomas in the following words: 'Look at the man (referring to Blochet). He won't give me such and such a ms.' Sir Thomas went up to the man and argued with him. But according to Sir Thomas, Blochet said, 'I won't give it to you,' and this finished the matter. I expressed some surprise that this could be possible between people whom one might call savants, but Sir Thomas said that facts were facts and that this was what had happened.

As a lesson from this, Sir Thomas strongly advised me to get a letter of introduction on the Librarian of the Bib. Nat. from the British Embassy. I asked how this was to be done. 'You are an Indian subject. Do you know anybody in the High Commissioner's Office? I' 'Why,' I said, 'I know Sir Atul Chander Chatterjee himself.' Alright. I should write to Sir Atul to give me a letter on the British Emb, and then everything would be alright.

I accordingly wrote a letter to the High Commissioner beginning 'Dear Sir Atul', and ending 'Yours sincerely'—I have risen to such terms of familiarity with the great since leaving India. Then the whole machinery of the Foreign Office and the diplomatic corps was set in motion. After about a month I received a letter from the office of the High Commissioner inclosing a copy of a letter signed (in the absence of the Secretary of State) by S. Gaselle and addressed to Nevile M. Henderson Esq., H. M. G. etc. etc. etc., Paris, saying

'I transmit to you herewith a copy of a letter no. . . . from the H. C. for India in connection with the desire of Mr Saif F. B. Tyabji to see the Rajput, Mughal and Persian miniatures in the Bib. Nat.

2. It will be observed that Mr Tyabji who is being instructed to call on his Majesty's embassy on his arrival in Paris may not require special facilities but I shall be glad if you will render him any assistance he may require.

3. A dispatch in similar terms is being addressed to his Majesty's representative at Vienna.'

Well, some time ago—about 10 days ago—I went over to the embassy and got the letter on the Librarian. Then to the Bibliotheque. There I was informed that I could have a Reader's ticket for the day on payment of 25 centimes (6 pies). If I wanted such a ticket for more than 3 days I must get a duplicate photograph of myself. 'Beastly nuisance', I said to myself, 'who is going to get oneself photographed and incur all this expense just to see a few silly pictures.' However I went into the Bibliotheque for the day and got thoroughly sick. They take about 1 hour to get out anything that you want.

In the Bib. Nat. there are as in the British Museum a number of depts. There is first of all the general reading room, very similar to the one in the British Museum in appearance. Then there is the Departement des Manuscrits. I suppose the room on the ground floor on the right in the British Museum where the mss are displayed would correspond to this. Another Dept. is the Departement des Estampes, corresponding to the department of which Lawrence Binyon was in charge. I was interested in the Departement des Mss and the Dep. Des Estampes. The second contains the comparatively few Indian paintings and the first the really fine collection of Persian miniatures, chiefly in the mss. Blochet by the way is in charge of the Departements des Mss.

The next day I met my Americans Dicus and King and I asked them by the way if it was possible to get oneself photographed easily and cheaply. Of course it was they said. You go to a Photomaton, sit on the chair, drop six francs into the slot and click click click, 6 photographs of you will be taken. You wait 4 minutes and your six pictures will drop out ready developed from another slot. If you move about while the pictures are being taken you will get photographed in different positions. And finally there was a photomaton in the Galeries Lafayette.

Well, the next day I wended my way to the G. L. The photographs were duly taken. Two were handed into the 'Secretariat' at the Bib. And on payment of 3 francs I received a card for 5 years. I went into the Dept des Estampes. That day they did not take so long to get me what I wanted. I found that the next volume of paintings was much better than the one I had seen the other day. And I generally felt satisfied with myself.

But I forget to tell you one thing. When in England I had formed very ambitious plans. It may be that Sir Thomas Arnold and Mr Percy Brown were treated with scant respect by Blochet. But they are not clever men. Now I am a clever man and we shall see whether Blochet is able to resist *me*. I shall first of all approach him in a reasonable manner. If Blochet does not respond to this, I shall summon flattery, if that does not work I shall use apology and in case even that fails, I shall employ rebuke (I don't think I have ever explained to you the weapon of Rebuke. It requires as you can well imagine delicate handling but when well handled it is wonderfully effective. It is essential that the patient should have no suspicion that the weapon is being used against him—but this is essential for the two other weapons too. Some other time I shall give you an a/c of my usual method of using the weapon of Rebuke.)

In fact I had intended stopping at nothing not directly contrary to the *Ahad* [vow taken at induction into Suleymani Bohra community] which I took just before leaving India to get round old Blochet.

In accordance with these plans, shortly after my arrival here I wrote to Blochet asking him for the pleasure of an interview with him. The letter was ordinary but ended with a short apology something like this: 'Before I end I must apologise for writing in English. But though I speak French a little I do so very incorrectly.' This was intended to lay stress on the fact that I was a very polite and considerate person. In reply to this I received a couple of days later a postcard in French about as gruff as it could be. M. Blochet acknowledged receipt of my letter, said there were very few Indian paintings in the Bib., and those in the Dep des Estampes. Finally, Rajput painting is not a variety of Persian painting but a form of Indian painting. This last was clearly intended as a snub for me, but I don't remember having ever said anything that was contrary to this statement of M. Blochet's.

I think I had mentioned this p. c. in one of my previous letters. However just then I was feeling a little depressed and my first idea was to give up M. Blochet. The next day I went into the Dept des Estampes again and asked for the album which I had only half seen the day before, and then I was informed that that volume formed part of the Reserve and was only given out on Mondays and Thursdays. Just imagine this. As most of the paintings are in the Reserve this means that anyone who comes here to look at them can only work two days a week from 10-4 and for the rest of the week he may wander about at will in Paris. Got thoroughly disgusted. However there was nothing to be done and so I went up to the Departement des Mss. There the first thing that I asked for was Blochet's catalogue of the mss which Sir Thomas had showed to me and which I had already used in the Deptmt des Estampes. They had a copy of it but none of the assistants knew where it was. I had better ask M.Blochet himself. I asked where M. Blochet was and he was pointed out to me sitting working at a corner seat in the general reading room of the Dept. I had imagined him as tightly shut up in his own particular den as the heads of depts. in the British Museum are. But it seems that this is not the practice in France.

I went up to him and started with 'Pardon, je vous derange beaucoup, Monsieur', etc. He turned round with a snarl and said, 'Oui, vous me derangez, Monsieur.' But this was nothing to get anxious about. He had merely mistaken me for somebody else. When I told [him] that I was the person who had written to him he almost put on a pleasant smile.

Blochet has got a fine appearance. A small man with a forehead something like Galsworthy's. A tinge of Gladstone in his way of holding the head but altogether he would remind one most of Max Muller. He is a very fine scholar. He has got a good knowledge of Arabic, Persian and Turkish and a fair knowledge of Sanskrit and Chinese. He wears a monocle in one eye. He would be much more famous if he had not his peculiar temperament. He has seldom worked outside the Bibliotheqeue and is therefore little known. Well I must end now. There is no more time.

Paris 29. 11.29

I am just now in a very happy mood. I am sitting in my shirtsleeves in my room. It's now 11.30 p.m. I was wondering how tremendously lucky I am. I can do exactly what I like. My dear Father and Mother have full confidence in me. I have sufficient money to live, at least as long as I stay in one place and don't travel about, almost extravagantly. This last by the way is one of the strong reasons which have made me give up the idea of going to Spain. When wandering about in England and Germany with all the carrying about myself of my suitcases to save porters etc. I spent more than 30 pounds for 2 months when I should have spent 23/. Here in Paris I have been living in a comfortable hotel with a large room with flowing hot and cold water, going about 5 times per week to the theatre, skating in the Palais de Glace, entertaining, and I shall spend less than 23 pounds.

Among my friends of artists and students I am considered rich. I have made lots of friends—some more some less attractive. This evening Sagheer Bhai introduced me to two Danish girls and it has been arranged that I should take them to the swimming bath the day after tomorrow. I haven't got a swimming costume and I must get one to-morrow. It seems a pity that just when I am really getting interested in Paris I should have to leave it. I leave on Tuesday 3rd When I came home this evening I found a letter from Edouard Loeb, the brother of Pierre Loeb, the art dealer of whom I think I have written to you, asking me to tea on Sunday. I am engaged on Sunday (with those Danish girls) and so I have just written off a note asking him to lunch with me on Sunday instead. I have not met Edouard yet but his brother Pierre was most interesting and there is no reason why he should not be

Paris 29.11.29

The address of the American Express Co. in Vienna is Kartnerring 14, Vienne 1.

I am going to bring the present of a wrist watch for mother. So if there is any question of her buying a watch now please don't do so.

For Haffoo I have got a set of the Temple Shakespeare.

For Daud Bhai I have got a pair of binoculars. These last are with me here and if, as it seems now quite possible Sagheer Bhai starts for India on the 1st December, I shall send them down with him so that they may be down in time. The other things will have to come with me as they are in London.

VI Zurich, Vienna

Zurich 5. 12. 29 from Amin Bhai's Flat

I came here the day before yesterday, i.e. the 3rd. *I went to a hotel first (I got into Zurich at about 4.15 p.m.) and then came straight to Amin Bhai's place. I found Sultana only. Amin Bhai came home later and I dined with them. They then pressed me to come and stay with them and so since yesterday morning I have been here.*

Amin Bhai is looking thin, Sultana nice—perhaps a little too nice. But to me the most interesting experience is that I have been quite charmed by Sultana. I have never liked her so much as I do now. Yesterday in the morning I went over with Amin Bhai to his laboratory and he showed me round there with great thoroughness. Except for his thin-ness Amin Bhai does not seem to have changed much. Yesterday in the evening a friend of Amin Bhai's, a chemist research assistant came after dinner for bridge. He is an ex-tremely nice person and a splendid bridge player. Amin Bhai is also very good and I must have been a bit of a nuisance for Sultana too is not bad.

My last week in Paris was just terribly interesting. But there is no time to write about it. I just want to tell you that I became friendly with Andre Weill who has been invited by Masood to Aligarh for two years as Prof of Maths. Particulars: Age about 23, knows English, German, and Italian fluently. Working knowledge of Swedish, Spanish and *Sanscrit*, the last language having been learnt by him in a vacation be-cause he felt 'interested in it'. Very thorough knowledge of French literature, music, painting, sculpture and architecture. Fair knowledge of English literature. Altogether a most charming person. He is daily expecting a cable from Aligarh when he will start. I have given him your address and said that you will help him, especially in getting an Indian outfit. He will probably write to you letting you know when he will get there. I should be very much obliged if you would do for him all that [you] can easily do, for I became fairly friendly with him and I like him very much.

Before I finish I must write that I feel very much ashamed of myself for one thing. I have evidently given you to understand that I am a little hard up for money. Thank you very much indeed for your extremely kind offer to increase my allowance. But I am returning home a month earlier to a very great extent because I want to return to India now

As to Italy I have in my final plans allotted 3 weeks to it, viz. Leave Zurich about 10th Dec.

Vienna from 10th Dec-10th Jan. Excursion to Budapest if I feel like it.

Berlin 10th Jan-10th Feb This will include a day or two for each of Prague, Dresden and Jena. Italy 10th Feb to 2nd March, when I embark from Naples.

I think I should feel very much ashamed of myself if I allowed you to send me further amounts of money. I have already had a glorious time.

P. S. I very probably write different things in each of my letters. But what I say in this page is the true thing.

Zurich 6.12.29

I don't remember where I ended my a/c of Blochet in my last letter. However, the ending was extremely happy. The old man came out of his shell and had lunch with me. Quite a connoisseur in food he turned out to be. In the hors d'oeuvre he would not touch the beetroot because it was so late in the season he said. I had till then always enjoyed my beetroot but after seeing him turn up his handsome nose I could no longer eat it and had to refuse it. We talked a great deal of other people and he was very amusing. I said that I wanted to meet Sylvain Levi and Fouchet: they are great scholars. 'Ewe!' Blochet replied. 'Ewe, ils voyagent, ils ne travaillent pas, pas du tout.' (They—they travel about—they don't work—not at all.). Sir Thomas Arnold: he does not know Persian (though he is Prof of Persian in the Oriental Institute), Strzygowski: he is mad. And in this manner for everyone. When I write this to you in this manner I am doing no justice to him. He was most amusing and his crisp short sentences in French, each delivered with a jerk of the head, kept me laughing continuously all the time I was with him.

I offered to identify some of the miniatures for him. However good he may be when once actually bearded he has certainly succeeded in keeping everybody away from the Bib. I notice that Coomaraswamy in his new book (Amin Bhai has curiously got a copy of it) does not even mention the Bib. Nat. as a place where there are some miniatures. Coomaraswamy is now the most famous authority on Indian art and Blochet told me that he had come to the Bib. Nat. 10 years ago but had not been there since. The pictures there have therefore been seen by few people.

You can then picture me sitting in the mss. Salon with an album before me and a piece of paper and pencil (you are not allowed ink there) writing something like this:

O. Dre *no* 5 Rajput school, probably late 18th or early 19th century. Note on picture says that the picture is by Bichitr but it cannot be by him as his work was much finer; compare Bichitr's pictures in the Johnstone Collect in the India Office

No. 6 Kangra School, early 15th century—good piece of work; subject—Rag Hindole (?) *etc.* I gave him 5 or 6 pages filled with this kind of stuff. Most of the remarks made for god alone knows what reason. But art critics don't give reasons. This reminds me that Coomaraswamy builds up a whole complicated theory on the origin of the Rajput school on the identification of a set of pictures as of the 16th cent and as he has handled thousands of pictures he ought to know. I thought this basis rather unsatisfactory till one day when I was talking about this to someone, one of the assistants in the Bodleian I think, and he pointed it out that this could be the only way which as a matter of fact existed for identification in a case like this, and after thinking about this I was to some extent reconciled to Coomaraswamy's method of working. (P. S. Reconciled so far in fact that I myself now make use of this method!)

Zurich I leave Zurich today at 4.20 for Vienna. I find that during the month and a half of Paris and learning of French I have forgotten my little German and though the words and conjugation come back to me fairly easily I have to go through the whole thing again.

The real news of Zurich would be an account of the friends of Amin Bhai whom I met. I am not just now feeling up to this but I might say that they are surprisingly good.—3 them especially. Of these 2 are assistants, in the chemical lab., another in the Biological lab and the 3rd is in the People's Bank. The man working in the biological lab has got European birds as his hobby and he is so good at this that he delivers lectures on them to the ornithological society at Basle.

Vienna 12th Your letters must be waiting for me at the Am. Exp., and I shall go and fetch them now. It is now 9 a.m., and I am sitting in my old overcoat used as a dressing gown—my dressing gown purchased in London is of artificial silk—having just had my coffee. I came here the day before yesterday at 10 a.m. I immediately called on the people on whom I had introductions and on Dr Molisch. Dr Molisch promised to take me the next day (yesterday) to introduce me to Prof Strzygowski. I also told him that I found living in a hotel expensive and wanted to go into 'apartments'. Yesterday morning therefore I was at Dr Molisch's at 10 a.m. He first of all took me to the porter of the school of medicine who had the names of people who might take me in. We then started out and the very first place where we came to was this. A huge room with palatial furniture, but no running water and no central heating. I have got so accustomed in Paris to having boiling water in my room all the time that this would have been unbearable if it had not been for the fact the room is cheap, cheaper than any room in which I have yet stayed in Europe. My landlady speaks only German and it is sometimes amusing, sometimes tiring making her understand what I want.

After this, Molisch took me to Strzygowski's institute of art studies. Strzygowski himself was not there but I met a young man named Staude of whom I had heard in London where he was working on the Akbar Nameh in the South Kensington Museum. He will get his degree of PhD in January [when] his thesis is ready. He speaks English well and we got on well together. In the afternoon at 4 I met him again in the University Hall and then he took me to Strzygowski's last lecture of the term.

Before the lecture he introduced me to the Prof. The lecture was on the Pompeian mosaics and the design of the pictures of Michelangelo, Leonardo da Vinci and Rafael. I could hardly follow anything except the names but the lantern slides were very interesting. Today at ten I have to be at Strzygowski's institute. Yesterday he gave me permission to use any books I wanted and to 'work' there. This evening I have to dine with Dr Molisch. I have purchased a ticket for 'Cosi Fan Tutti' (Mozart) at the Opera House for tomorrow. It is very different the opera here from Paris. This week's programme for instance includes besides 'Cosi Fan Tutti', 'Don Juan' (Mozart's masterpiece), 'Lohengrin' and the 'Mastersingers of Nurenburg' (the last two Wagner) and does not consist of 'Carmen' and 'Carmen' again as at Paris.

I was handed 4 letters, two from Som. Lodge, 2 from Vazir. I have now got all letters up to the mail of 23rd November.

Before I forget, my mail from the next month should be sent to Am. Exp. Co.

55 Charlottenstrasse Berlin, till the mail of 20 Jan. I shall be in Berlin till the 10th Feb.

After the 25th Jan till the 15th Feb letters should go c/o American Express Co, Piazzale Parini, Milan

I get into the steamer on the 2nd March from Naples, so no letters should be written to me after 15th Feb.

Of Vienna there is so much to write and so many things to write about that I hardly know where to begin. I posted my last letter on Thursday. That evening I dined with the Molisches. There were Dr Molisch, his wife (who can both speak a little English), his two sons (one of whom reads a great deal of English but has never had much practice reding [sic] English) and a niece and her husband. Molisch was extremely nice and kind. The others too were very nice and good but none of them have either the mind or the appearance of the old ex Rector of the University of Vienna.

On Friday night I went in the evening to 'Cosi Fan Tutti', a comic opera of Mozart. Very good. There is a new Director of the State Opera and the *mise-en-scene* was extremely good.

On Saturday at 10 I went again to the Kunst Historisches Institut (Art History Institute) of Strzygowski. I think I have already written that on the previous Wednesday Dr Molisch had taken me there to introduce me to Dr Strzygowski. Strzygowski was not there but I met him in the evening when I went with Staude—one of his pupils who is working on the *Akbar Nameh* in the South Kensington Museum—to hear him give his last lecture before the Christmas vacations at the university. Well, on Saturday I had a look at Strzygowski's book on the miniatures in Schonbrunn Palace and at Prof Gluck's book on a Hamza written and illustrated for Akbar. Of this book (the *Hamza*) about 60 pages are in Vienna, 10 in London and 5 or 6 distributed between Berlin, Paris, and Boston. Originally the volume consisted of 1115 pages and these few pages have been collected from such diverse places as Srinagar, the bazaar at Constantinople and a curiosity shop at Cairo.

On Sunday in the morning I went to the Art Museum here. At 12, I had to be at Staude's for lunch, or rather at Staude's mother's place. They do not live together: his mother has got a two-room flat and he had got a room opposite. But he takes his meals with her. Frau Staude does not speak English or French and so our conversation was rather limited. She gave us a splendid lunch. Not many courses but very good food. The Viennese feed themselves well. I as a matter-of-fact eat better food here than in Paris—and it was very good in Paris.

In the evening I was to go to hear the 'Meistersinger von Nurnburg' or the Mastersingers of Nurenburg which is supposed to be Wagner's masterpiece. So Staude played the different themes for me on the piano after lunch and also some of the more important parts so that I may know the music a little beforehand. We then adjourned to his room (Mrs Staude had left earlier) and then he showed me his notes for his work on the *Akbar Nameh*. Staude is a very interesting chap. He is 25 years old. Not very impressive to look at. He knows every nook and corner of London, Paris, Berlin, and Vienna and especially all the artists and musicians. He has been and is a student of art (He will get his PhD Feb) and so this is not surprising, but he also knows where the cheapest and best food is to be had, which are the restaurants with the prettiest waitresses, and which are the fastest cabarets. This last impressed me very much. He knows Europe so well that last summer he acted as courier for a tourist party organized by one of the tourist agencies in Paris.

We talked away till 5 when it was time for me to go to the opera. The 'Meistersingers' being Wagner's masterpiece begins at 5.30 and ends at 10.30. Staude has asked me to collaborate with him in his work on the *Akbar Nameh* in the transliteration of the names of the artists. He is to send me photographs of the pictures to Bombay. You now see why I am so keen that Vazir should be good at Persian. I shall make her do all the work and tell everyone that *I* did it. However this work is not difficult. As a matter of fact when in London I already wrote down for my own use the names of the artists.

Evening 'Meistersinger'. Absolutely magnificent. The music was just glorious. It is not surprising that this opera is considered Wagner's masterpiece. But I am hardly in a position to judge for I have never heard Wagner in an opera house of the standard of the Vienna Staats Opern Haus. The Paris opera though I went there so frequently was really very poor, especially the orchestra. Staude tells me that they always conduct Wagner too fast there and now I realise that the chief attraction of the Paris Opera house is the immense size and magnificence of the building.

On Monday at 2.30 I had an apptmt with Dr Mises. But this is a real adventure and I must commence from the beginning.

Dr Mises is a lawyer here—lawyer to the French embassy and doing international work and I got his name from Dr Kappel of Cologne of whom I have already written to you. Well, on Friday I called at his office duly provided with a copy of the letter from the Indian Merchants Chamber of the Manchester Chamber of Commerce, copies of which I have freely showered in every European town in which I have been. After much difficulty (my German is very weak) I was at last brought by the house porter to his flat (Dr Mises was away from office) where the Fraulein who speaks English would speak to me. I stood waiting in the entrance hall wondering whether it was worthwhile taking all this trouble when there was mighty little chance indeed of my ever getting any work from Vienna. After a short time, the Fraulein came: a dark Viennese, pretty, charmingly dressed, age about 18. She looked at me for a moment and then sort of fell on me. No, her father was not in office now, but would I come in and sit down for a few moments if I had time. Thank you very much, I said, and followed her into the sitting room. She offered me chocolates and cigarettes. I took a cigarette. Would I have a cognac or something. No thank you, I said. I was very businesslike. First of all, I explained what I was there for, gave my card with a short note on it. Then I spent about 20 minutes there. She asked me how long I was to stay here. About a month, I said. She said she hoped she would see me often. Thank you very much, I said. We described our respective tastes. She is not fond of music though she is Viennese. But she likes art (she used to attend some of Strzygowski's lectures in the University) and she loves sport. She skis, plays tennis and golf and motors (for motoring also is in Europe classed as sport). Well, after 20 minutes or half an hour of this kind of thing I left, saying that I would telephone to her father and make an appmt. I asked where her father's office was. Opposite, she said. I understood on the opposite side of the landing where the house porter had first taken me to.

Well, the next day I telephoned and I was given an apptmt for Monday at 2.30.

On Monday I went and knocked again. A maid appeared and after some vain conversation in German she left, as it appeared in a few moments, to fetch the Fraulein again. Fri Mises had evidently just come from her dressing room. No, her father's office was in the building opposite, on the 2nd floor. But she wanted to ask me one thing. Would I lunch with them next Sunday at one and (before I could well reply) and would I spend New Year's Eve with them? With the greatest pleasure, I said.

Well, I left and saw the father. A very nice man but nothing of much interest happening and I left thinking of what exactly was the matter with the Fraulein.

My first idea of course was that my personal charms were being now properly appreciated. But this hypothesis I had soon regretfully to give up. This incident took place on my 24th birthday and I think it must be admitted that one's personal charms do not sort of flower on any one day let alone a 24th birthday. The alternative hypothesis, that I have always had personal charms must also be given up for this reason: I don't remember any young lady particularly appreciating them before, at least, not in this manner, and this reason is again I am afraid conclusive. I thought, that I was an Indian and that she might have been interested in me as a person from a far-off land. But though she is evidently well educated and has interests and tastes, this interest could hardly be sufficiently strong to make her act as she did. Then I thought she might be lonely and without friends. But this again is hardly possible. She is young, rich (the flat was almost luxuriously furnished) and pretty. What on earth is the reason? I am looking forward to Sunday with great interest. In the meantime I am taking out my evening clothes to wear them for the first time on New Year's Eve.

Vienna 22.12.29

My dear Father

I am afraid that I have fallen from the heroic sentiments expressed in the letter before the last in which I said I would be no further burden on my parents and would not spend any more money in Europe.

My last programme as I had written to you was Vienna till the 10th Jan., Berlin till 10th Feb, and then till the 1st March in Italy. When I came to make out a detailed programme I found this practically impossible: there was much too little time for Italy where I would also spend a great deal of time in the train travelling. Besides, Feb has 28 days only. I also want to spend some little time in Dresden, Leipzig, Jena, and Prague, the last place chiefly on business.

So now I again alter my programme to what it was originally, viz. Vienna till 10th, Prague 11th, Dresden 13th, Berlin till 13th Feb., Leipzig 14th, Jena 15th, Munich 17th, and then in Italy till the 1st April.

You had offered to send me 50 pounds but I don't suppose that you had expected to spend 50 pounds more. I think that I shall require with my altered programme a maximum of 25 pounds more, but I hope to make it much less. In my estimates now I have allowed liberally for everything. Thus I have put aside 15 pounds for the duty and expenses on getting the 2 guns to India, and hope that this will be considerably less.

You would no doubt like to have some idea of how I have been doing financially. When I got to London I calculated that if I spent 23 pounds p.m., I could stay 10 months in Europe i.e. till 1st April But my expenditure was:

July 22. 15; Aug 24.15.6 1/2, trip to Camb and travel combined; Sept. 31.10.1/2; Oct. 33 pounds, 2.0; Nov. 22.10.0 in Paris

You see therefore that one month had to go. I cannot understand why the expenditure in Oct. was so high, for the hotels on the Rhine did not seem to be very expensive. But I paid a lot in train fares.

I hope that you generally approve of my scheme and above all that you don't think that I shall spend the extra money gallivanting in other places, a thing which you do not want me to do. If however you would like me to stick to the original programme or in any way to alter it please wire to me.

As to sending me the extra money I suggest that you ask the Bank of India to instruct their agents in Milan to pay me 25 pounds after the 1st Feb. I think the Am Exp. charge a little too much in commissions etc.

My idea of seeing Italy is something like this: Milan 2 or 3 days Venice 7 days Florence 7 days. Rome 14 days Naples 3 or 4 days. I would like to see some of the smaller cities like Pisa etc. But I have not yet made any definite plan.

I hope to make great economies in one thing. Till now I have been travelling 2nd but there is absolutely no reason why I should not travel 3rd and I think I shall do so in the future.

Vienna 22.12.29

During the last week it has been very cold, varying from –3 to –5 centigrade which is equivalent to 6–10 degrees of frost. However I don't seem to mind it. This is good for I have got a couple of months of temperatures of this kind before me.

My last letter was full of Fraulein Mises but since seeing her things have happened which have entirely thrown her into the shade.

I finished my last letter on Tuesday. I had to lunch with Mrs Wellecz (pronounce Willish). You remember her. I had been introduced to her by Staude (pronounce Shtowday) in the Bibliothek National where I had gone to see the two volumes of rather indifferent Indian pictures which they have here. Mrs Wellecz is really very fine-looking—beautiful I should say. She was dressed very plainly with a necktie on her blouse. I thought her about 30 years of age but she must be 40 or so for she has a married daughter of 20 years' age. At 10.30 I went down to Staude's place (he had also been invited) and at 11 we started for Mrs Wellecz's place. She had asked us to come at about 11.30 though lunch would be at 1.30.

Their house was extremely nice. Later on I learnt that the architect was Prof Hoffmann, one of the leaders of the modern school of architecture of Germany.

Before lunch we were chiefly employed in looking at Prof Strzygowski's reproductions of the miniatures in Schloss Schonbrunn. Mrs Wellecz is collaborating with Prof. Strzygowsky and Prof Gluck and Staude in producing a new book which is to give an account of all the Indian paintings in Vienna. I am proud to say that I was able to make some suggestions which were hailed as useful. Mrs Wellecz said that she would in her book acknowledge the help which she received from me. She said this last to the accompaniment of my loud 'No! No!'s.

At lunch I was introduced to Prof Wellecz and to their younger daughter aged about 18 and a friend of this younger dtr, a Scotch girl who is studying in Vienna and who had also been invited to lunch. Prof. Wellecz is Prof. of Music in the Univ. of Vienna. I learnt (only then) that he has discovered the clue to the Byzantine notation for music. He must be well-known in England for on the shelves I saw the translations into English of a number of his works. He seems to have done a lot of research on Byzantine music. But he is now best known for his operas which are performed a great deal in Berlin and south Germany, and which are—to quote Staude—very intellectual. I had never before met such an intellectual and eminent man on such intimate terms before. We talked only a little, for about half an hour or so, after lunch he had to go away.

This family is really very fine. Mrs Wellecz is a PhD in art of the Vienna University. She has been a pupil of Strzygowsky. She knows German and French extremely well and speaks English and Italian quite fluently. Besides she knows Latin and Greek sufficiently well to be able to speak them too. Her knowledge of European art seems to me to be almost exhaustive and her knowledge of Indian art history is by no means despicable. This term she started studying Sanskrit but she told me that she would have liked to commence Persian which would be most useful to her in her present study. As I have already said she is very goodlooking. And she is extremely charming and nice. Up till now in Europe it was I who had slightly to pursue the people whom I wanted to meet. But in Vienna it has been the other way. Staude immediately invited me to lunch and the very first time I met Mrs Wellecz she said she hoped I would go to her house. You will not therefore be surprised that I like Vienna and the Viennese very much.

A word about Miss Wellecz. She is extremely good-looking, with a huge mop of hair which is constantly tumbling over her forehead. I only spoke to her at lunch but she seems to be no less intellectual than her mother as she speaks Latin with her, though she said that she dislikes doing this tremendously. But her mother forces her to do so. She speaks English extremely well—the best in the family, as a matter of fact. She is also very charming.

The Scotch girl was indifferent. She spoke English with no trace of a Scotch accent.

I have seldom had such a fine time as at the Welleczs'. After lunch we finished looking at the Schonbrunn reproductions. I was there till about 4.30. It was agreed that we should go to Schloss Schonbrunn on Friday to look at the originals. This excursion wasn't up to much. The pictures are of little value. They have been so badly touched up. I told Mrs Wellecz that it seemed to me a pity that she was spending such an amount of scientific scholarship on such worthless pictures and she agreed with me. It was so frightfully cold in my room that I tore some sheets from my writing pad and I have come here to the Cafe Shottertor facing the University buildings. And supposed to be patronized by people having academical connections—though now, as I look round I don't see a single person who might be a student. To continue: Mrs Wellecz told me that she wanted to finish her part in this book 'anyhow' (a word which reminds me of Kihim, Daud Bhai and Venkat Rao) and then she wanted to make a 'mosaic' (again her own word) of Mughal history from the memoirs of Babur and Jehangir, the *Akbar Nameh* and the historians edited by Eliot and Dowson in their *'History of India as told by its own Historians'*. She asked for my approval of this scheme and I gave her a limited approval.

On the way back to the city from Schonbrunn Palace Mrs Wellecz told me that her brother was having the next day a party in the evening and that I might like to see his house and whether I would come. Her brother was a 'practical man' as compared to her husband, as he was Prof of Jurisprudence in the University. I said that I would come with great pleasure, only Staude had said that we might go to Prof. Gluck's in the afternoon to meet him (Prof. Gluck) and his wife (who is a Persian). This was really not the reason for hesitating. I had purchased a ticket for the opera and I could not decide at the moment whether I should sacrifice it. I didn't want to tell Mrs Wellecz the real reason as then that invitation might be withdrawn. However I told her I would telephone to her the next morning whether I could or could not come. Have you ever heard of such unmannerly behaviour before? I am invited by a lady on behalf of her brother. I say that I will keep the invitation and come if it is possible, telephoning the next day whether it *is* or *not* possible. On Saturday morning (the next day) I met Staude again in the National Bibliothek and he telephoned to Gluck to find out whether it would be convenient to him to receive us. In the meantime I had decided to sacrifice the opera ticket and go to Mrs Wellecz's brother's (=Prof Strauss). However, it turned out that Prof Gluck was not well and so we could not go to his house. I telephoned Mrs Wellecz that I would come.

In the afternoon I went to the Baroque Museum, a silly thing to do (I have finished the ink in my pen and so I am writing now with cafe writing material) as I had been having a very strenuous time for the last few days and I should have rested in the afternoon.

I had asked Mrs Wellecz whether I should come in evening dress to her brother's and she had said that I had better do so. Well, in the evening I donned my evening clothes for the second time in my life (I had put them on the previous day going to the opera in order to get a little accustomed to their feel), went to an automatic restaurant to have a little dinner and started off. It had been agreed that I should first go to Mrs Wellecz and then accompany them to her brother's as Prof. Strauss place was difficult to find.

I had been asked to spend the evening and I thought that it was an after dinner party. Hence my visit to the automatic restaurant (which last by the way I patronize a great deal). As a matter of fact it was to dinner that I had been invited and so the two schillings I spent in the aut. Rest were wasted. However I could pretend to be delicate and eat little. At dinner there was a very distinguished party. There were Prof and Mrs Strauss and Miss Strauss, the hosts, Prof Rendel who has recently lectured in Oxford and who is responsible for the article on 'Wai' in the Encyclopaedia Britannica and two other Profs with their wives and also a merchant and his wife. The names of all these I don't remember. I was really so tired and exhausted and sleepy that I did not take half the 'benefit' from the party that I might have done. However I enjoyed the evening which lasted from 8.30 till 12.30 very much. At dinner I sat between Miss Strauss (again extremely good-looking) and Mrs Wellecz. Miss Strauss is not so scholarly as the rest of Mrs Wellecz' family but quite as charming. I spent most of the evening talking with her. She told me all about her school and inter alia that she was 20 years old. She has been in England and Wales and she told me that she would never have thought that I was not a European. She would have taken me for a Welshman for the Welsh have often dark hair and skin. I must say that it has never been before suggested that I looked like a Celt.

The general conversation was in German and of course much too fast for me to follow. Mrs Wellescz and my host and hostess were extremely kind and they would always see that that I had someone to talk to in English. This however was not really a great task for as I said before Miss Strauss was always there.

Prof Rendel is evidently a wit and his German jokes (which I could not understand) were much appreciated. His English jokes (he knows English very well. He lectured at Oxford in English) however did not impress me. At table he made silly jokes of *hof machen* (hof = court, machen = to make) to me and Miss Strauss, when parting he pointed to a good oil sketch on the wall and said to me 'I painted this—two hundred years ago.' I asked whether it was his previous incarnation. But he did not wait to hear what I was saying and continued 'I am now 350 years old. I painted it when I was 150'.

However his German jokes were liked by Mrs Wellecz and I cannot think anything bad of Mrs Wellecz—not even bad taste in appreciating a joke.

I forgot to say that on the day of our visit to Schonbrunn Mrs Wellecz invited me to spend Christmas Eve in her house and see the Christmas tree in an Austrian house. She invited me with many hopes that I would not find it too dull as it was going to be merely a 'family party'.

Yesterday, Sunday, I lunched with the Mises. There was Dr and Mrs Mises, Fraulein Mises, another German lawyer and a French attaché of the Embassy. Conversation was in French. The meal was good but naturally rather colourless after my experiences of the two previous days. I found that Dr Mises is fond of obscure jokes. The Frenchman too said something which might possibly be said before French girls in a cafe in the Boulevard St Germain but which were hardly very funny. Miss Mises though very nice I found rather tame after the extremely charming and pretty girls whom I had met on Thursday and Saturday. However Miss Mises asked me whether I would go to the Eislaufverein this morning (Monday) to skate. I said yes, and so at 10.30 today I was again at their flat with my skates. The morning was not a success. Miss Mises skates very well and I can only get along. On the way home she said that the invitation for New Year's Eve was 'off'. It appears because there is some kind of disagreement between her mother and aunt. And a party cannot be got up. However I should telephone tomorrow morning at 9 to fix up an excursion during the 'holidays'.

I am glad of New Year's Eve for Staude wants me to go on that day to a concert which is to be very good. A good deal of Strauss and the 2nd symphony of Bruckner (whom I have never heard before. It is only in Germany that people are sufficiently intelligent musically to perform him) are on the programme.

Well, I must end now. It is 6.30 in the evening. At 7.30 I have to be at the opera house to hear Verdi's 'Troubadour'. Badr will be interested to hear that during the last week I heard 'Tosca', the 'Meistersingers of Nuremberg' (with E. Schumann singing the part of Eva and Rodec who took part in the Salzburg Festival in the part of Hans Sachs), 'Manon', 'Boris Goudonov', and 'Rosenkavelier'.

Now I must end.

Vienna 30.12.29

I have just received letters from home—very late, for today it is Monday and these are letters which I should have got last Monday. I received Vazir's and letters from Jabir Mamoo and Petit yesterday and I did not know why there was no letter from Somerset Lodge—but it had been understamped and was delayed.

The letter is full of interesting news. All the information of Haffoo's marriage and arrangements for it have made me feel homesick again. Just this morning I was saying to myself as I stood shivering before my washstand that I have now got over all homesickness (which had become a nuisance lately) thanks to Mrs Wellecz and her family and Staude and other Viennese friends. Mother's letter is particularly affecting especially when she relates all the changes which the new year is to bring [sister Hafiza's marriage].

The news that the motor cycles have been sold—the Douglas for a very good price I think—has pleased me immensely

Well, to give you my own news. The temperature has fortunately again gone below 0. For two or three days it used to be a little above 0 and the streets were full of a mixture of melting snow and mud—one of the most unholy things I have yet seen on the face of this fair earth. Now it is again hard and dry again [sic].

I think I ended my last letter on Tuesday. In the evening, Christmas Eve, I went to Mrs Wellecz. Before dinner, the Christmas tree was 'unveiled' to the sound of a march composed by Prof Wellecz for a Viennese festival of modern music and recently recorded by the Gramophone Co. The tree was admired and also the presents. I got a book, 'Caspar Hauser' by Jakob Wasserman, a novel which made a tremendous sensation in Germany when it appeared in 1908.

At dinner, the party was entirely a family party and I was the only outsider: Besides the house people (Mr and Mrs and Miss Wellecz) there was Mrs Wellecz' elder married daughter and her husband and Mr and Mrs Stross (the name of Mrs Wellecz's brother is Stross, not Strauss) and also Mrs Wellecz' mother, a most charming lady who however does not know English or at least knows only a few words.

A word as to Mrs Wellecz' elder daughter: Curiously I have not yet succeeded in catching her name. Her name is Mrs Pollaczek. She is the best-looking of the whole family and you already know my opinion of Mrs Wellecz and the younger daughter. She is the only member of the family who is shy, but her desire to please, and especially, to be pleased, makes her dangerously charming. But the most curious, or rather the most wonderful thing about her are her eyes. She is short-sighted and wears no glasses. Do you remember that portrait by Gainsborough in the National Gallery of a lady who was very influential at the English court and who had so to say, risen from the ranks. (I don't remember the name.) She was also very short sighted (you can see this in her portrait though she wears no glasses) and I remember in a short life of this lady which I had read somewhere it was stated that her eyes were the most charming part of her. (She had risen at the court entirely because of her charm). I could not understand how this could be till I met Mrs Wellecz Elder Daughter: She has got a curious way of looking away from you and then suddenly looking at you full in the eyes and smiling—a trick which I should advise all young ladies to learn if young men are at all like what I am.

After dinner, the merchant and his wife (whom I have mentioned before. They were also at Mr Stross (Mrs Wellecz' brother is not Prof.) two days before) and their two sons and dtr arrived. The dtr is a great friend of Miss Wellecz, and after her arrival we saw neither the one nor the other very much. I was chiefly with the E. D., her husband and the two sons of the merchant. I did not talk very much with Prof. or Mrs Wellecz who formed their own German-speaking group with Mrs Wellecz' mother and the other older people. But towards the end I was able to talk a little with Prof. Wellecz.

I don't think I have described him to you yet. He must be about 45, extremely nice and pleasant and with no unpleasant artisticness in his appearance. This last could hardly be when one remembers that he is a prof. of the University, a learned man, and has done lots of research on Byzantine and near Eastern music, and was familiar with Fox-Strangways' book. And he is a mild person. The first time I met him I asked him his opinion of modern English composers, a concert of the compositions by whom I had heard in London (one of the Promenade concerts of Sir Henry Wood) without much appreciation. Well, he gave his opinion. When we were coming away, Staude, who had been with us, said to me: 'There is one thing bad in Prof. Wellecz. He can never say anything bad about anyone'. Staude is not very firm in his English and as the sentence stands it is perhaps a little too strong. But you understand what I mean when I describe Prof Wellecz as mild.

With all this, Prof Wellecz is modern: modern in art, music, politics, and methods. I say 'with all this' because other modern people whom I have had the pleasure of meeting were by no means mild. Ede, I think the mildest of the other moderns, was quite ready to burn half the pictures in the Tate, the Leightons being placed at the top of the bonfire. But I must say that I never had the pleasure of meeting a modern of the eminence of Prof Wellecz before. It is a pleasure to go to his house. The architect was as I think I have already written, Hoffmann who is one of the leading 'modern' architects. The rooms are furnished in the very comfortable and the very tasteful style which I had seen and admired in the Salon d'automne in Paris. The drawing-sitting room has its walls on two sides covered with books from the floor to the ceiling, the third side has a piano and desks, the fourth is one large window.

Well I must end this letter quickly. I have no time but I shall give you a summary of what I have been doing.

25th morning Hofburg chapel, Mass by Bruckner My initiation into the mysteries of this composer who is in Austria and Germany placed in the same rank as Mozart and Brahms. Evening Opera: Ballet 'Joseph's Legend', music by Richard Strauss.

26th Art Museum Afternoon spent with Staude. Evening Opera: 'Don Juan'.

27th Morning Excursion to Coblenz castle with Dr Molisch. Evening 'Meistersingers von Nuremburg', Wagner, second hearing.

28th Morning Art Museum. Afternoon 2.30 I went to the Welleczs'. The whole Wellecz family was there and also Fraulein Stross. Fr. Stross and Fr. Wellecz sang together. Good. I have no idea too what the abbreviation for Fraulein is [in margin].

29th morning Hofburg Chapel Mass by Haydn. Afternoon concert with programme consisting of the 'Coriolan' overture of Beethoven and an oratorio-like 'Das Lied von der Erde' ('The Song of the Earth') by Mahler who, to quote Prof. Wellecz forms the 'direct line of Beethoven, Schubert, Brahms, Bruckner'.

30th (today) The morning I wasted, or rather I wrote letters. It is astounding what an amount of writing I have to do. For the last month I have been lazy but in London I frequently posted 5 or six letters at a time and I have posted 12 letters at a time.

I remember one week in London I calculated that I spent more on postage than on food.

In the afternoon

The Welleczs were to lunch with me but only the Prof. turned up. I then telephoned to Fraulein Stross to dine with me tonight and go to the opera. There is 'Cosi Fan Tutti', Mozart, tonight. Prof. Well. told me that his dtr wanted me to telephone to her. I did so and received an invitation to a party tomorrow evening.

31st. Today is New Year's Eve. A very happy new year to you. I write this in spite of the fact that my philosophy says that New Year and New Year's wishes are silly things. But distance from home makes you ... and sentimental. Besides I am in the land of New Year's Eves and you know 'In Rome etc.' I have as a matter of fact sent off New Year's cards to a number of people whose acquaintance I made during the last 6 months and whose acquaintance I want to keep up.

Last evening it was very nice. First of all, though, 'Cosi Fan Tutti' is really very good. Secondly, Miss Stross is very nice. She is the daughter of a rich house but she is a sport. And she can enjoy good things. She knows 'Cosi Fan Tutti' very well because she learnt two of the parts in it. She has been learning singing now for about 10 years, i.e., about as long as Haffoo, and sings in the same way that Haffoo does, viz. very well. But curiously, she had never heard the whole of 'Cosi Fan Tutti' before.

Miss Stross' house is really very fine. I think that after the house of the father of Mr W. Stanley in Cambridge, it is the best house I have been in in Europe, and I am not quite sure that it is not *the* best house which I have seen here.

Tonight as I wrote above, I have been invited by Miss Wellecz to an evening party to celebrate the New Year coming in. The party is to be of young people—'art students' they have been described to me. I assume they are friends of Miss Wellecz who is studying painting. Prof and Mrs Wellecz are going away to leave the house to us. Miss Stross is also coming. I told her that I was glad that she was coming and she seemed to be pleased at this.

There is one problem that I have not yet succeeded in solving for myself. That is how to flatter another without being too modest about your own merits. I hope soon to arrive at a rule, but at present the problem seems to be insoluble. If you flatter another, he gets so engrossed in himself that he forgets you. The end to be aimed at of course is that the man should be made to say 'I am a great man and you are a great man too. We are both great men'.

I note with deep regret that you seem to think that my a/c of my interview with Mr Meiningen was not quite accurate. It may be that my language [may have] been a little picturesque but I can assure you in all essential particulars it is quite accurate. It may surprise you that big businessmen should be so silly as to allow young men who say that they are big solicitors on the other side of the globe to stride up and down their office room and waste their cigarettes. But it is so. This may possibly be one of the reasons why Nana Sahib [Camruddin Latif, Saif Tyabji's maternal grandfather] never became a real millionaire. He was much too clever and with too much understanding. I would give 10 years of my life to see how Nana Sahib would treat a young man who behaved with him in the same manner as I did with Meiningen.

Well I must end now.

Vienna 4.1.30

I have had another extremely interesting and pleasant week here. Yesterday I was thinking whether merely the fact that I was enjoying myself very thoroughly in Vienna was sufficient reason for extending my stay here (I am extending my stay here.) but today I have spent such a useful day that it is really sufficient excuse to spend a fortnight in a place. This morning I LEARNT much.

But to commence from the commencement. 31 Dec. Tuesday I had written that in the evening I had been invited by Fraulein Wellecz to a Sylvester Abend (abend = evening) as it is called here. I got to their house at about 9.30. Fraulein Stross had told me the preceding evening when we had gone to the opera together that there would be a mixed lot and there was certainly a curious mixture of people. We were about 15 I think. First of all there was our young hostess and Fraulein Stross who was also almost a hostess because she is a first cousin and very intimate with the house—almost a dtr to Mrs Wellecz. Miss Stross was—by the way—the prettiest girl in the party and therefore much in demand. My first impression of her when I had dined at her place was, as I think I have already written, was that she was rather ingenuous and naive but she certainly knows how to manage young men. This must be, for she is a young lady of a rich house with good looks and must be having lots to do with young men, and she has, for instance, been in London two months by herself just at the time when I was there. Then there was the Scotch girl whom I had met before, 2 Americans, slightly better than the usual run of Americans. One of them, by the end of the evening (which ended at 5.30 in the morning) was so impressed by Miss Stross that he pursued Miss Stross round and round the 3 rooms where we were distributed. Asking her where he could telephone to her, how he could get into touch with her again, etc. Miss Stross put him off with answers which reminded me a little of the way in which Haffoo and Vazir used to treat some of our guests at the Judicial Commissioner's bungalow in Karachi at the time when you father and mother were in Simla and they were the ladies of the house. Thinking of this later on I was a little flattered to think that my conversation on the telephone with Miss Stross when I had asked her to come to the opera had been something like this: 'I say, are you free this evening?' (I telephoned at about 3 o'clock.) 'Oh! Ah! Yes!' 'Would you care to come to Cosi Fan Tutti then?' 'Oh! Thank you very much. With great pleasure.' 'Well then, look here. I shall come to your house at ... have you got a paper? Could you see at what time it begins?' She rushes off for the paper. It commences at 7. I said I would come at 5.30 to her house. 'Oh! Please do not take the trouble to come here. We are so far out of the city. I shall meet you at 6.45 in front of the opera.' 'But won't you dine with me?' 'Oh, thank you, yes.' Well, the appointment was made at 6.15 in front of the Rathaus Kellar (a restaurant). I did not then know that a girl does not usually dine with you if she goes to the theatre with you.

Contd 5. 1. 30 Well I find that I haven't got much time and if I write in this manner about all things I shall never finish.

Cont 6. 1. 30 At the party there were besides two communists. One of them is an artist whose studio I am sitting in as I write this letter. He is painting me. As this is the first time I have sat for my portrait in my life I am naturally excited. He is a young man of about 35, almost effeminately good-looking. He has travelled about a lot and is as poor as a rat. He travelled in Russia with Jawaharlal Nehru and Roy when they were in Russia in 1920 and he knows a good deal about India, specially about Indian and oriental art. This is why I find him so interesting. He is not like the great number of people whom I have met who have no idea that there is anything outside London or Paris as the case may be. And even this is saying much. Most of the people in Paris whom I met knew that there was a thing called Musee Guimet but no more. I don't think that Ede had ever been in the South Kensington Museum. Baur—the name of the artist—seems to me to be good. He has got ideas and I feel that he sees a little in his pictures 'into the heart of things'. As a communist too he seems to be fairly important. He is trying to persuade me to go to Russia. However I don't think I am very much interested in Russia. The other communist was not very interesting.

I got on fairly well. The Americans and others spoke English. Others spoke French so that I was able to converse with all.

I can't say that I liked the party very much. For me, the enjoyment was not sufficiently organized and hectic. There was too much waste of time. People danced a little, drank a little, ate a little. Somebody sang a song now and then. There were periodically discussions on art, Philosophy, Psychology, Politics, etc., all in a half-hearted manner

We dispersed at 5.30 in the morning.

At 1 I was at Staude's house, where I lunched with his mother and him. Later in the afternoon I was introduced to Blauensteiner, also a student in Strzygowski's institute and a great friend of Staude. He is I think one of the best-looking young men that I have ever seen. He looks like a young man that has just stepped out from one of Austin Reeds' advertisements. His face, figure, hands, all are perfect. And he is very nice. He has got large grey eyes which look earnestly in? '[sic]' you. But I am afraid that he is not very quick and that his sense of humour is not very keen.

In the evening we all, Mrs Staude, Staude, Blauensteiner, a Belgian girl friend of Staude's (fairly good looking and with a good sense of humour but she giggled too much) and myself went to a concert. Our language difficulty was considerable. Mrs Staude knows only German, Blauensteiner knows a little English but cannot understand French. The Belgian girl of course knew French and German well but could not understand English. I know English and a little French. The only person who was alright was Staude. Contd 7th *Absolutely no time*

2nd Lunched with Staude and Blauenstein. Spent afternoon with Baur. Saw his pictures and talked.

Evening Opera 'A Night in Venice', operetta by Johann Strauss

3rd Morning Visited Art History Museum with Mrs Wellecz. Very interesting. Afternoon took a man named Mody whom I had dug up here for Mrs Wellecz who wants some Gujarati inscriptions read to her in the National Bibliothek. Evening Opera 'The Prophet' by Meyerbeer.

4th Morning went to the Modern Gallery with Baur. Lunched with the Mises. After lunch, Fraulein Mises drove me to the Prater (something like Hyde Park) in their car. We spent the afternoon together and I returned to their flat and had tea with her. I was to spend the evening at Prof Glucks but was told that Prof Gluck had been suddenly called away. Went with some friends of the Kunsthistorisches Institut to a cinema.

5th Sunday morning. Hofburg Chapel Service. Really the church music here is magnificent. Lunched with Prof Gluck. HELPED HIM TO DECIPHER AN ARABIC INSCRIPTION. What does Asaf Bhai [Fyzee] say to this? Evening Opera 'Turandot' by Puccini

Oh by the way my reading of the Arabic inscription was making out that two letters were but as this simplified the whole thing it was a great thing and Prof Gluck was duly thankful.

Monday 6th Morning went to Baur to sit for my portrait. (Mrs Wellecz spoilt my whole taste for this painting by saying 'He is poor and models are expensive.') I wanted to finish this letter while he was painting but it was impossible to do so. We talked too much. He lives with a girl cousin who is studying sculpture here. She knows neither English or French so I told her funny stories of my landlady in German. I think I have written somewhere that Baur knows a little French, slightly less than what I know and we talk in French. From Baur's place I rushed off to the Stross' house where I had to lunch. At lunch Mr and Mrs Stross (a tall beautiful lady of 35–40. It is difficult to tell an age) and Miss Stross. I told them lots about India. They are really extremely nice people, with a great deal of ability and sense of humour. Mrs Stross is also very clever—not in the way Mrs Wellecz is—she is no scholar, but she has got a very quick mind. Mrs Stross said when I told her that from here I was going to Berlin that she would introduce me to Prof. Siegfried Bemfeld, her brother, who after Freud is perhaps the best-known psychoanalyst and who is in Berlin. She said that she was going to Berlin today for 3 days and she would speak to him about me and that I should call on him.

I was at the Strosses till about 3.30, then I got up and bid goodbye. When I was shaking hands with Miss Stross she said 'I hope to see you again before you go.' I had quite intended not seeing her and this took me a little unprepared. 'Oh yes', I said, 'I … hope you will come once again to the theatre or something with me.' This was the last thing I should have said. It is an expensive job taking a pretty girl to the Opera, even assuming it has Vazir's approval. I saw my mistake and to gain time I said I would telephone.

From the Stross' I took a taxi to the Wellecz where I had to be for tea. There were Prof and Mrs Wellecz in the drawing room. Prof Wellecz commenced on the 1st January a new opera which if ready by spring will be performed in the Berlin Opera— otherwise in autumn. At tea Miss Wellecz came in. After tea she had to go for her English lesson. When shaking hands she said 'I hope to see you again before you go.' Miss Wellecz is 3 years younger than Miss Stross (she is only 17). So to her I said 'Let us hope so though I don't know how we shall meet again'.

It is really extraordinarily interesting talking to Mr and Mrs Wellecz—of quite ordinary things—of friends in England, France and Germany, of the music and paintings which they like, of what they are reading. When I had gone with Mrs Wellecz to the Art Gallery, I had told her that I thought Prof Wellecz by far the most interesting man I had met in Europe and that what I liked in him was that he was both a scholar and an artist. In creating things he stood so to say on the pedestal already made by his predecessors. He had everything carefully thought out in his brain and if one asked him a question he had merely to take the answer out from one of the pigeon holes in his brain and hand it out. Mrs Wellecz, being a good wife must have told all this to her husband and the result is that Prof Wellecz now likes me very much.

After tea, Prof Wellecz played a few bars of music on the piano and asked me of what country I thought the music was. I said 'Of the North.' Then he told me it was from the overture of one of his operas, the libretto of which had an Indian subject. I said that the music had for me no suggestion of India, the strong harmonies being especially un Indian.

Time flew. It flew till Prof Wellecz said, 'I don't want to say anything but if you want to be in time for the opera you must go now.' I was going to see 'Lohengrin', which was to be conducted by Dr Richard Strauss. I cannot tell you how delighted Mr Wellecz had been when I had told him yesterday that I was going to hear Lohengrin and that it was to be conducted by Richard Strauss. This he said was one of the greatest things in music which Europe has got to offer. He had heard it when Strauss had conducted it on the 1st of Jan 1921 when he (Wellecz) had been still a critic and not a Prof.

Then to the opera and 'Lohengrin'. My impressions of the performance are not sufficiently homogeneous to be capable of being shortly described. My impression of the opera at Paris, especially of the overture which was done magnificently by Strauss, and especially the commencement and ending of the overture, was confirmed. But still I must say that to me the 'Meistersingers' seems to be a much greater thing. The 'Meistersingers' seems to me to be Shakespearean in its jewel-like beauty of every note. And then I missed the great humour of the 'Meistersingers'.

This morning I telephoned to Mr Wellecz. I had brought away by mistake a pair of gloves from their place thinking them to be mine. The first question of Prof Wellecz was: how did I like the opera last night.

Vienna 11.1.30

I am commencing this letter rather early in the week. Today is Sat. and it is not necessary to post till Wednesday. But I have got half an hour.

Tomorrow at 8 a.m. I leave Vienna for Prague where I shall get at 2 o'clock. I want to go to Prague chiefly because there is at present I believe a good deal of business done between Bombay and Prague. But Prague is also a very interesting town and it is possible that I may get an opportunity of hearing some Czech music. If I could hear an opera of Smetana or Dvorak it would be very interesting because they are not performed anywhere else outside Czechoslovakia half so well as there. Besides the new Exhibition bldg is said to be very interesting. It is made of just steel and glass.

My last week here has been as interesting as my last weeks in most [places] have been. I think I brought my last letter down to Monday 6th. On Tuesday in the morning after pottering about, at 12 I was at the Osterreiches Museum in Prof Gluck's room, where he had asked some of the students from Prof Strzygowski's institute (pronounce Shtrygofski). Prof Gluck had found some time back a lamp from Cairo in the mass of things lying in the Osterreiches Museum (Austrian museum) and after examining it he had discovered that the top part of it was of the early 13th century and the bottom of the middle 14th century. It was on this lamp that I had read the *be noon*. He, to use his own words, now wanted his pupils to find this out for themselves and he invited me to also attend the class.

My seeing—continued Hotel Wilson, Prague 13.1.30–7 p.m.—this was to me a revelation of what scientific scholarship can do. The first day Prof Gluck had told me about his conclusion I was a little surprised for this seemed to me then some Coomaraswamy business, where you think that a thing has been made in the middle 16th or early 17th century, and Prof. Gluck is in manner and appearance as unCoomaraswamy as possible. He had of course not then told me his reasons for his conclusions, but when he went through with them with his class I saw with what extraordinary care and minuteness he had studied the problems, the technique, the style and the artistic value and he had the history of the period both political and social at his fingers' ends.

It was amusing to hear him talk of Sir Thomas Arnold, Lawrence Binyon, Blochet. Of the first two he said: they can tell the date of a picture when there is an inscription on it. Of Blochet he spoke more kindly, not because his artistic estimates are any better, but because he is at least a good philologist and his work in the cataloguing of the oriental mss in the Bib. National is good. But I think we are a little unfair both to Sir Thomas and to Mr Binyon. The first is a Prof of Persian turned into an authority on Indian miniatures. The second is nothing in particular turned into an art critic. On the other hand Profs. Gluck and Strzygowsky have had a thorough training in the history of art (there is a faculty in Vienna in the subject) and they have specialized in this subject, the one for 25 years, the other for 45 years.

I am afraid I must end this letter quickly. There are so many interesting things to write about they will all have to wait.

8th Excursion to Melk where there is a Benedictine monastery in the Baroque style. Melk is about 50 miles from Vienna. Left Vienna 7.30 A.M., returned 6.30. Evening, dined at Prof Gluck's and spent an extremely interesting evening. There were Mr and Mrs Gluck (Mrs Gluck is half Persian, half Russian), Mrs Gluck's sister (who, I was told still continues to be Muslim), a Russian aunt, Staude and Blauensteiner. The last especially seems to be very much liked by Prof Gluck. I maintained that the Baroque style was a style without a backbone. When there was a clever architect he made a success of it, but as there was no driving force behind, at the slightest opportunity to go wrong the artist did go wrong. I cited as examples the roof of the Belvedere and the portico of the Karls church both of which are to quote Baedeker, 'masterpieces in the Austrian Baroque style'. Prof Gluck is a real Viennese and a great admirer of Austrian baroque and my criticism excited him very much. After some discussion Prof. Gluck admitted that the question of the portico was 'doubtful'. But 'What objection have you got to the roof of the Belvedere?' asked Prof. Gluck. Here the discussion was longer and a number of pictures of the building in books on art (Prof Gluck has a fine library) were referred to. But I am proud to say I again won. Prof. Gluck said 'but have got a good understanding in these matters', a compliment that pleased me greatly.

9th Went to the Art History Museum again, this time with Bauer, the artist communist. It was not very interesting for I had already so to say sounded his mind. The Primitive Germans, the Netherlandish portraits, but not landscapes, appealed to him, as they do it seems to all moderns. Rafael was 'crache de bonbons' (a very vulgar expression, it means sweets that have been chewed and then spat out) (you remember we spoke French, Bauer knows no English), Titian was better, Michelangelo and Perugino still better, the greatest Italians: Leonardo da Vinci and Grecco [sic]. We then lunched together. Staude also joined us and I introduced him to Bauer. I then left for the Am. Exp. Co. and then after wandering for an hour in the St Stephan's Cathedral which I like very much, I was at 5 o'clock at the Mises where I had tea. And I was there till nearly 7.20. When leaving, Miss Mises said, 'I hope I shall see you again before you go.' After shuffling about a few minutes I said, 'Alright, at 6 on Saturday we can go to a cinema'. A most foolish thing to say as you will see when I come to the a/c of what happened on Saturday.

Evening concert *Programme*
Debussy 'Ronde de printemps'-liked
Liszt Piano concerto—indifferent Bruckner 5th symphony—did not like
First piece of this composer about which I am not enthusiastic
10th I went in the morning to the Art History Museum, this time alone. In the afternoon I went to Prof Molisch to bid him goodbye. He asked me to dinner the next day (Saturday) when he was inviting a Japanese gentleman. I said I was already engaged—the first reason for being sorry for being engaged on Saturday—evening opera. 'Mignon' by Thomas (French)—very indifferent.

11th Sat Packed a little in the morning and wrote part of this letter. 12.30 at Bauer's to bid him goodbye and get letters from him on some communist and artist friends in Berlin. There I also met Staude and Blauensteiner who had both come there for the double purpose of bidding me goodbye and seeing Bauer's pictures. At 1.30 I was at Mrs Wellecz's (who is 2 minutes distance from Bauer's) where I was to lunch. After lunch I spent with Mr and Mrs Wellecz one of the most interesting afternoons that I ever have ever [sic] had. Mrs Pollaczek (the E.D.) was also there. I also met there Miss Stross who said she was waiting for me there to bid me goodbye. This reminds me that I am forgetting to write to you of one most interesting incident.
You remember I had told Miss Stross that I would telephone to her and that we might go to the opera again.

Well, after much deep thought 27th Monday. I got an inspiration. I had invited Staude to come to the concert of which I have already written and had accordingly got 2 tickets. When I met Staude I told him that he could not come as I was going to take a girl with me. He understood this with a knowing smile for he is the kind of man who powders his face in the morning (this reminds me to write to you that I have now become quite pink. I wonder whether the Red Sea will let me bring any of this colour home.) Then I telephoned to Miss Stross. But it was all a fiasco. She had a severe cold and could not come out in the evening in thin clothes. Poor girl. I pulled her out of her bed or at least her room because I could not understand what the servant was saying in German on the telephone, and insisted on speaking with Miss Stross herself. Well, the result was that I went to the concert alone, as Staude could also then not come. On the telephone Miss Stross said that if I could not find the time to see her I should at least telephone her to say goodbye. I was going to telephone to her on Saturday evening, but as I said I met her at the Welleczs'.

At about 5 Mrs Wellecz, Mrs Pollaczek (I shall always call her E.D., it is so much easier to pronounce) and I came back together to the city (Mrs Wellecz' house is in the suburbs). In the train, when bidding goodbye, the E.D. asked me what I was doing in the evening, but I could not accept her invitation to go with her as I had to go to that Jewess Mises. So I bid them both goodbye in the tram.

I was at the Mises' flat half an hour late, but this was alright because I had said that I would be a little late. We then went to the cinema, then I took her home, then I had something to eat (by the way in the restaurant I met a Sikh gentleman, the Managing proprietor of the Indian Steel Wire Products of Tatanagar, and made friends with him) then I came home and then I finally packed for the next day's journey. All very disgusting. The cinema was the usual American Jew??? direction, I was feeling sick not to have been able to go with Mrs Polaczek who is charming and as intelligent and well-educated as a daughter of Mrs Wellecz' ought to be, and Miss Mises was not even looking as well as she usually does.

Sunday 2 Left Vienna 8.30, Prague arrival 2.30. My first long journey 3rd. Not at all bad. I can't understand why I ever travelled 2nd. Afternoon, looked around. Evening Opera Wagner's 'Flying Dutchman'. But I was much too tired to be able to listen with attention as you must when you hear an opera for the first time. The opera house here is quite small, like an ordinary theatre, and also quite cheap.

Monday 13th today. I had got from Prof Molisch the name of a friend of his, the Editor of the 'Prag Tageblatt', and with his help I got into touch with much difficulty with the right man in the chamber of commerce here. I made my usual speech which I have now almost got by heart, explaining my scheme and assuring him

Alpha that the scheme is very good

Beta that I am a very clever person

Gamma that my social standing is very high

Delta that I shall do all and more than I promise. I left him and spent the rest of the day in looking at Prague. Came back to the hotel dead tired at 6 p.m. It is good that my room is nice and comfortable or else I would never write this letter. Well, it is 9 p.m. now and I have not had anything to eat yet. Goodbye.

Berlin 20.1.30

Today I received my letters of the mail of the 25th November. Just a week late: they must have been waiting for me in Berlin for 5 or six days. But I did not ask them to come to Prague because I don't speak Czech and I did not want to fumble about in the P.O. there and I did [not] ask them to come to Dresden out of pure laziness.

But to begin at the beginning:

My last letter I think I ended on Monday the 13th. Tuesday 14 Left Prague 9.30. Arrived Dresden 2. 15.

Really 3rd class travel is quite comfortable. What a fool I was not to have always travelled 3rd. It started like this. When I got into Hamburg I had quite decided to travel 3rd but when I got into the train for Cologne, I found the 3rd so crowded and so uncomfortable (and I think I was also a little tired on that day the result of some hectic wandering about in Hamburg the two previous days) that I could not think of the idea of sitting in the 3rd for 9 hours and in the train I changed into 2nd. The second in Germany is as you know father really very comfortable. You sit as in a drawing room, armchairs, probably one or two in a compartment for six.

But to proceed. There was not much time to do anything in Dresden on Tuesday as the galleries in Germany all close at 1. However I rushed from the Hospiz (houses belonging to the Protestant association of Saxony, comfortable and cheaper than ordinary hotels. I wonder whether you know them father) to the gallery and managed to get some 20 minutes there. Then I returned, had a bath and went off again to the opera. There was Mozart's 'Zauberflote' (the Magic Flute) and I wanted to hear it very much. I got a good ticket (the opera in Dresden is also cheap). Then there was the question of food. I went out of the theatre but Dresden is dark at night and was unfamiliar to me and I soon found that I was not up to searching out a reasonably cheap place to eat. So I returned to the cold buffet in the theatre and had something to eat which was both little and expensive. However Prof Wellecz' advice is that you must not listen to music with a stomach that is too full.

The 'Zauberflote' except for certain parts did not make such an impression on me as I expected but this was I think to a great extent due to the fact that I did not know the libretto and there had been no good Staude to play all the themes to me on the piano beforehand. I hope I shall get another opportunity of hearing it here. Prof. Wellecz told me that it is a popular opera here. You will be interested to hear of my musical development. I have from time to time written that such and such a piece made an impression on me but I don't think I have ever given a connected a/c.

As you know in Bombay my knowledge of music was derived from reading occasionally an article in Groves' dictionary and all that I had heard was our own records and Griffiths' records. In Bombay I was able to understand the thematic arrangement of simple pieces of music like the Kreutzer sonata and the two overtures of Mozart that we have got. In more complicated pieces like the Unfinished Symphony of Schubert that Badr and I heard twice at Griffiths I could follow the main themes. There remained therefore it seemed to me two things: the grand opera (which Wagner and also Prof. Wellecz consider to be the highest development of music) and religious music.

When I got to London (on the very evening I got there or it may be the next day I went to 'La Boheme'), I started trying to hear music. But I did not do much, firstly because the London musical season was over, secondly things are very expensive in London, and thirdly because the London theatres are extremely good as you know and I used to enjoy the plays immensely. However I was extraordinarily lucky in getting an opportunity of seeing and hearing the Serge Diaghileff Co. perform the Stravinsky and Debussy ballets. I say lucky because Serge Diaghileff, a rich Russian, who had this company more or less as a sacrifice to art, died shortly afterwards and I am told that the Co. has been dissolved. It was Serge Diaghileff who first brought Stravinsky forward and also induced Debussy and Stravinsky and others to write ballet music.

Now I find that I did not then understand the music very much but liked the whole extremely and as you may remember, I went 6 or 7 times to see them and I would have gone oftener if I had not been engaged in other theatres. The mise-en-scene and dancing was magnificent.

As to operas, there was a Carl Rosa Opera Co. going on then in London which also as I now realize was extremely bad. However, ignorance was bliss, and Wagner's 'Tannhauser' and 'Siegfried' and 'Valkyrie' pleased me tremendously, especially the first, which, by the way, was the first opera of Wagner that I heard. It makes me smile a little now when I remember that one day I saw that an opera by one Offenbach called 'Tales of Hoffman' was to be performed and I rushed to hear it as I had never heard of it and was very much pleased to find that two songs, records of which we have got at home were from it. Badr had of course played these records a million times but I had never taken the trouble to inquire what they were. This 'Tales of Hoffmann' (which is a pretty indifferent opera) had been pursuing me a great deal. When in Hamburg I heard it again, chiefly because I was so impatient to get my taste of the opera on the continent, and I could have heard it again when I got to Paris (many times in Vienna, Prague, and Dresden).

As to church music, in London in Westminster Cathedral, the early English composers (Purcell, etc.) were performed. I used to come home tired with intent listening for 2 or 2 1/2 hours, but the just following of music is hardly pleasure, at least not the kind of pleasure which I have since found that it is possible to get from European music. In St Paul's or Westminster Abbey Haydn was almost exclusively performed (Haydn is very popular in England). This I used to enjoy much more but the general effect was a little spoilt by the horribly ungodlike services that they have in Anglican churches. You can't have pieces of good music interspersed with a man getting up and speaking about God, His Son and the mother of his son in the same way as he would speak of his neighbours' family. I used to find the sermons very trying. I suppose I am truly 'religious'.

In Paris, so far as music was concerned I stagnated a little. The modern French opera of Messager etc. is not much to speak of, though 'Le Peau de Chagrin' to which I took Jami was not bad. In Paris I heard the 'Valkyrie' (Wagner) a great number of times, but the two really interesting things in the way of the opera was Mussorgsky's 'Boris Goudonov' (which I heard on the 1st or 2nd day of my arrival in Paris) and Richard Strauss' 'Rosenkavalier'. In Paris I was coming more and more to the opinion that the French and Italian opera is not worth going to and that the only real opera is the German opera. I remember I went with Sagheer Bhai to hear 'William Tell' and I decided never again to go to an opera by Rossini. To give the Italians another chance, a few days before I left I went to hear 'Rigoletto' and came back quite confirmed in my opinion. Why one should sit for 3 hours in an uncomfortable seat to hear song after song, each as meaningless in itself as it was without connection with the others sung by people dressed in curious costumes, I cannot explain to myself.

But towards the end in Paris it was a general period of depression for me. As a result of deep thinking (you must have gathered by now from my letters that I do DEEP thinking now) I had come to the conclusion that art, music etc. was all nonsense and children's play and the sooner we grew out of them the better. One of the corollaries of this proposition was that enjoyment for instance of the kind that we had last May at Kihim was also nonsense. When I came to this I began to have doubts of my sanity and I thought that the sooner I get out of this dangerous continent the better for my mental health. This was one of the reasons why I then decided to stay one month less in Europe. But besides this I used to ask myself why one should, as I said before, sit in an uncomfortable seat for 3 hours (Wagner's operas at Paris last 4 1/2 hours) to hear any opera, be it German or Italian and also why one should tire oneself to death by wandering from picture gallery to picture gallery instead of sitting at home in a comfortable chair and reading 'Lear' or 'Crotchet Castle' or the last number of Punch.

Well then, I came to Vienna with two propositions fairly clear to myself, 1stly that Italian and French opera was worthless, 2nd that operatic music was good so far as it went but that it did not go far.

But in my very first week in Vienna, I had the reply to the 1st question. One might sit in that uncomfortable chair instead of doing anything else to hear 'Cosi Fan Tutti' or the 'Mastersingers of Nuremberg'. And mind you the 'Mastersingers' lasts for a full 5 hours at Vienna where the intervals between the acts are not long. 'Cosi Fan Tutti' was the first Mozartian opera that I heard. Prof Wellecz told me that nowhere else is it done so well as in Vienna (and it is the same with the 'Mastersingers'). There is only one word for 'Cosi'—it is charming. I think it could be compared most with 'She

Stoops to Conquer' in literature. The music is quite wonderful. It takes you into the very spirit of light happiness. And you want to cry when it is over.

The 'Mastersingers' is Shakespearean. I so described it when speaking about my impressions of it to the Welleczes. The deep philosophical songs, for instance one in which Hans Sachs, one of the Mastersingers and a master cobbler, the real hero, sits in front of his cottage and says how he would like to not work but to sit and dream, is one of the most glorious pieces of music that I have yet heard.

But even a greater thing is the humour of the opera. I don't know whether humour is the right word. I explained what I meant to Prof. Wellecz by quoting Scene 1, Act V of the 'Merchant of Venice'. You remember it commences with the series of speeches with classical references. Lorenzo says (I shall quote from the book. I am very glad that I brought along those three volumes with me):

In such a night
Did Jessica steal from the wealthy Jew
And with an unthrift love did run from Venice
As far as Belmont.
(Lorenzo is out to make compliments, not so Jessica)
Jessica In such a night
Did young Lorenzo swear he loved her well
Stealing her soul with many vows of faith
And ne'er a true one.
Lor. In such a night
Did pretty Jessica, like a little shrew
Slander her love and he forgave it her.
Jess. I would out-night you, did no body come
But hark, I hear the footing of a man.

This, from the commencement of the scene I think one of the most wonderful pieces of work that Shakespeare has turned out (Do you think so too, Father?) Graphically I would describe this transition from the commencement of the scene up to where I have quoted something like this: [line drawing showing a graph]

In words I call this 'humour' for the want of a more expressive term. But this is exactly the kind of thing you have in the music of the 'Meistersingers'. I wish you could hear the 'Meistersingers'. I think I shall purchase some records, especially the overture and that song of Hans Sachs if it has been well recorded. But to me the hearing of the 'Meistersinger' was a revelation of what can be done in music.

What I have written above I told a couple of days after my second hearing of the 'Meistersingers' to Prof Wellecz. I was very much afraid that all this was 'imagination' on my part and I wanted very much to know what a man like Prof. Wellecz thought of it. For he was not only a composer of considerable standing but also Prof of 'Theory and Structure of Music' as his official title in the university goes. I quoted this passage of Shakespeare to describe what happens immediately after Hans Sachs concludes the song above referred to and I was greatly pleased when Prof. Wellecz said that it accurately describes the music.

Hullo, it is 11.30. I must end ... *and tomorrow is mail day and I have not yet written Vazir's letter.* It was a great thing in the Welleczs that they were so cultured. For instance, both Prof and Mrs Wellecz knew this passage from the 'Merchant of Venice' quite well.

VII Berlin, Reinhart Collection, Winterthur, Italy

Berlin 26.1.30

I am afraid you will find this letter very short. Father, you write one thing that has frightened me very much, viz. that you do not give my letters to any of my uncles or aunts. I thought that they would be hearing from you that I am hale and hearty and then would not mind my not writing to themselves very much. After writing 10 or 15 pages home and above all after writing the great number of letters on business and other purposes here, I find I have very little time left for further correspondence. As it is Haffoo reports that even Hanoo Phoophi's very kind heart is feeling sore.

Diary of last week

21st Tuesday Morning Met Prof Kuehnel (introduction from Prof Gluck and Dr Schmidt, both of Islamic Art) Looked at Kaiser Friedrich Museum Evening 'La Boheme'

22nd Kaiser Friedrich Museum—Dr Schmidt lunched with me—evening 'Salome' by Richard Strauss

23rd Ethnographical Museum—met Dr Cohn (Chinese and Indian art—introduction from Prof Gluck)—gave my opinion on two Rajput miniatures which he had just purchased—evening 'Schwande die Dudelsachpfeifer', a Czech opera by Weinberger—indifferent

24th Morning Kaiser Friedrich museum—lunched with the Zucherkandls (Dr Zucherkandl is a musical [sic] critic and the Welleczes' great friend). *Evening* 'Verkaufte Braut' by Smetana, another Czech opera—good

25th morning Ethnographical Museum. Afternoon called on the Schonbachs (letter from Amin Bhai) and had tea with them—extremely nice and cultured family—I don't know how Amin Bhai manages to make such good friends—Evening 'Kaiser von Amerika' (The Emperor of America), the German translation of the 'Apple Cart'. A great fall from the standard of the Malvern performance. These Germans have no sense of humour. They had made a very good piece into a farce.

26th Sunday (today) *Morning* Cathedral service, afternoon spent with Werner Saul, an artist (letter from Viktor Bauer of Vienna)—uninteresting young man. Returned home at 9 after wandering about a little in the fashionable quarters. *Wrote some letters. It is now 11.30 Hope will find some time to write more but don't expect to.*

I was entirely forgetting. Haffoo was married yesterday. Heartiest congratulations to all.

Berlin 1.2.30

I have got 5 minutes before I go to a place for tea so I commence a letter which will again be short.

27th Mond. Morning Kaiser Fried. Museu. 4 P.M. appointment at the entrance of the Viktoria Louise Underground station with Frau Schonwald, a lady whom I had made friends with in the opera house in Paris. I telephoned to her and this was the rendezvous that she gave—a rather curious place. She is over 35 and wishes to appear under 25. Otherwise good and also a little cultured. Had a 2 hours tete-a-tete with her in a cafe and was 2 marks 20 pfennigs the poorer at the end of it (1 cup of coffee = 1 mark 10 tip). However.

Continued after returning from the Rewalds. Oh, I am making a mistake. On Monday I went to her place for tea. It was again a tete-a-tete. However I was invited to dine on Friday when it was promised that I would be introduced to (1) Mr Schonwald (2) Mr Schonwald (jnr) (3) Miss Schonwald ('who is pretty and likes to dance') the last two being children of Mr Schonwald by his first divorced wife.

Evening 'Fra Diavolo' a light opera, quite an operetta, but quite nice. By the way, in the Kaiser Friedrich Museum I saw the frescoes brought from Kufan and Tushan (Central Asia) which are remarkably like the Ajanta paintings and remarkably good. They were done at about the same time. I had read of them, and seen reproductions in Sir Aurel Stein's book. (Did I write to you that I tried to meet Sir Aurel in Cambridge? But he was away from home.) and I had wanted to see the originals very much.

Tuesday Morning Volkerkunde Museum Dr Cohn had asked me to see him at 1 and when it was time I went down to his room. Invited to tea the next day.

Evening 'Palestrina' by Pfitzner, a really magnificent opera. I shall hear it again. Hearing it once is not sufficient because it is rather complicated and the music is difficult. Besides, it lasts 5 hours. I miss Staude here very much. He would have gone through all the music with me beforehand on the piano had he been here.

Wed. Kaiser Fried. Museum Islamic ceramics At 3.30 I went down to Saul's mother's flat to see 'modem apartments'. The façade of the huge block was very good. Had two cups of coffee and moderate amt of cake. At 5 for tea at Dr Cohn's. Mrs Cohn is a remarkably good looking and well-preserved woman and also very nice. Dr Cohn is also very good looking. There were for tea also another Prof (of Greek—he has specialized in Greek philosophy) and his wife, also Jews but as ugly a pair as Dr and Mrs Cohn are handsome.

Evening 'Carmen' I have not continued the story of my 'musical development' but you will be interested to hear that I am coming to believe that the 1st Act of 'Carmen' is about the greatest piece of operatic music that was ever written. I am looking forward to hearing it again next week with great excitement for I don't know what changes it may work in my musical opinions.

Thurd 30th

Morning National Gallery Lunched with the Zucherkandls. Really, they are extraordinarily nice people. The conversation is however very different from the kind of thing I used to have with Prof and Mrs Wellecz. In Vienna it used to be a respectable quiet interesting instructive conversation. Here Mrs and Dr Zucherhandl and myself, we all speak and if necessary shout at the same time. We each of us have our advantages. Mrs Zucherhandl being a lady we make way for her whenever we remember to do so. Dr Zucherhandl of course knows by far the most about the subject of our conversation—chiefly music, while I am the only person who is quite firm In English, the language of our conversation.

Evening 'Fidelio', Beethoven's one and only opera. I must say that I am very much disappointed with myself for being disappointed with it. For all critics say that of its kind it is the greatest piece of music written by the greatest master of music. However, I hope I shall get another opportunity to hear it.

Friday 31st

Morning, business of various kinds, and a couple of hours in the middle America section of the Volkerkunde Museum. *Evening* Dined with Schonwalds. I donned my evening clothes, chiefly because I thought I must make use of them and as I have my bath in the evening there is no trouble of changing. The Schonwalds are an interesting middle-middle-class family. Mr Schonwald owns a lady's hat factory. The son is in the N. A. G. automobile works. (He has promised to show me round.) The daughter, who now lives with a sister of the father, w-well I think I may say pretty?—but charming, frank, and unaffected. I have been invited to an English-speaking association of young Germans by son and dtr next Wednesday evening, and I shall go if there is nothing interesting in the opera.

Saturday 1st Feb

This morning has been rather important for me for today Giotto (Florentine, 1266–1337) succeeded a little in retrieving the honour or should I say rehabilitating, if there is such a word, the honour of Italian painting which had been very much lost with me. But I am still unable to understand what on earth Corregio, Andrea del Sarto, Perugino, etc. are driving at.

Afternoon had tea with the Rewalds (introduction from Gamadia). Love, adaabs P. S. I enclose—in order to make the letter fat—a letter from Prof Gluck. Isn't he nice. It was really my fault not going to his place to fetch the introduction but this was also due to that Miss Mises. I also enclose a pict. post c. of the Belvedere about the roof of which I had that discussion with Prof Gluck. Isn't the roof weak?

Berlin 9.2.30

After I had closed this letter it suddenly occurred to me as to what would happen if you did not get my letter asking for more money. For know, oh Father, that I had asked for more money. Some time in early January I decided that I should accept your offer to stay here another month and then I wrote to you to send me 25 pounds to Milan. I am afraid that now it may be necessary to send money by telegraph. No, I think if you could send the money to me at the American Exp. Co. Rome before the 15th Feb. it would be all right. Yes I had got at the commencement of this month about 45 pounds and this ought to carry me on easily for 1 1/2 months. Goodbye
Piece

Beethoven Leonora III Otto Klemperer and mitgl der Kapelle der Staats oper Berlin
with '*Nachtstraum (Mendelssohn) for the continuation, this is on 66603*
 Grm 66601
 66602
 Gram 66070 Georg Hoeberg, Copenhagen
 66071

8.2.30

[Account of Zeiss binoculars—various models for Haffoo.]
 To come to myself. I am enjoying Berlin. My friends here—especially the Zuckerhandls—are good and I am hearing also lots of good music and the museums etc. are interesting. But still I am feeling glad that the time for returning is now approaching. First of all I am getting tired of this eternal hunt for a restaurant. And I am not so unparticular about my food as I find I have been trying to make it out. I have for instance quite made up my mind as to what I shall eat when I am very rich and can afford to eat exactly what I want. I shall then live on a diet of lemon squash and *puran puri* interspersed with meals of beautifully cooked *dal chawal* and *gowarphalli* and yes, if Yacoob is still living and can be made to recover his old cunning hand I shall also eat large quantities of 'ladies fingers' *(bhendi)* cut into small pieces and fried as only Yacoob can do it.

Last Week's Diary
2nd Sunday I do not remember what I did in the morning. Evening 'Entfuhring aus dem Serail' 'Escape from the Serail'.Mozart
 3rd *Morning* inter alia 2 business calls. *Evening* Furtwangler concert. About this there is so much to write that I shan't write anything at all. However, I enclose a picture of Furtwangler, who by the way is the conductor of the Philharmonic Society of Berlin, which is the only picture that I have willingly purchased in Europe (the p.c. of the Belevedere which I sent you some time back I was *forced* to purchase). So you will realize the greatness of Furtwangler.
 4th *Tuesday* Morning some business calls, also Volkerkunde Museum. Evening 'Merry Wives of Windsor', an indifferent opera. But I was still suffering from mental fatigue from the Furtwangler concert so it was as well.
 5th *Wed* Dr Renpke of the Reichsverband der Deutschen lndustrie (=Federation of German Industry) lunched with me. He is a very nice man of about 37–40. He suggested that I should write a short pamphlet on Indian law so far as it interests the German merchants and he offered to translate it into German. I am dining with him next Saturday. *Evening* Went to the English-speaking club of which I have already written. Miss Schoenwald was not there and I was introduced by Mr Schoenwald jr. I wish I had the time to write a few pages about this evening. My experiences were most interesting and curious also Miss Schoenwald's behaviour.
 6th *Thursday* Went to Potsdam. Most unpleasant. Had my ears nearly frozen off. The middle of winter is not exactly the time to see beautiful parks. However, visited the chief places of interest.

7th *Friday* In the National Gallery which contains only German paintings of the 18th and 19th century. It was very interesting. This was my first visit to this gallery though I had already been twice or thrice to the building of the National Gallery where there are the modern paintings. In the afternoon I called again on the Schonbachs (distinguish from Schoenwalds), and was invited to tea next Tuesday.

8th *Today* I have now decided that it is not necessary to burn the pictures of Titian, Tintoretto, Veronese and of most of the Venetians. I am now slightly recovering from the anti-Italian mania caused by the overwhelming pictures of Netherlandish schools especially the Breughels in Vienna and the Van Eycks in Dresden. This was also I think to some extent caused by the company in which I was in in Paris and Vienna. For to the younger generation the Renaissance in Italians are as bad as the Romantic Wagner. Dr Zuckerhandl said the other day that this distaste of the Venetians, Florentines, and Romans of the 16th century and for Wagner is a fashion and will pass. I do not think that it is merely a fashion. In any case it is a fashion which has considerable foundation for it. But I was surprised to find myself sharing in this fashion. For I belong to another race and have nothing to do with the modern economic and social problems of Europe, and I ought to, it seems to me, be able to have a more impartial judgement. However there is no doubt that at present I greatly prefer Van Eyck (who is the only person it seems to me who has seen white light), the elder Breughel and the portraits of Durer to anything Italian. I also greatly prefer 'Don Juan', 'Cosi Fan Tutti' and 'Entfuhring' of Mozart to all Wagner except the last act of the 'Valkyrie' and the 'Meistersingers'. The 'Meistersingers' is also liked by the new generation and 'Valkyrie' is admitted to be 'beautiful'. On the other hand Rembrandt, who is the guru of the moderns, does not appeal to me so much. Nor was I overwhelmed by the 'Magic Flute' of Mozart and 'Fidelio' of Beethoven's which are the two greatest pieces of operatic music for the younger generation. But this last I should not say. I have heard them both only once and under unfavourable conditions.

You will be interested to hear that I shall go to Zurich again for one day. I have an introduction from Prof. Wellecz on Mr Werner Reinhart, one of the Proprietors of Volkart Bros. The other proprietors are his two brothers, George and Hans. Of these, Werner is a musician, Georg a collector of modern paintings and Hans a poet. I wrote to Mr Reinhart saying that I would like to see his brother's paintings. I have received a very nice reply and also a desire that I should give my opinion on some Indian miniatures that Mr Reinhart has got. Prof Wellecz had in his introduction written 'Indische Kunst sehr gut versteht' (understands Indian art very well). I don't feel nervous. I have now met most of the European experts on this subject and I find that I don't know very much less than any of them. So far as *ragamala* subjects are concerned I think I know more than most of them.

In any case, if I can become friendly with one of the proprietors of Volkart Bros it will be a great thing.

And Zurich is not very much out of my way from Munich to Milan.

17.2.30 Berlin

I received no letter from Somerset Lodge this mail. It has probably gone to Milan and I shall get it at Amin Bhai's where I have asked the letters at Milan to come. Vazir, to whom I sent no instruction as to posting, posted her letter to Berlin and so I got it alright.

I leave Berlin on the day after tomorrow by aeroplane for Leipzig. I hesitated some time before I decided to go by air. I do not believe that my education in life will be very much furthered by sitting in an aeroplane. However I shall be able to say that I have travelled by air and to be able to say that you have done a thing (whether the thing be a great thing or a silly thing) is a great thing. Then there is a considerable saving of time and the result will be that I shall be able to stay in Leipzig only one night. Finally, it is not very expensive. Berlin-Leipzig 3rd class is 7 marks, aeroplane fare is 25 marks, a difference of 18 marks. To this must be added the cost of sending my luggage separately, about 3 or 4 marks, say in all about 21 or 22 marks = about Rs 13 or 14. One pays I believe Rs 25 or 14 for sitting for half an hour in a plane in Bombay.

My diary:-

10th Monday I have no recollection what I did in the morning. Berlin museums are very interesting and I have been through them as well as one can go through them in a month. I had tea with Frau Schonbach. There was also another lady present who could speak English very well. I must say that everybody here is very nice to me and I enjoyed the afternoon in the company of these two ladies, neither of whom, by the way, is bad-looking. By the end I believe I had quite succeeded in convincing them that I was both good and clever. *Evening* I must have gone to the opera. I have no note of it in my diary.

11th Lunched with the Zucherhandls and there met a young man (Dr Schnitzler) evidently a great friend of the Zucherhandls and a very cultured man with a sound knowledge of literature and art. Also a good pianist. By profession an actor.

Evening Heard 'Otello'. Curiously up till now I had never heard any of the 'great Verdis' and this was my first.

12th Evening Went to the Komodia, one of the 'classical' theatres here. The Germans have no sense of humour. They like farces too much and make everything into a farce. This I think is almost a conclusive proof of the want of a sense of humour.

13th Thursday Oh yes on Monday morning I had gone to the Siemens Schubert works. I was treated with great consideration and I had lunch with the senior staff. Siemens now also produces aeroplane motors and I had said that I have an invention of a silencer to sell (you remember the expired patent of the Engineer at Hanumkonda whose name I now forget which I had unsuccessfully tried to sell to Wolseleys and Nortons). So I was given an apptmt on Thursday at 2.30 p.m. with the CE motor works. Well, I had a fair reception and I have received no definite reply yet. I was again treated with great consideration for though I am 25 I am told that I look like 28 and with an effort I can talk as if I was 38. I drove back from there to Dr Bernfeld's where I had an apptmt at 4 in one of the co.'s cars. I would have liked to have seen myself as I sat in the fairly big touring car with a thick woolly motoring rug on my legs and a huge Prussian in livery at the wheel. From Siemens Stadt to Charlottenburg where Dr Bemfeld stays is a long way and I was glad I got the car for otherwise I would have been late for my appt or have spent many marks on a taxi.

Dr Bemfeld is the psychoanalyst and the brother of Mrs Stross.

I had not been able to get in touch with him before for though I wrote to him and tried to telephone to him it seems that I wrote to the wrong address and telephoned to the wrong number. I would like to give you a full a/c of my conversation with Dr Bernfeld but I am afraid there is no time.

My knowledge of Maths came in useful and the fact that it was necessary to ... impressed me highly with the goodness of psychoanalysis.

Evening Mozart's 'Magic Flute' ('Zauberflote'). Marvellous.

14th Friday. Did nothing in particular. Ah yes, met Herwald? Walder, art dealer, publisher, poet, and above all the centre of 'modem movements' in art in Germany. He told me two things that made me fall on my feet with such a thud as there has not been for a long time. But it is 12 p.m. and I cannot elaborate.

15th Saturday Dined with Dr Renpke: an interesting penetration into German upper middle class life.

16th Sunday Morning. Visited an exhibition re: Japanese theatre. Afternoon 'the dansant' at Frau Schonbach's. I think the Schonbachs one may place in the upper Berlin society. If so, this was an interesting penetration into upper class life. *Evening* 'Palestrina' by Pfitzner. 2nd hearing. I like it immensely. Dr Zucherhandl thinks it to be the finest opera produced in the last 50 years. But I don't think I can say that I prefer it to Strauss' 'Rosenkavalier' and 'Egyptian Helena'.

17th Monday (today) *Morning* Palace museum, looking at Islamic (Egyptian and Spanish) Indian and Chinese stuffs and silks. I had to get special permission for this, but everybody is very kind to an 'Indian'. I penetrated into a very private exhibition of the paintings of Kokoschka (a modern painter) by saying that I was an 'Indian interested in modem art'. *Evening* Attended a lecture by Dr Bernfeld (he is not a prof. by the way). And then went to a cafe with him and a German lady and a young Egyptian (about 30 yrs) studying in the University here. Bid goodbye to Dr Bernfeld and exchanged cards and promises to meet again in Bombay or Alexandria as the case may be, with the Egyptian. It is 12.45 a.m. now so goodbye and love.

18.2.30

P. S. It is now 8.30 p.m. and this letter should have been posted at 4 p.m. to get this week's mail, but I have got quite callous now about missing mails. So long as I post one letter for every 7 days, I feel my conscience clear.

23.2.30

Munchen (letterhead)

23.2.31

My last letter I think ended with an a/c of my visit to the Shonbachs. That evening I heard 'Palestrina' by Pfitzner again. It was very good.

7th Monday. I was to lunch with the Zuckerhandls but in the morning Dr Z telephoned to me asking me whether I could postpone my farewell lunch visit (I never went to the Zucks except to lunch) till Tuesday. So I had the whole day free. I don't remember exactly what I did but I remember I was pretty busy. Yes, I made some arrangements for my travelling in Italy.

18th Frau Schonbach telephoned me in the morning but I was engaged for lunch and she was not free in the afternoon. So we bid each other goodbye on the telephone. I then telephoned to Dr Bernfeld. Hullo now I remember I have already written all this.

Wed. 19th Left Berlin by air. The interesting part is only the getting off and landing. I got into Leipzig at 12.30 and met Dr Fratzzacher, a friend of Staude to whom I had sent from Berlin the letter of introduction. He was waiting for me at the place where the car from the aerodrome bringing me (I was the only passenger for Leipzig) stopped. He took me to the Hospiz in Leipzig (extremely good and cheap) and I had lunch. He had then to go to work (he is in a publishing firm) and he promised to meet me there again at 7. I went up to my room to rest a little (the aeroplane had given me a headache) and dozed off. When I got up I had to hurry to keep the 3 business apptmts that I had. At 7 Fratzscher arrived and we had dinner together and then we went to a concert by the University students. There was Bach and Handel on the programmes. It was extremely good and to quote myself—terribly enjoyable. Really the standard of music attained by these University music unions is very high and I was told that the Leipzig students are particularly good. Some orchestra pieces of Bach and a concerto (piano) of Handel were performed. The idea was to play these compositions on instruments of the same period as the compositions themselves so as to get the true tone and effect intended by the composers. So the piano and other instruments were of the time of Bach and Handel and were brought down from the Museum for the music.

We then went about the town a little and then to a cafe. I returned home at about 12.30. I have now got very lazy so I decided to take the 8.10 train the next morning for Jena instead of the 6.12 train.

Thursday 20th It was rather unsatisfactory at Jena as I got very little time. I came to Nurnburg by the 2 o'clock train. I enclose a form in English which I got in Jena.

Friday The Hospiz at Nuremburg was even better than the one at Leipzig. Nuremburg was an extraordinarily fascinating town for me. I have been as I think I have written to you been taking a great deal of interest in the art of the German Renaissance and at this period Nuremburg and Augsburg were the two great cities. I saw the places where Albrecht Durer, Peter Vricher, and Hans Sachs lived, and the places where Wagner has placed the scenes of his opera. The scene of the second Act (in front of Hans Sachs' house) has been to some extent restored to its original condition and you can see the cobbler's apron and the tools with which Sachs worked.

At 7.30 I left for Munich and got here at 10.30.

Sat 22nd I spent almost the whole day in the New Gallery where the modern paintings are. The collection here is very fine, indeed much better than that in Vienna or Berlin or Paris in any one place. In the Tate Gallery they have some good pictures of the French Impressionists (1860–1890) but they have practically no XXth century pictures.

Sunday (today) I was again in the New Gallery and then in the Glyptothek where the classical sculptures are. The Glyptothek is not heated and so after suffering torture for some time I left. Then I went to another exhibition. It is now 4.30 p.m. At 6 I am going to hear Wagner's 'Tristan and Isolde'. It is the height of Wagner's romanticism and was intensely disliked by all my friends in Vienna and Berlin. I have heard it once before in Paris where I had liked it. I am going to listen with great attention today to see what happens.

'Lohengrin' for instance I had liked in Paris but I was bored with it (especially the very long 2nd and Act) in Vienna where as a matter fact it was much better done. Richard Strauss had conducted it.

Well now goodbye.

Letterhead: Albergi Agnello and Duomo Milano

I received 3 letters from Somerset at Zurich and one from Vazir I found waiting for me here. This gives me a very good idea of the marriage celebrations and I see them from three quite distinct points of view—Mother's, Father's and Vazir's. I suppose Haffoo is coming back to Bombay again from Delhi. What about Sarhan M.'s transfer to B'by.

My last letter I think I posted on Sunday last at Munich. I was in Munich on Sat. Sund. Mond. Tuesd. and Wed till 1 p.m. I was afraid that this would not be sufficient time but I think I have seen everything satisfactorily. I would have liked to have a couple of days more for the Old Pinakothek and the National Museum (Old Masters and German art—sculpture etc chiefly Gothic and Renaissance—respectively). At 8 p.m. on Wed I was in Zurich.

Amin Bhai had written to me that he would not be at home but I found both him and Sultana there as the excursion on which he was to go had been put off. We sat up talking till about 12.30 or later. Bad thing to do for I am never in the best form when I have been up till late

Mr Reinhart had written to me that there was a train from Zurich to Winterthur at 10.12. I first of all went down to the Italian Railways and got a copy of their hotel guide. There was still some time so I wandered about a little in a quarter of Zurich in which I had no occasion to go when I was formerly there. At Winterthur I asked the porter for the offices of Gebruder Volkart and a fine new building within a 100 yards of the station was pointed out to me. It was really a most beautiful building. I went up and was shown into Mr Reinhart's office by a bowing clerk.

I am afraid that from my descriptions of the people whom I have lately met you will think that I have got into the habit of praising people. It is now 3 days since I met Mr Reinhart and I have been thinking a good deal about him and I think that I am justified in lavishing every praise on him. A finely set-up quite good-looking man of 40 or 45 or 50, a bachelor (so far as I could see), quite a good musician himself (authority: Prof. Wellescz), taking a great interest in music (Prof. and Mrs Wellescz had been his guests last summer), very good knowledge of art, has travelled about a great deal in India and seen most of our monuments etc. I feel that if I was placed in his position I would like to live to a great extent as he does.

We spoke together for a few minutes and then he said that as his brother was ill and Thursday was the Ind. Mail day he would be obliged if I would excuse him till 12 (it was 11.15 then). I might possibly be interested in the Museum where there were a good collection of modem pictures. His car was waiting for me below and would take me to the museum and then he would join me at 12 and we could then go for lunch to his house.

I found the museum at Winterthur very interesting. It owes its existence chiefly to the generosity of the Reinhart brothers, and the picture gallery of modern painting which was all that I saw is certainly not inferior to any other that I have seen. Mr Reinhart came punctually and then showed me the board room etc., of the museum. By the way he had already telephoned to the museum that I was coming there so I had to pay nothing for entrance. In Switzerland they skin you on this as on every other expense. We then motored to his house.

I was greatly impressed by what I saw there. No liveried fuss, just 2 or 3 maids and the chauffeur: In the hall (baroque style) there were some fine Chinese screens and 2 large pictures by Hadler [sic] [correctly, Hofer]. [Hofer] is now one of the leading painters in Germany and Central Europe (which you must remember is slightly separated from Paris and the art of Paris). He was discovered some 20 years ago by Reinhart the father,—now dead—in Berlin and really established by him. [Hofer] has, Reinhart told me, travelled with him in India and painted there. The collection of [Hofers] in the possession of the Reinhart family is in number and it seemed to me also in quality greatly superior to the pictures in the Vienna or Berlin or Munich Galleries.

I had lunch on finer crockery than I have ever eaten off before. I asked him what was the style of the cutlery called. It was Goldsmith and Silversmith 'Shell' pattern and had been in the family 40 years. We then adjourned for coffee into a small study painted a dark green with brownish red lacquer furniture and a Chinese carpet. The furniture had been designed and the colours been matched by Mr Reinhart and an artist friend of his. We first of all looked at the Indian miniatures hung up in the room which were really the best of his collection. There was one *ragmala* painting (I forget which one it was) in the early Rajput style which was really very fine. Mr Reinhart told me that he had purchased it in 1908 or so from a man in Lahore for a rupee or two. Now because of the recent tremendous vogue for our miniatures I do not think that one could purchase such a thing for less than Rs 500 or 1000.... But you will be glad to hear that I think that I have really become good friends with Mr Reinhart. I was chiefly keen on meeting him because he was such a big man as far as Indian business was concerned. But now I place him possibly a little lower than Professor Wellescz but certainly not lower than Dr Zuckerhandl among the really good friends that I have made in Europe. And I think that this friendship will also be a lasting one. He has taken my address in Bombay with a keenness which seems to show that he too liked me and has promised to see me when he is in Bombay again which will probably be in the next year.

Letterhead: Hotel Gabruielli Sandwirth Venezia

This afternoon when I was in the San Marco I saw an Indian gentleman and lady and I recognized Daphtary. I went upto him and he said, 'Have you met your uncle?' 'My uncle,' I said, 'Which uncle?' 'Why your uncle Latifi.' Well, I rushed to Cook's office where Daphtary said Alma Mamoo was and we then spent some 3 hours together. I saw him off on his train to Paris and London. It was really most lucky meeting him like this. He missed his train in the morning or he would have left Venice at 12 noon, ½ hour after I got into Venice.

I am here in a very comfortable and quite cheap hotel. It is certainly true that Italy is cheap. By the way, Badr will be interested to hear that I heard 'William Tell' and 'La Boheme' in the Scala at Milan. It was really magnificent.

Florence 10.3.30

I have got very little news to give and still less time to give it to you in. I left Venice on the 7th and am now seeing Florence as well as it is possible to see it in a week.

Just now I am going to Mrs Elmquist (it is 8 p.m. and I must dine first) on whom Prof Gluck had given me a letter. I was to have gone to her place in the suburbs last Sunday but when I did go there I found the house closed and nobody in sight except 3 girls aged respectively 12, 14, and 16 (I estimate) playing in the garden. Now I know no Italian and the girls were giggling girls. And I have always said: From plague, pestilence and giggling girls, Oh Lord protect us. It was with some difficulty therefore that I obtained Mrs Elmquist's new address for Mrs Elmquist has moved.

Roma 18.3.30 Hotel Pension Suez Pagnini

I have been learning much in Europe. For example, I have learnt what it is to have corns and I am learning what it is to get bald. This last, by the way, is causing me more sorrow than I thought it would.

I am fairly comfortably settled here. I am not in [a] pension. I find that it is by no means cheaper to be in pension. Provided that you are prepared to go into the smallplaces not usually frequented by foreigners you can be much better off than in a pension. Here it is slightly more difficult because I don't know the language but both in Paris and in Germany I used to eat better and more cheaply than what was offered to me in the pensions. However by now I have got up sufficient Italian to be able to order a meal.

I saw Florence fairly well. I am going through Rome thoroughly. I find that provided you start fairly early and don't waste time over lunch (I go into a cafe and have coffee and cakes) you can see a good deal before it gets too dark to see any more.

In Florence, besides Mrs Elmquist I made two other friends: Prof Soulier of the French Institute and Prof Cellestine of the Accademia di Belle Arte, who is himself an artist. Soulier (aged about 60) has it seems (I had not heard of him till I got to Florence) written a great deal on Oriental influences on European art ... and on Tuscan art in particular. He is a great friend of Mrs Elmquist's and when he learnt that I was coming to Vienna [sic] (I had written to Mrs Elmquist beforehand from Venice), he asked me to go to his house. When Mrs Elmquist informed me of his invitation I felt quite sick because I did not want to leave Florence at 3 o'clock in the afternoon to go to meet him and miss 3 good hours of daylight. However, I thoroughly enjoyed my excursion. Prof Soulier lives in a very old villa situated on the heights over Florence and he, his wife, his villa, the view and the tea which he gave me were all very nice and good. He had quite a good collection of antiquities, small pieces of art, etc. and I enjoyed myself going through them. I must say that he did not impress me as a very accurate or scientific worker, but I must not judge him after a couple of more or less casual conversations and without having read his books. On the other hand it was what he showed me of his books that made the worst impression on me. For example, he had reproduced in his book a picture of Duccio's (a leading Sienese painter of the 14th cent., and the last and most important man to paint in what is called the Byzantine manner) and a Moghul miniature. Reproduced in black and white they certainly looked similar, and he accordingly said that Duccio was 'influenced' by Oriental art. As to the small difficulty that the miniature was painted some 4 hundred years later he said that I should read his whole book and look at the original pictures and compare the colours.

There seem to be 3 kinds of people who are working on art history. First of all there are those who see 'Hellenistic influences' in every thing. This has I think become a little less recently but did I write to you that Dr Goetz (who is now the best man in Berlin for Indian art of the Mughal period) told me that two years ago Blochet had published an article in which he traces Hellenistic influences in Persian and Mughal miniatures of the 17th–19th centuries. Then there are people who see 'Oriental influences' in everything. I asked Prof Soulier how if China could exert an influence over Tuscany through the intervening Turkistan, Persia, the Ottoman empire and half the Mediterranean, it was possible for Florence, Siena, Perugia, Bologna, and Venice, each of them to have such distinct styles of painting. He explained this by the strong personalities of the artists at these centres. But it seems to me that this answer is not satisfactory. If these differences were merely due to particular artists they should die with them and it should be impossible for Venice for instance to have its own distinct rich golden style during the course of some 2 hundred years.

Prof Cellestine I came to know in a different way. Walking in the streets of Florence, I saw in a window photographs of some mise en scenes and these I liked so much that I wrote down the name of the artist which was given below. When I met Mrs Elmquist I asked her about him and she told me that he was Prof Cellestin, a fairly well-known aqua artist who had recently taken to making mise en scenes. She gave me a card on him and I called on him. He certainly impressed me very much. Oh yes, the day before I met him I was at Prof Soulier's. It seemed that Prof Soulier was a great friend of Prof Cellestin's and had a considerable number of his aqua-forts. I thought these extremely good and made up my mind to buy one or two. When however the next day on asking Prof Cellestin their prices I was informed that they ranged between lire 300 and 500 (3–5 pounds), I decided that they were not for me for the present. But I have quite made up my mind that when my clients start paying their bills I shall send for some of those which I liked. As a man Prof Cellestin impressed me extremely. With clear ideas, earnestness, and a good sense of humour he seemed to combine a certain romantic religiousness which I met I might almost say for the first time in a man of his academic standing and education in Europe. I discovered this (his rom. relig.) when I turned the conversation on to the religious pictures of Fra Angelico, a trick which I had tried the day before on Prof Soulier without reaping much harvest. Well, I must end now. I must write to Vazir and then study my Baedeker for tomorrow. This visiting 10 or 12 churches per day requires lots of previous preparations if no time is to be lost.

24.3.30

The chief news to give you is that in spite of the fact that all my introductions to people in Rome had busted I have managed to make friends—a young man of about 26, 27 and his wife, both of Jewish descent, the man born in America, the girl a Russian. His name is Krauss, so he must have come from somewhere in Germany. I must say that they entirely shame me. They live on black bread and coffee (I am not quite sure even of the coffee) and they always walk for they can't afford tram fares. Krauss is or wants to be an author. The wife I understand sings. I hope I shall get an opportunity to hear her. She is extremely nice and quite good-looking. Krauss himself did not at first attract me very much. He looks too poetic and I have discovered that he suffers from 'art for art's sake' and attendant manias. However, I have great hopes of him. He is a scholar, or rather, wants to be one. He knows quite well English French and German, and he works hard. And I think he has got a logical mind. I saw him first in a gallery in Florence. There I saw him again twice or thrice. When I came to Rome I saw him again 2 times and the 3rd time I accosted him with 'We seem to be following each other about'. Tonight after dinner we have got a rendezvous in a cafe. As to the rest of my news you might just as well read Baedeker and put Monday—Rome, Part I routes A, B, and C Tuesday " " route D, E, and F, etc. Love Saif.

Notes

Introduction

1. Tyabji (1952).
2. These have been closely studied by Uma Chakravarty, Rosalind O'Hanlon, and Sudhir Chandra, among others.
3. Dobbin (1972).
4. See Ahmed (2017), for an understanding of the widespread Muslim fear and distrust of Western habits of clothing and eating. On the other hand, the young Camruddin Tyabjee in his London diary 1851–52, has no such inhibitions—except in the matter of being bareheaded ('Diary', London, 1851–52).

Chapter 1

1. See Fyzee (1964). I have used Asaf Fyzee's spelling 'Bohora' in preference to the more common 'Bohra'.
   Of the many studies of political and social change in the Bombay region in the nineteenth century, Christine Dobbin's study of Bombay provides an excellent background to the political awakening of that area during the latter half of the nineteenth century, as does Uma Chakravarti's.
2. See family tree from Fyzee (1964), p. 24.
3. In addition, Camruddin Latif's family, which was closely linked by marriage to Badruddin's, maintained an *akhbar* at their family home Latifia, in Kihim. The Shujauddin Tyabji branch's *Akhbar-nama-e Ahmadganj—Murud-Jazira*, 3 vols., 1896–98, 1898–1904, and unspecified but 1906–09, corresponding to the European years of Atiya Fyzee and the rest, also includes some letters by Hassanali Fezhyder. I owe this information to Dr Sunil Sharma, Boston.
4. They were Amirunissa, daughter of Shujauddin, Bhoymeeah's eldest son, and mother of Zohra, Atiya and Nazli Fyzee, and Camrunissa, daughter of Kulsum, Tyabjee's third daughter. They were probably instructed in the language at home, either by their husbands, or possibly by an English lady. Yet the women were far behind other Bombay communities in terms of formal, institutional western education. Cornelia Sorabjee had graduated from the University in Bombay by 1887, obtaining a first; in 1901, two more young Gujarati women, Vidyagauri Nilkanth and Sharda Mehta from Ahmedabad, granddaughters of a reformer and one of the founders of the Prathna Samaj in Gujarat, took their degrees.

5. Now housed in the Bombay University Library, Asaf Fyzee collection.

6. The Bohoras are Ismaili Muslims, originally of the Hindu trader caste, converted by missionaries from Yemen who had travelled to Cambay in the eleventh century; they were persecuted severely for their unorthodox beliefs both in Yemen and in Gujarat under the Sunni Sultanate in the fifteenth century, when they were forced to go into hiding, their mosques fell into disuse, and they had to practise the doctrine of dissimulation. Traces of this fear of persecution by more orthodox Islam persist to this day. See Fyzee (1960).

7. One of the most successful alliances, which continued for several generations, was with the family of Amiruddin Abdul Latif, a prosperous merchant trading in cotton, carnelian, and opium with China in the nineteenth century. Amiruddin's son, Camruddin, was trained in the law, and became the advisor to the Sultan of Zanzibar in about 1880. He and his wife spent long periods in England, their three sons were educated at Cambridge, Heidelberg, and London universities, and three of their children married Badruddin's children. In 1905, Badruddin sent two of his younger daughters, both affianced to Camruddin Latif's elder sons, to England to school, in the company of their future parents-in-law. See Amiruddin Abdul Latif, 'Life', dictated to Camruddin Latif, 1898, NMML, Delhi.

In 1906, another cousin, Atiya Fyzee, went on a Government of India scholarship to London for a year, together with Sarojini Das. It was then that Atiya met the poet and philosopher Iqbal, who was about to take his degree at Cambridge.

8. See Yatuk (1990).

9. By that time, the *akhbar* written by the *akhbarnavis,* official *akhbar* writers, had changed considerably to suit the purposes of rival courts seeking first-hand and confidential information about other centres of power (see Fisher 1993).

10. Although the genuineness of the Timur MS is doubtful.

11. Perhaps some reference to it exists in the first *akhbar* book started c. 1860.

12. See Safia Jabir Ali, Memoirs, Chapter 4.

13. Fyzee (1964), p. 3.

14. Sakina, Badruddin's second daughter (1871–1960), married a first cousin, Badruddin Lukmani, who had studied medicine in England. She played an active part in the non-cooperation movement and in social work in the 1920s and 1930s. Husain was Badruddin's second son (1873–1973), B. A. Cantab., who practised at the Bar in Bombay, and finally retired as Judge of the Small Causes Court, Bombay.

15. Yet the men, specifically Camruddin and Badruddin, would have been actively involved in spreading awareness on these issues. The Rakhmabai case, where a young woman who had been married at the age of 13 refused to accept the validity of her marriage and to live with her husband, led to a nationwide debate on the binding nature of the Hindu practice of child marriage; this was fuelled

in 1889 by a furious controversy over the death of the 10-year-old Phulmoni following the forced consummation of her marriage. This for the reformers constituted rape, but was justified on the grounds of being legitimate intercourse between a legitimately married couple.

The Parsi reformer Malabari's tracts on child marriage, and the Government of India's attempts to intervene through legislation were criticized by the orthodox as attacks by an alien (Christian) government on practices that were sanctified by ancient law. Camruddin, Badruddin's solicitor brother, was active on the Rakhmabai Appeal Committee, Badruddin himself was a close friend of Ranade's, and together with Telang and Pherozeshah Mehta, was in the forefront of progressive change in Bombay.

16. Mohsin, Badruddin's eldest son (1866–1917) B.A. Oxon., ICS.

Chapter 2

1. In the 1880s, Badruddin began with Charles Ollivant, a senior ICS official, to give large mixed parties at which judges, barristers and solicitors, Europeans and Indian 'gentlemen' were present. 'These mixed gatherings ... are now becoming an institution in Bombay. Mr Ollivant and Mr Tyabji have set a very pleasant example, which might be usefully followed by other public men in Bombay'. *The Times of India,* Bombay, January 8, 1863, quoted by Tyabji (1952), p. 56.

2. Of the books kept by Badruddin at his three homes, the Bombay one was the most neglected. The older married daughters who lived in Bombay rebelled at having to spend part of their Sunday, which they traditionally spent with their parents, writing—Surayya in particular wrote characteristically decisively about this.

3. For instance, Faiz's elder sister, Sakina, in every way the mistress of the household (described as 'able and wilful' by her brother Husain) had decided to punish a defaulter, who happened to be the leader ('General'), of the family troop. The culprit denied that Sakina had any right to judge or punish him, and by virtue of being the leader of the gang, decided to turn the tables, and punish the lady for her effrontery in reprimanding him. She was made to walk to one of their favourite points from which there was a view of the hills and greenery cascading below Matheran, write her confession of guilt at having tried to bully him, put it into a matchbox, and throw it off the point, vowing never to make such a mistake again, on pain of a terrible but unspecified punishment. What's at stake here was not male against female, elder against younger, but, it appears, beneath the horseplay and tamasha, a reassertion of the authority of the group 'Leader'. He was the one who decided what the day's activities were to be, what was 'sporting' or not, what was out of sync with the family culture that was being evolved through games, walks, and other entertainments, a status that was unquestioningly given Faiz, and that probably led to his autocratic decisions being accepted with reasonable good will.

315

4. A detailed account is given in Safia Jabir Ali's memoir, Chapter 4.
5. Scott (1994), pp. 19, 92–3.
6. Amiruddin Tyabji, 'Letters from Havre', 1870.
7. See for instance Ramabai Ranade's account of how seriously Ranade took his wife's education, in Ranade (1963).
8. Scott (1994), pp. 92–3.
9. See Bano Ahmed (n.d.).
10. The Allana family were extremely successful Khoja merchants and philanthropists, in the forefront of social and political reform. One member of the family, Qasim Ali, was one of the earliest graduates from Wilson College in Bombay.
11. See Safia Jabir Ali's account of the Akhde Surayya, MS. The club minutes covering the period about 1889–1965 were meticulously kept and are in a private collection in Bombay.
12. His eldest daughter Amina was married at the age of 13, but subsequently his daughters Sakina and Surayya were 18 and more at their marriage. Amina's husband was a first cousin, the only son of Badruddin's elder brother Shumsuddin, who had lost his first wife, and was considerably older. These circumstances seem to have been outweighed for both Badruddin and his wife by the fact that Abbas was 'family', moreover a highly educated, very liberal young man, who had a bright future ahead of him at the Bar. Being family implied that their daughter would be marrying a man who would treat her well, with respect, she would not be subjected to the kind of neglect or humiliating treatment that was associated with *zamindari* families in Badruddin's and Rahat's mind. Not a single one of Badruddin's daughters was married outside the *jamaat*, into aristocratic Sunni families, although it appears (verbal comm. Laeeq Futehally) that a number of such proposals had been made.
13. Camruddin's daughter, Dilshad, was married to the Nawab of Murshidabad, was tragically unhappy, and spent most of her married life away from her husband, in Bombay (personal communication, Safia Tambi Mattoo). The second case was of Nazli Fyzee, granddaughter of Badruddin's eldest brother, Shujauddin, who married the Nawab of Janjira. This marriage appeared to be a happy and successful one, but ended in divorce when the Nawab insisted on marrying a second time to beget an heir.
14. Maulana Shibli Nemani (1857–1914), an extremely distinguished and influential scholar of Arabic, Urdu, Persian and Turkish, a poet, historian, biographer, critic, and theologian, taught at Aligarh in its early years, and later at Osmania University in Hyderabad. From 1905 till 1913 he was the Principal of Nadwatul Uloom in Lucknow, and a close associate of Maulana Azad, whom he invited to edit the journal *al-Nadwa*.
15. Sayid (1998).
16. See Tyabji (1952), pp. 310–311.

17. The first member of the Tyabji clan to appear at a large mixed evening party in India was Amena (Lady Hydari), at an evening party at Jamshedji Tata's. *The Daily Graphic,* London, reported that the Tyabji family was the first to abandon purdah; in Egypt it was not till 1919, when Madame Zaghlul, did so Tyabji (1952), pp. 79–80.

18. Bhoymeeah's contemporary, Amiruddin Abdul Latif, was summoned with other leading Muslim citizens by Charles Forjett, the Police Commissioner, and warned in the severest and most direct manner of the consequences of any attempt to sympathize with the rebels—they would be strung up on the lamp-posts outside their mansions. Daniyal Latifi, verbal communication. Amiruddin's son, Camruddin, who was then a child of six or seven, never forgot this extraordinary announcement of summary punishment. His jubilation at the British defeat at the Dardanelles (Dar-I Daniyal) in 1916 made him name his new-born grandson Daniyal.

19. See Fyzee (1964).

20. Biography, p. 12.

21. Scott (1994), pp. 16–17, 87.

22. Ibid.

23. Saeeda Bano Ahmed in her memoir *Degar Se Hat Kar* gives a graphic account of her childhood pastimes in Bhopal, contrasting them with the refined indoor pursuits that were acceptable in the aristocratic Lucknow family she had married into.

24. See Tyabji (1952), especially pp. 175–228, and Dobbin, for a fuller discussion of this issue.

Chapter 3

1. Dost Mohammad Allana (b. 1869) was a very successful Khoja businessman, a philanthropist who established the Dost Mohammad Allana orphanage of Pune; Haji M. Ismail (1800–1912) was the founder of the Bombay Steam Navigation Company, father of Sir Mohammad Ismail who made the initial endowment for the Ismail Yusuf College in Bombay in 1914; Kazi Kabiruddin of Kalyan, the first Konkani Muslim barrister, whose daughters were the poet and writer Sultana Fyzee (A. A. A. Fyzee's wife), and Khurshid, wife of Agha Kashmiri the playwright; Ba Akaza from Surat, author of the *Haqiqat-I Surat*; Nakhuda Mohammad Ali Rogay, first Vice-President of the Anjuman-i-Islam, member of the Governor's Council. I am indebted to A. M. I. Dalvi for this information.

Chapter 4

1. See Ali (1981), pp. 4–6, for a graphic account of Chembur and Deonar in those days.

2. See Haeems (2000).

3. Amtussalaam, one of the leading nationalist workers of the time, accompanied Gandhi to Noakhali. Gandhiji attributed his success there largely to her presence. She later founded an ashram at Rajpura in Haryana. I am indebted to Anil Nauriya for this information.

4. Rehatsek (1964).

5. Two very prominent Khoja social workers. See Forbes (1987) for a detailed account of Kulsum Sayani's achievements. Fatima Ismail founded the pioneering Fellowship of the Physically Handicapped in Bombay. She was later nominated to the Rajya Sabha.

6. Jabir returned with a degree in the Natural Sciences Tripos (geology, botany, zoology), and a Diploma in Agriculture.

7. Mehta and Patwardhan (1942). This was written in prison by two of the leading socialists within the Congress Party. Asoka Mehta (1911–84), worked with Jayaprakash Narayan to organize the socialist wing of the Congress Party. Achyut Patwardhan (1905–92), one of the founders of the Indian Socialist Party, concentrated on social and educational work after 1947.

8. Nagardas Gandhi, who later founded the Department of Geology at Banaras Hindu University, was also a fine sportsman.

9. Mehar Mohammad Khan Shahab 'Maler Kotlavi', a versatile linguist and scholar of comparative religion, migrated from Maler Kotla to Bombay, where he taught Persian; he translated Suniti Chitre's autobiography into Urdu from the Marathi.

10. Moinuddin Harris, a Konkani Muslim from Lala Sopara, a Gandhian and socialist, was President of the Anjuman-i-Islam for six years, from June 1977 till August 1983. He published the Urdu daily *Ajmal* (after Hakim Ajmal Khan), having worked earlier on the *Bombay Chronicle* with Abdullah Brelvi.

11. Nazar Futehally (1910–92) founded his factory, Dynacraft, in Bombay in 1942, and despite some very rocky periods, steered it successfully till the 1980s. He depended entirely on indigenous know-how, and built the first conveyor systems, escalators, and microprocessor-controlled electronic systems, developed wholly in India.

12. Passages I have deleted for this translated version contain an account of a visit to Sarhan Latif's house, Saloma, at One Tree Hill in Matheran. This is followed by an account of her son's (and her own) immediate ancestors:

> 'So, my dear child, let me tell you about your great-grandfather. Perhaps he had Arab ancestors, who may have come to India to trade, and then settled and intermarried in Gujarat, in Cambay. They had a lot of trade with China. Dadasaheb Tyabally wasn't rich, and in fact at one time he was a small trader, but he was highly regarded for his integrity, and trustworthiness, and competence. He rose in the world very fast, and became a very wealthy man. His children [sons] were: 1) Shujauddin, 2) Shumsuddin, 3) Camruddin, 4) Najmuddin, 5) Badruddin, 6) Amiruddin. The daughters were Zainab, Kulsum, Sakina, and Nudrat-ul-Naim.

'I Of the sons, Shujauddin had only one child, a daughter called Amirunissa (who was your friend Nafisa's great-grandmother), that is to say Asaf Bhai's grandmother. She married a cousin, Hasan Ali, and their children called themselves 'Fyzee'. They had the following children: (1) Ali Akbar, (2) Ali Asghar, (3) Zahra, (4) Nazli, (5) Atiya, (6) Azhar, (7) Athar (these two made a name for themselves as tennis champions, and were known as the 'Fyzee brothers').

'II Shumsuddin. You have a special interest in him, because he was your grandmother Zeenuth's father. He had two children, Abbas and Zeenuthunissa. Sadly you never knew your grandmother, and I myself only remember her from when I was a child. But you'll remember Abbas Mamoo, from Baroda, where you'd gone and stayed once, when Kamal [Habib] was there, and you'd played together. And once you went from Gwalior.

'Both these two, Shuja and Shums, were merchants and very successful, and traded and travelled to Europe and goodness knows where else. They owned their own ships, and being well-travelled and educated, they moved in the first rank of modern and progressive society. Their homes, their wives' appearance and behaviour, and clothes, and education were all affected by their experience of Europe, especially of France, and in particular, Paris, where they had occasion to travel frequently, and they were at home there, and at ease speaking French, and in the French culture. And when they came home, they wanted their wives [to follow those fashions].

'I've heard a lot of praise of Shumsuddin, his goodness, and especially of his [munificence?]. He was also very sociable and affectionate, but he died very young, at the age of 42. [Dates of birth and death left blank]… He married twice, by his first wife he had a son (Abbas) and a daughter (your grandmother) Zeenuthunissa, he had no living child by the second wife, Hamida Begum.

'III This uncle [Camruddin] was also very brilliant and successful. He became a solicitor and was perhaps the first Indian to become one. He was extremely successful, and more than that, made a name for himself (among Muslims as well as others). He became very wealthy and spent lavishly on himself and lavishly on others. He lived in a very splendid fashion all his life. He was divorced from his first wife, and his second wife was a Mughal, called Qadar Sultana Begum, and we used to call her 'Chachani Saheba Begum'. Unfortunately, I never knew any of these uncles. My older brothers and sisters, Ameena, Sakina, Surayya, were very fond of him, and he was a very affectionate man, who had the gift of making people enjoy themselves. He lived in Khetwadi, in a house known as 'Sion ka Bangla'. This was quite a big house, magnificently furnished in his days, of which there was just a faint glimmer in my time, 'of which only a dying lamp is left', because none of his children had his talents. He had six surviving children of which there were two by his first wife: Hyder and Ashraf, by the second (Mughal) wife he had four: Shuffi (Mirza Aqa), Hadi (Aga Koochik), Kazim (Mirza Jan), and Dilshad Begum.

'Dear Amir, of these the ones you're closest to are Hadi, whom you know as Agha Koochik Mamoo. His wife, Atika, is his second wife, he'd first been married to my sister Jamila, who was a little older than Halima. They had one child who died in infancy, and Jamila, her mother, died a year later of grief. Akoochik and Atika have two children, Hanif and Safia.

'Oh yes, of the two children by the first wife, Hyder died childless, and Ashraf had two children by Abbas, called Shumsuddin (Mukhlis' father), and Shujauddin (whom you know as Shujoo Phupa). When his first wife, Ashraf, died Abbas married my elder sister Ameena.

'Now, to Shuffi Camruddin Tyabjee's family: he married Khadija [Najmuddin], and they had a son called Camruddin, and a daughter called Sultana. They're both married—the son to his cousin Najmunissa [daughter of Muhammad Akbar Hydari], and they have four children: Munira, Shuffi, Masud, and Mazhar. Sultana has no children so far. Shuffi Tyabjee died young, about twenty years ago [in the '20s] and his wife Khadija [one of the founders of the Women Graduates' Union, set up in Pune in 1927] turned to social work, and has made quite a name for herself in Bombay for the steadfast way in which she has worked, which is very unusual amongst Muslims. All praise to her.

'Camar Tyabjee is an agent for the Nizam, sadly, we have very little contact with him or his wife, so dear Amir, you probably don't know them. It was in their home that Azeem and Amena's marriage took place, and a very splendid party it was, with the garden looking quite marvellous—perhaps you might remember it? You'd come too. And so had Ustad Sahib (Samad) You were given a car as a present.

'The wedding of Amena's was on behalf of Sir Akbar and Lady Hydari—Amena's clothes, jewellery, dowry, everything was given by them. Now these two (which the family can pride itself on) are both dead.

'IV The fourth son was Najmuddin, who had one son, Ali, and the rest were daughters: (1) Safia (who married Faiz Muhammad Fatehali) by whom she had two daughters, Atika, now Mrs Hadi Tyabjee, and Saada, Mrs Salman B. Tyabji, (2) Fatima, wife of Ali Asghar Fyzee, who had a son, Rashid, who died young of *diq*, (3) Saada, who was engaged to Mohsin B. Tyabji, but died at the age of 16 or 17, (4) Amena (Lady Hydari) whose children are: Salah, now a very senior ICS officer [later governor of Assam in independent India], Maryam (Mrs Hatim B. Tyabji), Najmunissa (Mrs Camar Tyabji), whose children are Ali, Iqbal, and Masud, (5) Khadija, whose children are Camar and Sultana (wife of Fazle Husain), and (6) Munira.

'The son Ali married Surayya B. Tyabji, but died young, leaving her with two children, Fatima and Salim, both of whom have had tragic lives—there is nothing one can say about them! What a fate for children of such illustrious parents! God help those who are high who fall so low! They are now in Poona, aged about 45 and 43. Such pretty healthy children they were. Strange are God's ways. May He have mercy on them.

'Najmuddin was also a merchant. When he was young luck was with him. He had an Arab wife, Mariam Khatoon, whom he had met on his travels in Arabia and brought home. She was a beautiful woman, big and strong, and very generous and hospitable. She had great charm, and people were devoted to her. All this is what I've heard—I was only five or so when she died, and I have only a very faint picture of her in my mind. What tragedies these people endured, to have lost three young daughters, one after the other, because of *diq,* the eldest daughter, Safia, died leaving two young children, Atika and Saada, Fatima left a young son, Rashid, and Saada died unwed. ("Alas, the buds that wither away") [Ghalib]. [Later] his business also suffered and I heard they were in great difficulties financially. As if that was not enough, his only son fell into bad company and caused his parents great grief. He was quite charming and good-looking, and died young. Perhaps his mother had died before him. Uncle Najmuddin, beset with problems, then married again, a lady from the *jamaat,* this girl was very young and ignorant and not very competent, but Uncle Najmuddin could not have borne his sorrows alone, and died very soon after his second marriage.

'Now, about Chacha Sahib Najmuddin. He was a great scholar of Arabic and Persian, and taught a great deal to our young people, one of whom is Hamid [Ali], who is deeply indebted to him. He was a very fine and dedicated teacher. I have very faint memories of him,—he used to visit us in Matheran, and we children would crowd round him, and pour *jamuns* into his lap. I can visualize him quite clearly, his face, his expression, but there's nothing much more I can say about him.'

The variety of other topics covered by Safia's memoir; and her wide-ranging interests, can be gauged by the synopsis given below:

An account of Sarhan Latif's household, Alma Latif's marriage to Helen, Hazrat's reluctance to perform the *nikah* because of their lack of contact with the *jamaat.*

Description of daily routine, books, papers, writing, servants. Pages 72–90 deal with Raffoo's wedding, 1909, her departure for Nizamabad, Safia's visit to them there, birth of Vazir, 1912, p. 72 Safia's wedding, 1915, Rafia's wedding and children, etc., p. 75 Frank Moraes (Editor of the *Times of India*) asked to write Badruddin's biography, p. 76 Alma and Helen Latif's wedding 'Iqrar nikah' conducted by Faiz, 1942, p. 82 at Somerset Lodge (Faiz Tyabji's home), rediscovers Chowk Hall (Matheran) *Akhbar ki kitab* 1900–06, which she glances through, p. 88 Read at Asaf Fyzee's 'Dada Sahib Tyabali's Akhbar books' function. Comments on his autobiography, and Camruddin's comments on Badruddin's achievements in taking part in French, Greek, Latin and English plays at school, within a year of joining, p. 90 Fatima Farid out of gaol.

Account of Shamima and Zafar's visit, joy of Urdu poetry, Ustad Samad's presence increasing it, Badr Lukmani and his poet friends, especially Shibli. Visit to brother Mohsin in Mahabaleshwar, to sister Ameena, to Kihim, Porbunder, stay at Somerset for some months, when there was no tenant.

Account of visitors, and preparations for Mohsin and Shafiqa's wedding in Karachi. Account of Aamir Ali, Jabir's younger brother, his way of talking, joking.

Read a new Urdu magazine, *Nai Zindagi*, which had a couple of interesting articles, one on Pakistan (opposing it), and one on Ghalib's poetry. Mohsin's wedding party leaving from Bombay Central, spat with husband over treatment of servants, visit to the cinema.

Reading Lin Yutang, Ian Hay, Sylvia Thomson, Urdu, literary history, Josh, periodical *Madina*. Visit of Salim Ali, with friend Lok, birdwatching, Salim to meet Rao of Kutch to arrange for visit to Kutch in monsoon, collecting for drought-affected in Bijapur, books by Sylvia Thomson, Lin Yutang, Joan Butler, Urdu *mushaira*, Hafiz Jalandhari, Jigar, Ahsan, Akhtar, Majaz, and others taking part, night spent with three other sisters at Halima Fyzee's. *Mushaira* at Bandra to which entire family went. Party for Mohsin and Shafiqa at Somerset Lodge.

Amir's return from boarding school, Farhat and Shuja's visit, family parties in Kihim, Asaf Fyzee, Haffoo. Visit by poet Mahir, eating mangoes, reading poetry, informal behaviour, visit by F. B. T., Shakespeare reading at Somerset Lodge, Akhde Surayya's debate on 'The Good Old Days were the Best', with a lively exchange between Sultana Fyzee, the President, and her husband, Principal of the Law College, with her calling him to order: Faiz Tyabji's intervention, and her own comments on the seriousness of this issue, and her pride at her son's speech against it.

Faiz Tyabji's account of their maternal uncle, Jafar Ali's, eulogies on her parents, especially her mother. Amir taught Urdu by her when Jabir in gaol, Shakespeare reading at Somerset Lodge, purdah *mushaira* in Badr Bagh, Sakina Lukmani points out that poetry can and should inspire people and the country.

Reading of the *Taming of the Shrew*, Amir returns to school with 4 other cousins, heavy rains, visits to family in Andheri and Bandra.

Relations with friends from Tavoy, Akhde Surayya *mela* to raise funds for Bengal famine, servants, Samad and Amir, Chembur, Id gathering at Alma Latifi's, Raihana singing, Jabir's character.

Travels in Punjab, to Agra, Aamir's death, Laila and Hasan Latif's marriage. Zafar and Laeeq's wedding, Akhde Surayya meeting, Saif Tyabji speaking on the Anjuman. Sakina and Badr Lukmani's 50th wedding anniversary, Rs 1500 collected, for Women's Home in Chembur, fruit and vegetable show, Jabir's talks on AIR, Ghalib's *Aakhr i Mushaira*, Ghalib Day, Talk on Akhde Surayya's history, Akhde Surayya, English and Urdu literary circles, should a new edition of Ghalib's works be produced? 1944 bomb explosion, Ladies' Meeting, Sarojini Naidu, Leela Naidu, Rameshwari Naidu present, Raihana sings.

Id, film on Madame Curie with Greer Garson, party at Juhu, reading *I Believe*. Own family's comments, her longing to have large function for Badruddin, Jabir's suggestion to contribute to the Gymkhana, Welfare Centre for *mahars* in Chembur, physical education for children in Kurla, Shaikh Abdullah at Somerset Lodge: very interested in his accounts, what a huge big man he is—all of us look like pygmies in front of him!

Mushaira at Saboo Siddiq with Kaifi Azmi, Jigar Muradabadi, Josh Malihabadi, and Sagar Nizami, as well as a number of young local poets, also Sardar Jafri, Hasrat Mohani presiding.

Conclusion

1. In the early 1890s, the Rakhmabai case where a young woman who had been married at the age of 13 but refused later to accept the validity of her marriage and to live with her husband, led to a nationwide controversy on the nature and binding qualities of the Hindu practice of child marriage.

   Earlier, in 1889, a furious controversy had arisen over the death of the young Phulmoni at the age of 10, following the forced consummation of her marriage. This was seen to constitute rape, but was justified on the grounds of legitimate intercourse between a legitimately married couple.

   The Parsi reformer Malabari's tracts on child marriage, and the Government of India's attempts to intervene through legislation were criticized by the orthodox as attacks by an alien (Christian) government on practices that were sanctified by ancient law.

   Camruddin, Badruddin's solicitor brother, was active on the Rakhmabai Appeal Committee, Badruddin himself was a very close friend of Ranade's, and together with Telang and Pherozeshah Mehta, was in the forefront of progressive leaders in Bombay. See Chandra, Chakravarty.

2. Tyabji (1952), pp. 194–203.

3. See Fyzee (1964), 'Tyabjee Bhoymeeah', for a translation of Bhoymeeah's memoir.

4. For instance: his eldest son, Shujauddin's daughter Amirunissa, his grandchildren, Nazli and Atiya Fyzee, and their nephew Asaf Fyzee, the second son, Shumsuddin's, son Abbas Tyabji, Abbas's daughters Sharita and Raihana, Amena (later Hydari) by his fourth son, Najmuddin, Akbar Hydari, his grandson through his eldest daughter Zainab, Sakina and Ameena, daughters of his fifth son, Badruddin; Badruddin's grandson Saif; Bhoymeeah's youngest son Amiruddin, childless himself, who became a father to Shumsuddin's grandchildren, among whom are Jabir, Salim and Hamid Ali.

5. Saif Tyabji's is an interesting case. He had joined the Muslim League on Gandhiji's advice that he could best serve the nation by serving his own community (Vazir Tyabji, 1960, personal communication). He resigned from the League in 1940 when the Lahore resolution for Pakistan was passed. In 1957, he stood for Parliament as a Congress candidate, having remained a very active member of the Anjuman-i-Islam throughout. See Tyabji, Desnavi and Ali (1959); see also Guha (2007), pp. 370–71.

6. Two other senior members of the *khandaan* who were posted in Karachi at the time of Partition, Hatim Tyabji and Sarhan Latif, stayed on in the new country.

One of Husain Tyabji's sons, who had married into a Lucknow family, and was in the Indian Railways, opted for Pakistan.

7. Camruddin's second wife, known as Begum Sahiba, was a 'Mughlani', of Persian descent; two of his children married into North Indian aristocratic families—matches of the kind Badruddin's family had rejected. His grandson, Iskander Mirza (1899–1969), became Governor-General, then the first President of Pakistan, 1956–58.

Bibliography

MS Sources

Nehru Memorial Museum and Library

Urdu

Tyabji, Abbas. 'A Biography'. In *Khilafat*, Bombay, edited by M. Hadi Dehlawi. Abbas Tyabji Papers, no. 29, New Delhi.

Tyabji, Amiruddin. *Letters Written from Havre, France* (English, Urdu, Gujarati), 1870.

Tyabji, Amiruddin. *Akhbar-I Amiri*, 1877–1944, copied by Safia Jabir Ali 1958 (Badruddin Tyabji Family Papers VI).

Tyabji, Amiruddin. *Wynad Akhbar*, 1876 copied by Safia Jabir Ali, 1958 (Badruddin Tyabji Family Papers VI).

Tyabji, Badruddin. *Bombay, Matheran and Mahableshwar Akhbar ki Kitab*, 1880–1906, 4 vols., copied by Safia Jabir Ali 1958 (Badruddin Tyabji Family Papers VI).

Safia, Jabir Ali. 1) *Devnar, Chabootra par shuroo ke saal: 1924–1946;* 2) *Khandaan-e taybji ka kuchh haal;* 3) *Badruddin Tyabji ki awlad; Somerset House ki Zindagi;* 4) *Chabootra ka Roznamcha* (Badruddin Tyabji Family Papers VI), Acc. no. 1602.

English

Amiruddin Abdul Latif, 'Memoir', dictated to Camruddin Latif, Bombay, 1898.

Bombay University Library

Urdu

Yali *Akhbar ki Kitab*, 3 vols., 1892–1962.

Private Collections

English

Tyabji, Faiz B. *Letter to Badruddin, 1902.*

Tyabji, Saif. *Letters Home*, 1929–30.

Published Works

English

Abida, Sultaan. *Memoirs of a Rebel Princess,* Introduction by Siobhan Lambert-Hurley. New York: Oxford University Press, 2008.

Ahmad, Aziz. *Islamic Modernization in India and Pakistan, 1857–1964.* London: Oxford University Press, 1967.

Ahmad, lmtiaz, ed. *Caste and Social Stratification among Muslims in India.* New Delhi: Manohar Publishers, 1978.

Ahmad, lmtiaz, ed. *Modernization and Social Change among Muslims in India.* New Delhi: Manohar Publishers, 1983.

Ahmed, Akbar S., and David M. Hart, eds. *From the Atlas to the Indus.* London: Routledge and Kegan Paul, 1984.

Ahmed, Tufail. *Towards a Common Destiny, A Nationalist Manifesto.* Translated by Ali Ashraf. Delhi: People's Publishing House, 1994.

Ali, Salim. *The Fall of a Sparrow.* Delhi: Oxford University Press, 1981.

Basu, Aparna. 'A Century's Journey: Women's Education in Western India, 1820–1920'. In *Education, Socialization and Women; Explorations in Gender Identity,* edited by Karuna Chanana, 181–210. New Delhi: Orient Longman, 1988.

Basu, Aparna. 'Reformed Families, Women Reformers', *Samaya Shakti,* New Delhi: Centre for Women's Development Studies, 1991.

Borthwick, Meredith. *The Changing Role of Women in Bengal 1849–1905.* Princeton: Princeton University Press, 1984.

Chakravarty, Uma. *Rewriting History: The Life and Times of Pandita Ramabai.* Delhi: Kali for Women, 1998.

Chandra, Sudhir. *Enslaved Daughters: Colonialism, Law and Women's Rights.* Delhi: Oxford University Press, 1996.

Conlon, Frank. 'Into the City, Early Saraswati Encounters with Urban Life, 1864–1900'. In *A Caste in a Changing World: The Chitrapur Saraswat Brahmans, 1700–1935,* Ch. 6. Delhi: Thomson Press, 1977.

Datta, V. N. *Maulana Azad.* Delhi: Manohar, 1990.

Dobbin, Christine. *Urban Leadership in Western India: Politics and Communities in Bombay City, 1840–1885.* London: Oxford University Press, 1972.

Edib, Halide. 1937, *Inside India,* new ed. 2002 with an Introduction by Mushirul Hasan. Delhi: Oxford University Press, 2002.

Encyclopedia of Islam, 3rd ed. Leiden: EJ Brill, 1960.

Forbes, Geraldine. 'Women in Modern India'. In *The New Cambridge History of India,* Vol. 4, Part 2. Cambridge: Cambridge University Press, 1996.

Fyzee, A. A. A. 'Bohoras'. *Encyclopaedia of Islam,* Vol. IV, 1960.

Fyzee, A. A. A. 'The Autobiography of Tyabjee Bhoymeeah, edited with an Introduction and Notes'. *Journal of the Asiatic Society of Bombay* (N.S) Volume 36–37, Supplement, April 1964.

Fyzee, A. A. A. 'The Study of the Literature of the Fatimid Da'wa'. In *Arabic and Islamic Studies in Honour of Hamiiton A. R. Gibb,* edited by G. Makdisi, 232–50. Leiden: Brill, 1965.

Fyzee-Rahamin, Atiya Begum. *The Music of India* (with illustrations from 17th century miniatures, photographs of musicians, paintings by Fyzee-Rahamin). London: Luzacs and Co, 1925.

Fyzee Rahamin, Samuel. *Daughter of Ind, A Play in Three Acts, Music by Atiya Begum.* Bombay: New Book Company, 1940.

Fyzee-Rahamin, Atiya Begum. *Iqbal.* Bombay: Academy of Islam Publication, 1947.

Guha, Ramachandra. *India after Gandhi: The History of the World's Largest Democracy.* New Delhi: Picador, 2007.

Haeems, Nina. *Rebecca Reuben, 1889–1957: Scholar, Educationist, Community Leader.* Mumbai: Vacha Trust, 2000.

Hasan, Zoya, ed. *Forging Identities: Communities and the State.* New Delhi: Kali for Women, 1994.

Karlekar, Malavika. *Voices from Within: Early Personal Narratives of Bengali Women.* Delhi: Oxford University Press, 1993.

Kellock, James. 'The Social Reformer, Efforts, Achievements and Principles'. In *Mahadeo Govind Ranade, Patriot and Social Servant*, Ch 7. Calcutta: Association Press, 1926.

Kumar, Ravinder, ed. *Essays on Gandhian Politics: The Rowlatt Satyagraha of 1919.* Oxford: Oxford University Press, 1971.

Kumar, Ravinder, ed. *Essays in the Social History of Modern India.* New Delhi: Oxford University Press, 1983.

Levy, Reuben. *The Social Structure of Islam* (being the second edition of *The Sociology of Islam*). Cambridge: Cambridge University Press, 1957.

Lokhandwala, S. T., ed. *India and Contemporary Islam: Proceedings of a Seminar.* Simla: Indian Institute of Advanced Study, 1971.

Masselos, J. C. *Towards Nationalism: Group Affiliations and the Politics of Public Associations in Nineteenth Century Western India.* Bombay: Popular Prakashan, 1974.

Mehta, Asoka, and Achyut Patwardhan. *The Communal Triangle in India.* Allahabad: Kitabistan, 1942.

Metcalf, Barbara Daly. *Islamic Revival in British India: Deoband, 1860–1900.* Princeton: Princeton University Press, 1982.

Minault, Gail. *Secluded Scholars: Women's Education and Muslim Social Reform in Colonial India.* Delhi: Oxford University Press, 1998.

Minault, Gail. *The Khilafat Movement; Religious Symbolism and Political Mobilization in India.* Delhi: Oxford University Press, 1999.

Misra, Satish C. *Muslim Communities in Gujarat: Preliminary Studies in their History and Social Organization.* Bombay: Asia Publishing House, 1964.

Mujeeb, M. *The Indian Muslims.* London: George Allen and Unwin, 1967.

Mukerjee, Meenakshi. 'The Unperceived Self: A Study of Five Nineteenth-Century Autobiographies'. In *Education, Socialization and Women; Explorations in Gender Identity*, edited by Karuna Chanana, 249–69. New Delhi: Orient Longman, 1988.

Mukherjee, S. N. 'Class, Caste and Politics in Calcutta, 1815–38'. In *Elites in South Asia*, edited by E. Leach and S. N. Mukherjee, 33–78. Cambridge: Cambridge University Press, 1970.

Natarajan, S. 'Bombay in the Making'. In *A Century of Social Reform in India*, Ch. 3, 52–129. Bombay: Asia Publishing House, 1959.

Pearson, Gail. 'The Female Intelligentsia in a Segregated Society-Bombay: A Case Study'. In *Women in India and Nepal*, edited by M. Allen and S. N. Mukherjee, 136–54. Canberra: Australian National University, 1983.

Ranade, Ramabai. *His Wife's Reminiscences,* Translated by Kusumvati Deshpande from Ramabai Ranade's Marathi original, *Amchya Ayushatil kalu Athavani.* Delhi: Publications Division, Ministry of Information and Broadcasting, Government of India, 1963.

Rehatsek, Edward. *The Gulistan or Rose Garden of Sa' di.* London: George Allen and Unwin, 1964.

Roy, S. *The Dawoodi Bohras: An Anthropological Perspective.* New Delhi: B. K. Publications, 1984.

Sadiq Ali, Shanti. *The African Dispersal in the Deccan from Medieval to Modern Times.* New Delhi: Orient Longman, 1995.

Saiyad, Dushka. *Muslim Women of the British Punjab: From Seclusion to Politics.* London: Macmillan, 1998.

Sangari, Kumkum, and Suresh Vaid, eds. *Recasting Women: Essays in Colonial History.* New Delhi: Kali, 1989.

Scott, Nora. *An Indian Journal,* edited by John Radford. London: The Radcliffe Press, 1994.

Seal, Anil. *The Emergence of Indian Nationalism, Competition and Collaboration in the Later Nineteenth Century.* Cambridge: Cambridge University Press, 1966.

Shahinda (Begum Fyzee-Rahamin). *Indian Music,* preface by F. Gilbert Webb and illustrations by S. Fyzee-Rahamin (b/w in classical ragini miniature style). London: William Merchant and Co., 1914.

Shakir, Moin. *Muslims and the Indian National Congress: Badruddin Tyabji and His Times.* New Delhi: Ajanta, 1987.

Shinde, Tarabai. *A Comparison between Women and Men: Tarabai Shinde and the Critique of Gender Relations in Colonial India.* Translated by Rosalind O'Hanlon. Madras: Oxford University Press, 1994.

Telang, K. T. *Select Writings and Speeches,* Vol. I, edited by V. N. Naik. Bombay: Gaud Saraswat Brahmin Mitra Mandal, 1916.

Tucker, Richard P. *Ranade and the Roots of Indian Nationalism.* Bombay: Popular Prakashan, 1977.

Tyabji, Badruddin, S. S. Desnavi, and Jabir A. Ali. *Saif Tyabji (Three Memoirs).* Foreword by Laeeq Futehally. Bombay: Privately Published, 1959.

Tyabji, Husain B. *Badruddin Tyabji, A Life.* Bombay: Thacker and Co., 1952.

Wright, Theodore. 'Muslim Kinship and Modernization: The Tyabji Clan in Bombay'. In *Family Kinship and Marriage among Muslims in India,* edited by Imtiaz Ahmed, 217–38. Delhi: Manohar, 1976.

Yatuk, Sylvia. 'Schooling for What? The Cultural and Social Context of Women's Education in a South Indian Muslim Family'. In *Women, Education, and Family Structure in India,* edited by C. C. Mukhopdhyay and S. Seymour, 135–64. Boulder: Westview, 1994.

Urdu

Ahmed, Deputy Nazeer. *Ibn ul Waqt.* Delhi: Maktaba Jamia. Reprint. 2017.

Bano Ahmed, Saeeda. *Degar se Hat Kar.* Delhi: Sajjad Publishing House, n.d.

Mohsini, Shamsur Rehman. *Life of Abdullah: Dr Shaikh Mohammad Abdullah, Padma Bhushan.* Aligarh: Female Education Association, n.d.

Shibli, Maulana. *Khutoot-I Shibli, be nami-Atiya Begam Fyzee Sahib,* edited by Md. Amin Zuberi. Foreword by Abdul Haq. Lahore: Taj Co. Ltd., 1935.

Articles and Papers

Engels, Dagmar. 'The Age of Consent Act of 1891: Colonial Ideology in Bengal'. *South Asia Research* 3, no. 2 (November 1983): 107–34.

Fisher, Michael. 'The Office of *Akhbar Navis*: The Transition from Mughal to British Forms'. *Modern Asian Studies* 27, no. 1 (February 1993): 45–82.

Fyzee, A. A. A. 'Three Sulaymani Dais: 1936–1939'. *Journal of the Bombay Branch of the Royal Asiatic Society* 26 (1940): 101–104.

Ghadially, Rehana. 'Veiling the Unveiled: The Politics of Purdah in a Muslim Sect'. *South Asia: Journal of South Asian Studies* 12, no. 2 (December 1989): 33–48.

Heimsath, Charles. 'Origin and Enactment of the Age of Consent Bill, 1891'. *Journal of Asian Studies* 1, no. 4 (August 1962): 491–504.

Karlitzky, Maren. 'The Tyabji Clan—Urdu as a Symbol of Group Identity'. *The Annual of Urdu Studies 17*. http://www.urdustudies.com/Issue17/index.html accessed on 16 April 2015.

Kishwar, Madhu. 'Gandhi on Women'. *The Economic and Political Weekly* 20, no. 40 (5 October 1985): 1753–58.

Patterson, Maureen L. P. 'Changing Patterns of Occupation among Chitpavan Brahmans'. *Indian Economic and Social History Review* 7, no. 1 (1970): 375–96.

Sarkar, Tanika. 'Rhetoric against Age of Consent'. *Economic and Political Weekly* 28, no. 36 (4 September 1993): 1869–78.

Subrahmaniam, Lakshmi. 'Banias and the British: The Role of Indigenous Credit in the Process of Imperial Expansion in Western India in the Second Half of the Eighteenth Century'. *Modern Asian Studies* 21, no. 3 (1987): 473–510.

Yatuk, Sylvia. 'The Cultural Construction of Shared Identity: A South Indian Family History'. *Social Analysis* 287 (1990): 114–31.

About the Author

Salima Tyabji (1939–2013) was educated at the universities of Bombay and Oxford, taught for a short time at school and university in Bombay and then worked with the Oxford University Press in Delhi, specialising in history and art history.

She lived in Delhi and amongst her many passions were gardening, classical music, reading (English and Urdu) and, generally, having fun.